ADVENTURE CLASSICS

Graphic Classics Volume Twelve

2005

Edited by Tom Pomplun

EUREKA PRODUCTIONS

8778 Oak Grove Road, Mount Horeb, Wisconsin 53572

www.graphicclassics.com

THE WIND BLEW SHRILL AND SMART

by Robert Louis Stevenson / Illustrated by Skot Olsen

The wind blew shrill and smart,
And the wind awoke my heart
Again to go a-sailing o'er the sea,
To hear the cordage moan
And the straining timbers groan,
And to see the flying pennon lie a-lee.

O sailor of the fleet,
It is time to stir the feet!
It's time to man the dingy and to row!
It's lay your hand in mine
And it's empty down the wine,
And it's drain a health to death
before we go!

To death, my lads, we sail;
And it's death that blows the gale
And death that holds the tiller
as we ride.
For he's the king of all
In the tempest and the squall,
And the ruler of the Ocean
wild and wide!

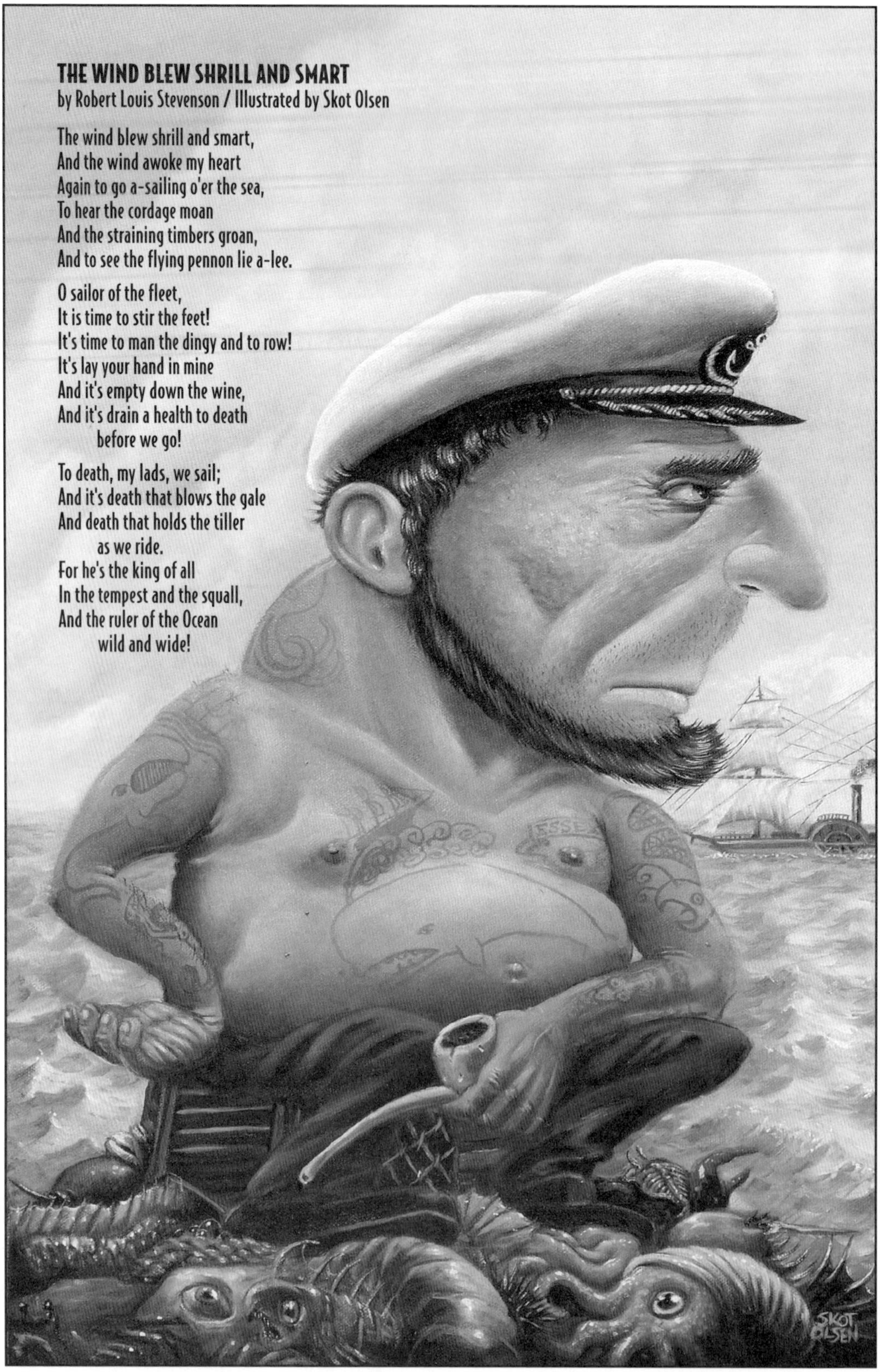
SKOT OLSEN

ADVENTURE CLASSICS

Graphic Classics Volume Twelve

Cover illustration by Chris Moore / Back cover illustration by Don Marquez

Adventure Classics: Graphic Classics Volume Twelve is published by Eureka Productions. ISBN #978-0-9746648-4-7. Price US $11.95. Available from Eureka Productions, 8778 Oak Grove Road, Mount Horeb, WI 53572. Tom Pomplun, designer and publisher, tom@graphicclassics.com. Eileen Fitzgerald, editorial assistant. This compilation and all original works ©2005 Eureka Productions. All rights revert to creators after publication. Graphic Classics is a trademark of Eureka Productions. The Graphic Classics website is at http://www.graphicclassics.com. Printed in Canada.

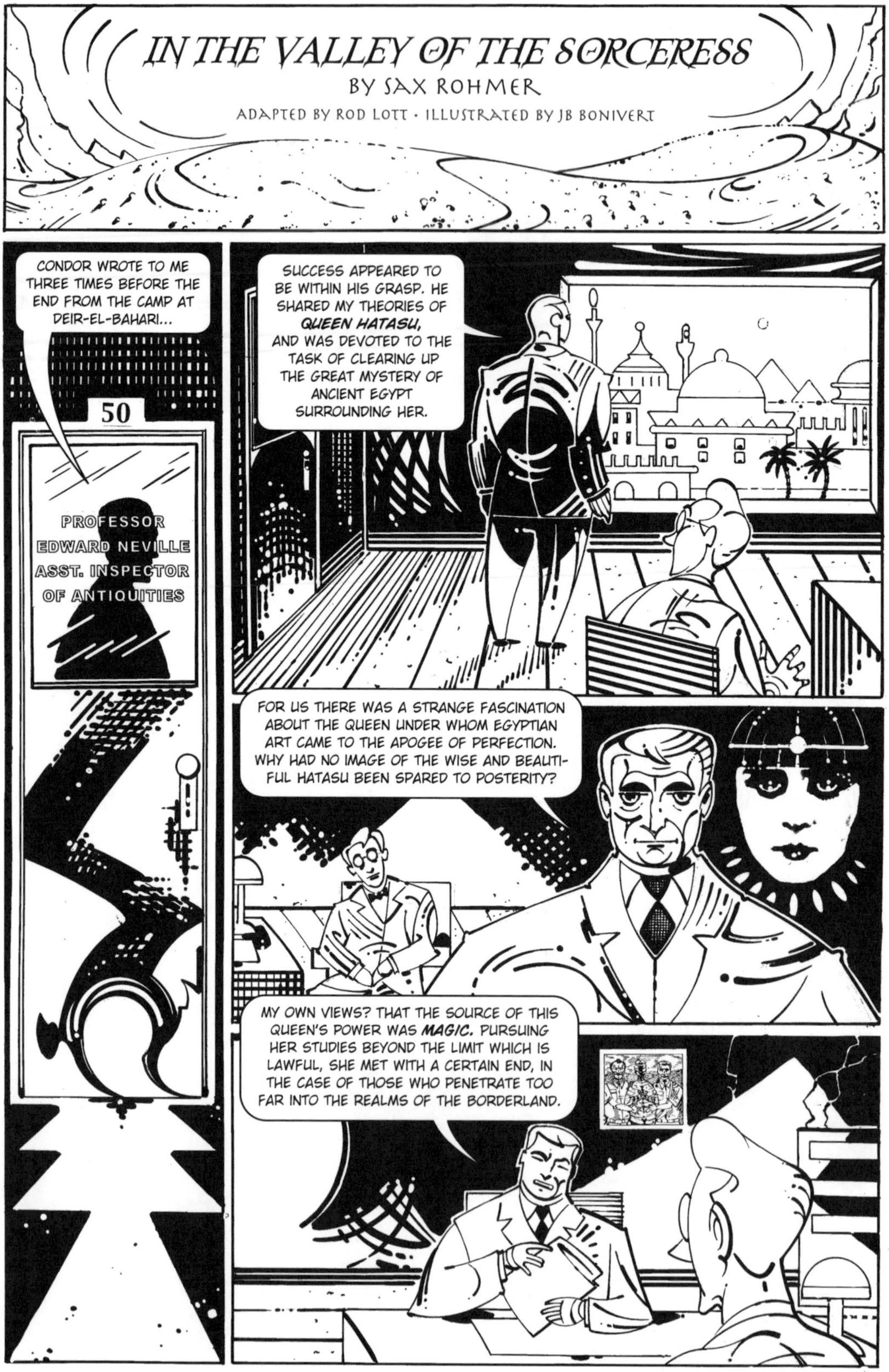
IN THE VALLEY OF THE SORCERESS
BY SAX ROHMER
ADAPTED BY ROD LOTT • ILLUSTRATED BY JB BONIVERT
CONDOR WROTE TO ME THREE TIMES BEFORE THE END FROM THE CAMP AT DEIR-EL-BAHARI...
50
PROFESSOR EDWARD NEVILLE ASST. INSPECTOR OF ANTIQUITIES
SUCCESS APPEARED TO BE WITHIN HIS GRASP. HE SHARED MY THEORIES OF QUEEN HATASU, AND WAS DEVOTED TO THE TASK OF CLEARING UP THE GREAT MYSTERY OF ANCIENT EGYPT SURROUNDING HER.
FOR US THERE WAS A STRANGE FASCINATION ABOUT THE QUEEN UNDER WHOM EGYPTIAN ART CAME TO THE APOGEE OF PERFECTION. WHY HAD NO IMAGE OF THE WISE AND BEAUTIFUL HATASU BEEN SPARED TO POSTERITY?
MY OWN VIEWS? THAT THE SOURCE OF THIS QUEEN'S POWER WAS MAGIC. PURSUING HER STUDIES BEYOND THE LIMIT WHICH IS LAWFUL, SHE MET WITH A CERTAIN END, IN THE CASE OF THOSE WHO PENETRATE TOO FAR INTO THE REALMS OF THE BORDERLAND.

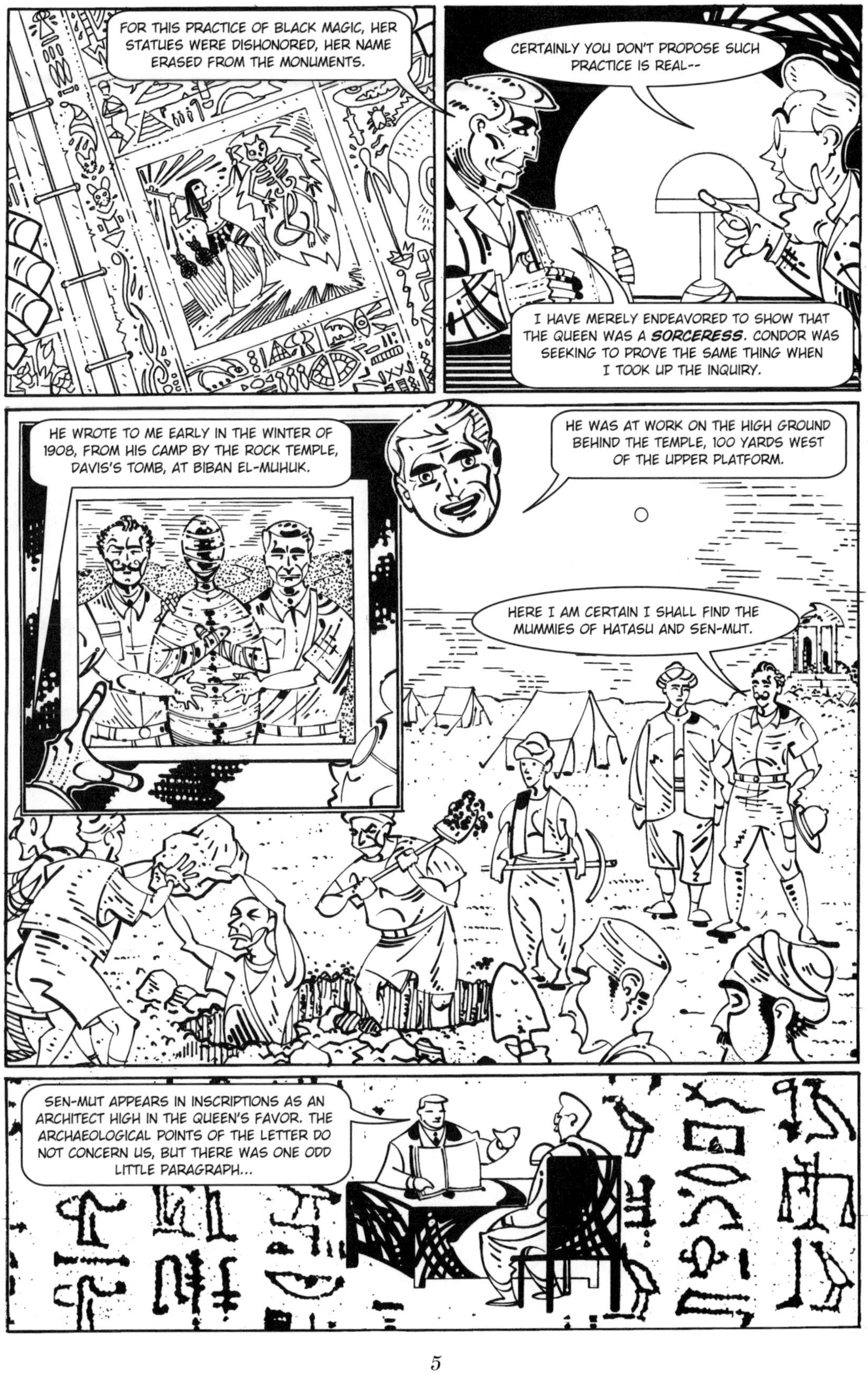
FOR THIS PRACTICE OF BLACK MAGIC, HER STATUES WERE DISHONORED, HER NAME ERASED FROM THE MONUMENTS.
CERTAINLY YOU DON'T PROPOSE SUCH PRACTICE IS REAL--
I HAVE MERELY ENDEAVORED TO SHOW THAT THE QUEEN WAS A ***SORCERESS***. CONDOR WAS SEEKING TO PROVE THE SAME THING WHEN I TOOK UP THE INQUIRY.
HE WROTE TO ME EARLY IN THE WINTER OF 1908, FROM HIS CAMP BY THE ROCK TEMPLE, DAVIS'S TOMB, AT BIBAN EL-MUHUK.
HE WAS AT WORK ON THE HIGH GROUND BEHIND THE TEMPLE, 100 YARDS WEST OF THE UPPER PLATFORM.
HERE I AM CERTAIN I SHALL FIND THE MUMMIES OF HATASU AND SEN-MUT.
SEN-MUT APPEARS IN INSCRIPTIONS AS AN ARCHITECT HIGH IN THE QUEEN'S FAVOR. THE ARCHAEOLOGICAL POINTS OF THE LETTER DO NOT CONCERN US, BUT THERE WAS ONE ODD LITTLE PARAGRAPH...

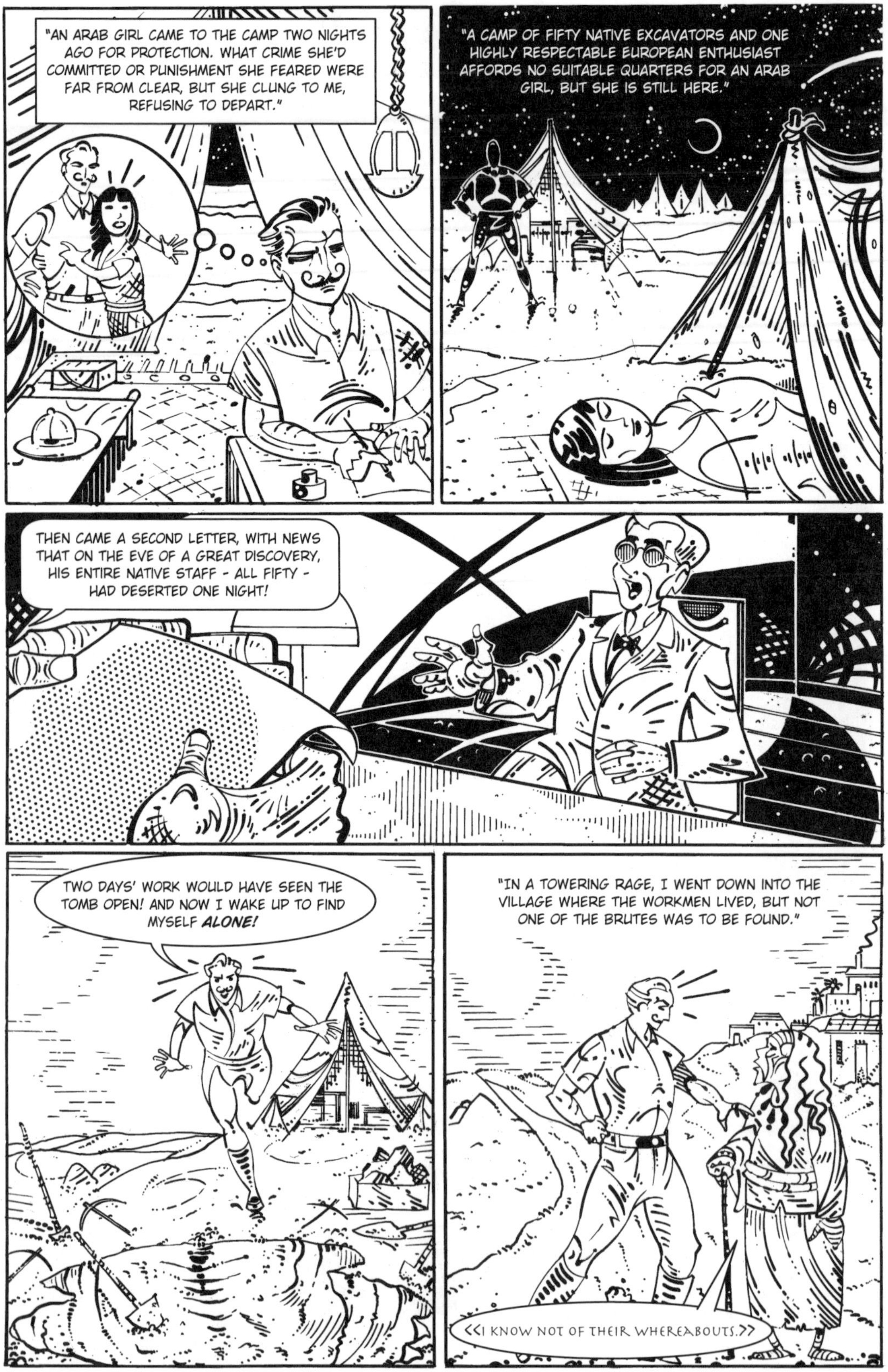
"AN ARAB GIRL CAME TO THE CAMP TWO NIGHTS AGO FOR PROTECTION. WHAT CRIME SHE'D COMMITTED OR PUNISHMENT SHE FEARED WERE FAR FROM CLEAR, BUT SHE CLUNG TO ME, REFUSING TO DEPART."
"A CAMP OF FIFTY NATIVE EXCAVATORS AND ONE HIGHLY RESPECTABLE EUROPEAN ENTHUSIAST AFFORDS NO SUITABLE QUARTERS FOR AN ARAB GIRL, BUT SHE IS STILL HERE."
THEN CAME A SECOND LETTER, WITH NEWS THAT ON THE EVE OF A GREAT DISCOVERY, HIS ENTIRE NATIVE STAFF - ALL FIFTY - HAD DESERTED ONE NIGHT!
TWO DAYS' WORK WOULD HAVE SEEN THE TOMB OPEN! AND NOW I WAKE UP TO FIND MYSELF ***ALONE!***
"IN A TOWERING RAGE, I WENT DOWN INTO THE VILLAGE WHERE THE WORKMEN LIVED, BUT NOT ONE OF THE BRUTES WAS TO BE FOUND."
<<I KNOW NOT OF THEIR WHEREABOUTS.>>

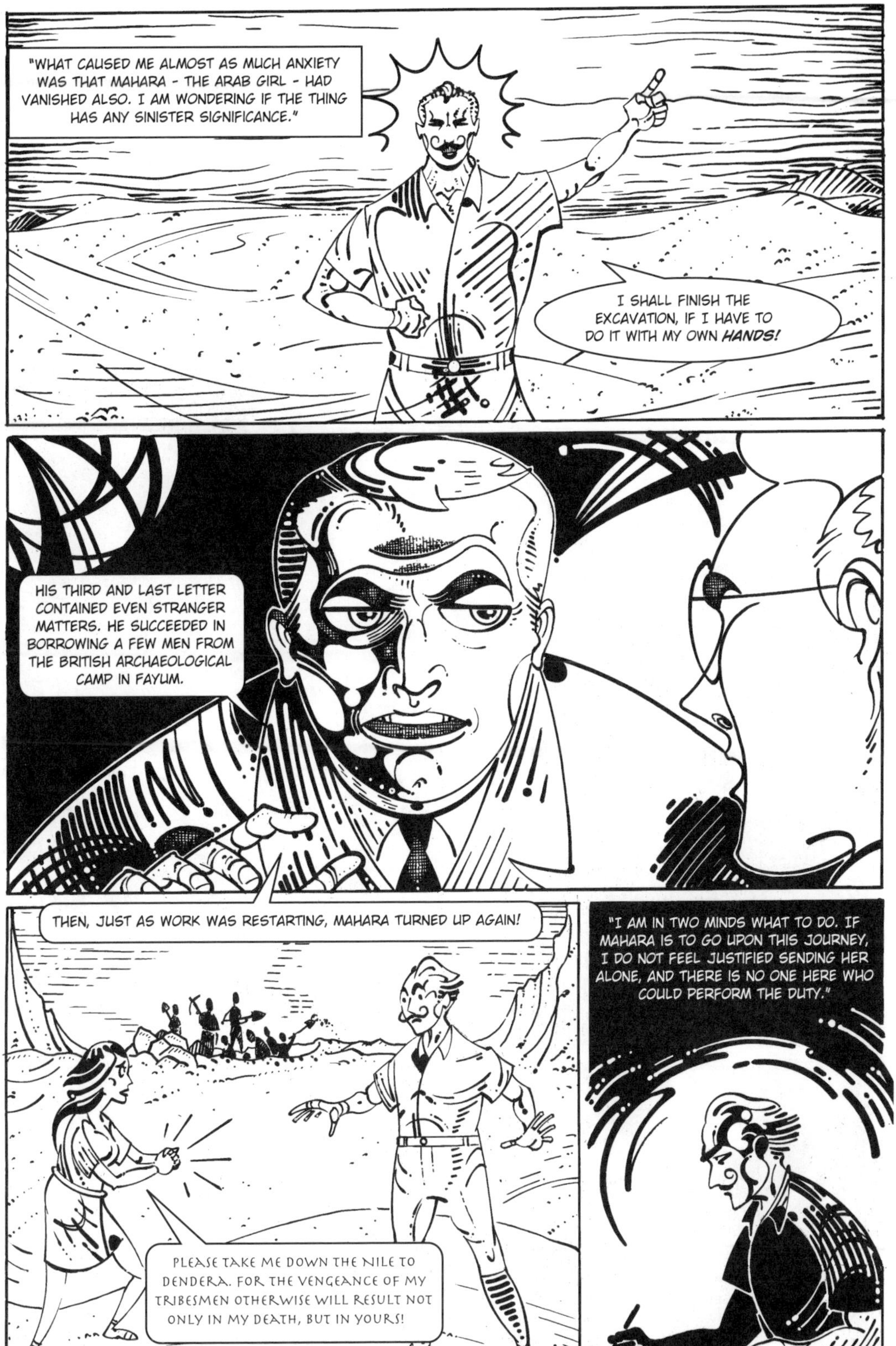
"WHAT CAUSED ME ALMOST AS MUCH ANXIETY WAS THAT MAHARA - THE ARAB GIRL - HAD VANISHED ALSO. I AM WONDERING IF THE THING HAS ANY SINISTER SIGNIFICANCE."
I SHALL FINISH THE EXCAVATION, IF I HAVE TO DO IT WITH MY OWN ***HANDS!***
HIS THIRD AND LAST LETTER CONTAINED EVEN STRANGER MATTERS. HE SUCCEEDED IN BORROWING A FEW MEN FROM THE BRITISH ARCHAEOLOGICAL CAMP IN FAYUM.
THEN, JUST AS WORK WAS RESTARTING, MAHARA TURNED UP AGAIN!
PLEASE TAKE ME DOWN THE NILE TO DENDERA. FOR THE VENGEANCE OF MY TRIBESMEN OTHERWISE WILL RESULT NOT ONLY IN MY DEATH, BUT IN YOURS!
"I AM IN TWO MINDS WHAT TO DO. IF MAHARA IS TO GO UPON THIS JOURNEY, I DO NOT FEEL JUSTIFIED SENDING HER ALONE, AND THERE IS NO ONE HERE WHO COULD PERFORM THE DUTY."

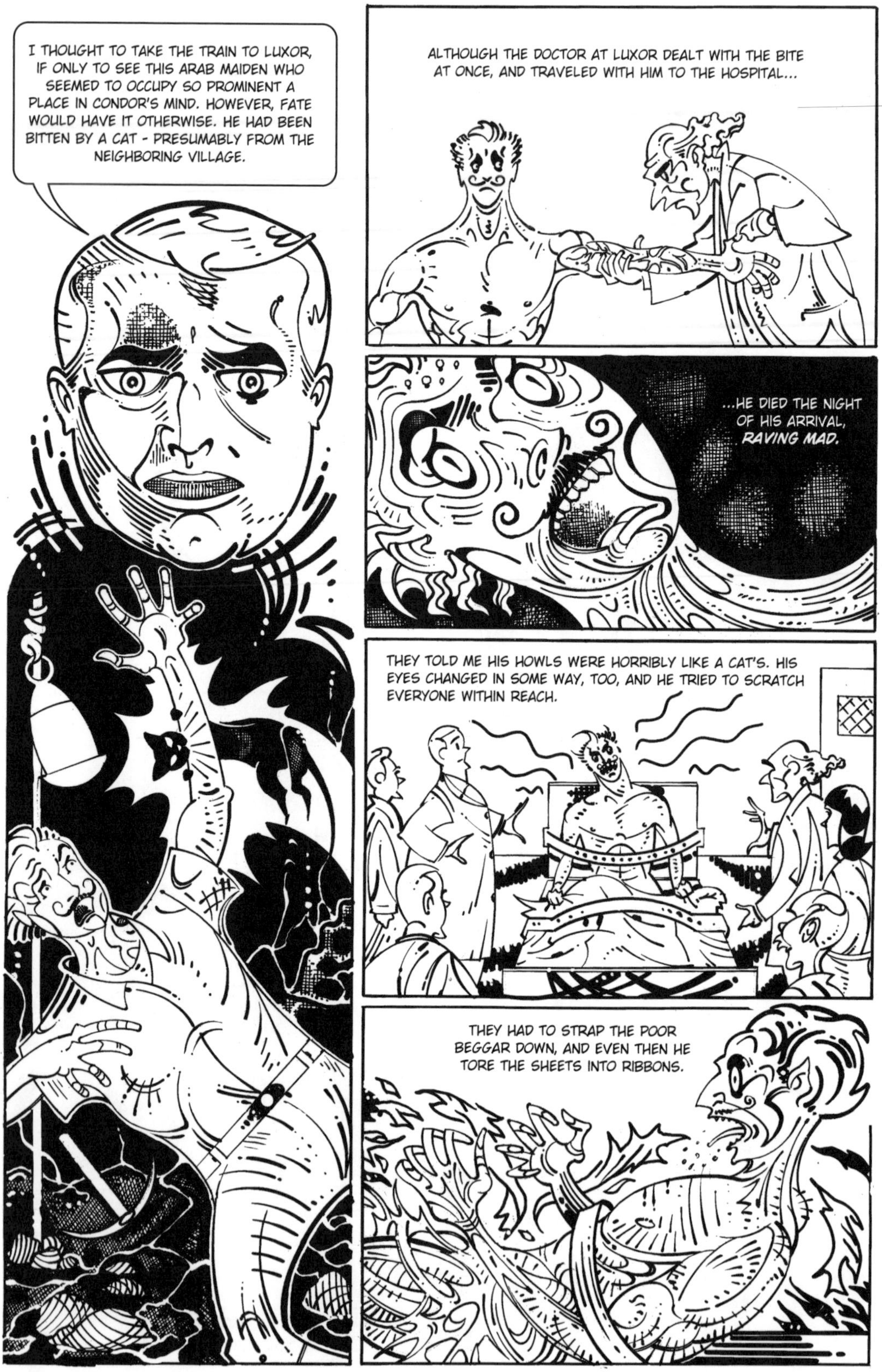
I THOUGHT TO TAKE THE TRAIN TO LUXOR, IF ONLY TO SEE THIS ARAB MAIDEN WHO SEEMED TO OCCUPY SO PROMINENT A PLACE IN CONDOR'S MIND. HOWEVER, FATE WOULD HAVE IT OTHERWISE. HE HAD BEEN BITTEN BY A CAT - PRESUMABLY FROM THE NEIGHBORING VILLAGE.
ALTHOUGH THE DOCTOR AT LUXOR DEALT WITH THE BITE AT ONCE, AND TRAVELED WITH HIM TO THE HOSPITAL...
...HE DIED THE NIGHT OF HIS ARRIVAL, ***RAVING MAD.***
THEY TOLD ME HIS HOWLS WERE HORRIBLY LIKE A CAT'S. HIS EYES CHANGED IN SOME WAY, TOO, AND HE TRIED TO SCRATCH EVERYONE WITHIN REACH.
THEY HAD TO STRAP THE POOR BEGGAR DOWN, AND EVEN THEN HE TORE THE SHEETS INTO RIBBONS.

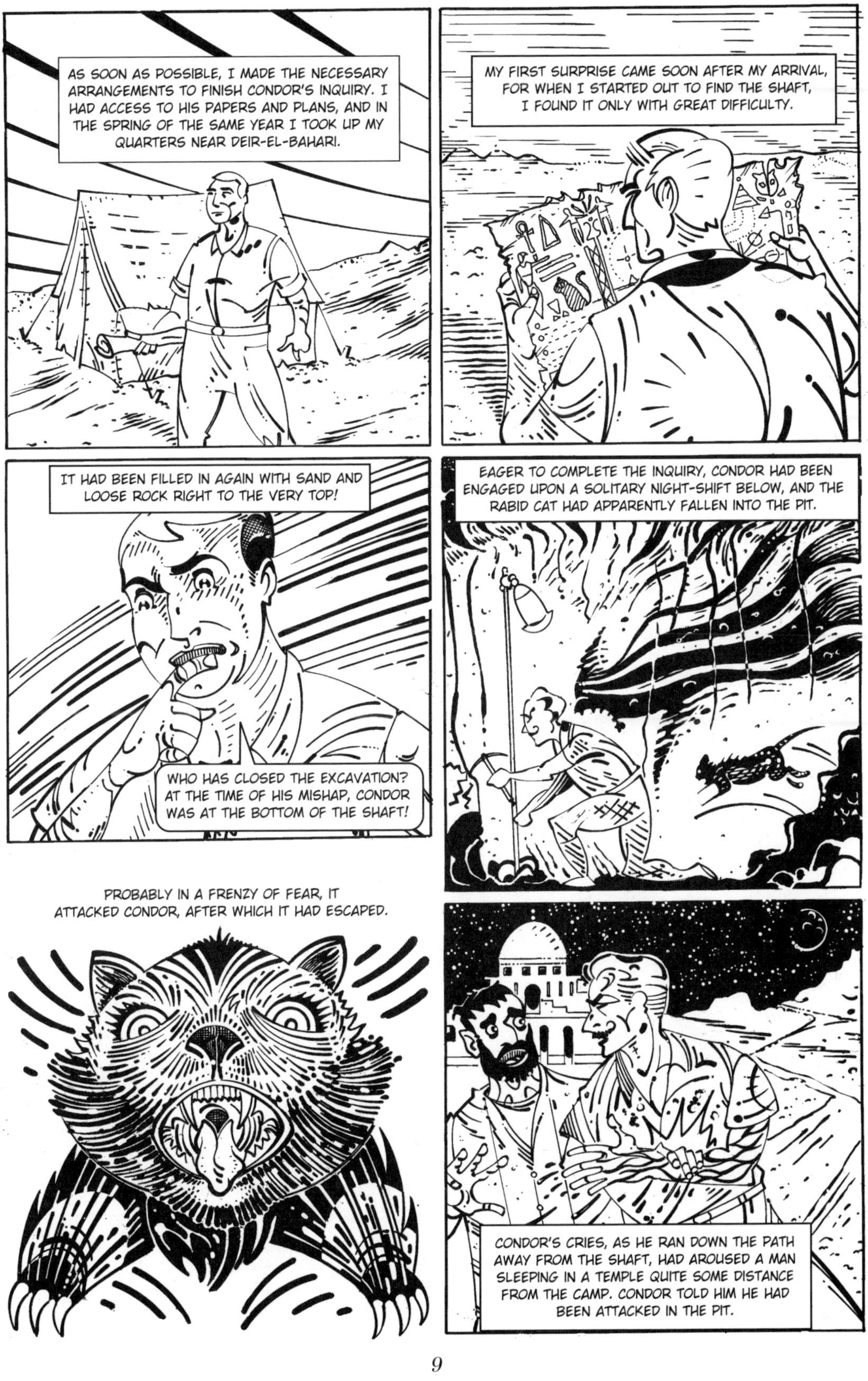
AS SOON AS POSSIBLE, I MADE THE NECESSARY ARRANGEMENTS TO FINISH CONDOR'S INQUIRY. I HAD ACCESS TO HIS PAPERS AND PLANS, AND IN THE SPRING OF THE SAME YEAR I TOOK UP MY QUARTERS NEAR DEIR-EL-BAHARI.
MY FIRST SURPRISE CAME SOON AFTER MY ARRIVAL, FOR WHEN I STARTED OUT TO FIND THE SHAFT, I FOUND IT ONLY WITH GREAT DIFFICULTY.
IT HAD BEEN FILLED IN AGAIN WITH SAND AND LOOSE ROCK RIGHT TO THE VERY TOP!
WHO HAS CLOSED THE EXCAVATION? AT THE TIME OF HIS MISHAP, CONDOR WAS AT THE BOTTOM OF THE SHAFT!
EAGER TO COMPLETE THE INQUIRY, CONDOR HAD BEEN ENGAGED UPON A SOLITARY NIGHT-SHIFT BELOW, AND THE RABID CAT HAD APPARENTLY FALLEN INTO THE PIT.
PROBABLY IN A FRENZY OF FEAR, IT ATTACKED CONDOR, AFTER WHICH IT HAD ESCAPED.
CONDOR'S CRIES, AS HE RAN DOWN THE PATH AWAY FROM THE SHAFT, HAD AROUSED A MAN SLEEPING IN A TEMPLE QUITE SOME DISTANCE FROM THE CAMP. CONDOR TOLD HIM HE HAD BEEN ATTACKED IN THE PIT.

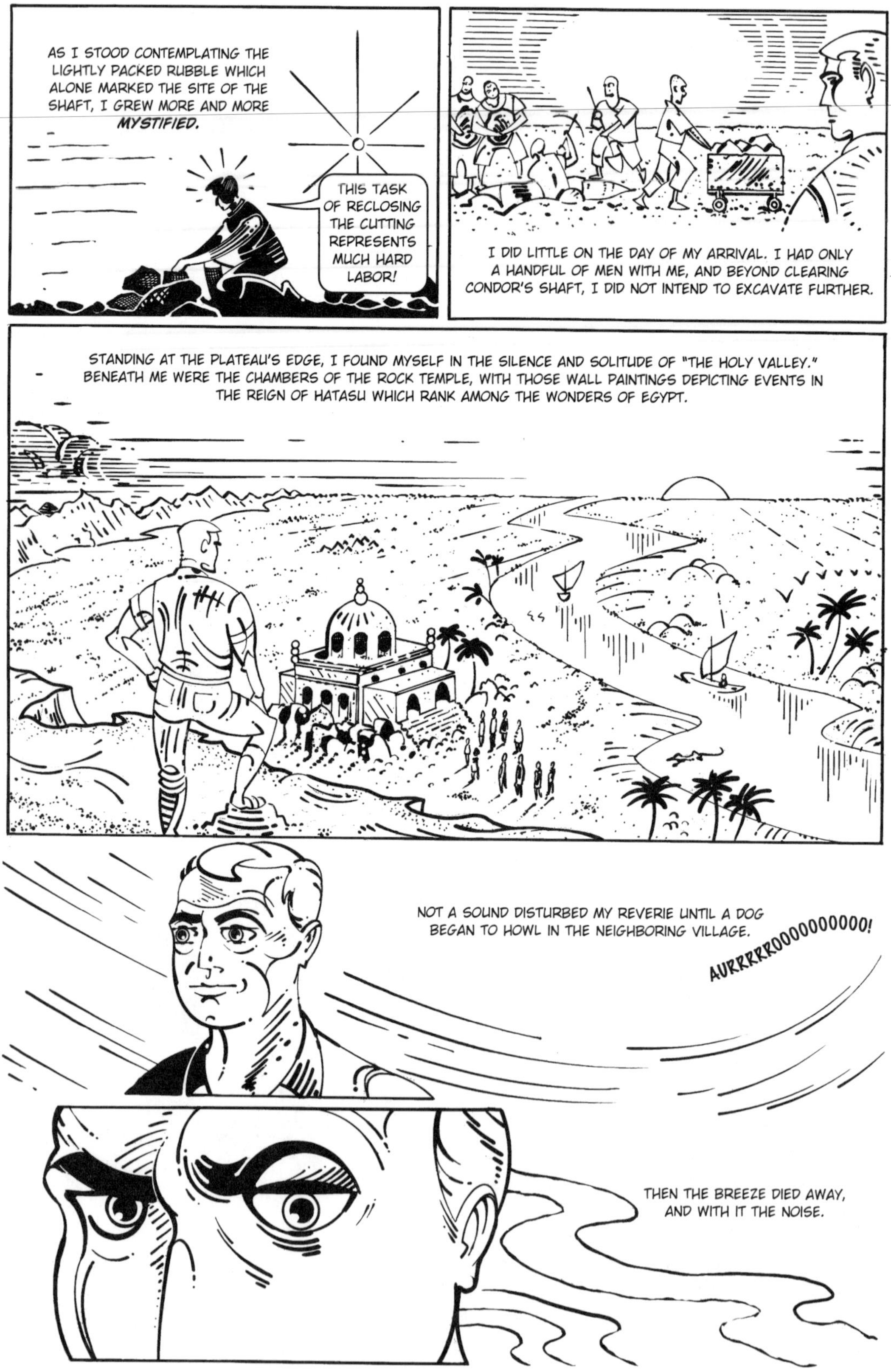
AS I STOOD CONTEMPLATING THE LIGHTLY PACKED RUBBLE WHICH ALONE MARKED THE SITE OF THE SHAFT, I GREW MORE AND MORE MYSTIFIED.
THIS TASK OF RECLOSING THE CUTTING REPRESENTS MUCH HARD LABOR!
I DID LITTLE ON THE DAY OF MY ARRIVAL. I HAD ONLY A HANDFUL OF MEN WITH ME, AND BEYOND CLEARING CONDOR'S SHAFT, I DID NOT INTEND TO EXCAVATE FURTHER.
STANDING AT THE PLATEAU'S EDGE, I FOUND MYSELF IN THE SILENCE AND SOLITUDE OF "THE HOLY VALLEY." BENEATH ME WERE THE CHAMBERS OF THE ROCK TEMPLE, WITH THOSE WALL PAINTINGS DEPICTING EVENTS IN THE REIGN OF HATASU WHICH RANK AMONG THE WONDERS OF EGYPT.
NOT A SOUND DISTURBED MY REVERIE UNTIL A DOG BEGAN TO HOWL IN THE NEIGHBORING VILLAGE.
AURRRRROOOOOOOOOOO!
THEN THE BREEZE DIED AWAY, AND WITH IT THE NOISE.

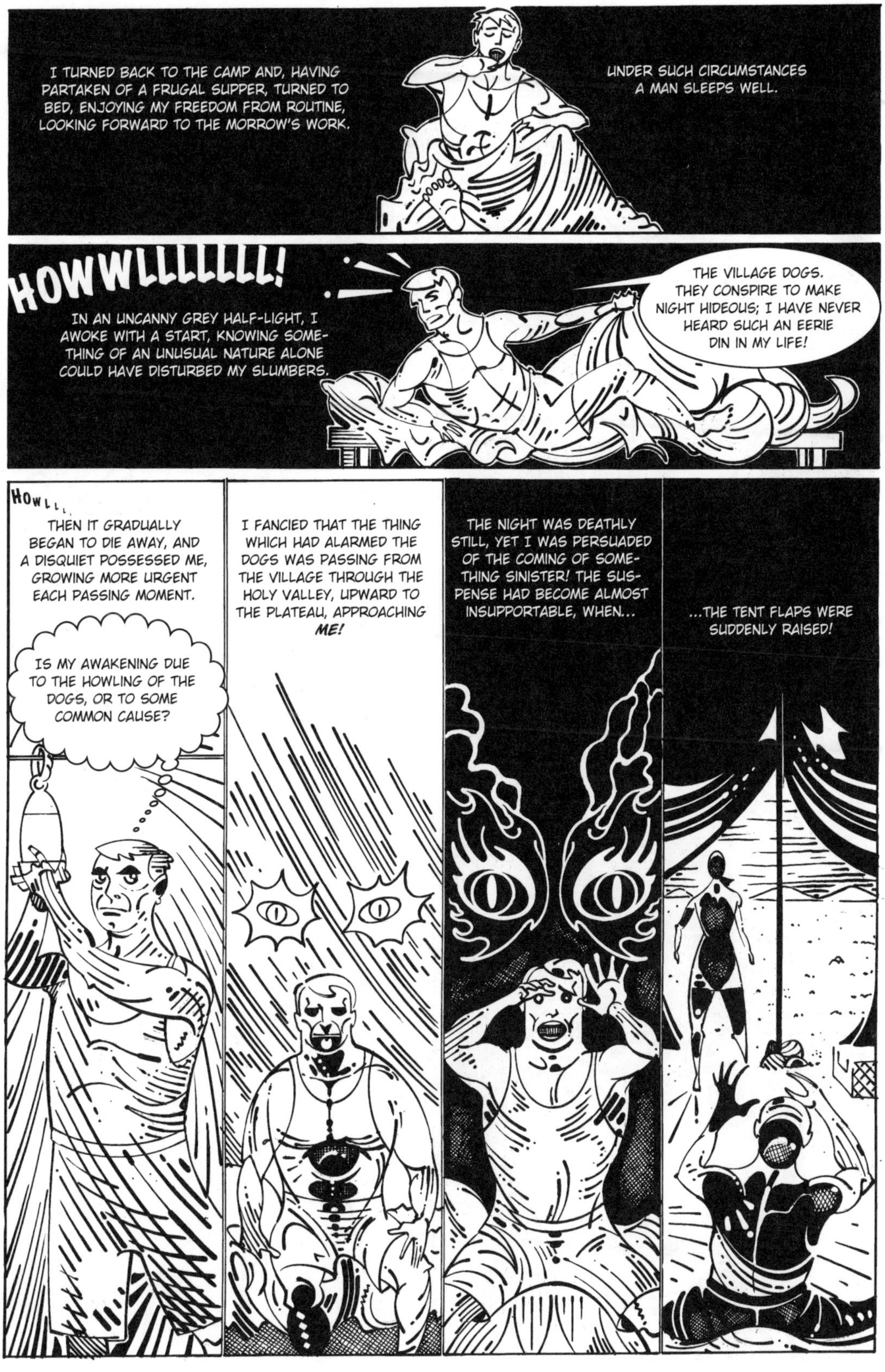
I TURNED BACK TO THE CAMP AND, HAVING PARTAKEN OF A FRUGAL SUPPER, TURNED TO BED, ENJOYING MY FREEDOM FROM ROUTINE, LOOKING FORWARD TO THE MORROW'S WORK.
UNDER SUCH CIRCUMSTANCES A MAN SLEEPS WELL.
HOWWLLLLLLL!
IN AN UNCANNY GREY HALF-LIGHT, I AWOKE WITH A START, KNOWING SOMETHING OF AN UNUSUAL NATURE ALONE COULD HAVE DISTURBED MY SLUMBERS.
THE VILLAGE DOGS. THEY CONSPIRE TO MAKE NIGHT HIDEOUS; I HAVE NEVER HEARD SUCH AN EERIE DIN IN MY LIFE!
HOWL…
THEN IT GRADUALLY BEGAN TO DIE AWAY, AND A DISQUIET POSSESSED ME, GROWING MORE URGENT EACH PASSING MOMENT.
IS MY AWAKENING DUE TO THE HOWLING OF THE DOGS, OR TO SOME COMMON CAUSE?
I FANCIED THAT THE THING WHICH HAD ALARMED THE DOGS WAS PASSING FROM THE VILLAGE THROUGH THE HOLY VALLEY, UPWARD TO THE PLATEAU, APPROACHING *ME!*
THE NIGHT WAS DEATHLY STILL, YET I WAS PERSUADED OF THE COMING OF SOMETHING SINISTER! THE SUSPENSE HAD BECOME ALMOST INSUPPORTABLE, WHEN…
…THE TENT FLAPS WERE SUDDENLY RAISED!

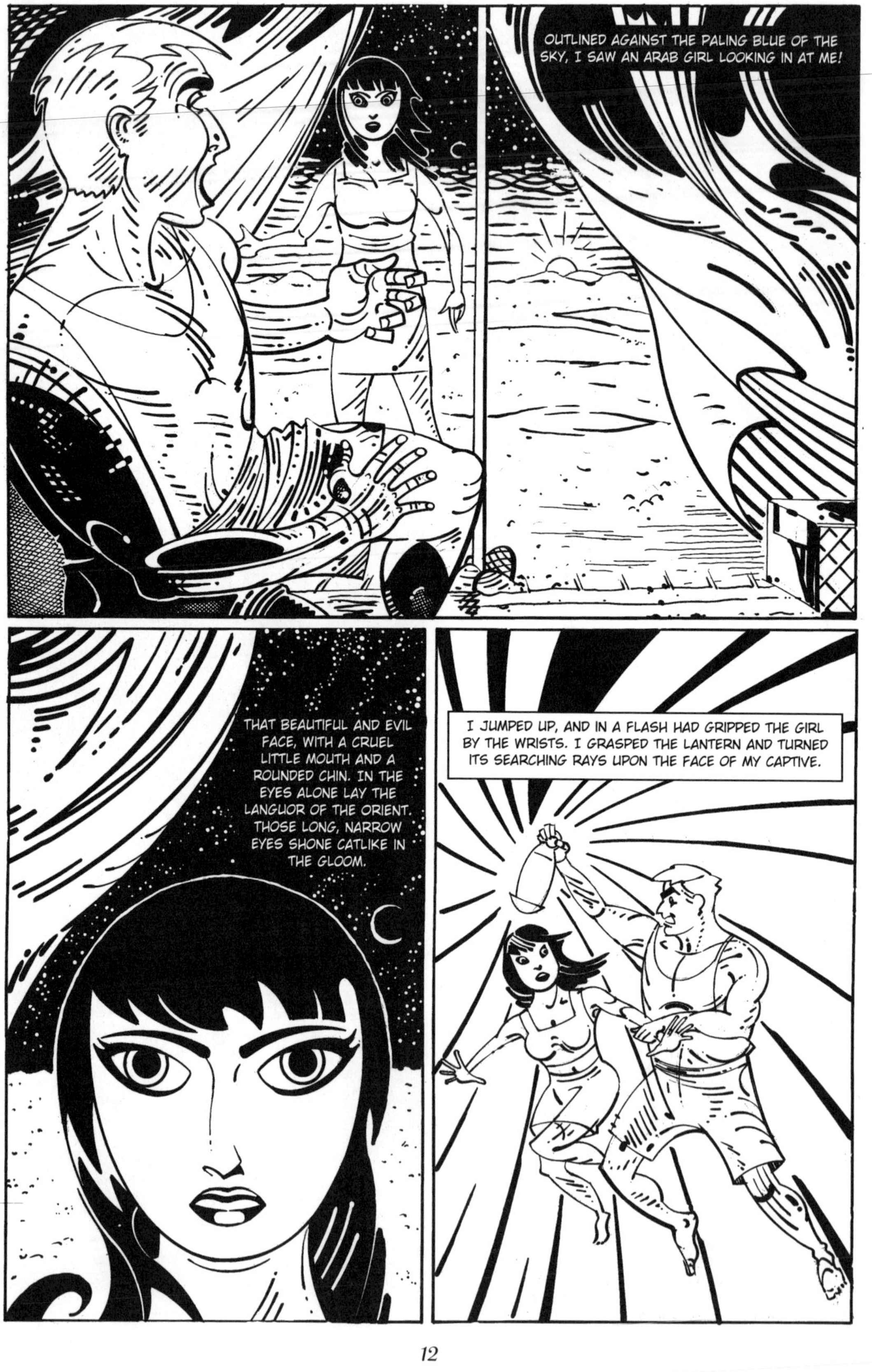
OUTLINED AGAINST THE PALING BLUE OF THE SKY, I SAW AN ARAB GIRL LOOKING IN AT ME!
THAT BEAUTIFUL AND EVIL FACE, WITH A CRUEL LITTLE MOUTH AND A ROUNDED CHIN. IN THE EYES ALONE LAY THE LANGUOR OF THE ORIENT. THOSE LONG, NARROW EYES SHONE CATLIKE IN THE GLOOM.
I JUMPED UP, AND IN A FLASH HAD GRIPPED THE GIRL BY THE WRISTS. I GRASPED THE LANTERN AND TURNED ITS SEARCHING RAYS UPON THE FACE OF MY CAPTIVE.

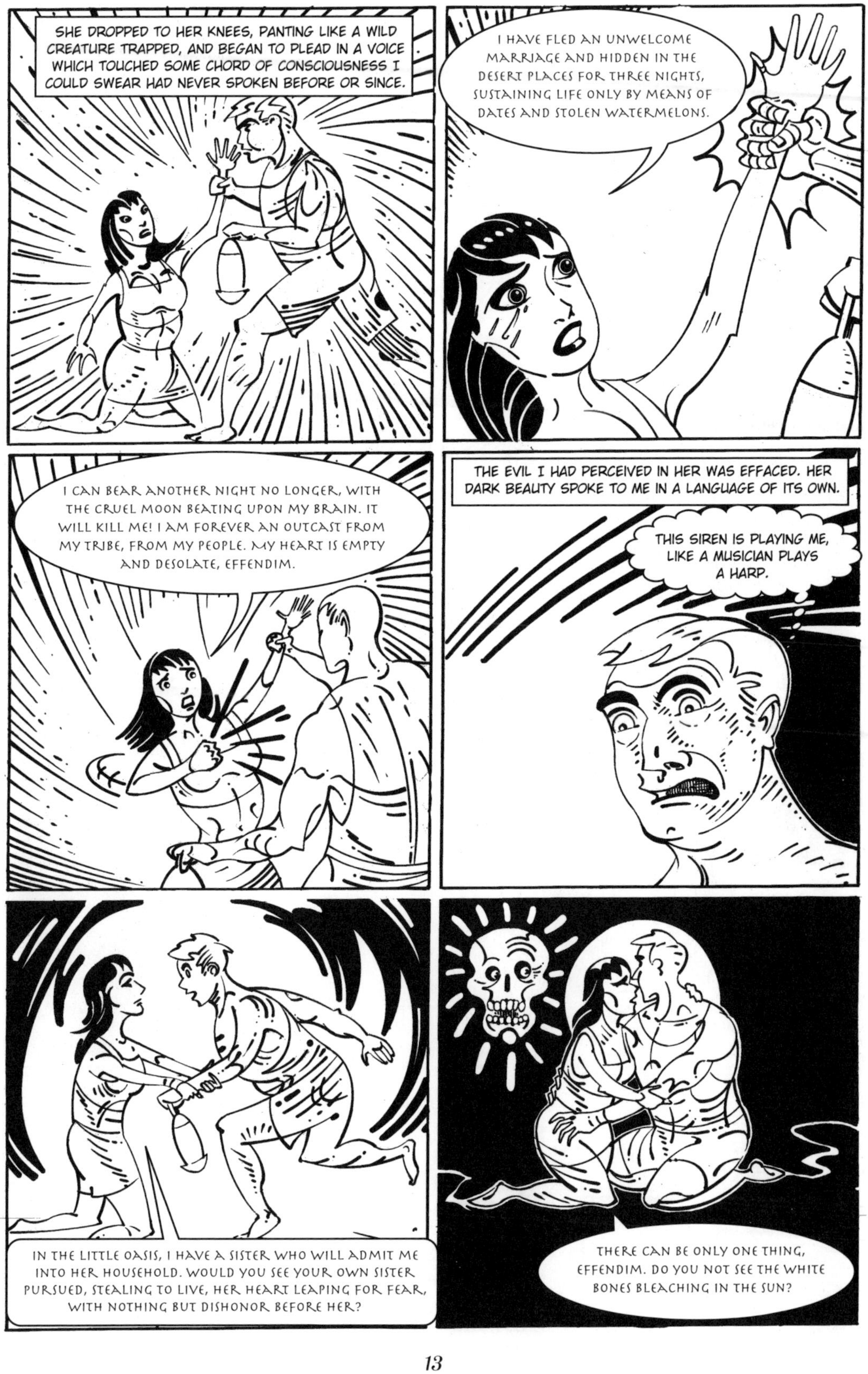
SHE DROPPED TO HER KNEES, PANTING LIKE A WILD CREATURE TRAPPED, AND BEGAN TO PLEAD IN A VOICE WHICH TOUCHED SOME CHORD OF CONSCIOUSNESS I COULD SWEAR HAD NEVER SPOKEN BEFORE OR SINCE.
I HAVE FLED AN UNWELCOME MARRIAGE AND HIDDEN IN THE DESERT PLACES FOR THREE NIGHTS, SUSTAINING LIFE ONLY BY MEANS OF DATES AND STOLEN WATERMELONS.
I CAN BEAR ANOTHER NIGHT NO LONGER, WITH THE CRUEL MOON BEATING UPON MY BRAIN. IT WILL KILL ME! I AM FOREVER AN OUTCAST FROM MY TRIBE, FROM MY PEOPLE. MY HEART IS EMPTY AND DESOLATE, EFFENDIM.
THE EVIL I HAD PERCEIVED IN HER WAS EFFACED. HER DARK BEAUTY SPOKE TO ME IN A LANGUAGE OF ITS OWN.
THIS SIREN IS PLAYING ME, LIKE A MUSICIAN PLAYS A HARP.
IN THE LITTLE OASIS, I HAVE A SISTER WHO WILL ADMIT ME INTO HER HOUSEHOLD. WOULD YOU SEE YOUR OWN SISTER PURSUED, STEALING TO LIVE, HER HEART LEAPING FOR FEAR, WITH NOTHING BUT DISHONOR BEFORE HER?
THERE CAN BE ONLY ONE THING, EFFENDIM. DO YOU NOT SEE THE WHITE BONES BLEACHING IN THE SUN?

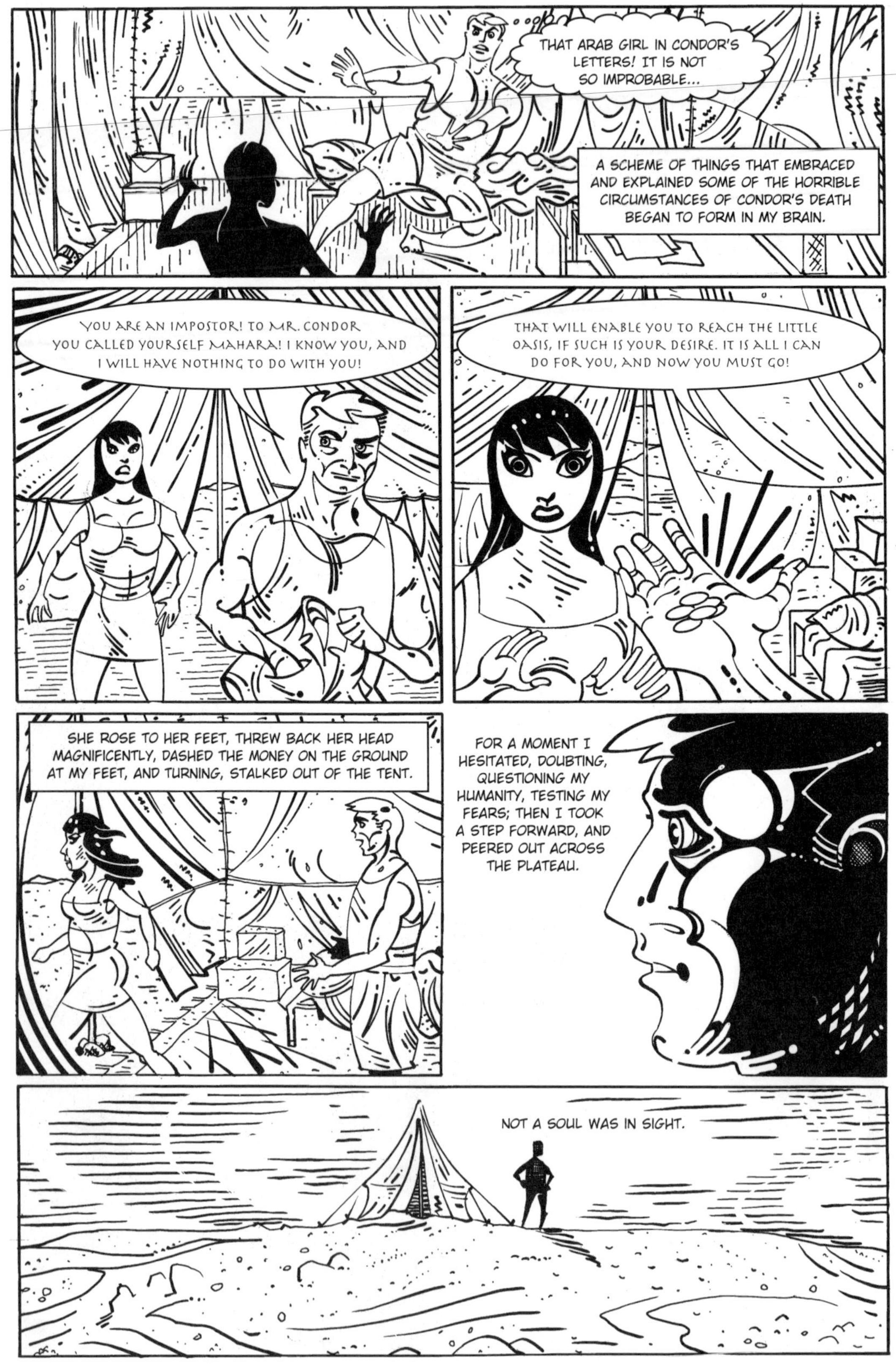
THAT ARAB GIRL IN CONDOR'S LETTERS! IT IS NOT SO IMPROBABLE...
A SCHEME OF THINGS THAT EMBRACED AND EXPLAINED SOME OF THE HORRIBLE CIRCUMSTANCES OF CONDOR'S DEATH BEGAN TO FORM IN MY BRAIN.
YOU ARE AN IMPOSTOR! TO MR. CONDOR YOU CALLED YOURSELF MAHARA! I KNOW YOU, AND I WILL HAVE NOTHING TO DO WITH YOU!
THAT WILL ENABLE YOU TO REACH THE LITTLE OASIS, IF SUCH IS YOUR DESIRE. IT IS ALL I CAN DO FOR YOU, AND NOW YOU MUST GO!
SHE ROSE TO HER FEET, THREW BACK HER HEAD MAGNIFICENTLY, DASHED THE MONEY ON THE GROUND AT MY FEET, AND TURNING, STALKED OUT OF THE TENT.
FOR A MOMENT I HESITATED, DOUBTING, QUESTIONING MY HUMANITY, TESTING MY FEARS; THEN I TOOK A STEP FORWARD, AND PEERED OUT ACROSS THE PLATEAU.
NOT A SOUL WAS IN SIGHT.

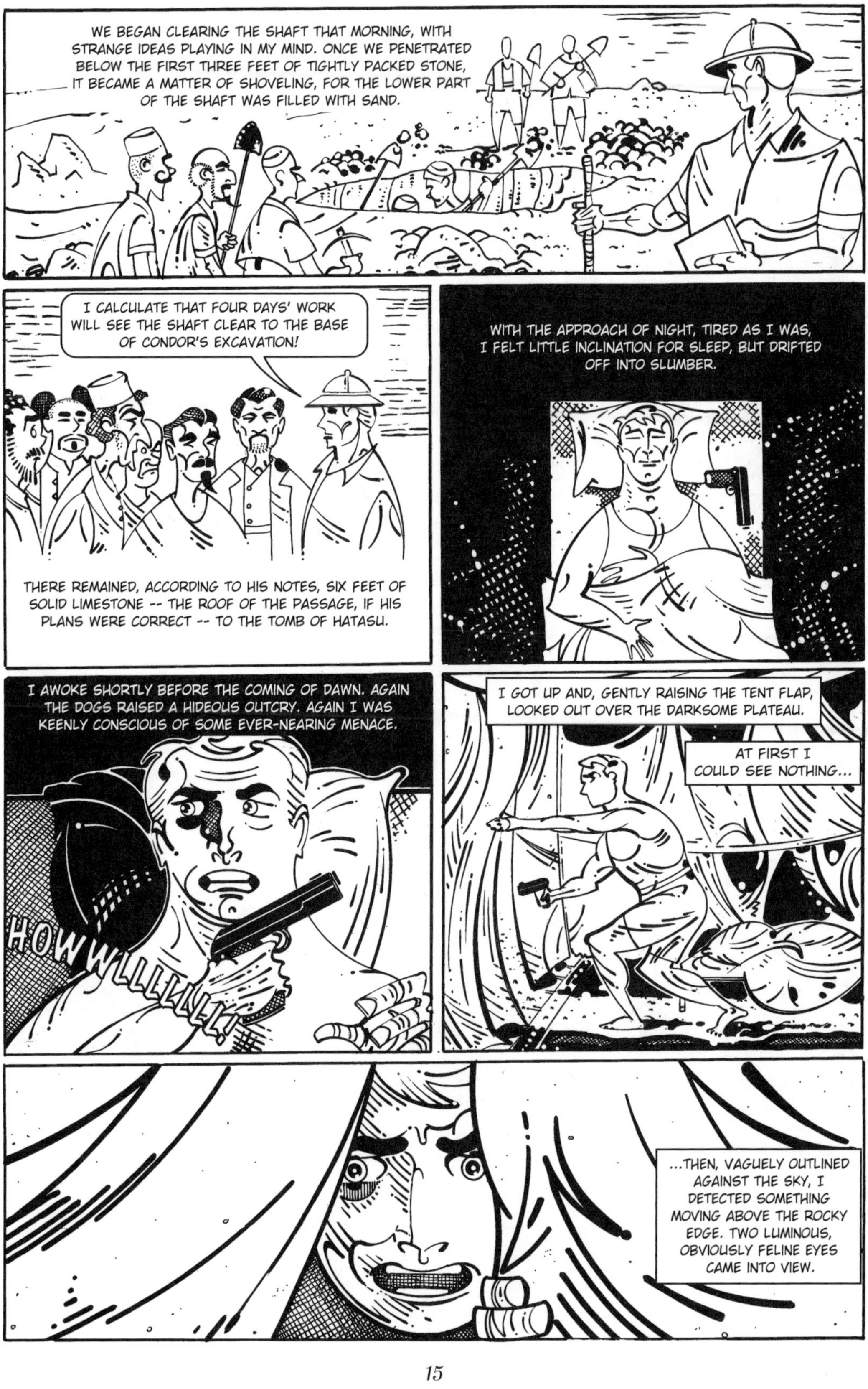
WE BEGAN CLEARING THE SHAFT THAT MORNING, WITH STRANGE IDEAS PLAYING IN MY MIND. ONCE WE PENETRATED BELOW THE FIRST THREE FEET OF TIGHTLY PACKED STONE, IT BECAME A MATTER OF SHOVELING, FOR THE LOWER PART OF THE SHAFT WAS FILLED WITH SAND.
I CALCULATE THAT FOUR DAYS' WORK WILL SEE THE SHAFT CLEAR TO THE BASE OF CONDOR'S EXCAVATION!
THERE REMAINED, ACCORDING TO HIS NOTES, SIX FEET OF SOLID LIMESTONE -- THE ROOF OF THE PASSAGE, IF HIS PLANS WERE CORRECT -- TO THE TOMB OF HATASU.
WITH THE APPROACH OF NIGHT, TIRED AS I WAS, I FELT LITTLE INCLINATION FOR SLEEP, BUT DRIFTED OFF INTO SLUMBER.
I AWOKE SHORTLY BEFORE THE COMING OF DAWN. AGAIN THE DOGS RAISED A HIDEOUS OUTCRY. AGAIN I WAS KEENLY CONSCIOUS OF SOME EVER-NEARING MENACE.
HOWWLLLLLLL
I GOT UP AND, GENTLY RAISING THE TENT FLAP, LOOKED OUT OVER THE DARKSOME PLATEAU.
AT FIRST I COULD SEE NOTHING...
...THEN, VAGUELY OUTLINED AGAINST THE SKY, I DETECTED SOMETHING MOVING ABOVE THE ROCKY EDGE. TWO LUMINOUS, OBVIOUSLY FELINE EYES CAME INTO VIEW.

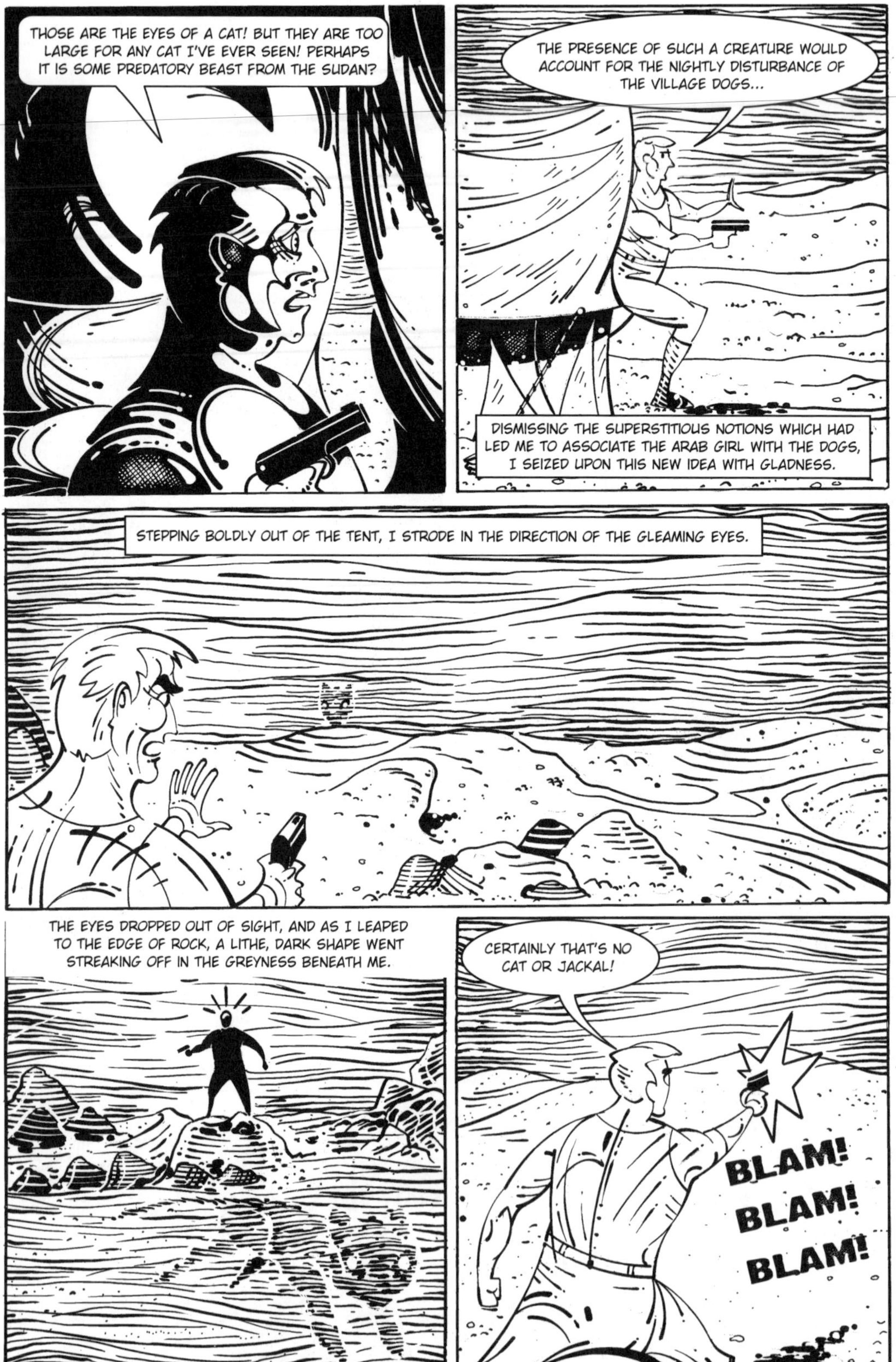
THOSE ARE THE EYES OF A CAT! BUT THEY ARE TOO LARGE FOR ANY CAT I'VE EVER SEEN! PERHAPS IT IS SOME PREDATORY BEAST FROM THE SUDAN?
THE PRESENCE OF SUCH A CREATURE WOULD ACCOUNT FOR THE NIGHTLY DISTURBANCE OF THE VILLAGE DOGS...
DISMISSING THE SUPERSTITIOUS NOTIONS WHICH HAD LED ME TO ASSOCIATE THE ARAB GIRL WITH THE DOGS, I SEIZED UPON THIS NEW IDEA WITH GLADNESS.
STEPPING BOLDLY OUT OF THE TENT, I STRODE IN THE DIRECTION OF THE GLEAMING EYES.
THE EYES DROPPED OUT OF SIGHT, AND AS I LEAPED TO THE EDGE OF ROCK, A LITHE, DARK SHAPE WENT STREAKING OFF IN THE GREYNESS BENEATH ME.
CERTAINLY THAT'S NO CAT OR JACKAL!
BLAM!
BLAM!
BLAM!

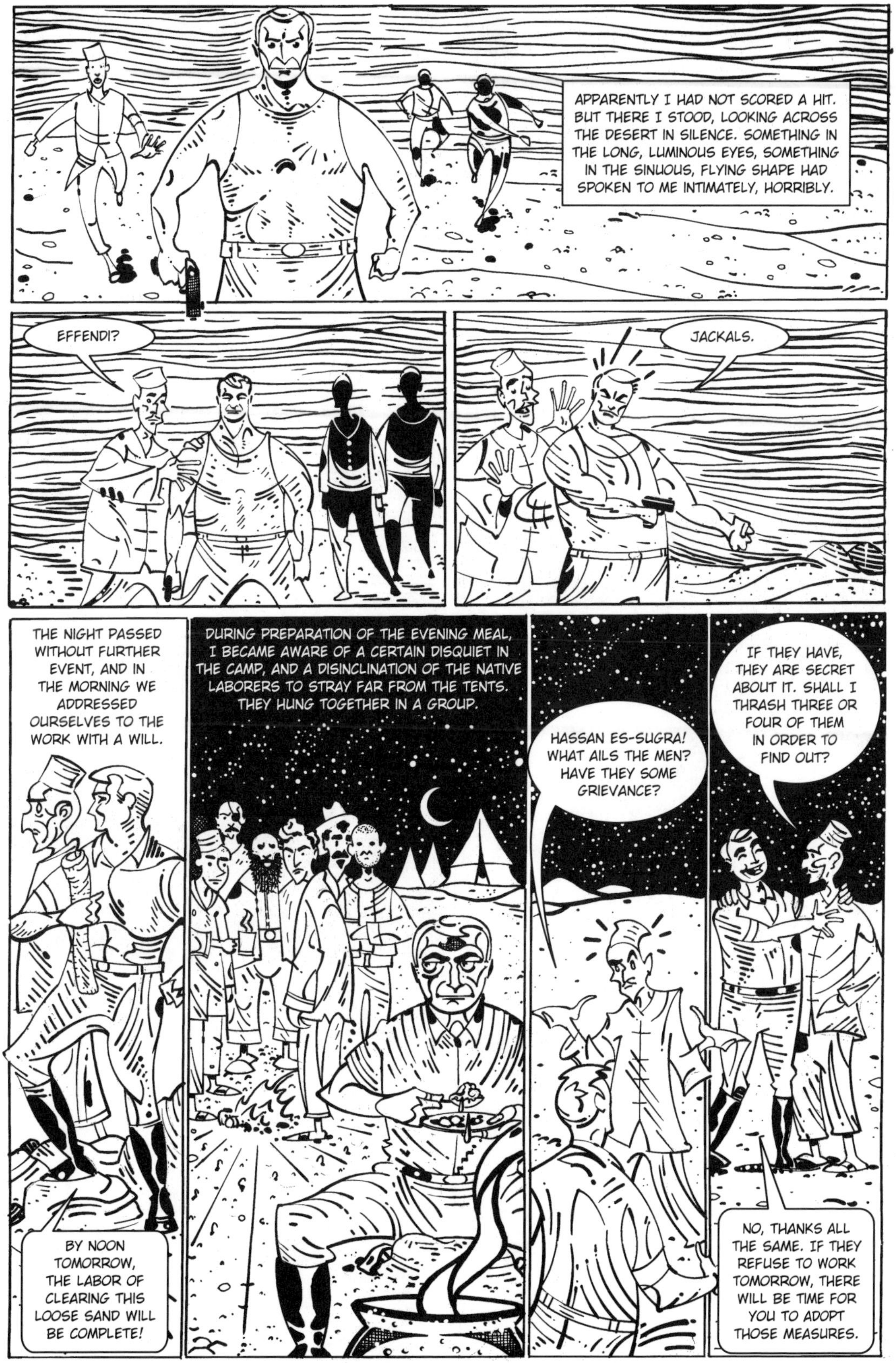
APPARENTLY I HAD NOT SCORED A HIT. BUT THERE I STOOD, LOOKING ACROSS THE DESERT IN SILENCE. SOMETHING IN THE LONG, LUMINOUS EYES, SOMETHING IN THE SINUOUS, FLYING SHAPE HAD SPOKEN TO ME INTIMATELY, HORRIBLY.
EFFENDI?
JACKALS.
THE NIGHT PASSED WITHOUT FURTHER EVENT, AND IN THE MORNING WE ADDRESSED OURSELVES TO THE WORK WITH A WILL.
BY NOON TOMORROW, THE LABOR OF CLEARING THIS LOOSE SAND WILL BE COMPLETE!
DURING PREPARATION OF THE EVENING MEAL, I BECAME AWARE OF A CERTAIN DISQUIET IN THE CAMP, AND A DISINCLINATION OF THE NATIVE LABORERS TO STRAY FAR FROM THE TENTS. THEY HUNG TOGETHER IN A GROUP.
HASSAN ES-SUGRA! WHAT AILS THE MEN? HAVE THEY SOME GRIEVANCE?
IF THEY HAVE, THEY ARE SECRET ABOUT IT. SHALL I THRASH THREE OR FOUR OF THEM IN ORDER TO FIND OUT?
NO, THANKS ALL THE SAME. IF THEY REFUSE TO WORK TOMORROW, THERE WILL BE TIME FOR YOU TO ADOPT THOSE MEASURES.

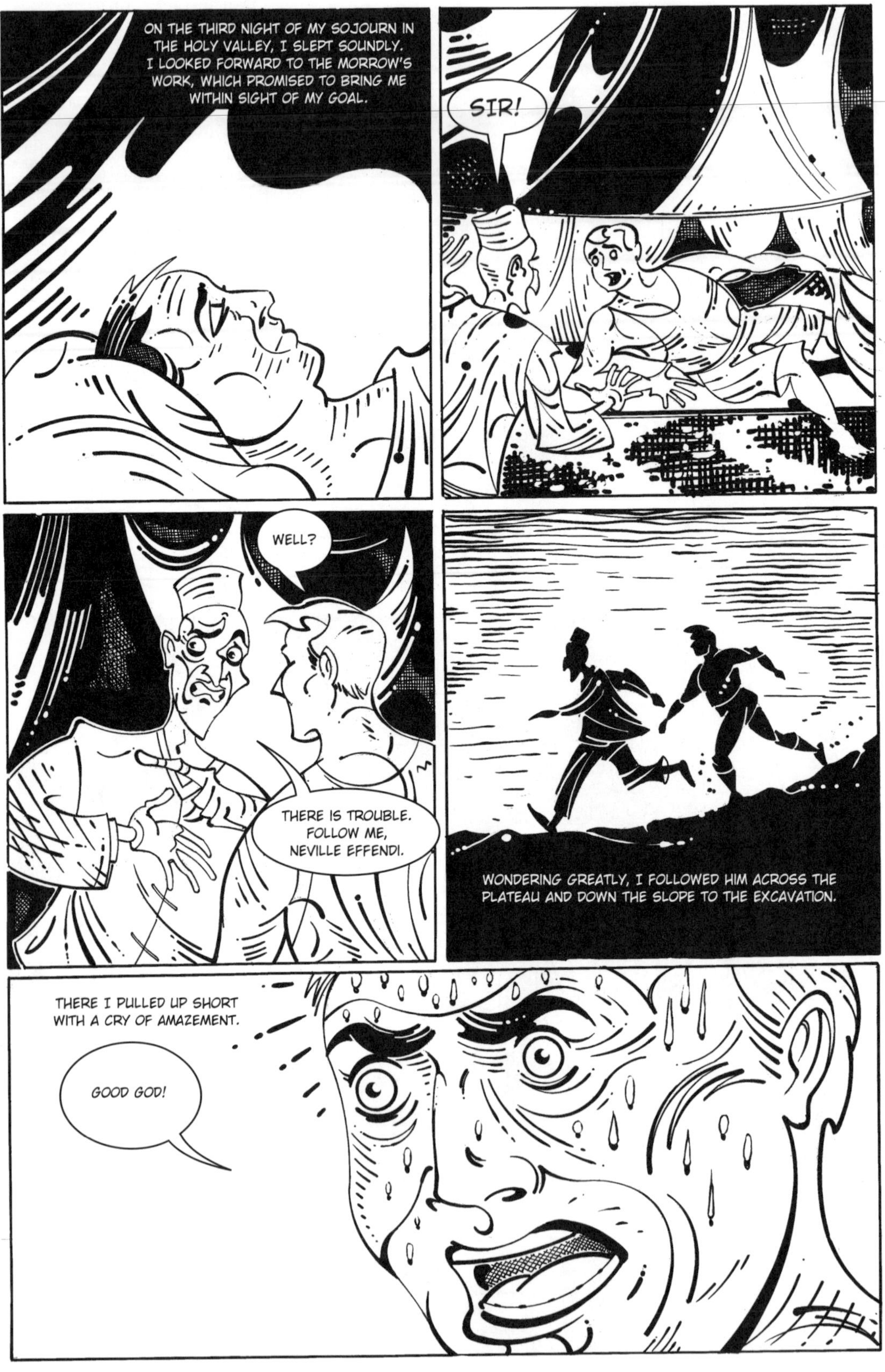
ON THE THIRD NIGHT OF MY SOJOURN IN THE HOLY VALLEY, I SLEPT SOUNDLY. I LOOKED FORWARD TO THE MORROW'S WORK, WHICH PROMISED TO BRING ME WITHIN SIGHT OF MY GOAL.
SIR!
WELL?
THERE IS TROUBLE. FOLLOW ME, NEVILLE EFFENDI.
WONDERING GREATLY, I FOLLOWED HIM ACROSS THE PLATEAU AND DOWN THE SLOPE TO THE EXCAVATION.
THERE I PULLED UP SHORT WITH A CRY OF AMAZEMENT.
GOOD GOD!

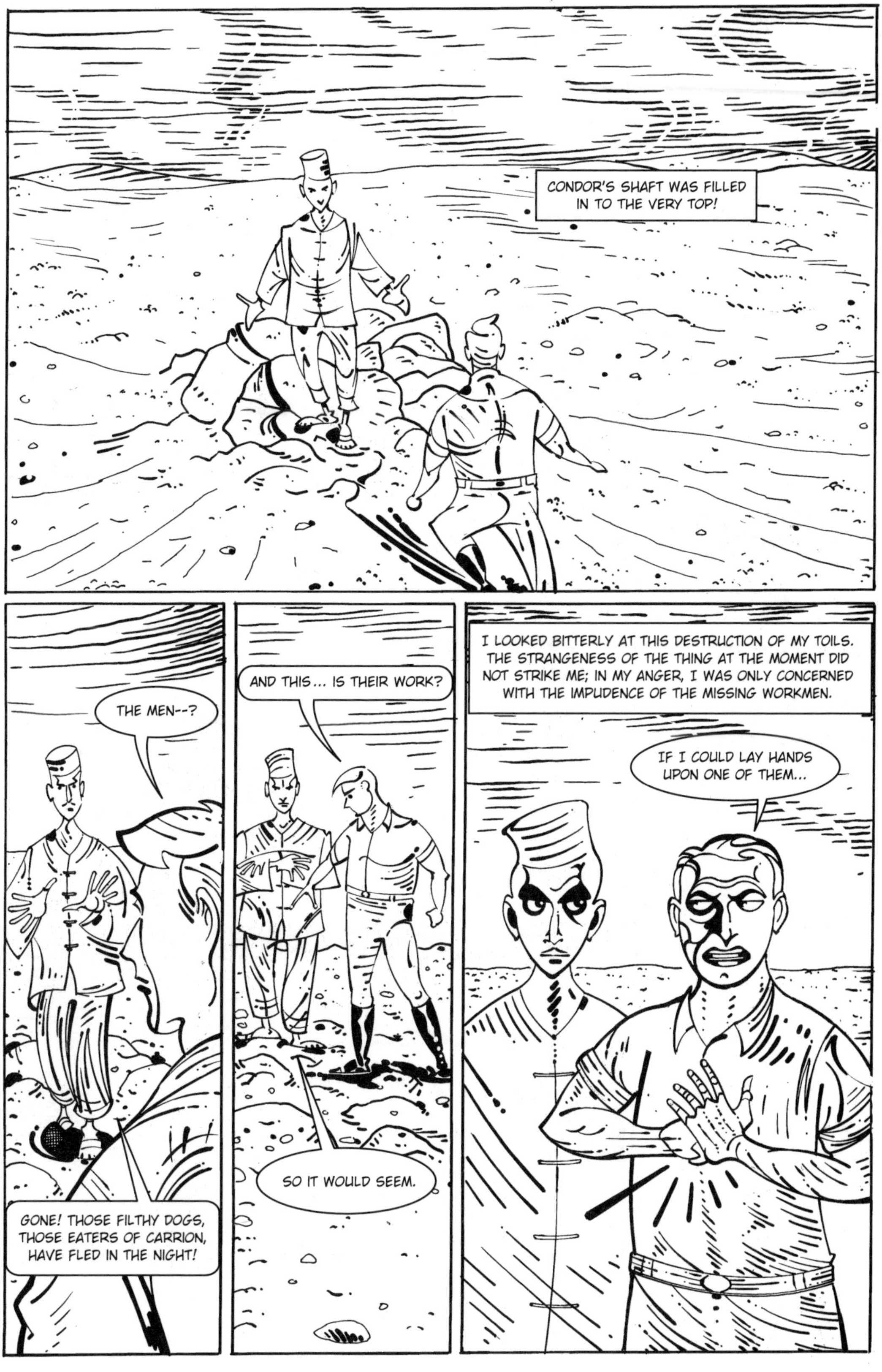
CONDOR'S SHAFT WAS FILLED IN TO THE VERY TOP!
THE MEN--?
GONE! THOSE FILTHY DOGS, THOSE EATERS OF CARRION, HAVE FLED IN THE NIGHT!
AND THIS... IS THEIR WORK?
SO IT WOULD SEEM.
I LOOKED BITTERLY AT THIS DESTRUCTION OF MY TOILS. THE STRANGENESS OF THE THING AT THE MOMENT DID NOT STRIKE ME; IN MY ANGER, I WAS ONLY CONCERNED WITH THE IMPUDENCE OF THE MISSING WORKMEN.
IF I COULD LAY HANDS UPON ONE OF THEM...

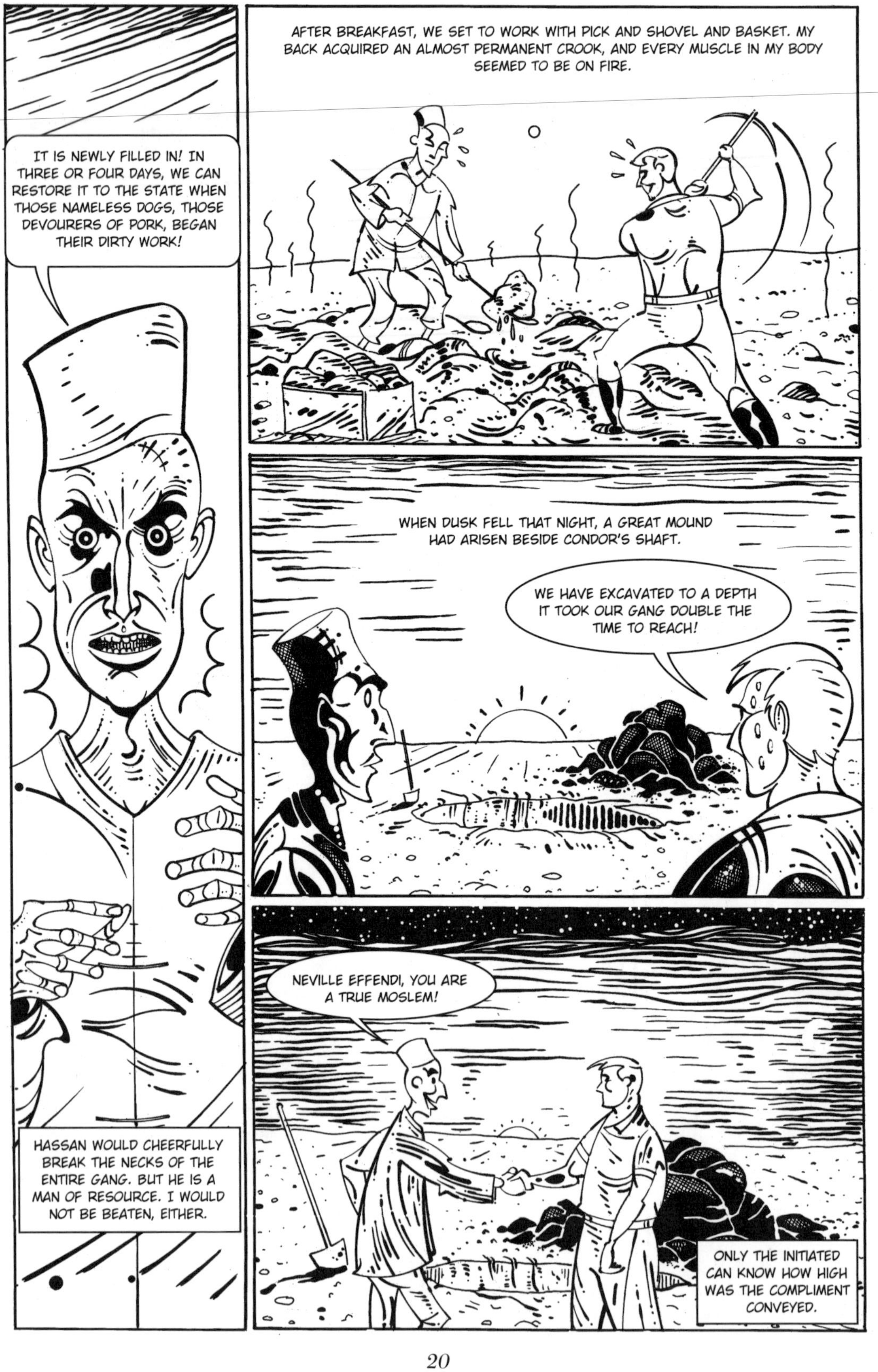
IT IS NEWLY FILLED IN! IN THREE OR FOUR DAYS, WE CAN RESTORE IT TO THE STATE WHEN THOSE NAMELESS DOGS, THOSE DEVOURERS OF PORK, BEGAN THEIR DIRTY WORK!
HASSAN WOULD CHEERFULLY BREAK THE NECKS OF THE ENTIRE GANG. BUT HE IS A MAN OF RESOURCE. I WOULD NOT BE BEATEN, EITHER.
AFTER BREAKFAST, WE SET TO WORK WITH PICK AND SHOVEL AND BASKET. MY BACK ACQUIRED AN ALMOST PERMANENT CROOK, AND EVERY MUSCLE IN MY BODY SEEMED TO BE ON FIRE.
WHEN DUSK FELL THAT NIGHT, A GREAT MOUND HAD ARISEN BESIDE CONDOR'S SHAFT.
WE HAVE EXCAVATED TO A DEPTH IT TOOK OUR GANG DOUBLE THE TIME TO REACH!
NEVILLE EFFENDI, YOU ARE A TRUE MOSLEM!
ONLY THE INITIATED CAN KNOW HOW HIGH WAS THE COMPLIMENT CONVEYED.

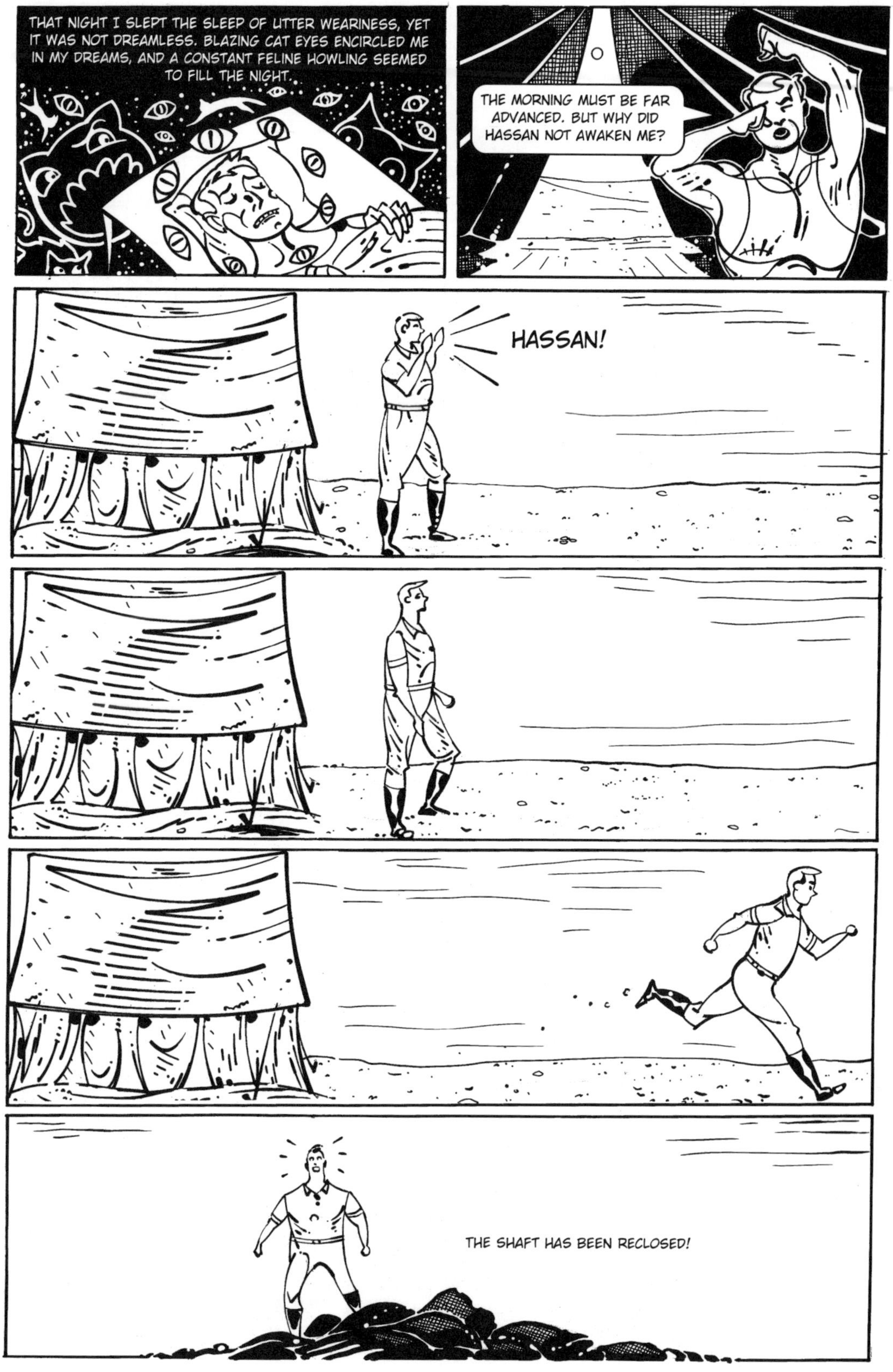
THAT NIGHT I SLEPT THE SLEEP OF UTTER WEARINESS, YET IT WAS NOT DREAMLESS. BLAZING CAT EYES ENCIRCLED ME IN MY DREAMS, AND A CONSTANT FELINE HOWLING SEEMED TO FILL THE NIGHT.
THE MORNING MUST BE FAR ADVANCED. BUT WHY DID HASSAN NOT AWAKEN ME?
HASSAN!
THE SHAFT HAS BEEN RECLOSED!

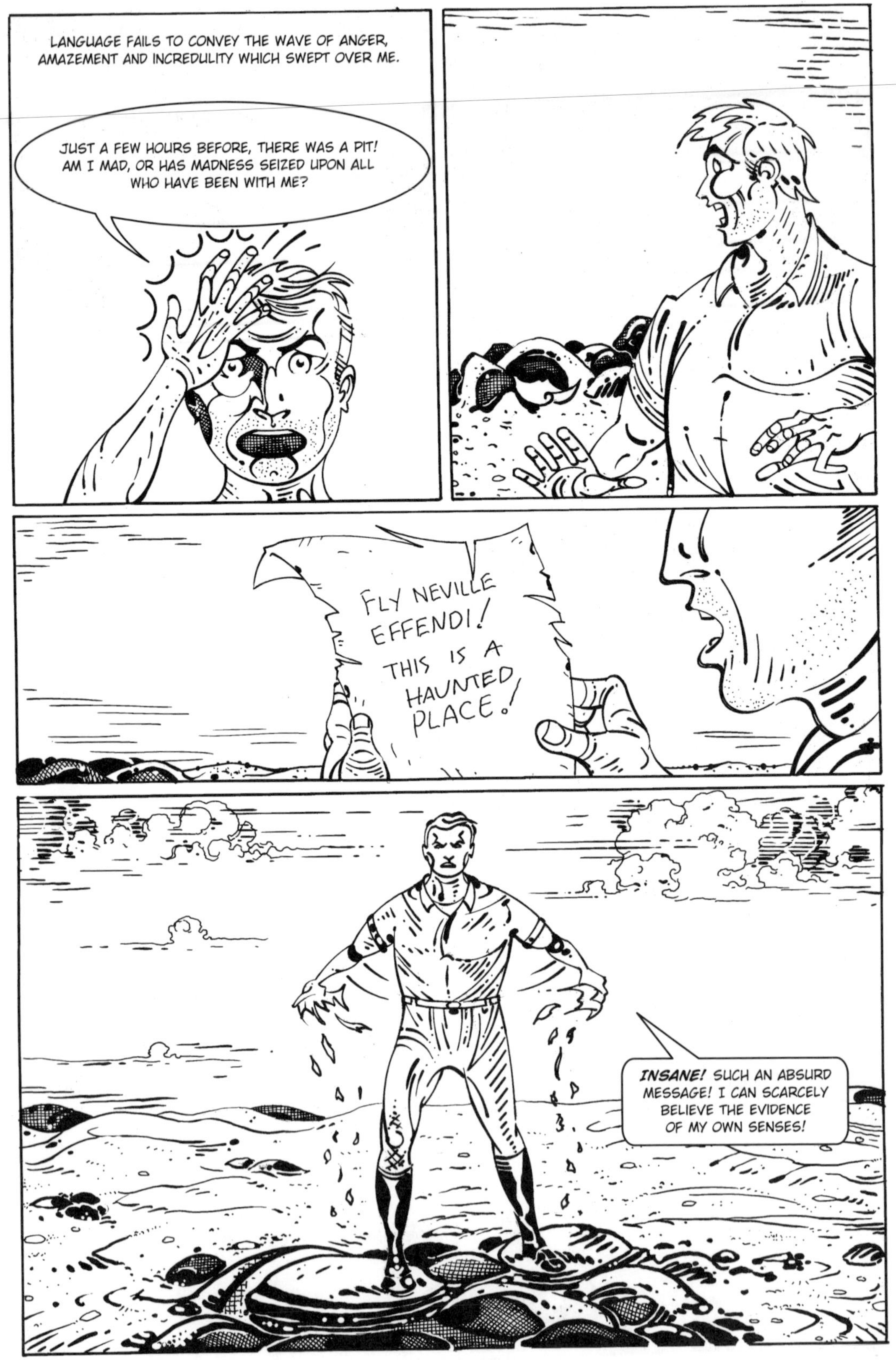
LANGUAGE FAILS TO CONVEY THE WAVE OF ANGER, AMAZEMENT AND INCREDULITY WHICH SWEPT OVER ME.
JUST A FEW HOURS BEFORE, THERE WAS A PIT! AM I MAD, OR HAS MADNESS SEIZED UPON ALL WHO HAVE BEEN WITH ME?
FLY NEVILLE EFFENDI! THIS IS A HAUNTED PLACE!
INSANE! SUCH AN ABSURD MESSAGE! I CAN SCARCELY BELIEVE THE EVIDENCE OF MY OWN SENSES!

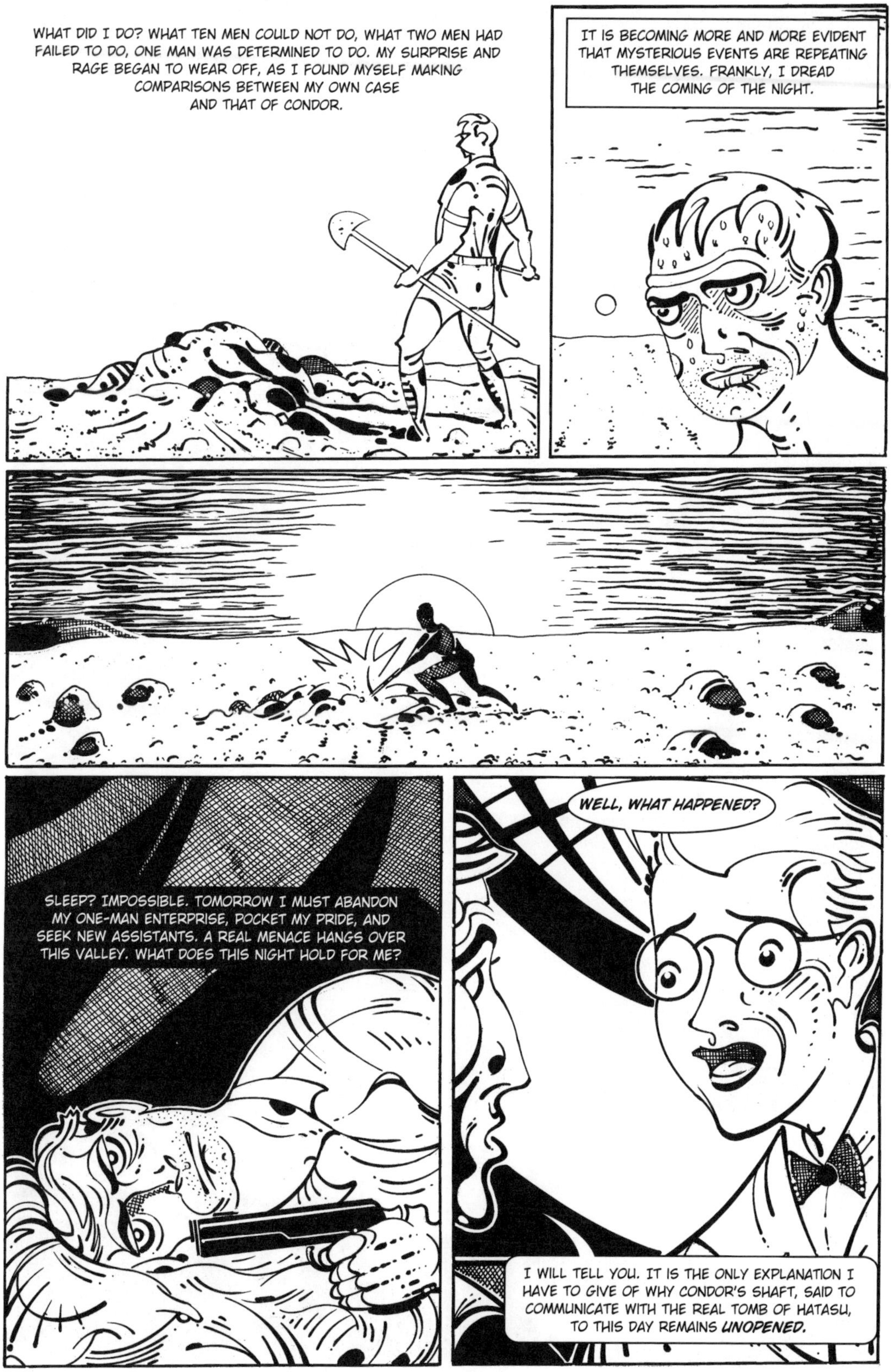
WHAT DID I DO? WHAT TEN MEN COULD NOT DO, WHAT TWO MEN HAD FAILED TO DO, ONE MAN WAS DETERMINED TO DO. MY SURPRISE AND RAGE BEGAN TO WEAR OFF, AS I FOUND MYSELF MAKING COMPARISONS BETWEEN MY OWN CASE AND THAT OF CONDOR.
IT IS BECOMING MORE AND MORE EVIDENT THAT MYSTERIOUS EVENTS ARE REPEATING THEMSELVES. FRANKLY, I DREAD THE COMING OF THE NIGHT.
SLEEP? IMPOSSIBLE. TOMORROW I MUST ABANDON MY ONE-MAN ENTERPRISE, POCKET MY PRIDE, AND SEEK NEW ASSISTANTS. A REAL MENACE HANGS OVER THIS VALLEY. WHAT DOES THIS NIGHT HOLD FOR ME?
WELL, WHAT HAPPENED?
I WILL TELL YOU. IT IS THE ONLY EXPLANATION I HAVE TO GIVE OF WHY CONDOR'S SHAFT, SAID TO COMMUNICATE WITH THE REAL TOMB OF HATASU, TO THIS DAY REMAINS UNOPENED.

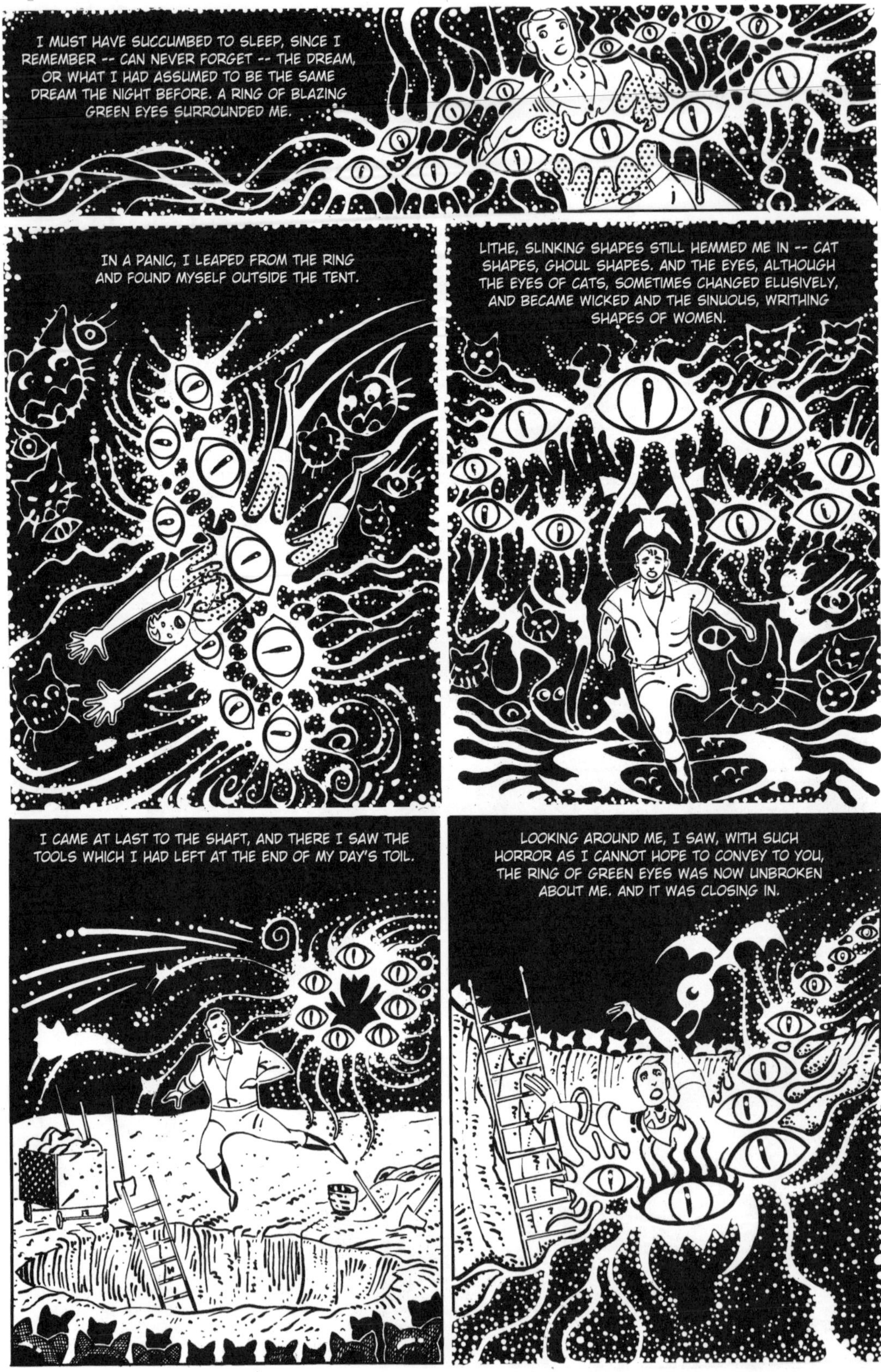
I MUST HAVE SUCCUMBED TO SLEEP, SINCE I REMEMBER -- CAN NEVER FORGET -- THE DREAM, OR WHAT I HAD ASSUMED TO BE THE SAME DREAM THE NIGHT BEFORE. A RING OF BLAZING GREEN EYES SURROUNDED ME.
IN A PANIC, I LEAPED FROM THE RING AND FOUND MYSELF OUTSIDE THE TENT.
LITHE, SLINKING SHAPES STILL HEMMED ME IN -- CAT SHAPES, GHOUL SHAPES. AND THE EYES, ALTHOUGH THE EYES OF CATS, SOMETIMES CHANGED ELUSIVELY, AND BECAME WICKED AND THE SINUOUS, WRITHING SHAPES OF WOMEN.
I CAME AT LAST TO THE SHAFT, AND THERE I SAW THE TOOLS WHICH I HAD LEFT AT THE END OF MY DAY'S TOIL.
LOOKING AROUND ME, I SAW, WITH SUCH HORROR AS I CANNOT HOPE TO CONVEY TO YOU, THE RING OF GREEN EYES WAS NOW UNBROKEN ABOUT ME. AND IT WAS CLOSING IN.

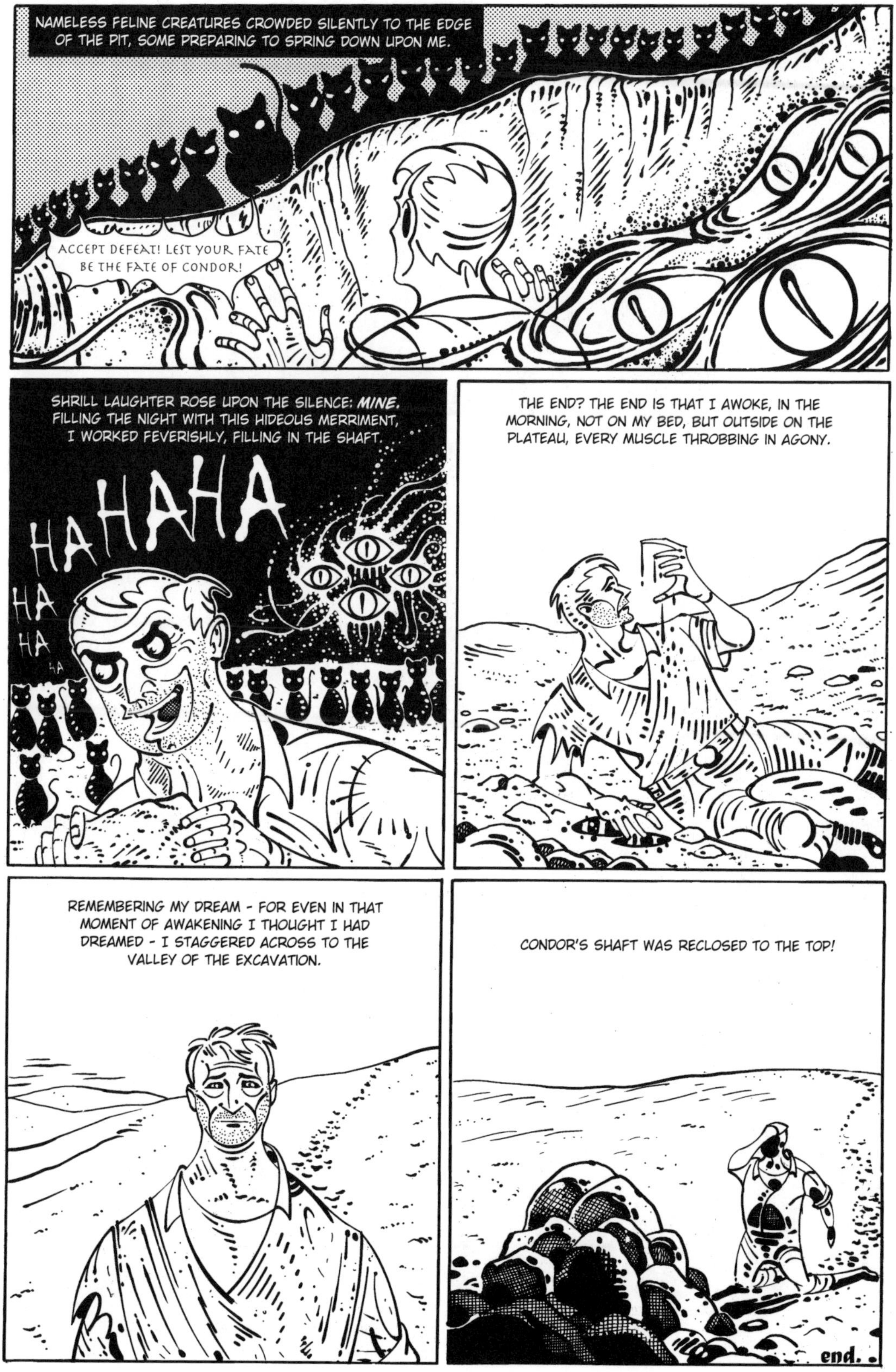
NAMELESS FELINE CREATURES CROWDED SILENTLY TO THE EDGE OF THE PIT, SOME PREPARING TO SPRING DOWN UPON ME.
ACCEPT DEFEAT! LEST YOUR FATE BE THE FATE OF CONDOR!
SHRILL LAUGHTER ROSE UPON THE SILENCE: *MINE.* FILLING THE NIGHT WITH THIS HIDEOUS MERRIMENT, I WORKED FEVERISHLY, FILLING IN THE SHAFT.
HAHAHA
HA
HA
HA
THE END? THE END IS THAT I AWOKE, IN THE MORNING, NOT ON MY BED, BUT OUTSIDE ON THE PLATEAU, EVERY MUSCLE THROBBING IN AGONY.
REMEMBERING MY DREAM - FOR EVEN IN THAT MOMENT OF AWAKENING I THOUGHT I HAD DREAMED - I STAGGERED ACROSS TO THE VALLEY OF THE EXCAVATION.
CONDOR'S SHAFT WAS RECLOSED TO THE TOP!
end.

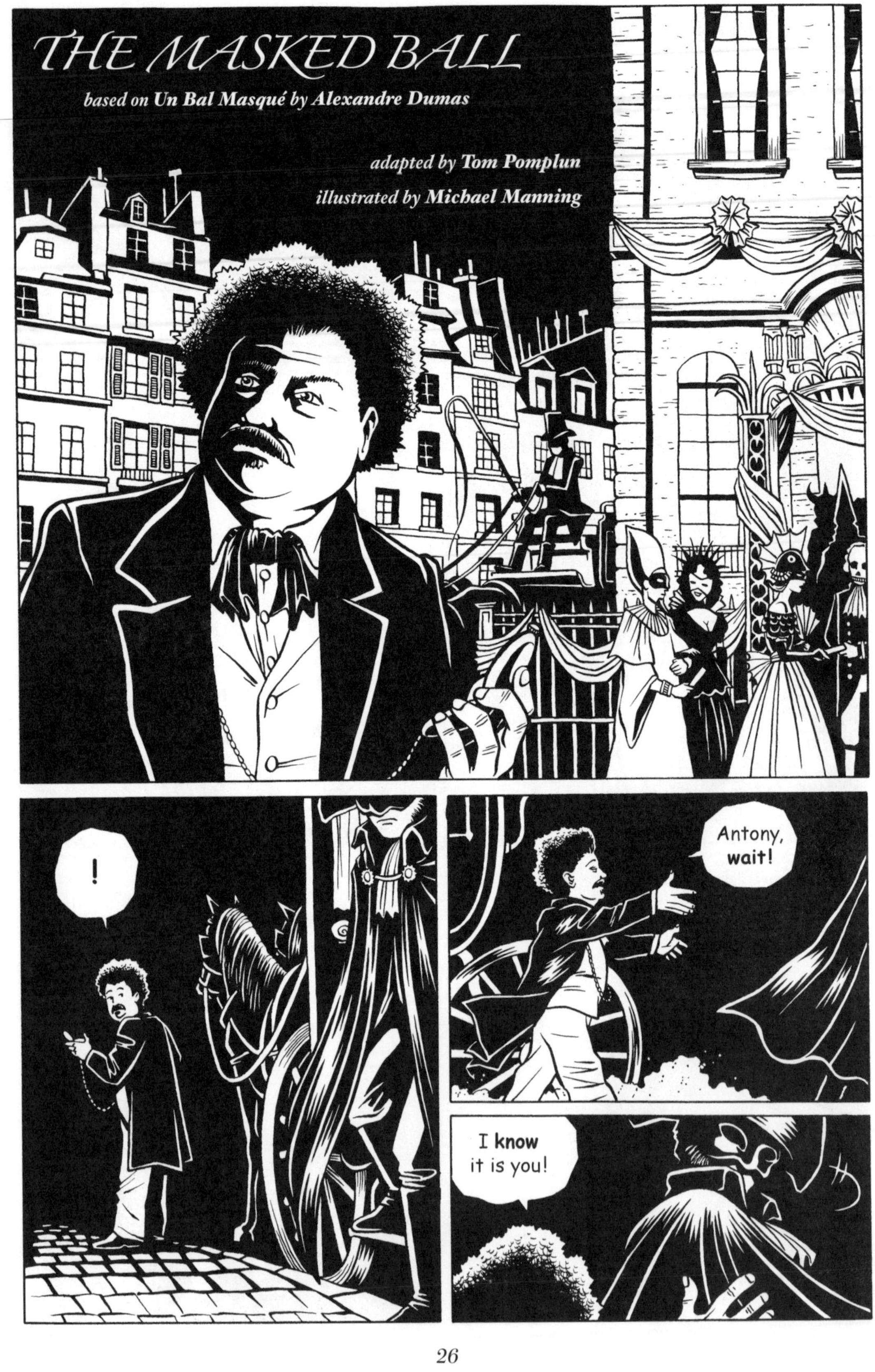
THE MASKED BALL
based on Un Bal Masqué by Alexandre Dumas
adapted by Tom Pomplun
illustrated by Michael Manning
!
Antony, wait!
I know it is you!

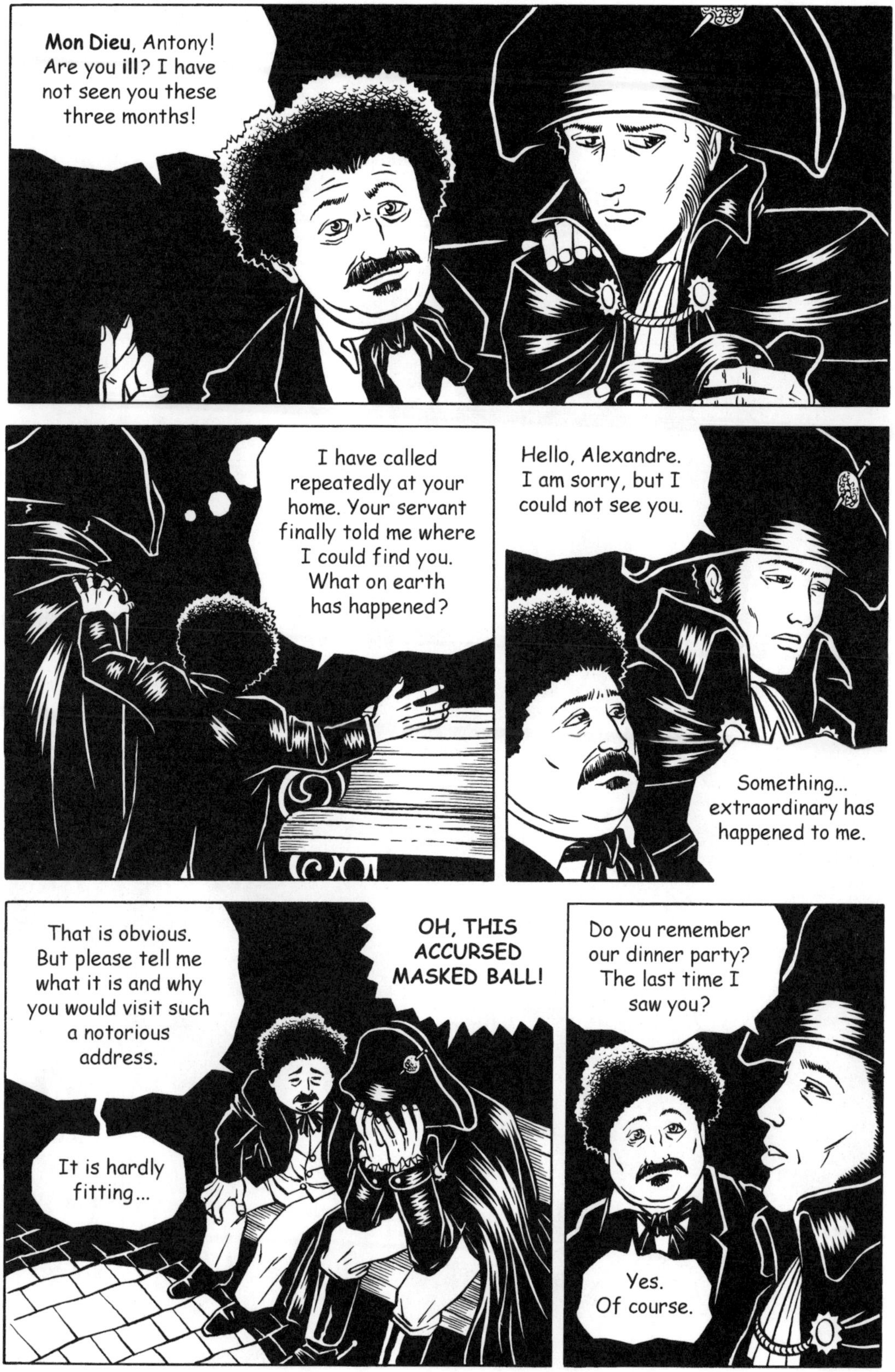
Mon Dieu, Antony! Are you ill? I have not seen you these three months!
I have called repeatedly at your home. Your servant finally told me where I could find you. What on earth has happened?
Hello, Alexandre. I am sorry, but I could not see you.
Something... extraordinary has happened to me.
That is obvious. But please tell me what it is and why you would visit such a notorious address.
It is hardly fitting...
OH, THIS ACCURSED MASKED BALL!
Do you remember our dinner party? The last time I saw you?
Yes. Of course.

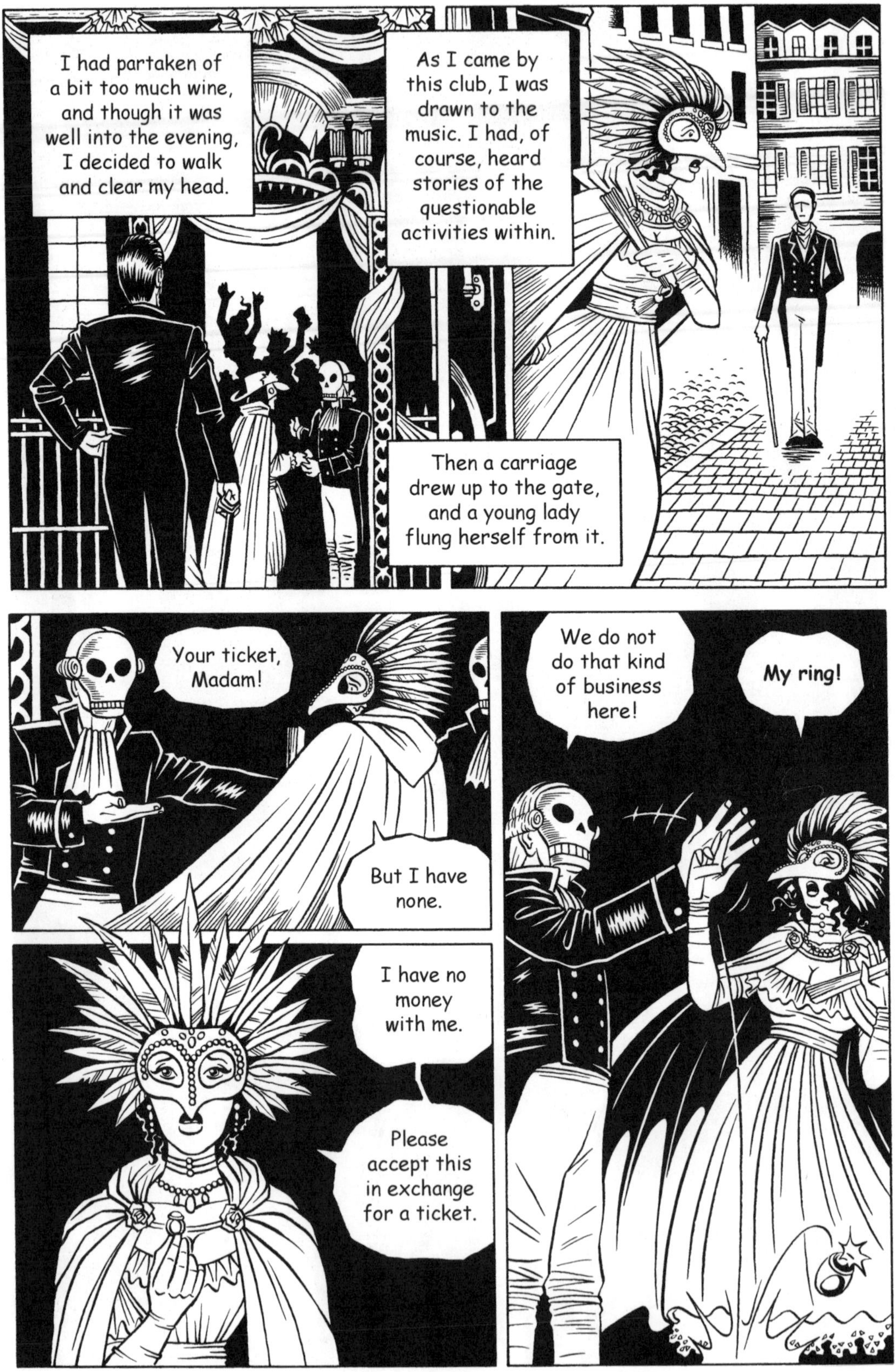
I had partaken of a bit too much wine, and though it was well into the evening, I decided to walk and clear my head.
As I came by this club, I was drawn to the music. I had, of course, heard stories of the questionable activities within.
Then a carriage drew up to the gate, and a young lady flung herself from it.
Your ticket, Madam!
But I have none.
I have no money with me.
Please accept this in exchange for a ticket.
We do not do that kind of business here!
My ring!

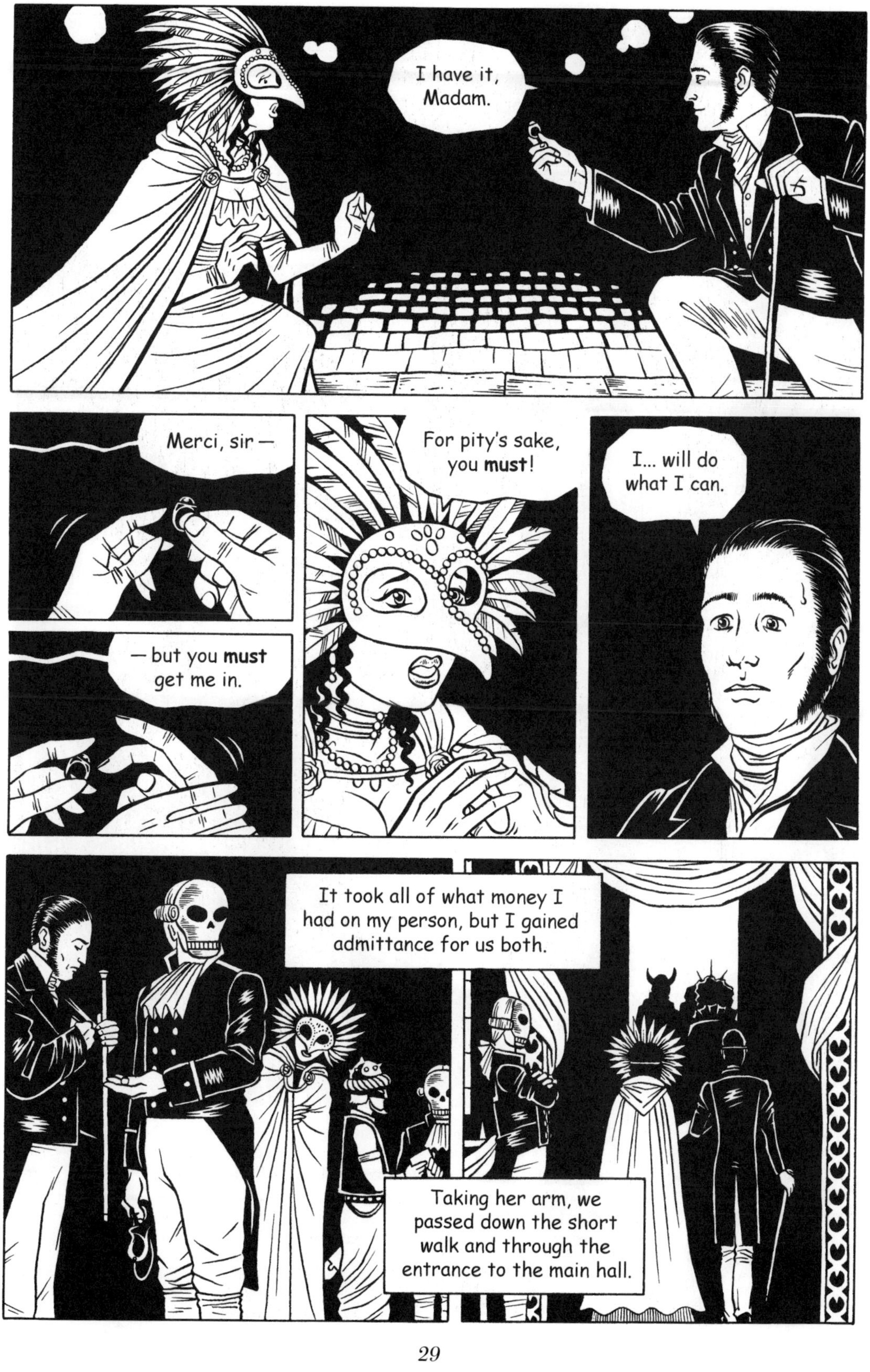
I have it, Madam.
Merci, sir —
— but you **must** get me in.
For pity's sake, you **must**!
I... will do what I can.
It took all of what money I had on my person, but I gained admittance for us both.
Taking her arm, we passed down the short walk and through the entrance to the main hall.

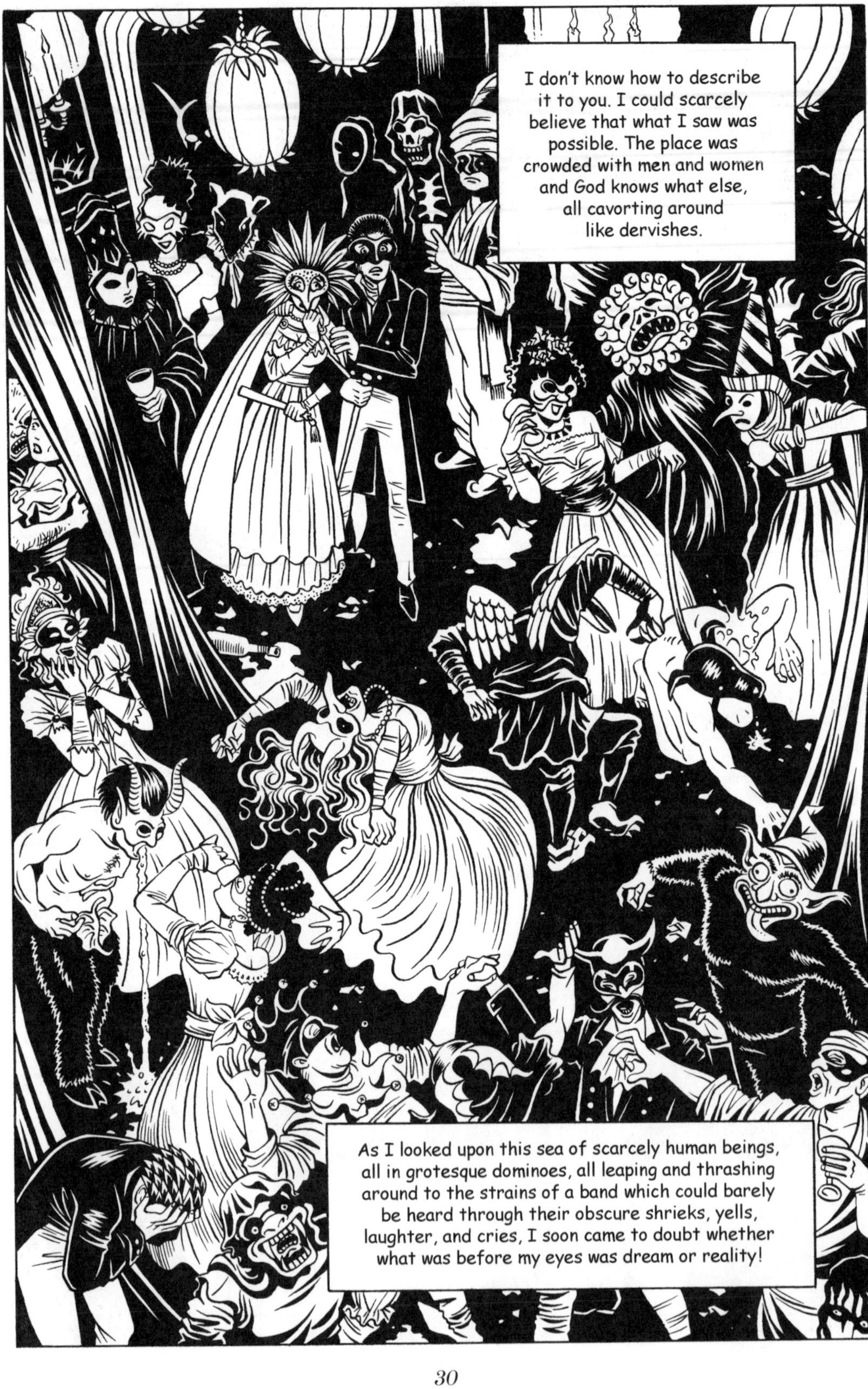
I don't know how to describe it to you. I could scarcely believe that what I saw was possible. The place was crowded with men and women and God knows what else, all cavorting around like dervishes.
As I looked upon this sea of scarcely human beings, all in grotesque dominoes, all leaping and thrashing around to the strains of a band which could barely be heard through their obscure shrieks, yells, laughter, and cries, I soon came to doubt whether what was before my eyes was dream or reality!

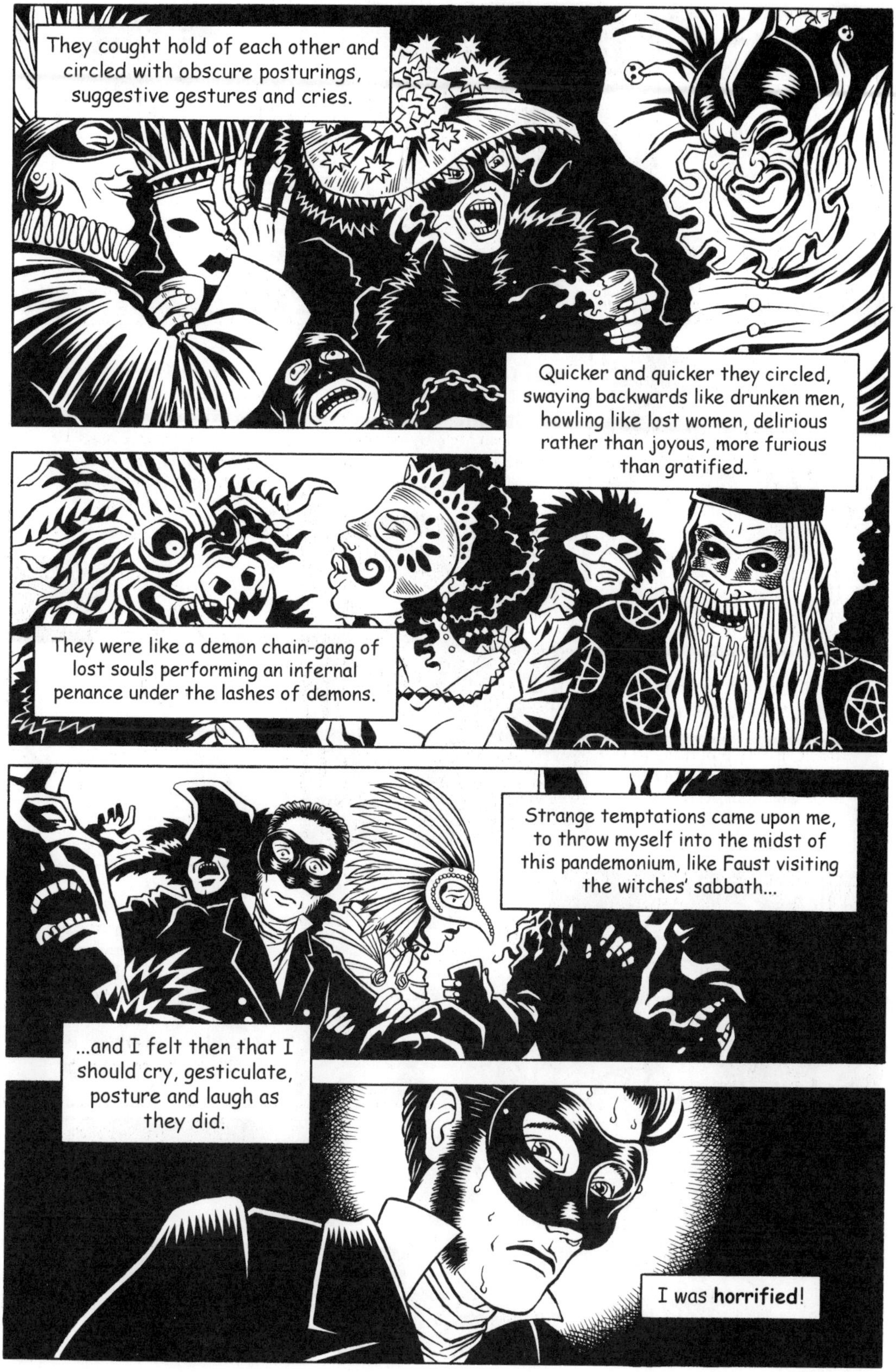
They cought hold of each other and circled with obscure posturings, suggestive gestures and cries.
Quicker and quicker they circled, swaying backwards like drunken men, howling like lost women, delirious rather than joyous, more furious than gratified.
They were like a demon chain-gang of lost souls performing an infernal penance under the lashes of demons.
Strange temptations came upon me, to throw myself into the midst of this pandemonium, like Faust visiting the witches' sabbath...
...and I felt then that I should cry, gesticulate, posture and laugh as they did.
I was **horrified**!

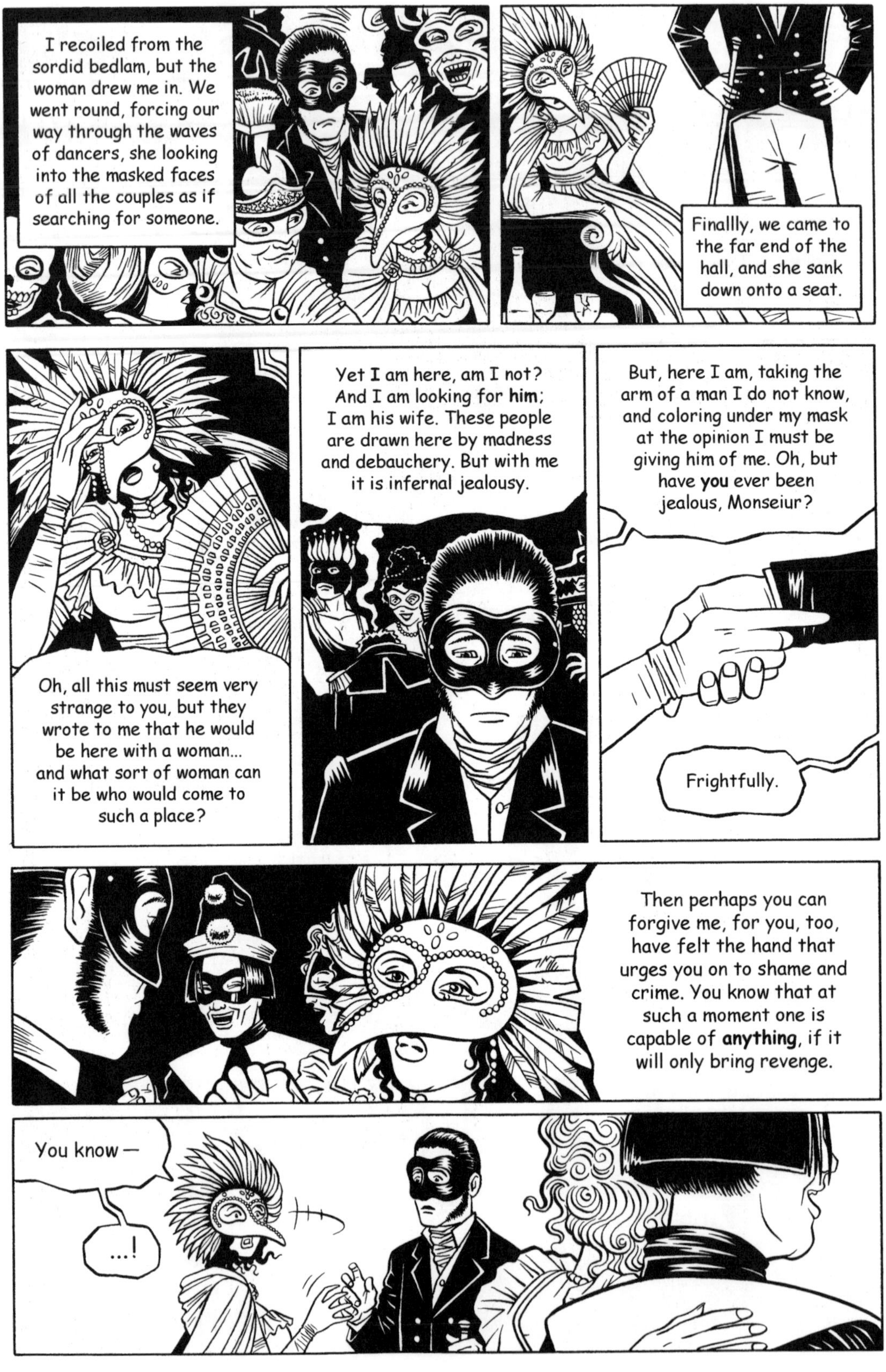
I recoiled from the sordid bedlam, but the woman drew me in. We went round, forcing our way through the waves of dancers, she looking into the masked faces of all the couples as if searching for someone.
Finallly, we came to the far end of the hall, and she sank down onto a seat.
Oh, all this must seem very strange to you, but they wrote to me that he would be here with a woman... and what sort of woman can it be who would come to such a place?
Yet I am here, am I not? And I am looking for **him**; I am his wife. These people are drawn here by madness and debauchery. But with me it is infernal jealousy.
But, here I am, taking the arm of a man I do not know, and coloring under my mask at the opinion I must be giving him of me. Oh, but have **you** ever been jealous, Monseiur?
Frightfully.
Then perhaps you can forgive me, for you, too, have felt the hand that urges you on to shame and crime. You know that at such a moment one is capable of **anything**, if it will only bring revenge.
You know —
...!

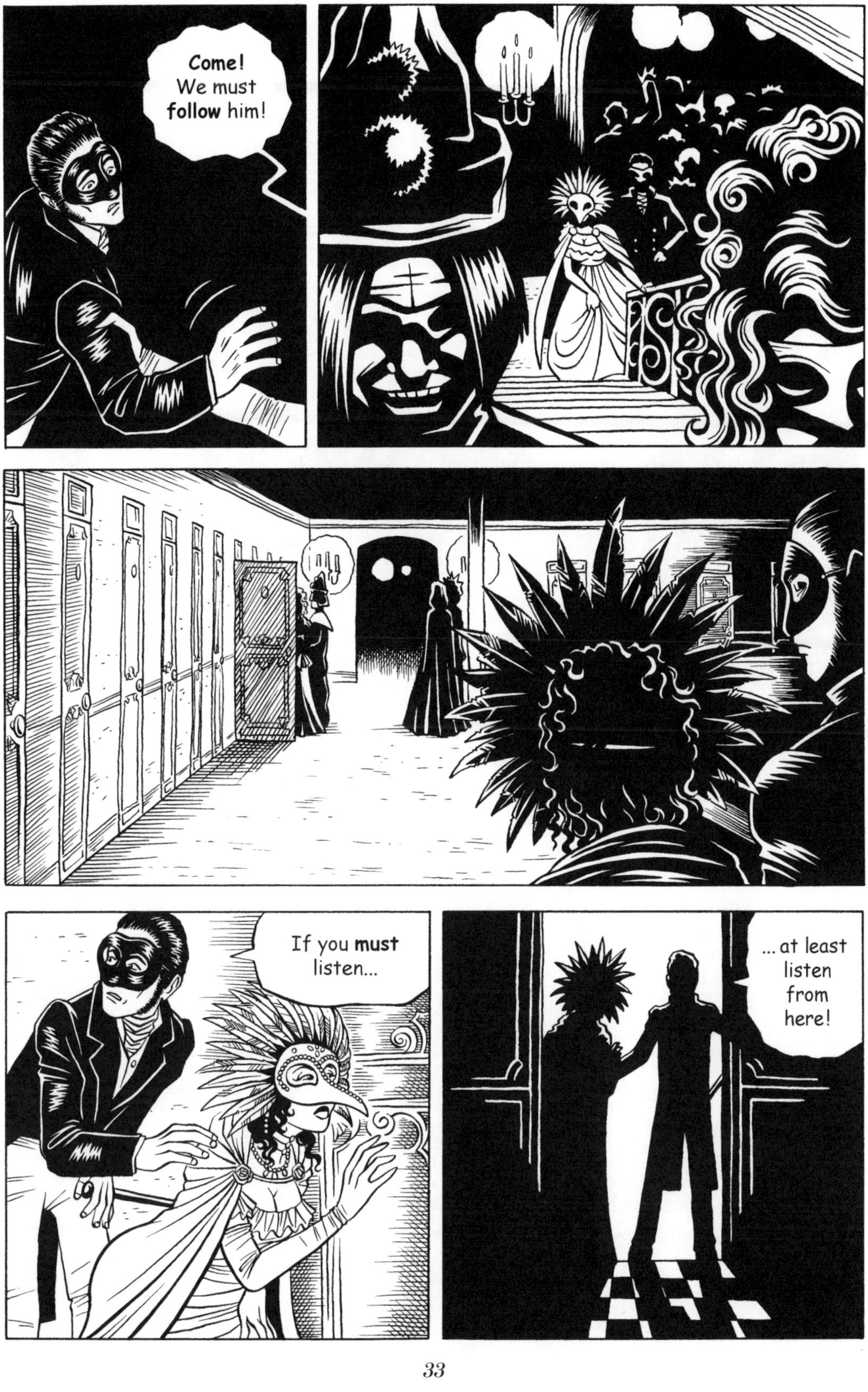
Come! We must follow him!
If you must listen...
... at least listen from here!

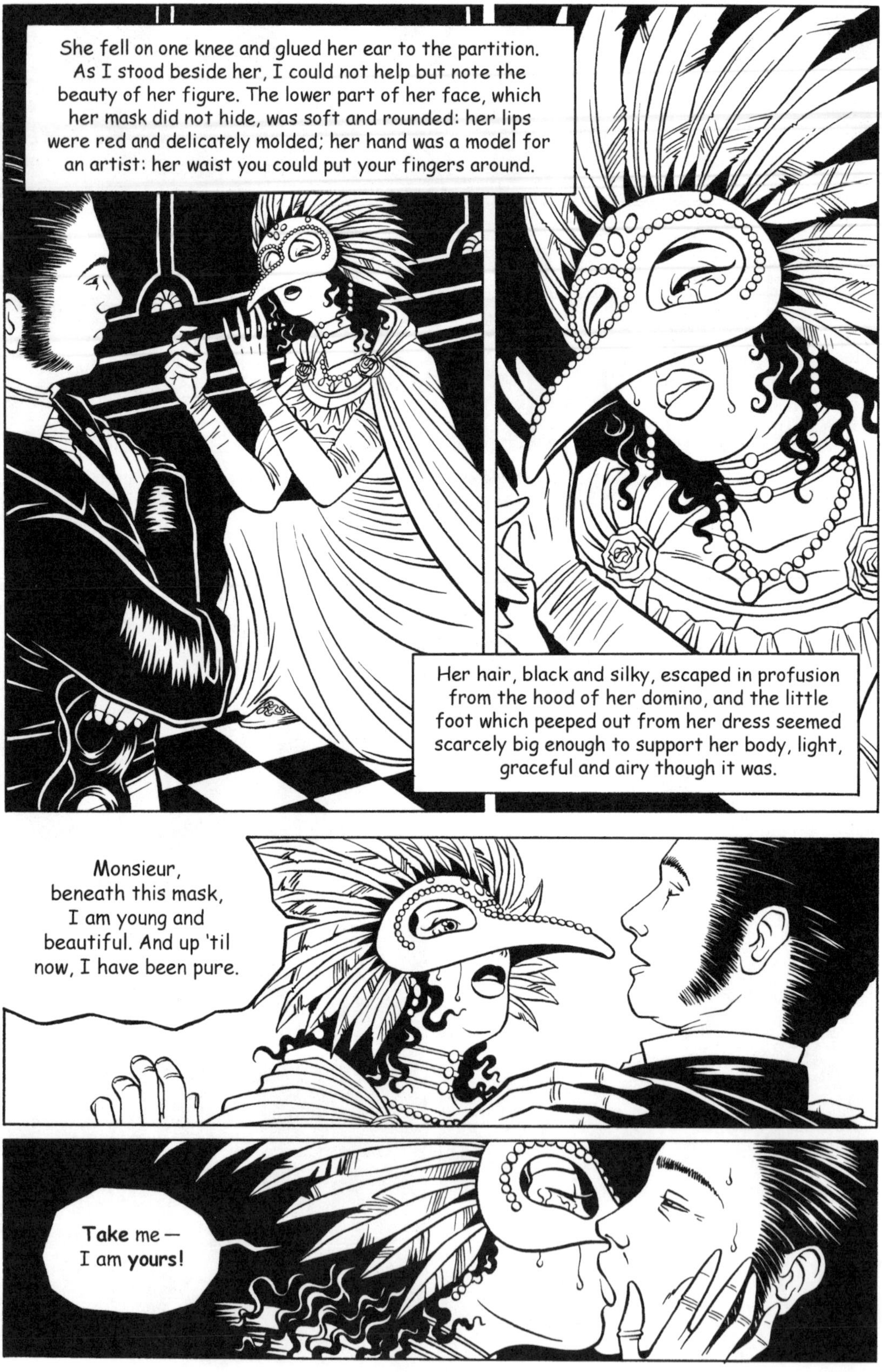
She fell on one knee and glued her ear to the partition. As I stood beside her, I could not help but note the beauty of her figure. The lower part of her face, which her mask did not hide, was soft and rounded: her lips were red and delicately molded; her hand was a model for an artist: her waist you could put your fingers around.
Her hair, black and silky, escaped in profusion from the hood of her domino, and the little foot which peeped out from her dress seemed scarcely big enough to support her body, light, graceful and airy though it was.
Monsieur, beneath this mask, I am young and beautiful. And up 'til now, I have been pure.
Take me — I am **yours**!

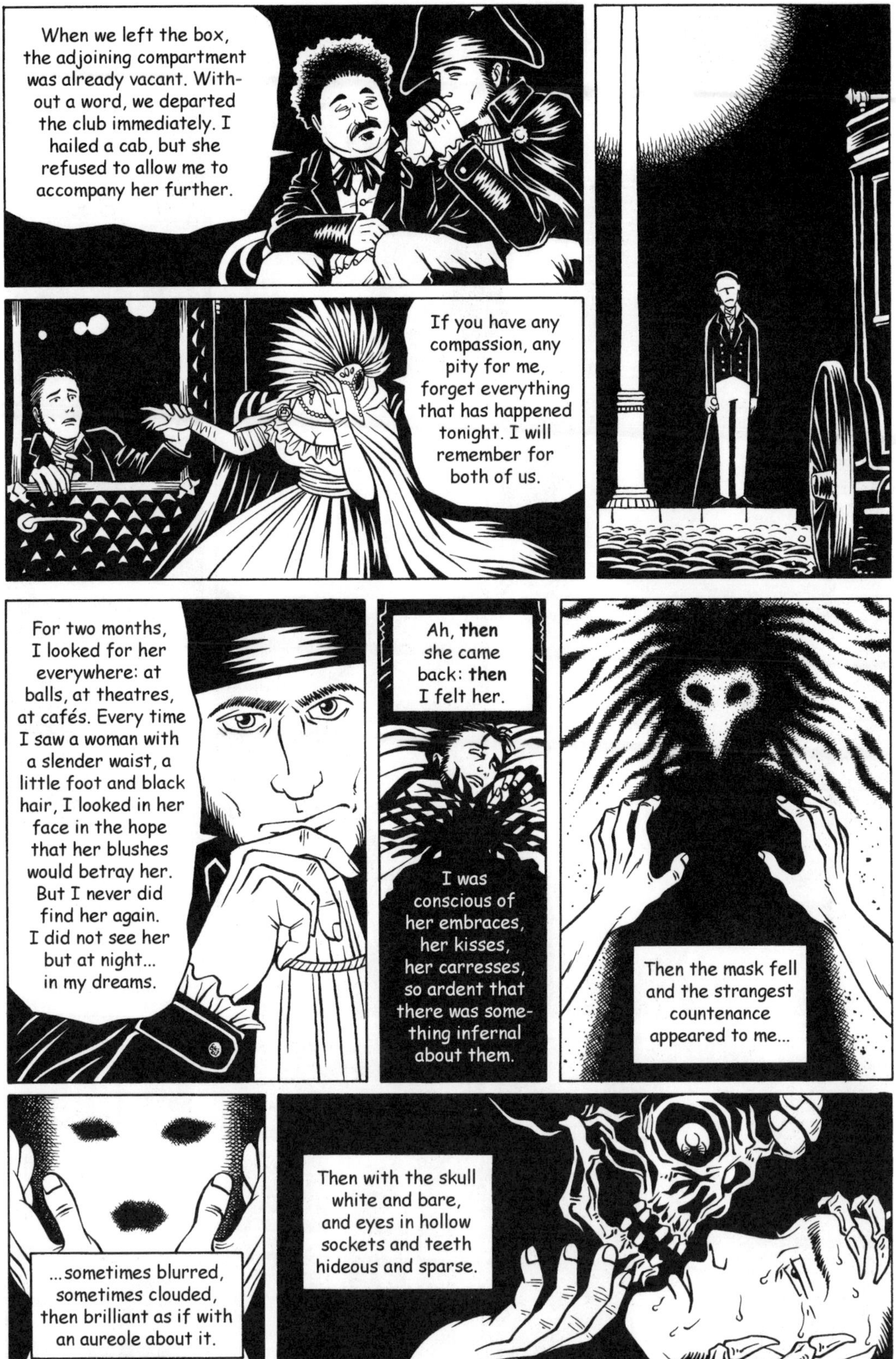
When we left the box, the adjoining compartment was already vacant. Without a word, we departed the club immediately. I hailed a cab, but she refused to allow me to accompany her further.
If you have any compassion, any pity for me, forget everything that has happened tonight. I will remember for both of us.
For two months, I looked for her everywhere: at balls, at theatres, at cafés. Every time I saw a woman with a slender waist, a little foot and black hair, I looked in her face in the hope that her blushes would betray her. But I never did find her again. I did not see her but at night... in my dreams.
Ah, **then** she came back: **then** I felt her.
I was conscious of her embraces, her kisses, her carresses, so ardent that there was something infernal about them.
Then the mask fell and the strangest countenance appeared to me...
...sometimes blurred, sometimes clouded, then brilliant as if with an aureole about it.
Then with the skull white and bare, and eyes in hollow sockets and teeth hideous and sparse.

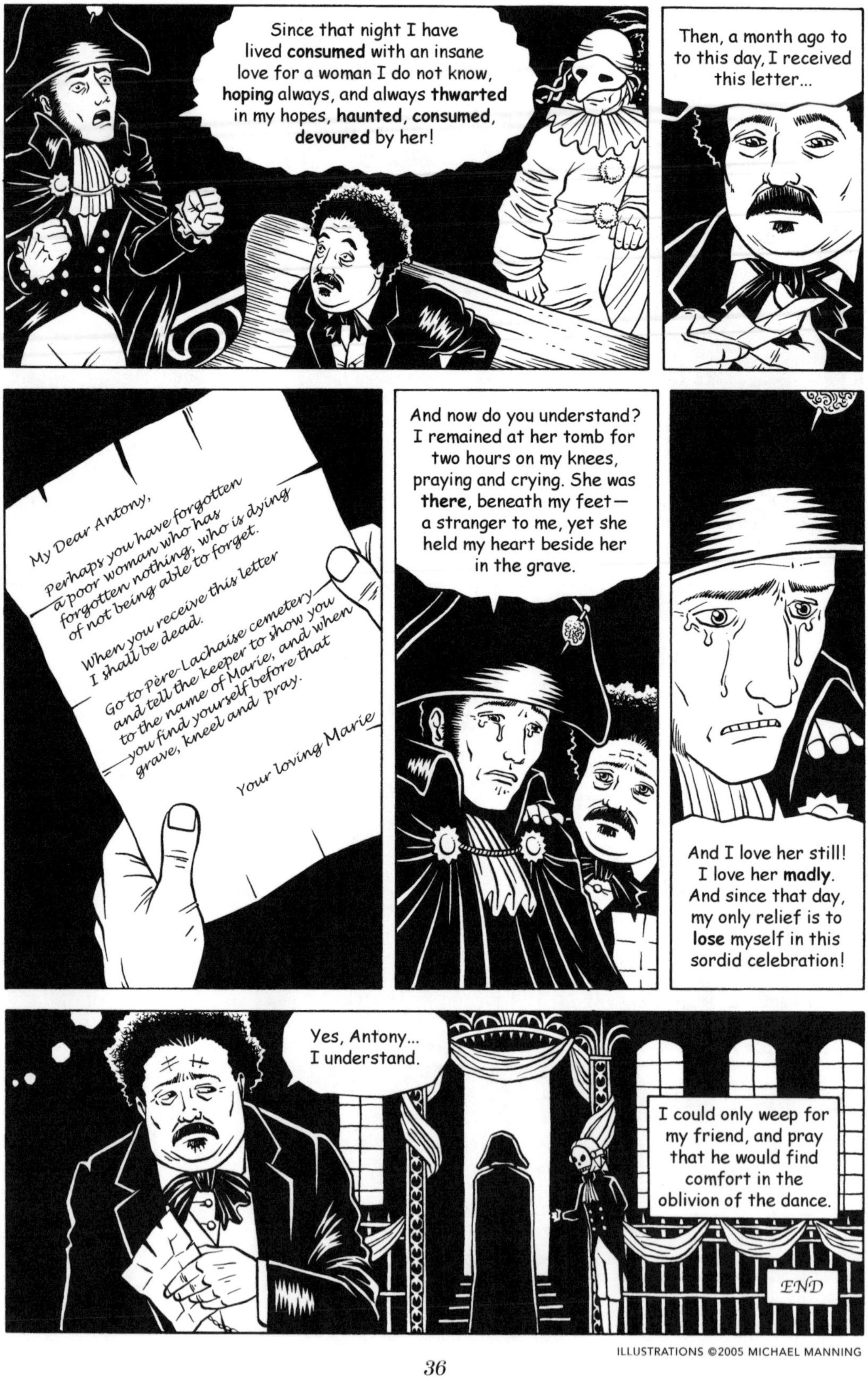
Since that night I have lived consumed with an insane love for a woman I do not know, hoping always, and always thwarted in my hopes, haunted, consumed, devoured by her!
Then, a month ago to to this day, I received this letter...
My Dear Antony,
Perhaps you have forgotten a poor woman who has forgotten nothing, who is dying of not being able to forget.
When you receive this letter I shall be dead.
Go to Père-Lachaise cemetery and tell the keeper to show you to the name of Marie, and when you find yourself before that grave, kneel and pray.
Your loving Marie
And now do you understand? I remained at her tomb for two hours on my knees, praying and crying. She was there, beneath my feet— a stranger to me, yet she held my heart beside her in the grave.
And I love her still! I love her madly. And since that day, my only relief is to lose myself in this sordid celebration!
Yes, Antony... I understand.
I could only weep for my friend, and pray that he would find comfort in the oblivion of the dance.
END

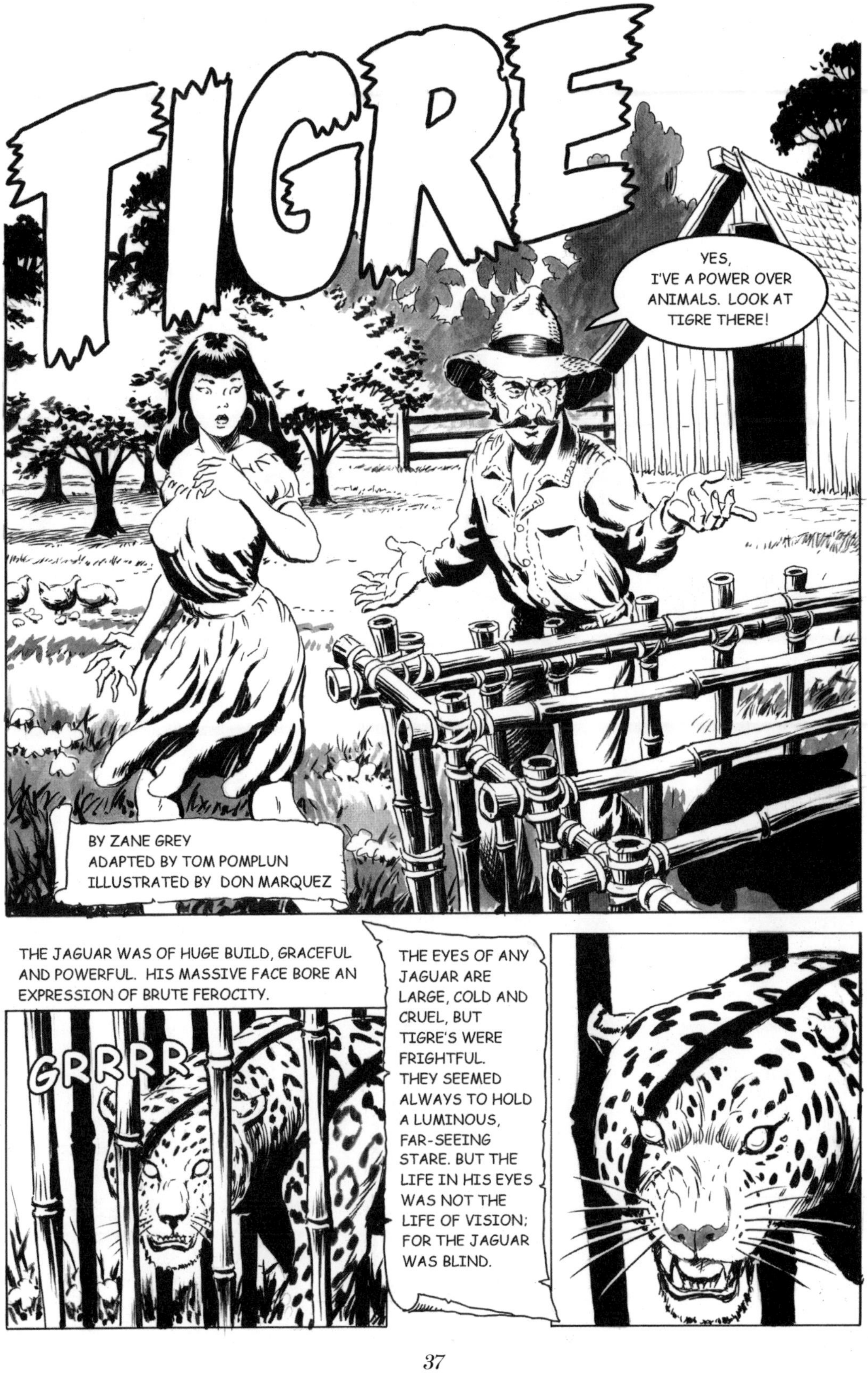
TIGRE
YES, I'VE A POWER OVER ANIMALS. LOOK AT TIGRE THERE!
BY ZANE GREY
ADAPTED BY TOM POMPLUN
ILLUSTRATED BY DON MARQUEZ
THE JAGUAR WAS OF HUGE BUILD, GRACEFUL AND POWERFUL. HIS MASSIVE FACE BORE AN EXPRESSION OF BRUTE FEROCITY.
GRRRR
THE EYES OF ANY JAGUAR ARE LARGE, COLD AND CRUEL, BUT TIGRE'S WERE FRIGHTFUL. THEY SEEMED ALWAYS TO HOLD A LUMINOUS, FAR-SEEING STARE. BUT THE LIFE IN HIS EYES WAS NOT THE LIFE OF VISION; FOR THE JAGUAR WAS BLIND.

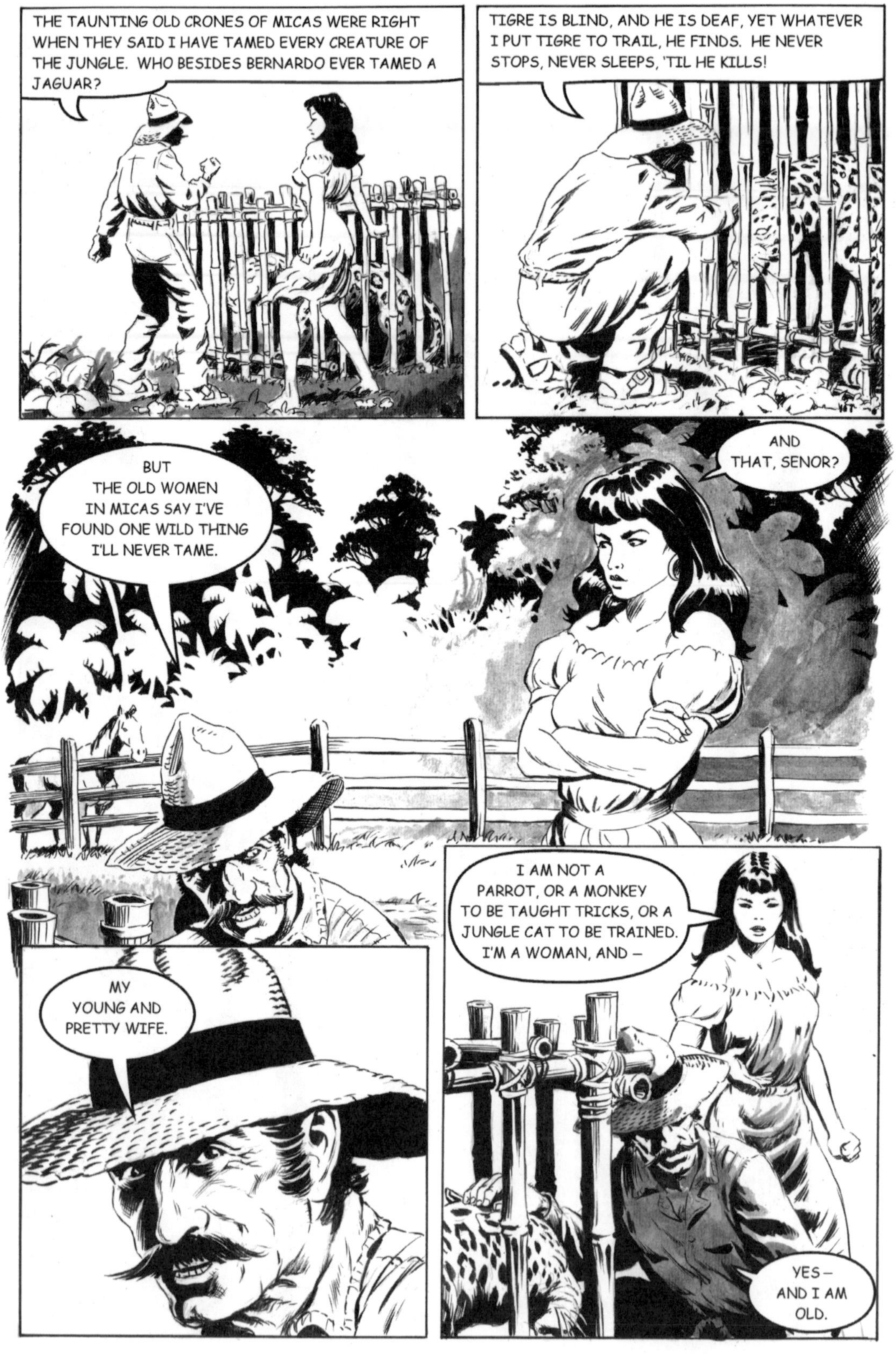
THE TAUNTING OLD CRONES OF MICAS WERE RIGHT WHEN THEY SAID I HAVE TAMED EVERY CREATURE OF THE JUNGLE. WHO BESIDES BERNARDO EVER TAMED A JAGUAR?
TIGRE IS BLIND, AND HE IS DEAF, YET WHATEVER I PUT TIGRE TO TRAIL, HE FINDS. HE NEVER STOPS, NEVER SLEEPS, 'TIL HE KILLS!
BUT THE OLD WOMEN IN MICAS SAY I'VE FOUND ONE WILD THING I'LL NEVER TAME.
AND THAT, SENOR?
MY YOUNG AND PRETTY WIFE.
I AM NOT A PARROT, OR A MONKEY TO BE TAUGHT TRICKS, OR A JUNGLE CAT TO BE TRAINED. I'M A WOMAN, AND –
YES – AND I AM OLD.

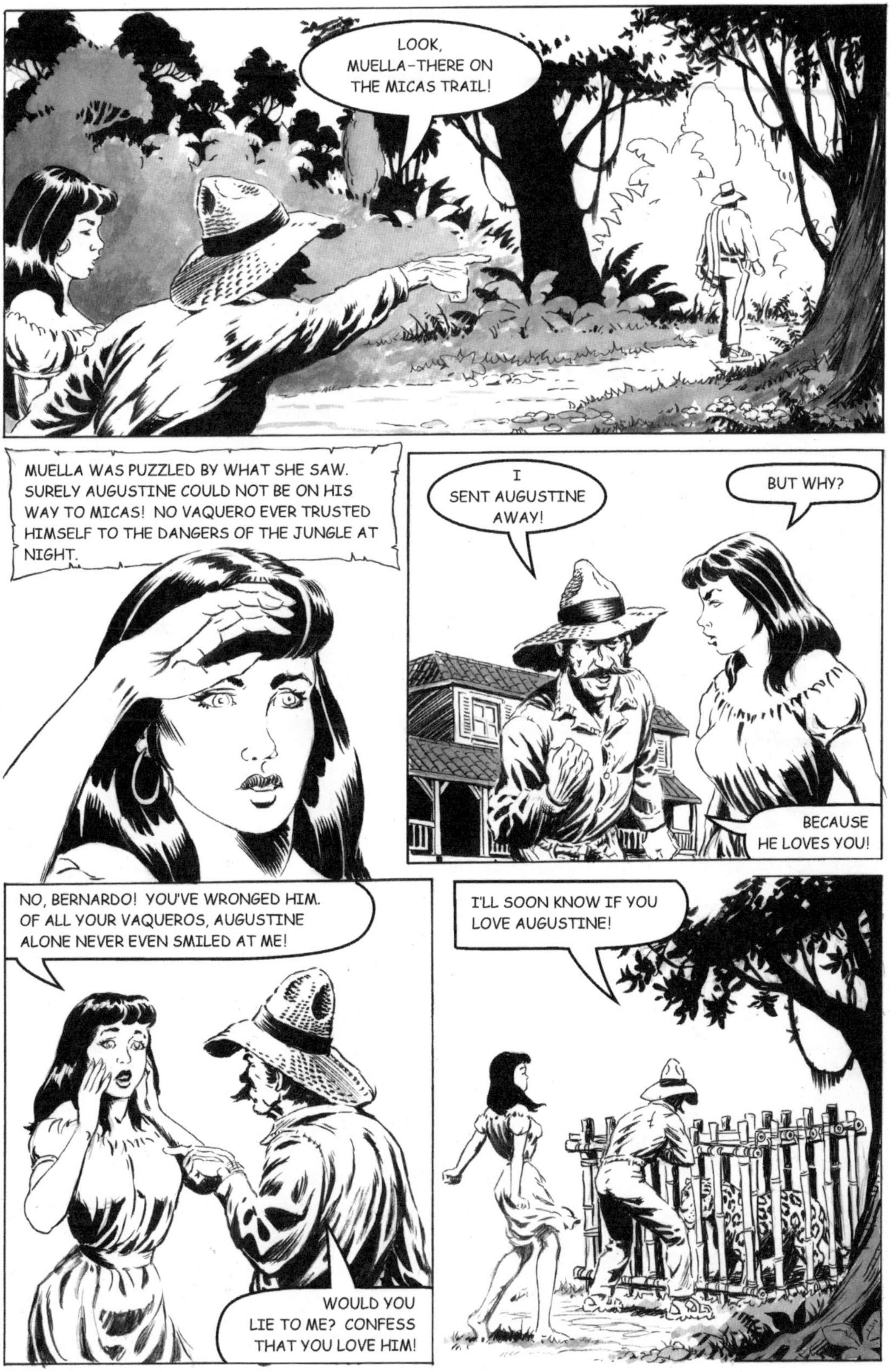
LOOK, MUELLA–THERE ON THE MICAS TRAIL!
MUELLA WAS PUZZLED BY WHAT SHE SAW. SURELY AUGUSTINE COULD NOT BE ON HIS WAY TO MICAS! NO VAQUERO EVER TRUSTED HIMSELF TO THE DANGERS OF THE JUNGLE AT NIGHT.
I SENT AUGUSTINE AWAY!
BUT WHY?
BECAUSE HE LOVES YOU!
NO, BERNARDO! YOU'VE WRONGED HIM. OF ALL YOUR VAQUEROS, AUGUSTINE ALONE NEVER EVEN SMILED AT ME!
WOULD YOU LIE TO ME? CONFESS THAT YOU LOVE HIM!
I'LL SOON KNOW IF YOU LOVE AUGUSTINE!

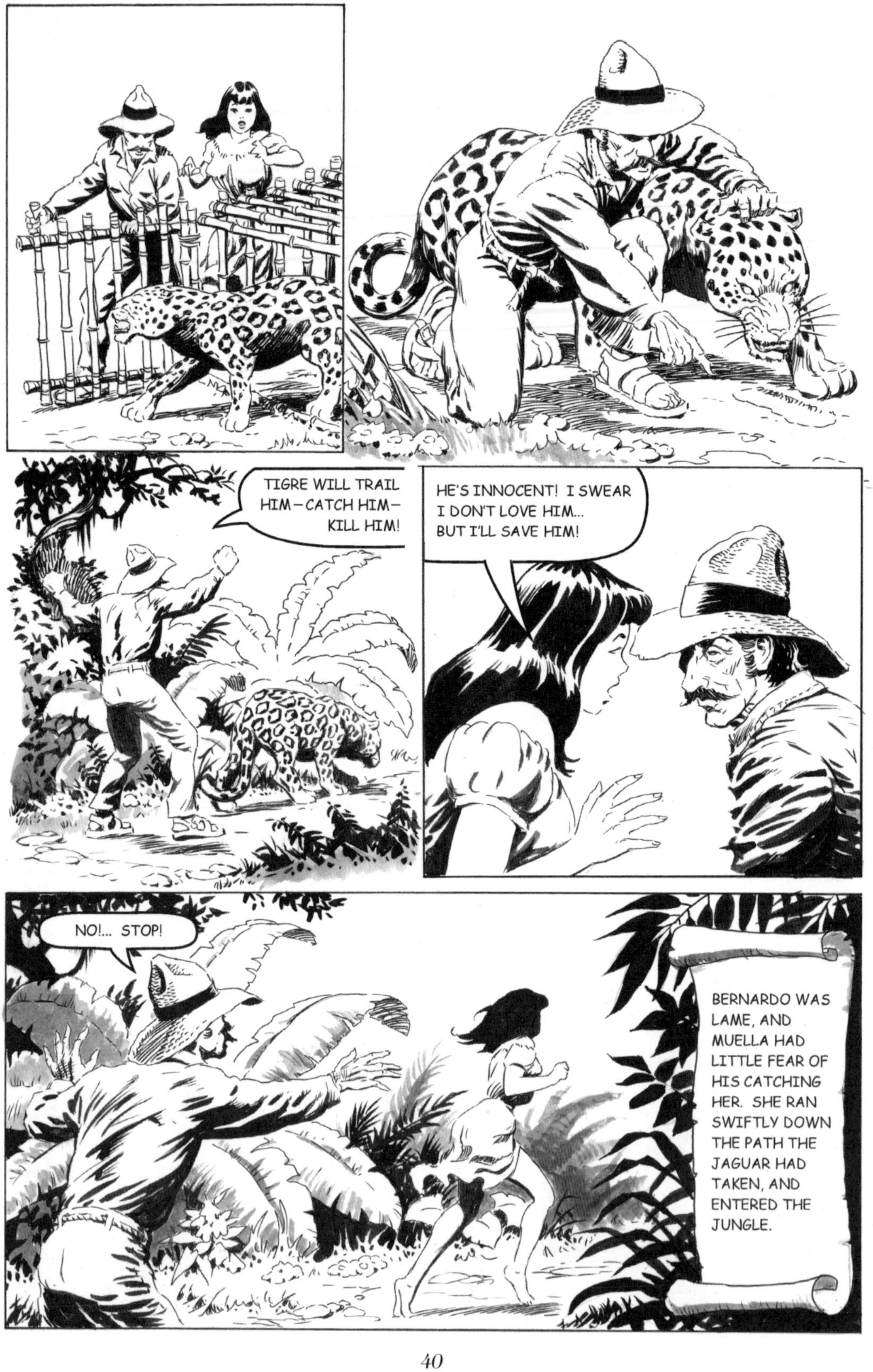
TIGRE WILL TRAIL HIM–CATCH HIM–KILL HIM!
HE'S INNOCENT! I SWEAR I DON'T LOVE HIM... BUT I'LL SAVE HIM!
NO!... STOP!
BERNARDO WAS LAME, AND MUELLA HAD LITTLE FEAR OF HIS CATCHING HER. SHE RAN SWIFTLY DOWN THE PATH THE JAGUAR HAD TAKEN, AND ENTERED THE JUNGLE.

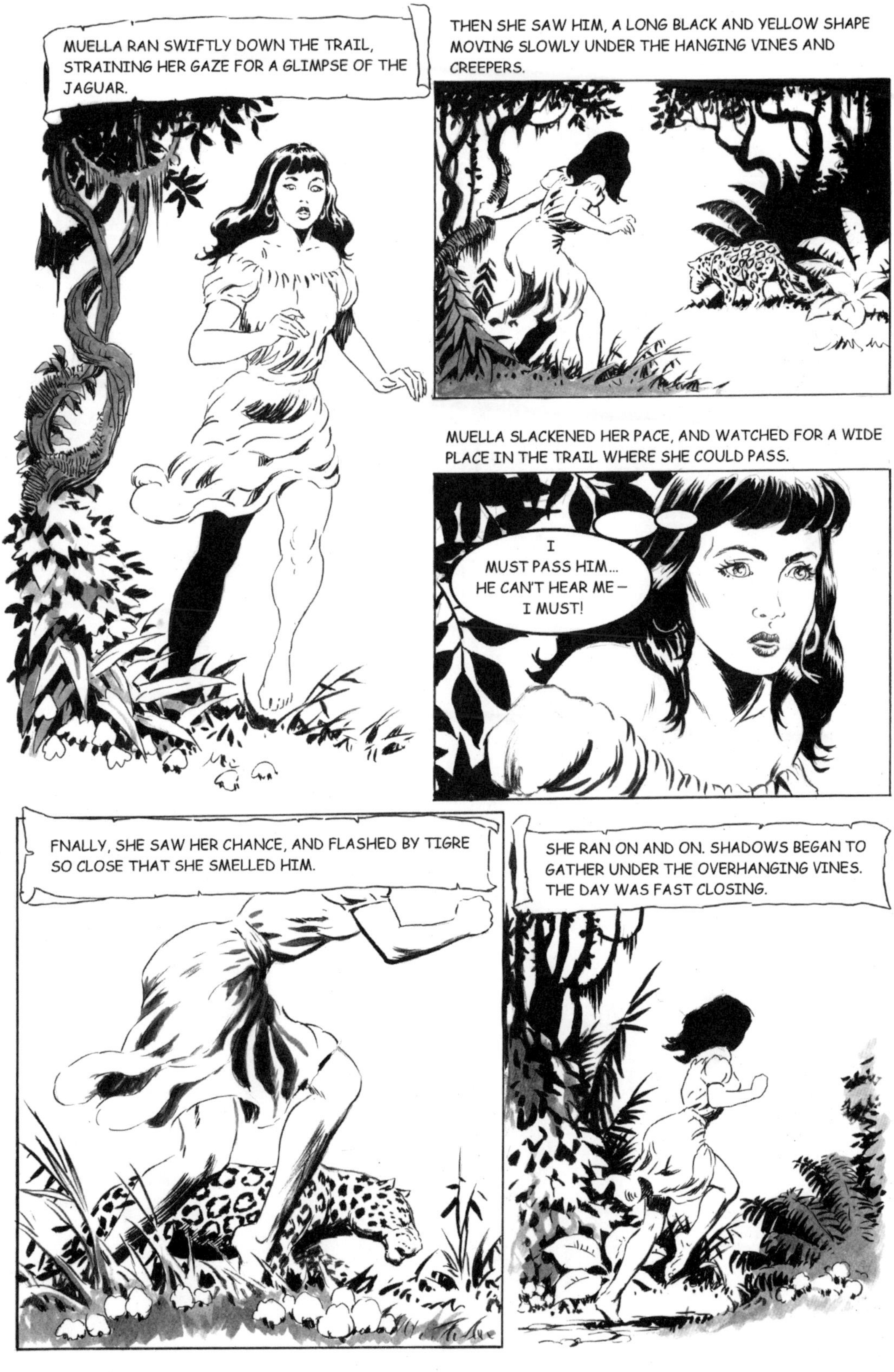
MUELLA RAN SWIFTLY DOWN THE TRAIL, STRAINING HER GAZE FOR A GLIMPSE OF THE JAGUAR.
THEN SHE SAW HIM, A LONG BLACK AND YELLOW SHAPE MOVING SLOWLY UNDER THE HANGING VINES AND CREEPERS.
MUELLA SLACKENED HER PACE, AND WATCHED FOR A WIDE PLACE IN THE TRAIL WHERE SHE COULD PASS.
I MUST PASS HIM... HE CAN'T HEAR ME – I MUST!
FNALLY, SHE SAW HER CHANCE, AND FLASHED BY TIGRE SO CLOSE THAT SHE SMELLED HIM.
SHE RAN ON AND ON. SHADOWS BEGAN TO GATHER UNDER THE OVERHANGING VINES. THE DAY WAS FAST CLOSING.

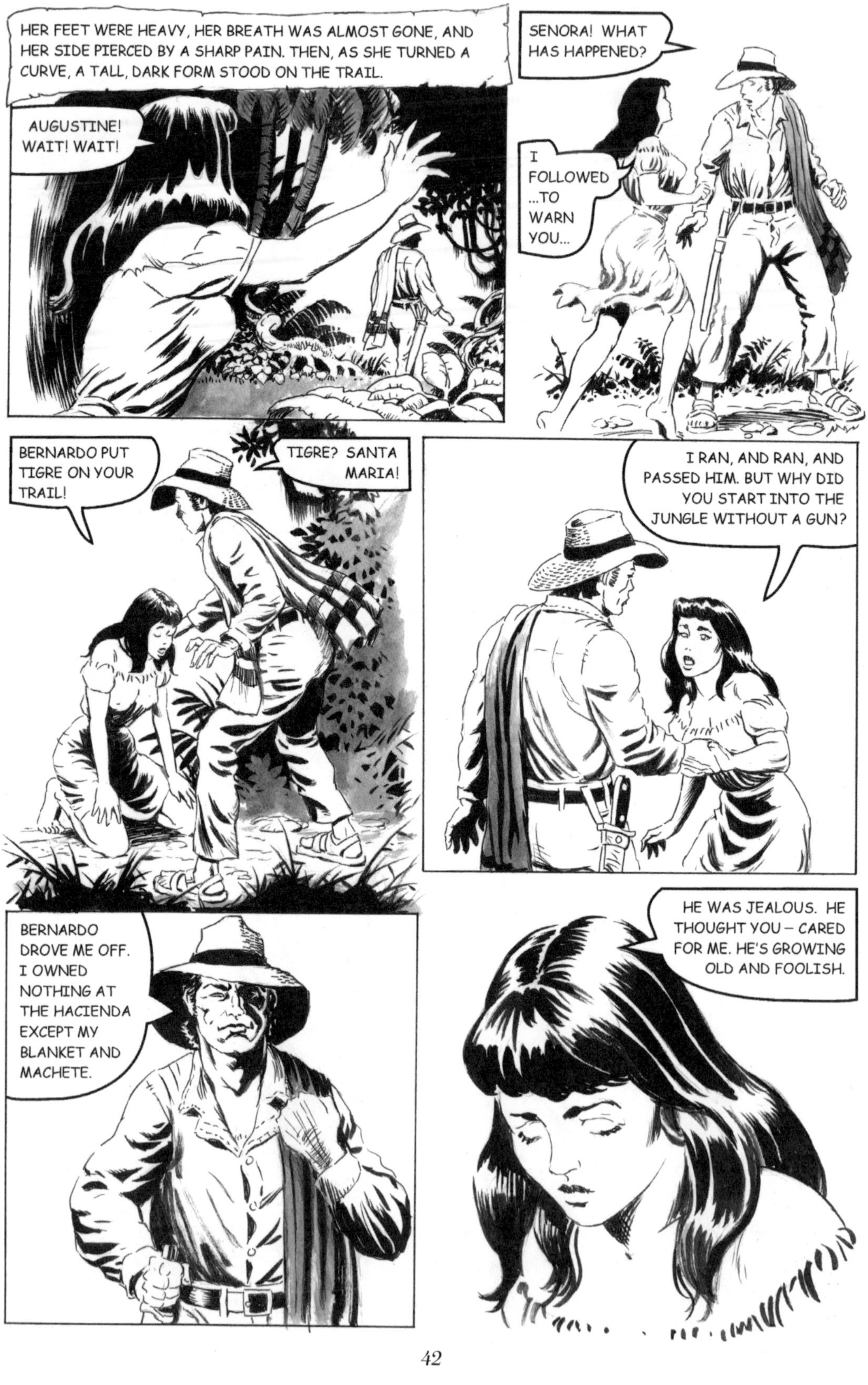
HER FEET WERE HEAVY, HER BREATH WAS ALMOST GONE, AND HER SIDE PIERCED BY A SHARP PAIN. THEN, AS SHE TURNED A CURVE, A TALL, DARK FORM STOOD ON THE TRAIL.
AUGUSTINE! WAIT! WAIT!
SENORA! WHAT HAS HAPPENED?
I FOLLOWED ...TO WARN YOU...
BERNARDO PUT TIGRE ON YOUR TRAIL!
TIGRE? SANTA MARIA!
I RAN, AND RAN, AND PASSED HIM. BUT WHY DID YOU START INTO THE JUNGLE WITHOUT A GUN?
BERNARDO DROVE ME OFF. I OWNED NOTHING AT THE HACIENDA EXCEPT MY BLANKET AND MACHETE.
HE WAS JEALOUS. HE THOUGHT YOU – CARED FOR ME. HE'S GROWING OLD AND FOOLISH.

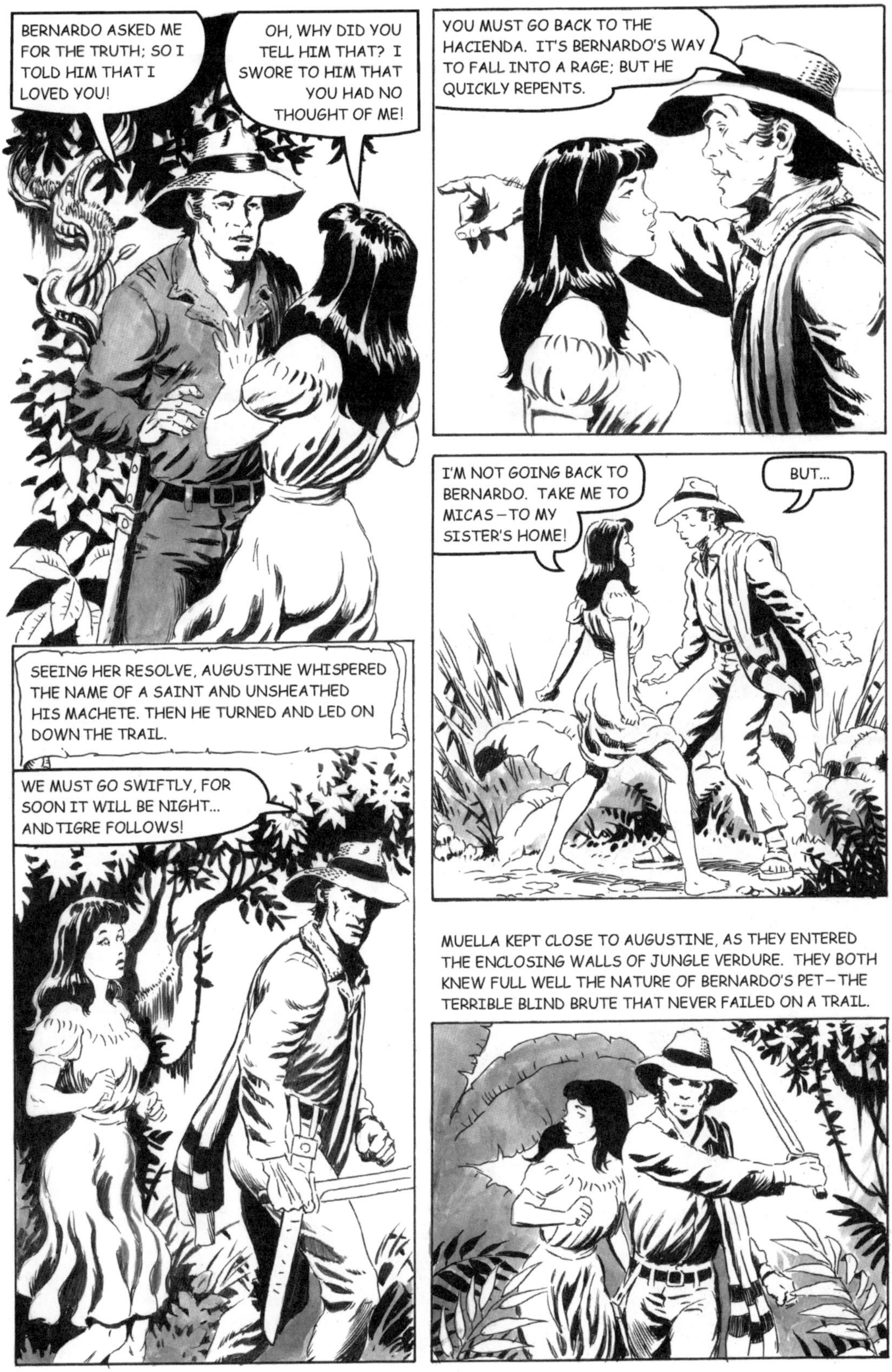
BERNARDO ASKED ME FOR THE TRUTH; SO I TOLD HIM THAT I LOVED YOU!
OH, WHY DID YOU TELL HIM THAT? I SWORE TO HIM THAT YOU HAD NO THOUGHT OF ME!
YOU MUST GO BACK TO THE HACIENDA. IT'S BERNARDO'S WAY TO FALL INTO A RAGE; BUT HE QUICKLY REPENTS.
I'M NOT GOING BACK TO BERNARDO. TAKE ME TO MICAS—TO MY SISTER'S HOME!
BUT...
SEEING HER RESOLVE, AUGUSTINE WHISPERED THE NAME OF A SAINT AND UNSHEATHED HIS MACHETE. THEN HE TURNED AND LED ON DOWN THE TRAIL.
WE MUST GO SWIFTLY, FOR SOON IT WILL BE NIGHT... AND TIGRE FOLLOWS!
MUELLA KEPT CLOSE TO AUGUSTINE, AS THEY ENTERED THE ENCLOSING WALLS OF JUNGLE VERDURE. THEY BOTH KNEW FULL WELL THE NATURE OF BERNARDO'S PET—THE TERRIBLE BLIND BRUTE THAT NEVER FAILED ON A TRAIL.

NIGHT FELL, AND WITH IT CAME A BLINKING OF STARS THROUGH DENSE FOLIAGE OVERHEAD. THE STRANGE NIGHT NOISES FRIGHTENED MUELLA, AND INSTINCTIVELY SHE SHRANK CLOSER TO AUGUSTINE.

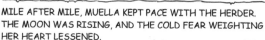

MILE AFTER MILE, MUELLA KEPT PACE WITH THE HERDER. THE MOON WAS RISING, AND THE COLD FEAR WEIGHTING HER HEART LESSENED.

WHEN SHE QUESTIONED HIM, THE HERDER MUMBLED A REPLY THAT SHE DID NOT UNDERSTAND.

IT IS NEAR DAWN. OH, HOW GOOD THE LIGHT WILL BE! WE SHALL BE SAFE IN MICAS SOON, SHALL WE NOT?

HMPHGM SMD BRAGFRM...

AS THE DAYLIGHT CAME, IT STRUCK MUELLA THAT THE TRAIL HAD BECOME ROUGH AND UNFAMILIAR TO HER. BUT SHE PRESSED ON, TRUSTING AUGUSTINE'S SKILLS.

WITH THE HEAT OF DAY CAME THE JUNGLE FLIES AND MOSQUITOES. MUELLA WALKED ON, AND BEGAN AGAIN TO LOOK BACK...

...WHEN SHE CAUGHT AUGUSTINE DOING LIKEWISE, SHE GAVE WAY TO DREAD.

AUGUSTINE! YOU HAVE LOST YOUR WAY!

44

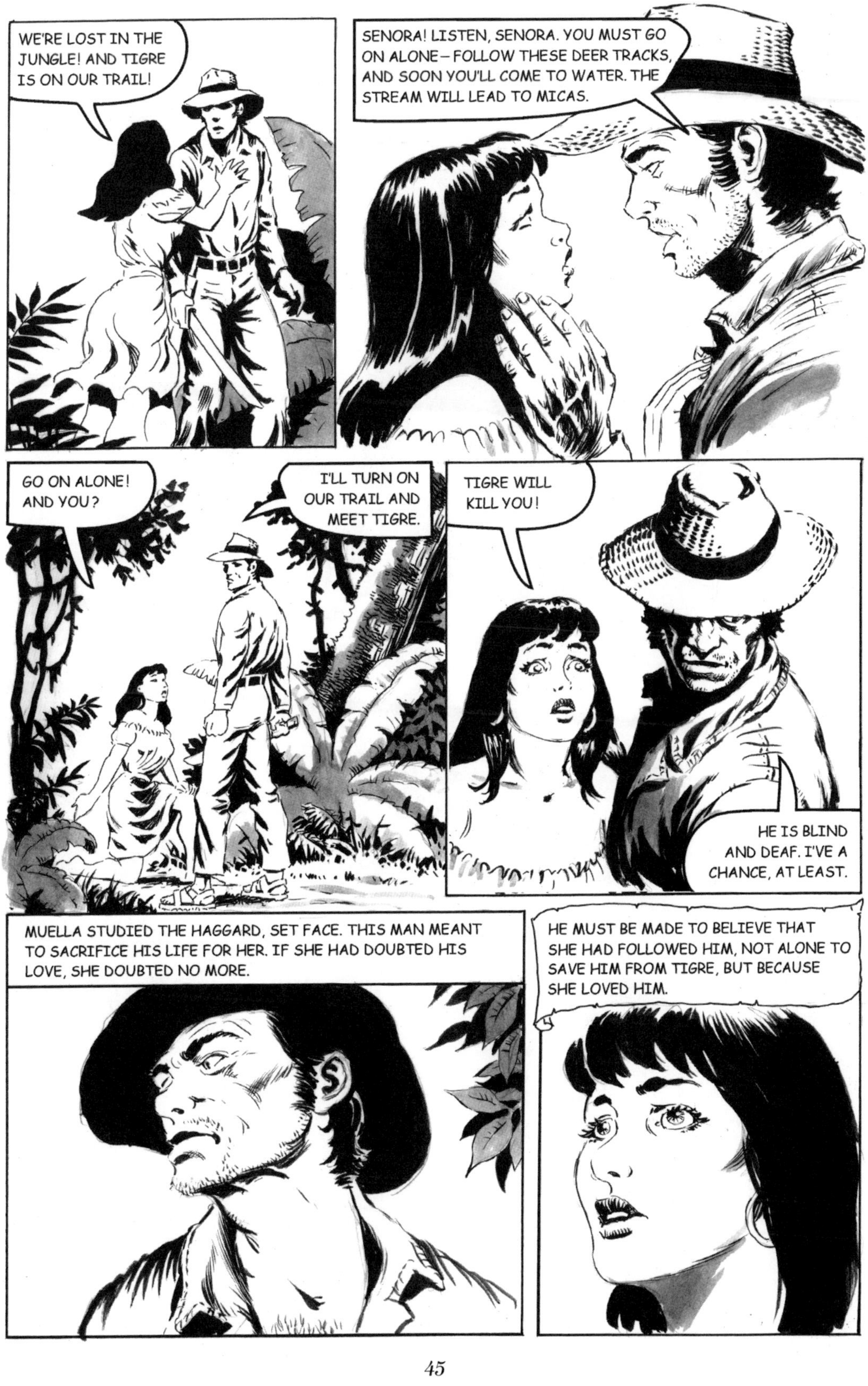
WE'RE LOST IN THE JUNGLE! AND TIGRE IS ON OUR TRAIL!
SENORA! LISTEN, SENORA. YOU MUST GO ON ALONE—FOLLOW THESE DEER TRACKS, AND SOON YOU'LL COME TO WATER. THE STREAM WILL LEAD TO MICAS.
GO ON ALONE! AND YOU?
I'LL TURN ON OUR TRAIL AND MEET TIGRE.
TIGRE WILL KILL YOU!
HE IS BLIND AND DEAF. I'VE A CHANCE, AT LEAST.
MUELLA STUDIED THE HAGGARD, SET FACE. THIS MAN MEANT TO SACRIFICE HIS LIFE FOR HER. IF SHE HAD DOUBTED HIS LOVE, SHE DOUBTED NO MORE.
HE MUST BE MADE TO BELIEVE THAT SHE HAD FOLLOWED HIM, NOT ALONE TO SAVE HIM FROM TIGRE, BUT BECAUSE SHE LOVED HIM.

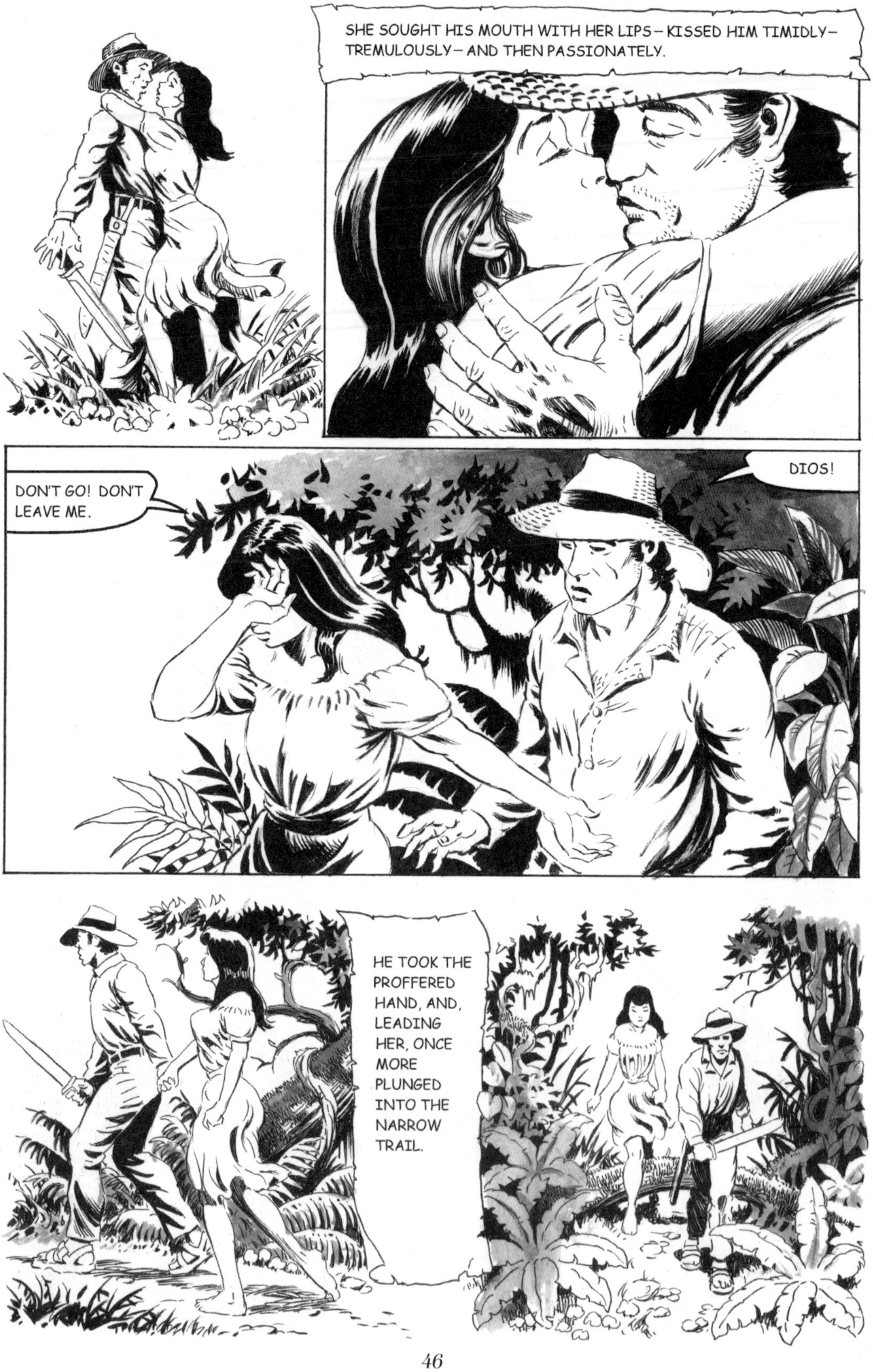
SHE SOUGHT HIS MOUTH WITH HER LIPS—KISSED HIM TIMIDLY—TREMULOUSLY—AND THEN PASSIONATELY.
DON'T GO! DON'T LEAVE ME.
DIOS!
HE TOOK THE PROFFERED HAND, AND, LEADING HER, ONCE MORE PLUNGED INTO THE NARROW TRAIL.

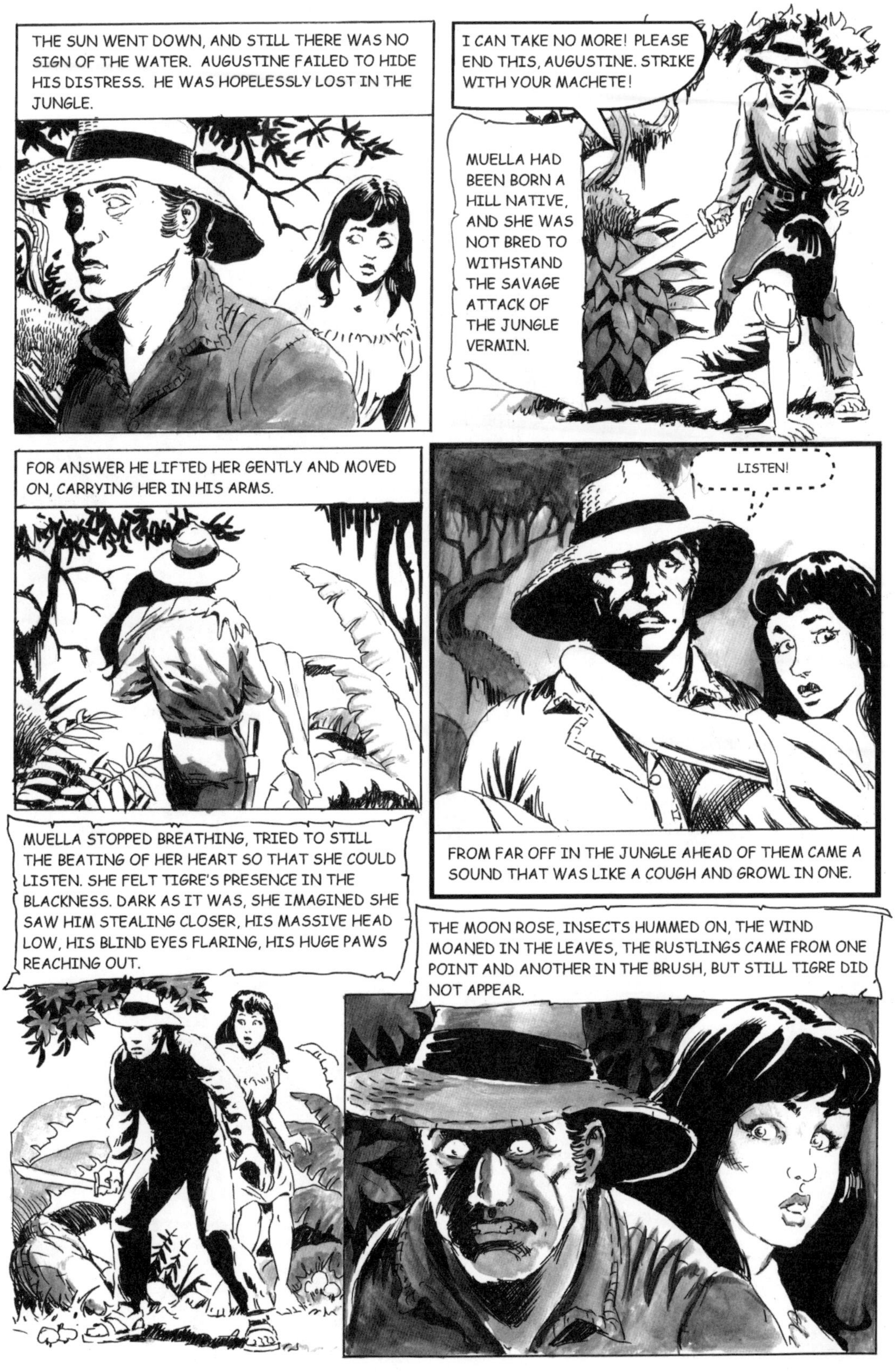
THE SUN WENT DOWN, AND STILL THERE WAS NO SIGN OF THE WATER. AUGUSTINE FAILED TO HIDE HIS DISTRESS. HE WAS HOPELESSLY LOST IN THE JUNGLE.
I CAN TAKE NO MORE! PLEASE END THIS, AUGUSTINE. STRIKE WITH YOUR MACHETE!
MUELLA HAD BEEN BORN A HILL NATIVE, AND SHE WAS NOT BRED TO WITHSTAND THE SAVAGE ATTACK OF THE JUNGLE VERMIN.
FOR ANSWER HE LIFTED HER GENTLY AND MOVED ON, CARRYING HER IN HIS ARMS.
LISTEN!
FROM FAR OFF IN THE JUNGLE AHEAD OF THEM CAME A SOUND THAT WAS LIKE A COUGH AND GROWL IN ONE.
MUELLA STOPPED BREATHING, TRIED TO STILL THE BEATING OF HER HEART SO THAT SHE COULD LISTEN. SHE FELT TIGRE'S PRESENCE IN THE BLACKNESS. DARK AS IT WAS, SHE IMAGINED SHE SAW HIM STEALING CLOSER, HIS MASSIVE HEAD LOW, HIS BLIND EYES FLARING, HIS HUGE PAWS REACHING OUT.
THE MOON ROSE, INSECTS HUMMED ON, THE WIND MOANED IN THE LEAVES, THE RUSTLINGS CAME FROM ONE POINT AND ANOTHER IN THE BRUSH, BUT STILL TIGRE DID NOT APPEAR.

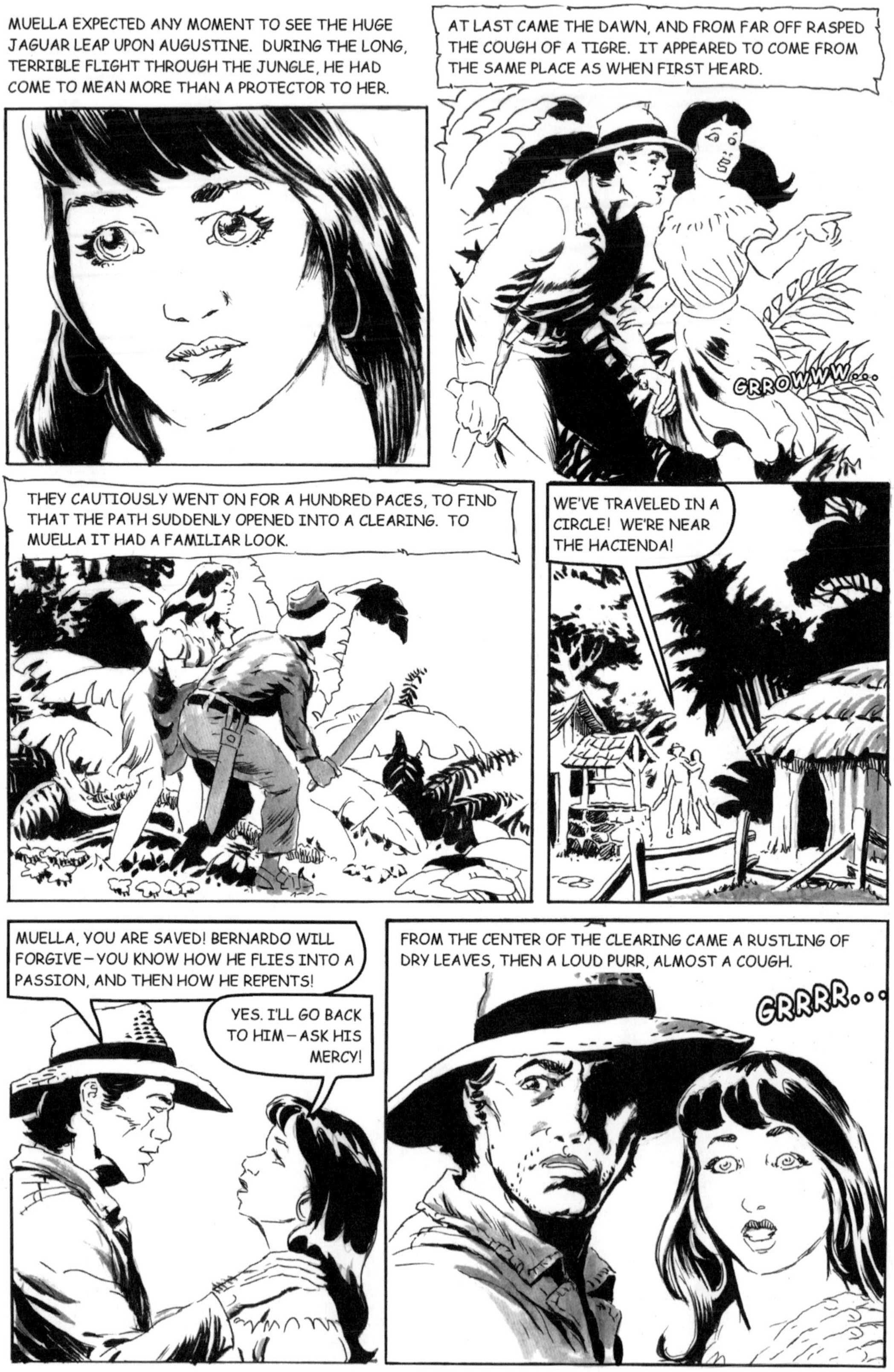
MUELLA EXPECTED ANY MOMENT TO SEE THE HUGE JAGUAR LEAP UPON AUGUSTINE. DURING THE LONG, TERRIBLE FLIGHT THROUGH THE JUNGLE, HE HAD COME TO MEAN MORE THAN A PROTECTOR TO HER.
AT LAST CAME THE DAWN, AND FROM FAR OFF RASPED THE COUGH OF A TIGRE. IT APPEARED TO COME FROM THE SAME PLACE AS WHEN FIRST HEARD.
GRROWWW...
THEY CAUTIOUSLY WENT ON FOR A HUNDRED PACES, TO FIND THAT THE PATH SUDDENLY OPENED INTO A CLEARING. TO MUELLA IT HAD A FAMILIAR LOOK.
WE'VE TRAVELED IN A CIRCLE! WE'RE NEAR THE HACIENDA!
MUELLA, YOU ARE SAVED! BERNARDO WILL FORGIVE—YOU KNOW HOW HE FLIES INTO A PASSION, AND THEN HOW HE REPENTS!
YES. I'LL GO BACK TO HIM—ASK HIS MERCY!
FROM THE CENTER OF THE CLEARING CAME A RUSTLING OF DRY LEAVES, THEN A LOUD PURR, ALMOST A COUGH.
GRRRR...

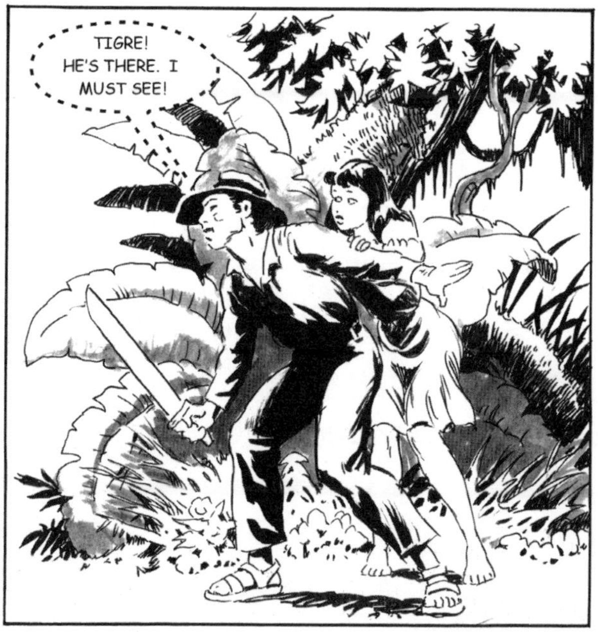
TIGRE!
HE'S THERE. I MUST SEE!

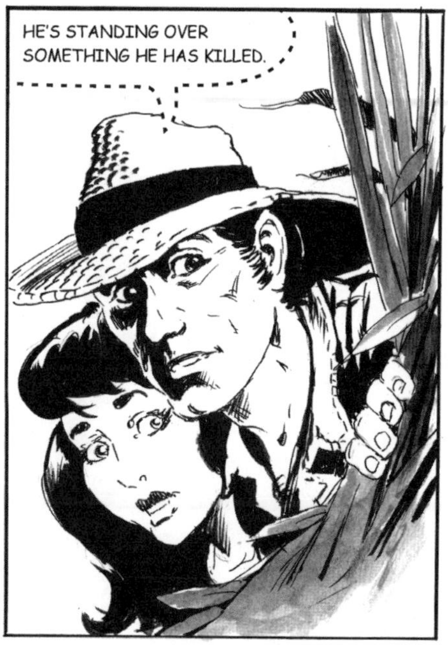
HE'S STANDING OVER SOMETHING HE HAS KILLED.

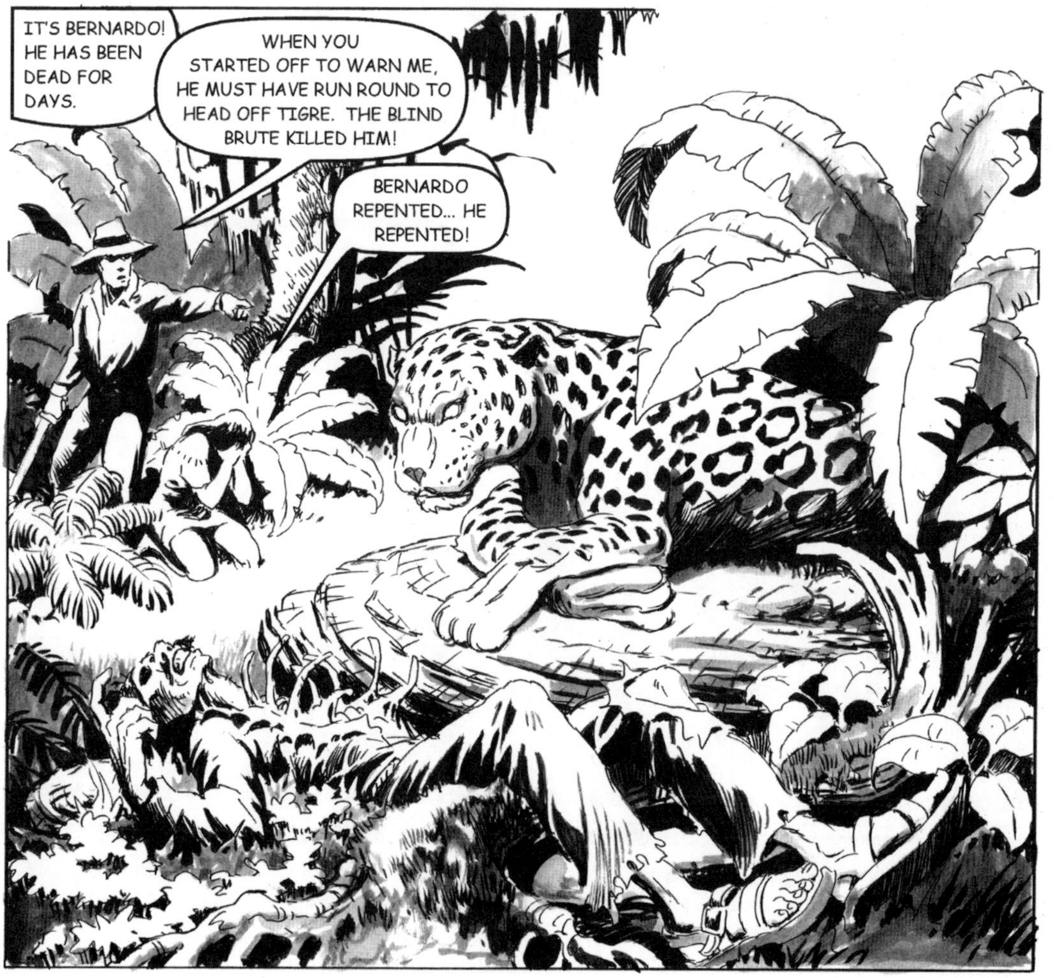
IT'S BERNARDO! HE HAS BEEN DEAD FOR DAYS.
WHEN YOU STARTED OFF TO WARN ME, HE MUST HAVE RUN ROUND TO HEAD OFF TIGRE. THE BLIND BRUTE KILLED HIM!
BERNARDO REPENTED... HE REPENTED!

THE SHOOTING OF DAN McGREW

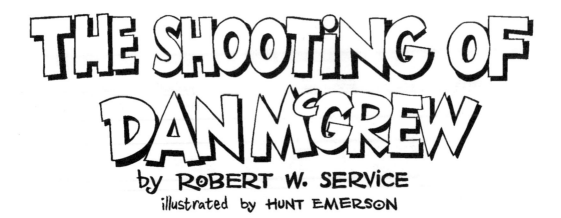

by ROBERT W. SERVICE

illustrated by HUNT EMERSON

WHOOP! WHOOP WHOOP WHOOP
WHOOP
WHOOP

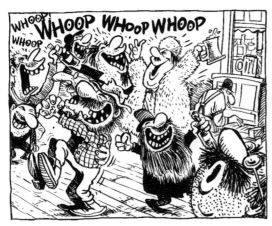

A bunch of the boys were whooping it up
in the Malamute saloon;
The kid that handles the music-box
was hitting a jag-time tune;

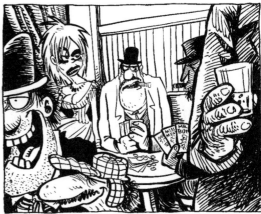

Back of the bar, in a solo game,
sat Dangerous Dan McGrew,
And watching his luck was his light-o'-love,
the lady that's known as Lou.

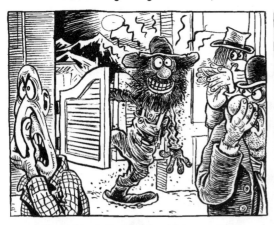

When out of the night, which was fifty
below, and into the din and the glare,
There stumbled a miner fresh from the
creeks, dog-dirty, and loaded for bear.

DRINKS ON ME BOYS!

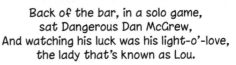

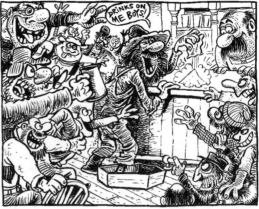

He looked like a man with a foot in the grave
and scarcely the strength of a louse,
Yet he tilted a poke of dust on the bar,
and he called for drinks for the house.

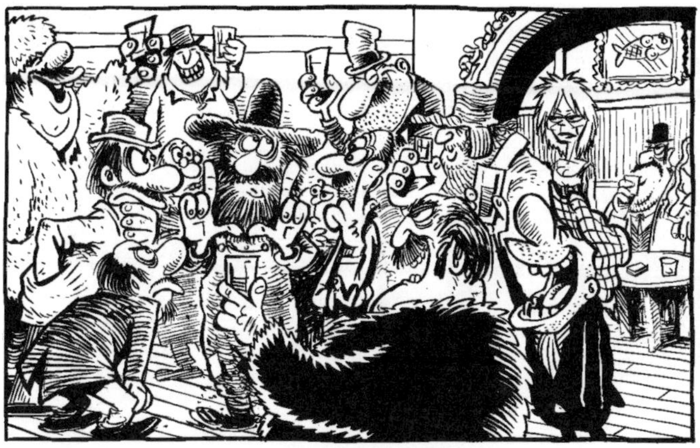

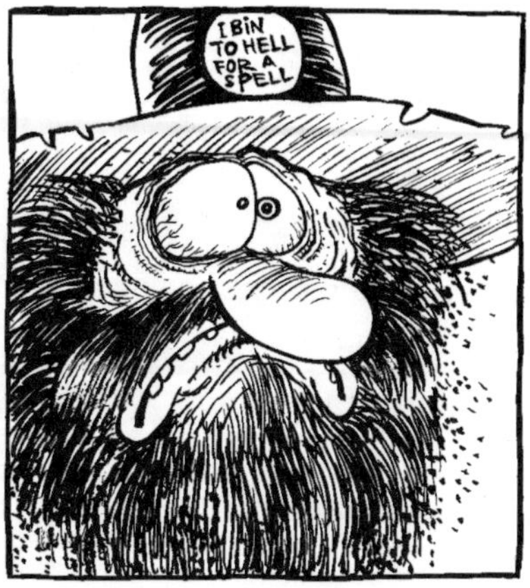
I BIN TO HELL FOR A SPELL

There was none could place the stranger's face,
though we searched ourselves for a clue;
But we drank his health, and the last to drink
was Dangerous Dan McGrew.

There's men that somehow just grip your
eyes, and hold them hard like a spell;
And such was he, and he looked to me
like a man who had lived in hell;

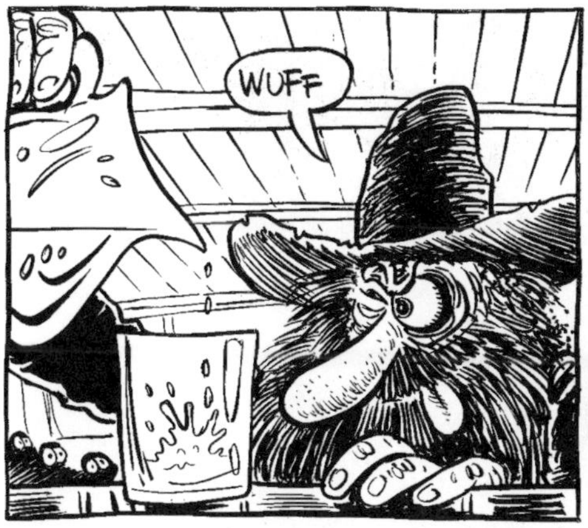
WUFF

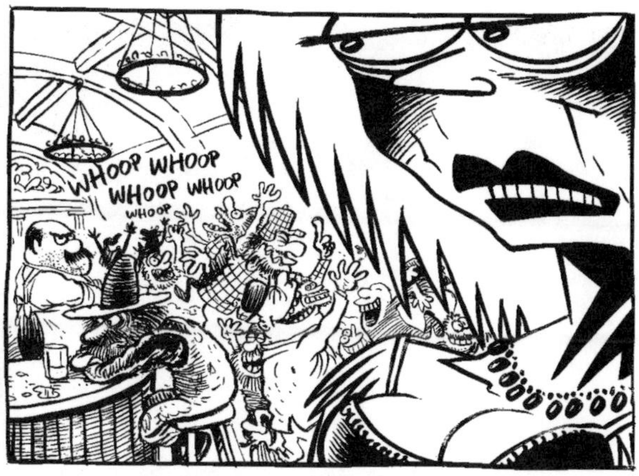
WHOOP WHOOP
WHOOP WHOOP
WHOOP

With a face most hair, and the dreary stare
of a dog whose day is done,
As he watered the green stuff in his glass,
and the drops fell one by one.

Then I got to figgering who he was,
and wondering what he'd do,
And I turned my head — and there watching
him was the lady that's known as Lou.

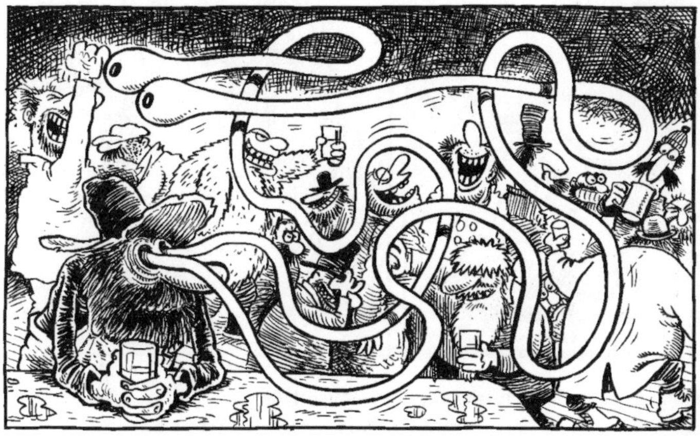

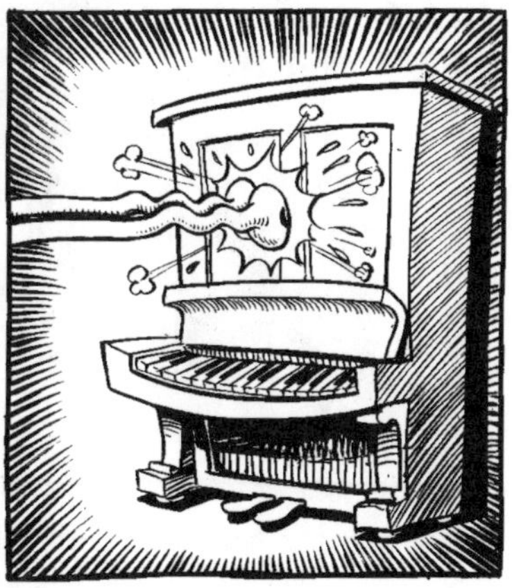

His eyes went rubbering round the room, and he seemed in a kind of daze,
Till at last that old piano fell in the way of his wandering gaze.

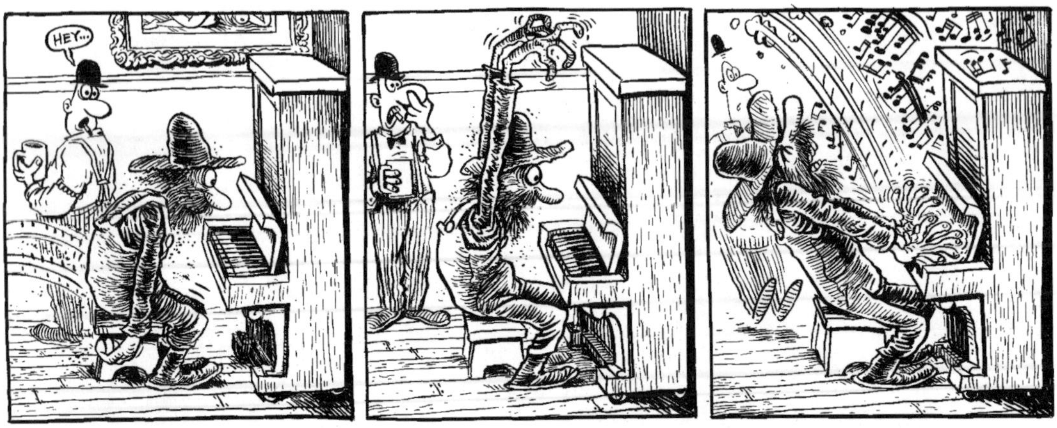
HEY...

The rag-time kid was having a drink;
there was no one else on the stool,
So the stranger stumbles across the room,
and flops down there like a fool.

In a buckskin shirt that was glazed with dirt
he sat, and I saw him sway;
Then he clutched the keys with his talon
hands — my God! but that man could play.

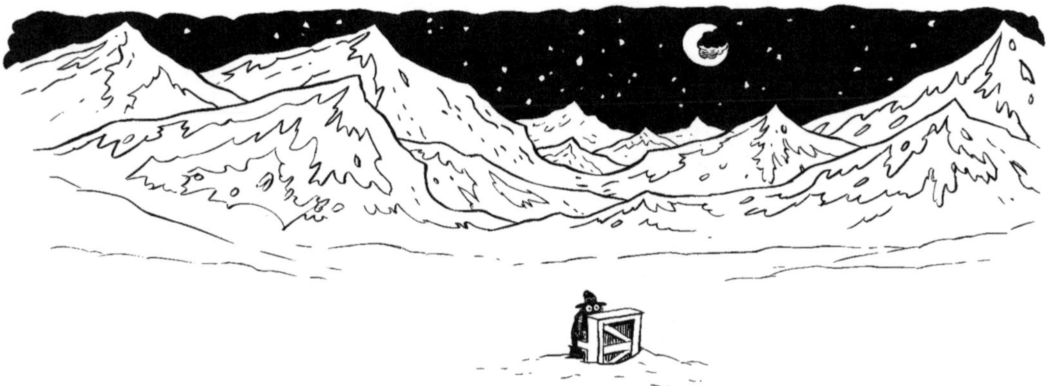

Were you ever out in the Great Alone, when the moon was awful clear,
And the icy mountains hemmed you in with a silence you most could HEAR;

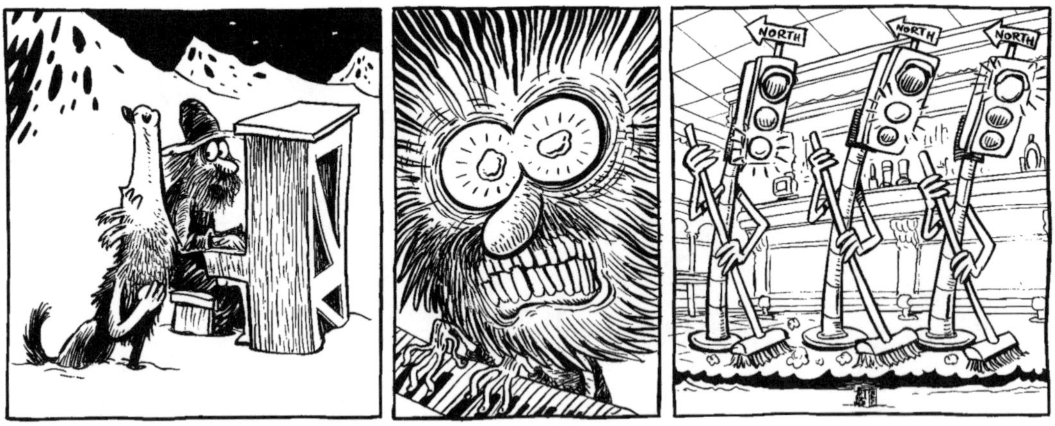
NORTH
NORTH
NORTH

With only the howl of a timber wolf, and you
camped there in the cold,
A half-dead thing in a stark, dead world,
clean mad for the muck called gold;

While high overhead, green, yellow and red,
the North Lights swept in bars? —
Then you've a hunch what the music meant
...hunger and night and the stars.

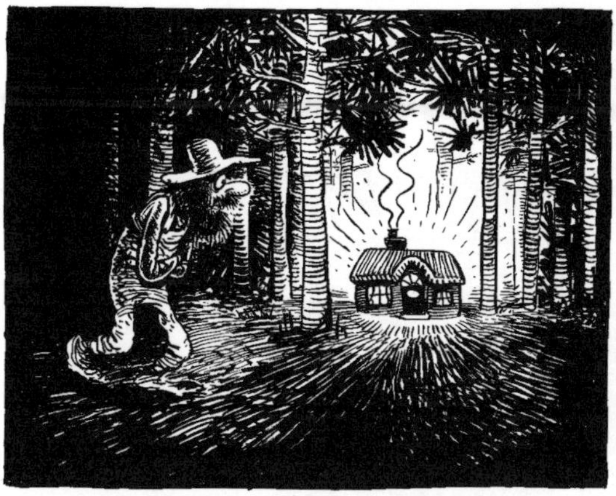

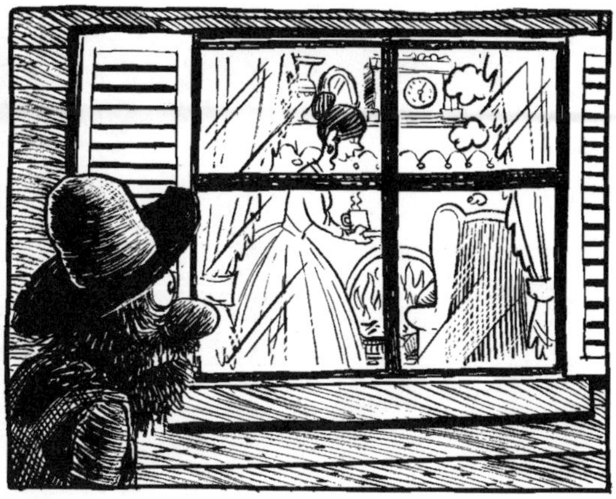

And hunger not of the belly kind,
that's banished with bacon and beans,
But the gnawing hunger of lonely men
for a home and all that it means;

For a fireside far from the cares that are,
four walls and a roof above;
But oh! so cramful of cozy joy,
and crowned with a woman's love —

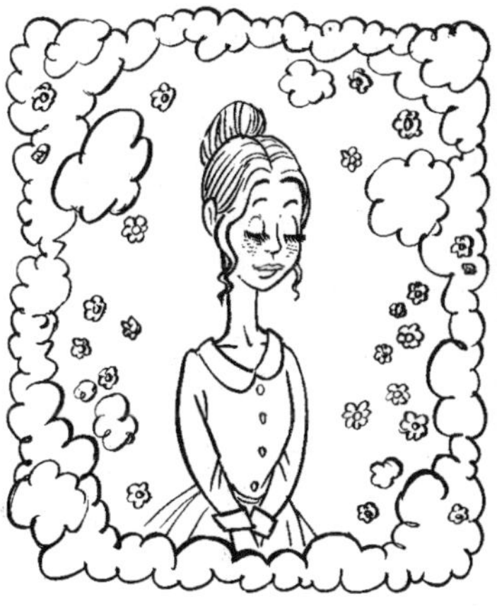

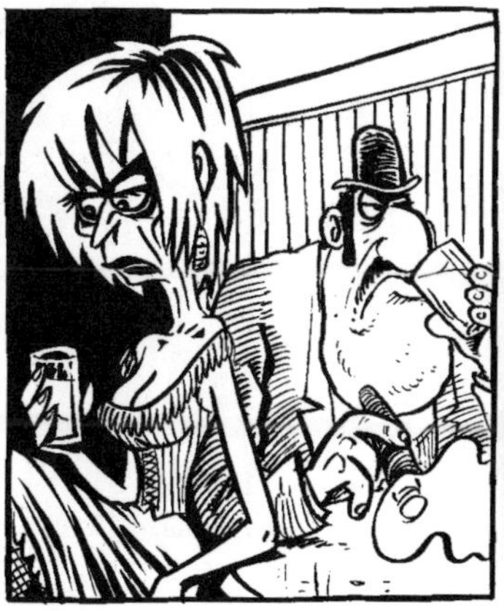

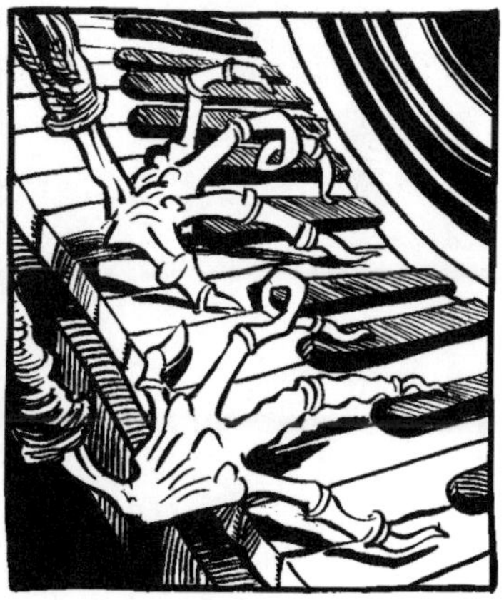

A woman dearer than all the world,
and true as Heaven is true —
(God! how ghastly she looks through her
rouge, — the lady that's known as Lou.)

Then on a sudden the music changed,
so soft that you scarce could hear;
But you felt that your life had been looted
clean of all that it once held dear;

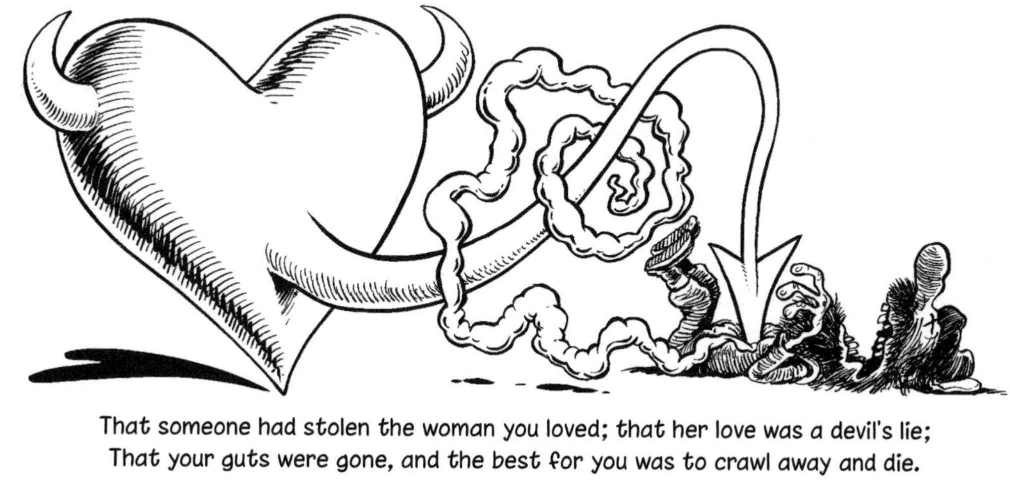

That someone had stolen the woman you loved; that her love was a devil's lie;
That your guts were gone, and the best for you was to crawl away and die.

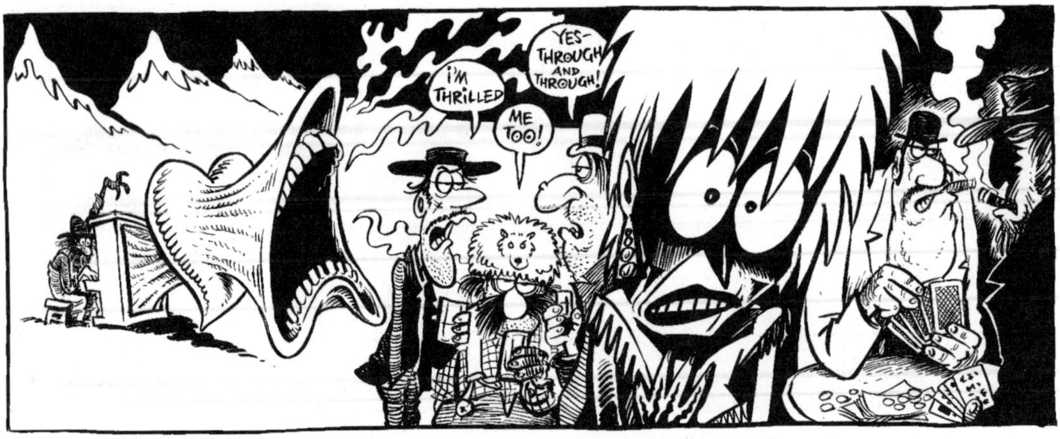
I'M THRILLED
ME TOO!
YES- THROUGH AND THROUGH!

'Twas the crowning cry of a heart's despair, and it thrilled you through and through --
"I guess I'll make it a spread misère," said Dangerous Dan McGrew.

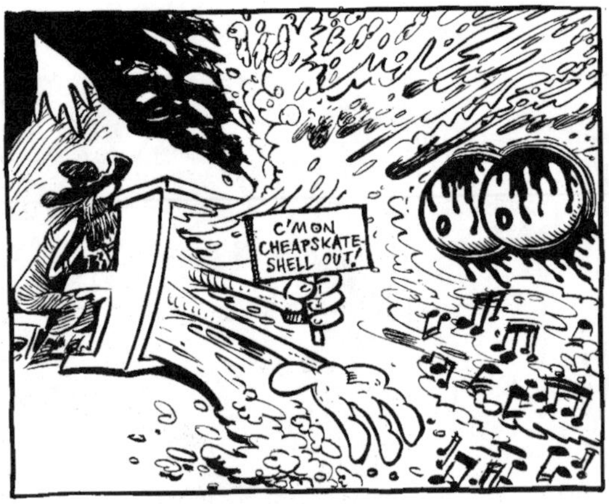
C'MON CHEAPSKATE SHELL OUT!

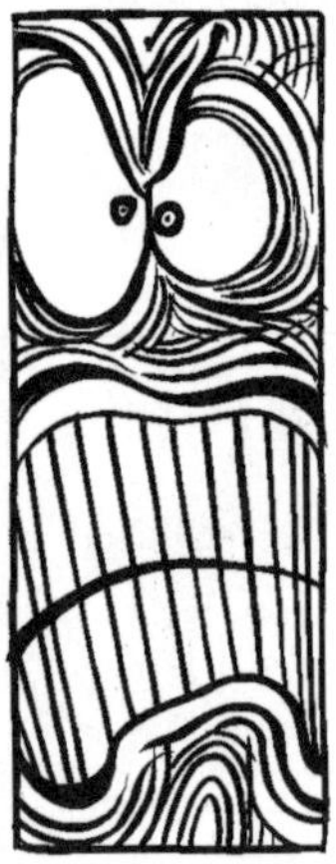

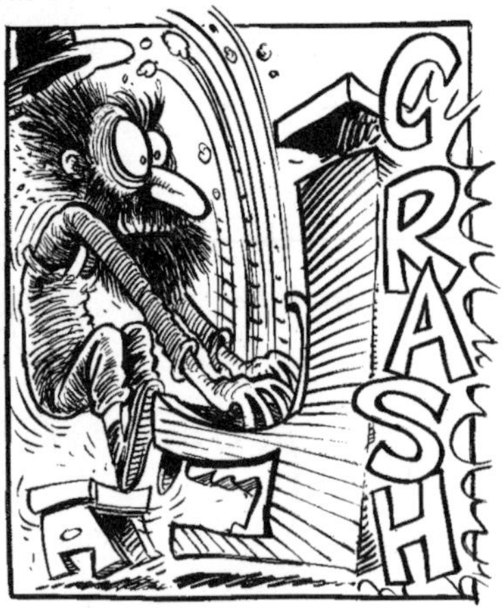
CRASH

The music almost died away... then it burst
like a pent-up flood;
And it seemed to say, "Repay, repay,"
and my eyes were blind with blood.

The thought came back of an ancient wrong,
and it stung like a frozen lash,
And the lust awoke to kill, to kill...
then the music stopped with a crash,

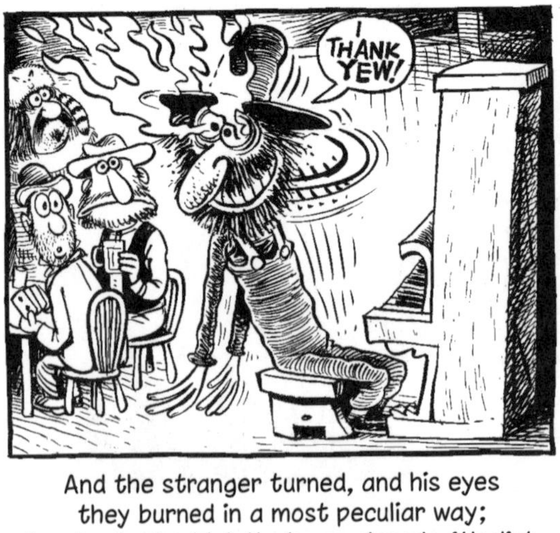
I THANK YEW!

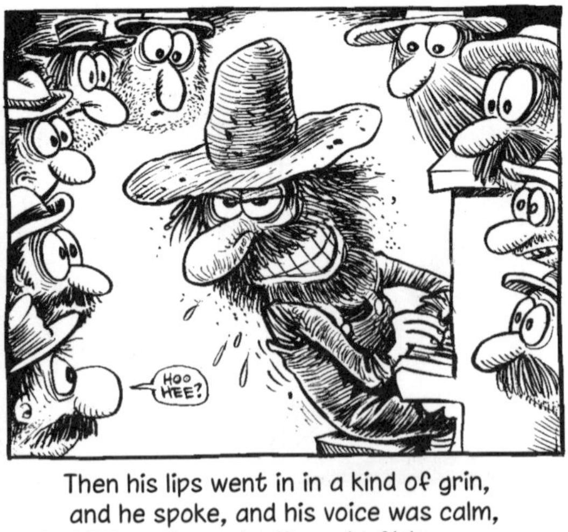
HOO HEE?

And the stranger turned, and his eyes
they burned in a most peculiar way;
In a buckskin shirt that was glazed with dirt
he sat, and I saw him sway;

Then his lips went in in a kind of grin,
and he spoke, and his voice was calm,
And "Boys," says he, "you don't know me,
and none of you care a damn;

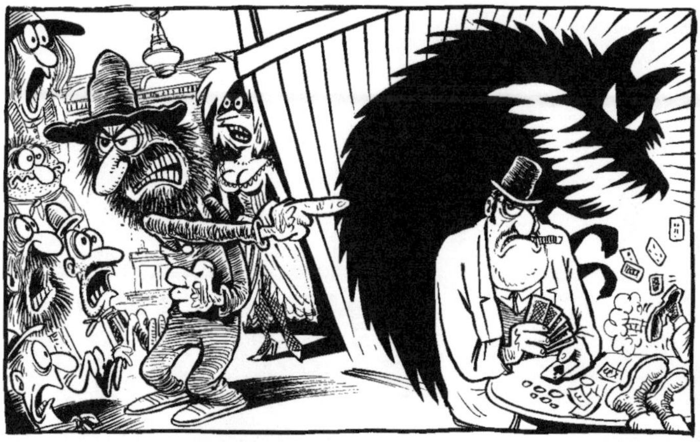

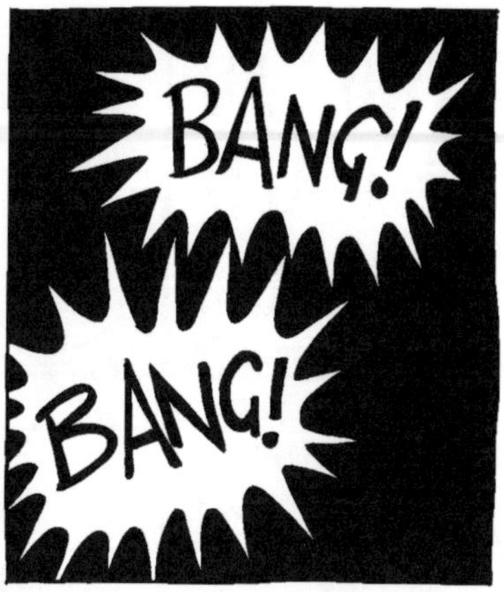
BANG!
BANG!

"But I want to state, and my words are straight, and I'll bet my poke they're true, That one of you is a hound of hell... and that one is Dan McGrew."

Then I ducked my head, and the lights went out, and two guns blazed in the dark, And a woman screamed, and the lights went up, and two men lay stiff and stark.

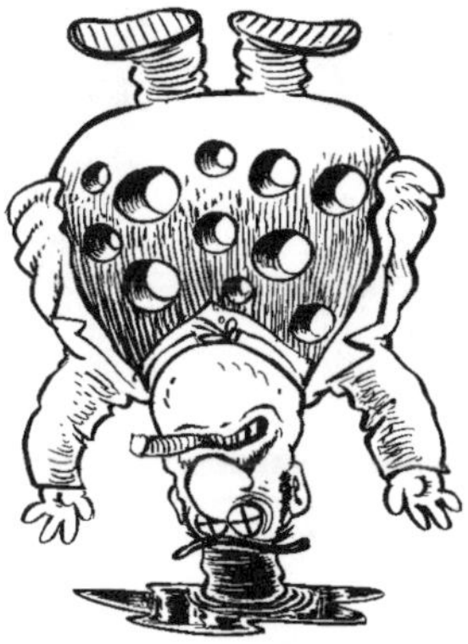

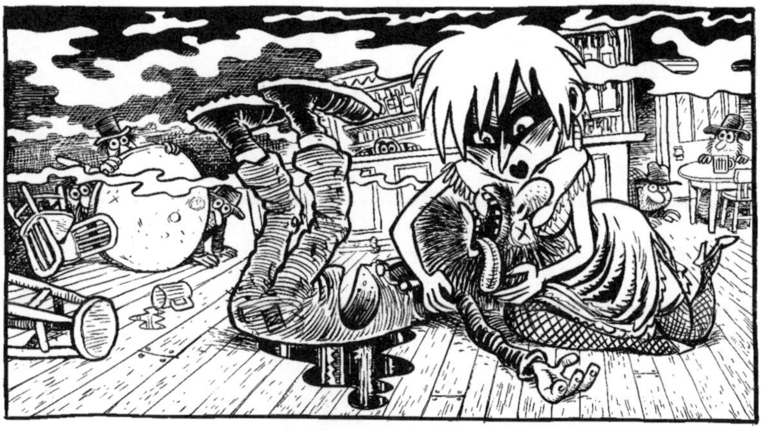

Pitched on his head, and pumped full of lead, was Dangerous Dan McGrew, While the man from the creeks lay clutched to the breast of the lady that's known as Lou.

These are the simple facts of the case, and I guess I ought to know. They say that the stranger was crazed with "hooch", and I'm not denying it's so.

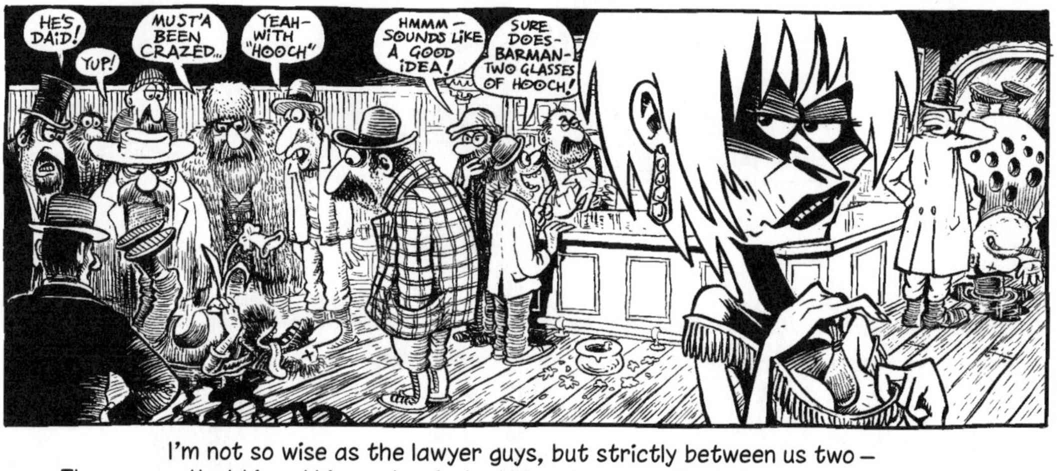
HE'S DAID!
YUP!
MUST'A BEEN CRAZED..
YEAH- WITH "HOOCH"
HMMM- SOUNDS LIKE A GOOD IDEA!
SURE DOES- BARMAN- TWO GLASSES OF HOOCH!

I'm not so wise as the lawyer guys, but strictly between us two –
The woman that kissed him and – pinched his poke – was the lady that's known as Lou.

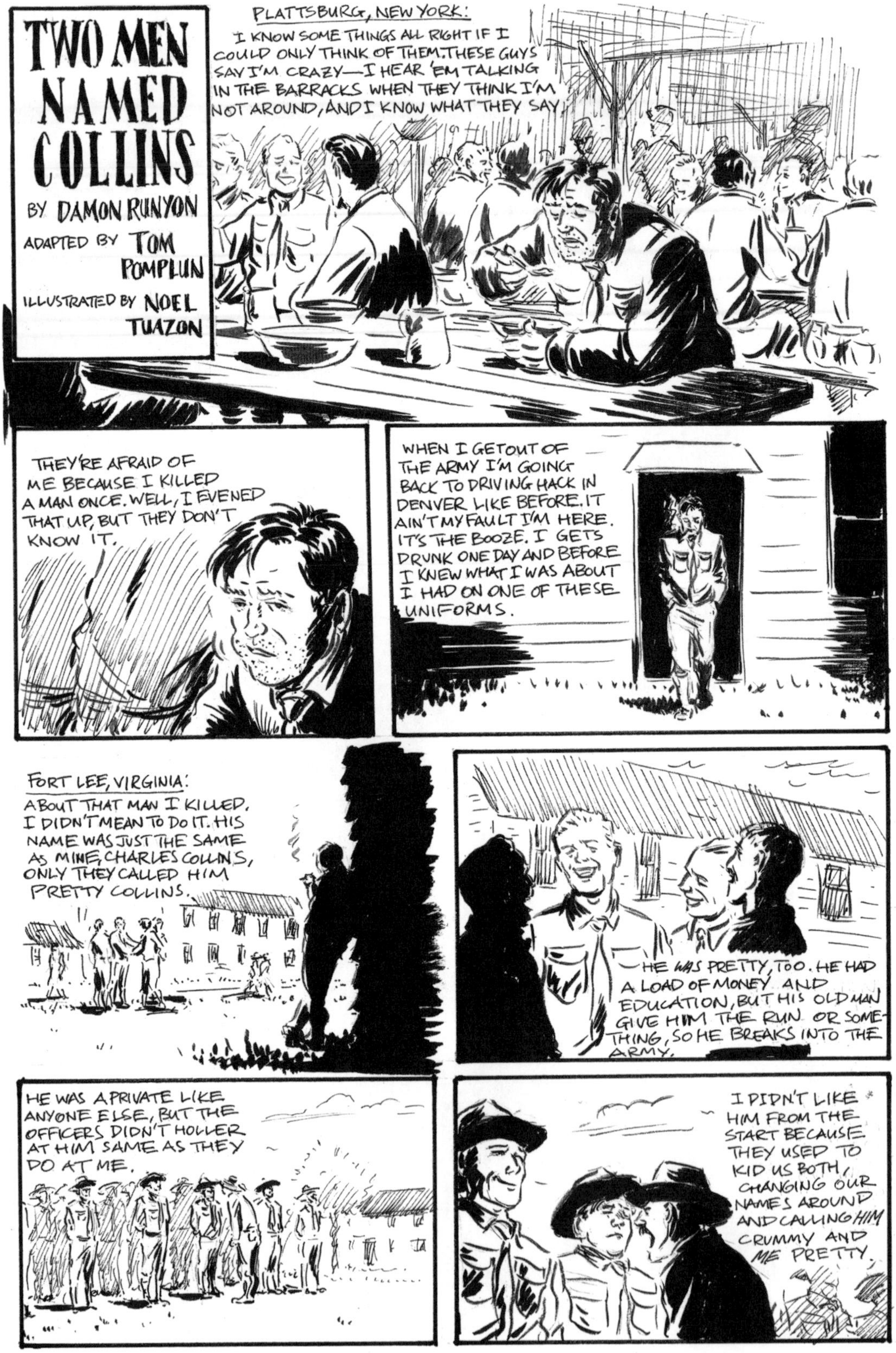
TWO MEN NAMED COLLINS
BY DAMON RUNYON
ADAPTED BY TOM POMPLUN
ILLUSTRATED BY NOEL TUAZON
PLATTSBURG, NEW YORK:
I KNOW SOME THINGS ALL RIGHT IF I COULD ONLY THINK OF THEM. THESE GUYS SAY I'M CRAZY—I HEAR 'EM TALKING IN THE BARRACKS WHEN THEY THINK I'M NOT AROUND, AND I KNOW WHAT THEY SAY.
THEY'RE AFRAID OF ME BECAUSE I KILLED A MAN ONCE. WELL, I EVENED THAT UP, BUT THEY DON'T KNOW IT.
WHEN I GET OUT OF THE ARMY I'M GOING BACK TO DRIVING HACK IN DENVER LIKE BEFORE. IT AIN'T MY FAULT I'M HERE. IT'S THE BOOZE. I GETS DRUNK ONE DAY AND BEFORE I KNEW WHAT I WAS ABOUT I HAD ON ONE OF THESE UNIFORMS.
FORT LEE, VIRGINIA:
ABOUT THAT MAN I KILLED. I DIDN'T MEAN TO DO IT. HIS NAME WAS JUST THE SAME AS MINE, CHARLES COLLINS, ONLY THEY CALLED HIM PRETTY COLLINS.
HE WAS PRETTY, TOO. HE HAD A LOAD OF MONEY AND EDUCATION, BUT HIS OLD MAN GIVE HIM THE RUN OR SOMETHING, SO HE BREAKS INTO THE ARMY.
HE WAS A PRIVATE LIKE ANYONE ELSE, BUT THE OFFICERS DIDN'T HOLLER AT HIM SAME AS THEY DO AT ME.
I DIDN'T LIKE HIM FROM THE START BECAUSE THEY USED TO KID US BOTH, CHANGING OUR NAMES AROUND AND CALLING HIM CRUMMY AND ME PRETTY.

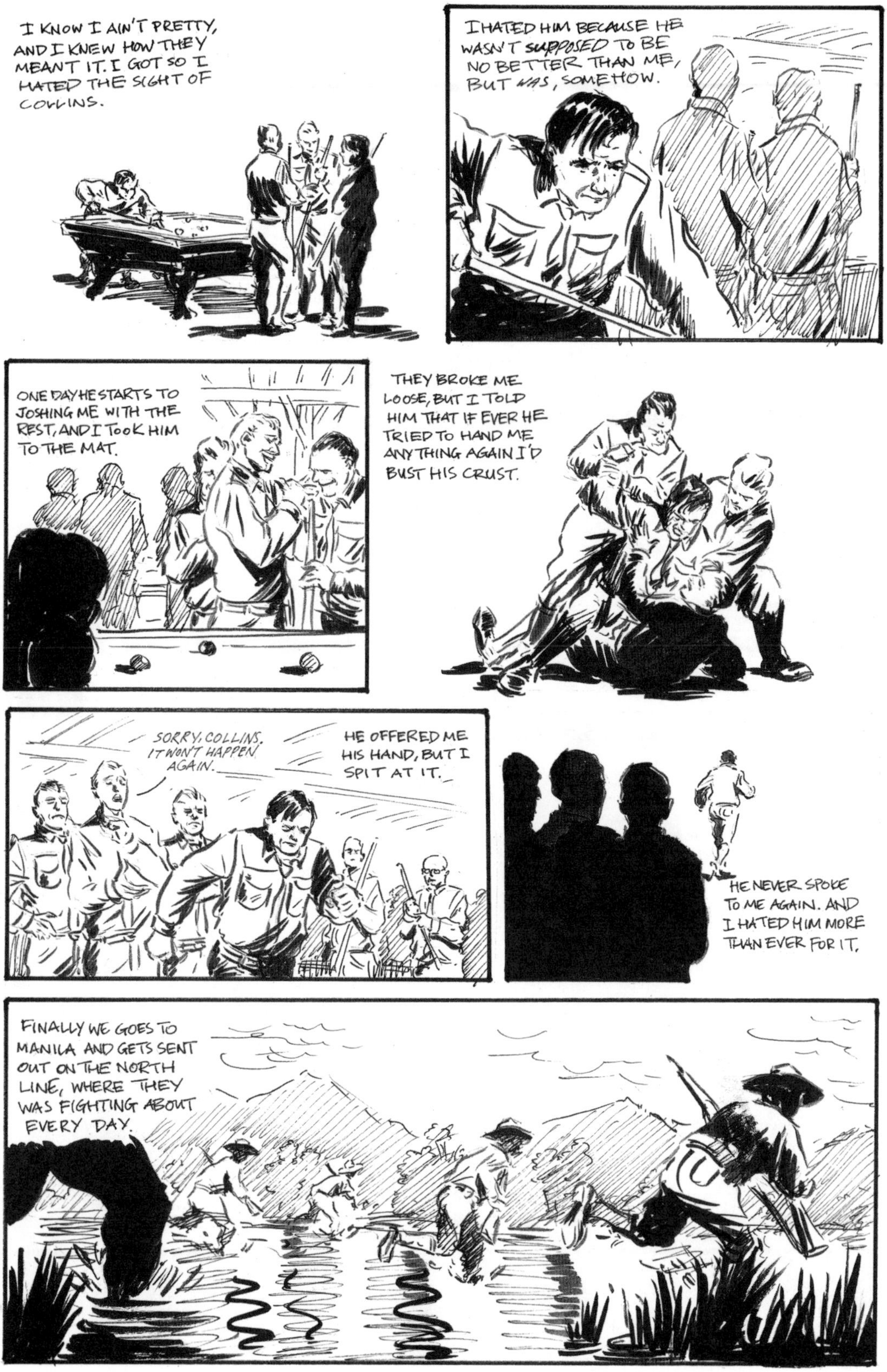
I KNOW I AIN'T PRETTY, AND I KNEW HOW THEY MEANT IT. I GOT SO I HATED THE SIGHT OF COLLINS.
I HATED HIM BECAUSE HE WASN'T SUPPOSED TO BE NO BETTER THAN ME, BUT WAS, SOMEHOW.
ONE DAY HE STARTS TO JOSHING ME WITH THE REST, AND I TOOK HIM TO THE MAT.
THEY BROKE ME LOOSE, BUT I TOLD HIM THAT IF EVER HE TRIED TO HAND ME ANYTHING AGAIN I'D BUST HIS CRUST.
SORRY, COLLINS. IT WON'T HAPPEN AGAIN.
HE OFFERED ME HIS HAND, BUT I SPIT AT IT.
HE NEVER SPOKE TO ME AGAIN. AND I HATED HIM MORE THAN EVER FOR IT.
FINALLY WE GOES TO MANILA AND GETS SENT OUT ON THE NORTH LINE, WHERE THEY WAS FIGHTING ABOUT EVERY DAY.

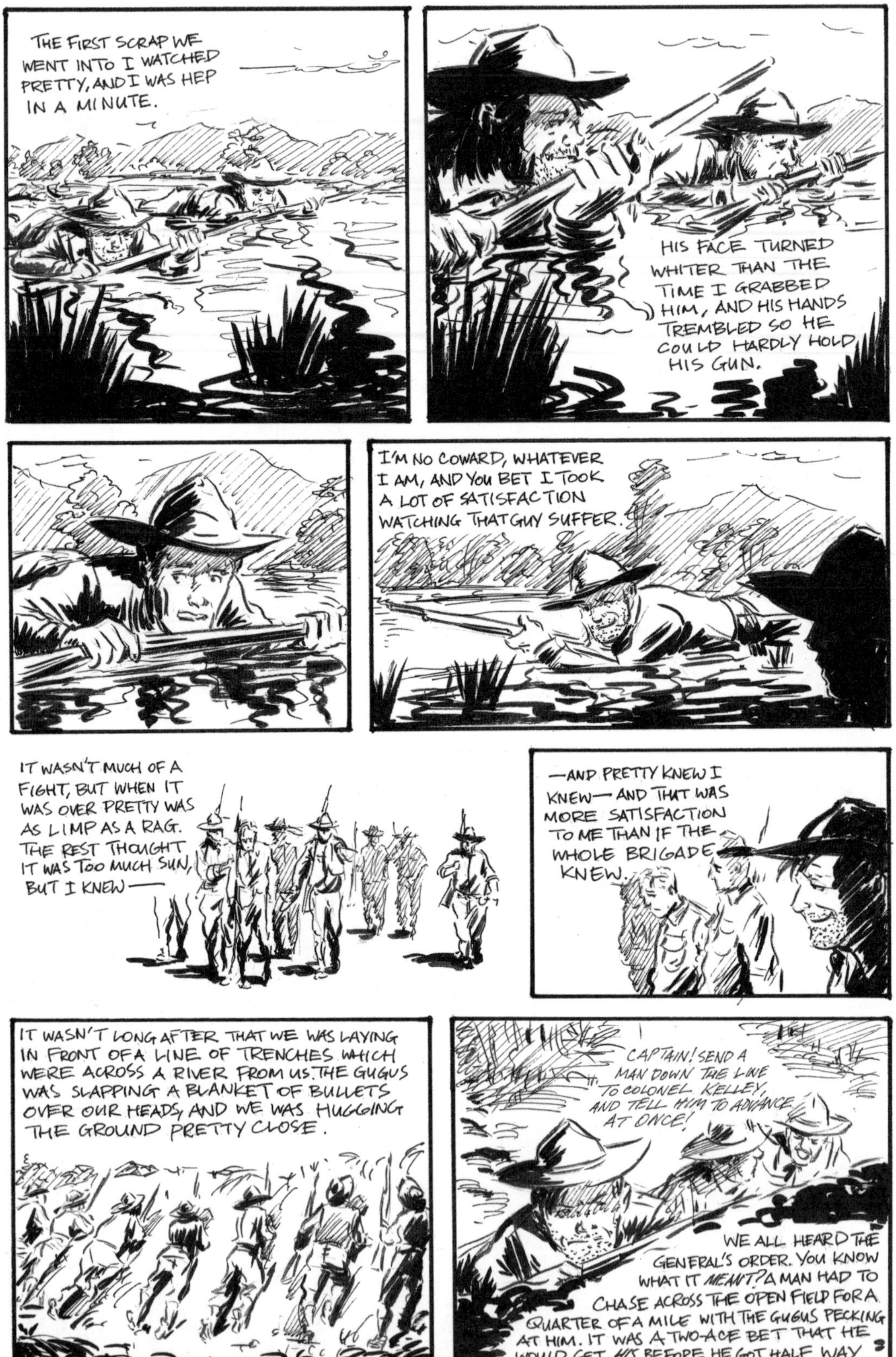
THE FIRST SCRAP WE WENT INTO I WATCHED PRETTY, AND I WAS HEP IN A MINUTE.
HIS FACE TURNED WHITER THAN THE TIME I GRABBED HIM, AND HIS HANDS TREMBLED SO HE COULD HARDLY HOLD HIS GUN.
I'M NO COWARD, WHATEVER I AM, AND YOU BET I TOOK A LOT OF SATISFACTION WATCHING THAT GUY SUFFER.
IT WASN'T MUCH OF A FIGHT, BUT WHEN IT WAS OVER PRETTY WAS AS LIMP AS A RAG. THE REST THOUGHT IT WAS TOO MUCH SUN, BUT I KNEW—
—AND PRETTY KNEW I KNEW— AND THAT WAS MORE SATISFACTION TO ME THAN IF THE WHOLE BRIGADE KNEW.
IT WASN'T LONG AFTER THAT WE WAS LAYING IN FRONT OF A LINE OF TRENCHES WHICH WERE ACROSS A RIVER FROM US. THE GUGUS WAS SLAPPING A BLANKET OF BULLETS OVER OUR HEADS, AND WE WAS HUGGING THE GROUND PRETTY CLOSE.
CAPTAIN! SEND A MAN DOWN THE LINE TO COLONEL KELLEY, AND TELL HIM TO ADVANCE AT ONCE!
WE ALL HEARD THE GENERAL'S ORDER. YOU KNOW WHAT IT MEANT? A MAN HAD TO CHASE ACROSS THE OPEN FIELD FOR A QUARTER OF A MILE WITH THE GUGUS PECKING AT HIM. IT WAS A TWO-ACE BET THAT HE WOULD GET HIS BEFORE HE GOT HALF WAY.

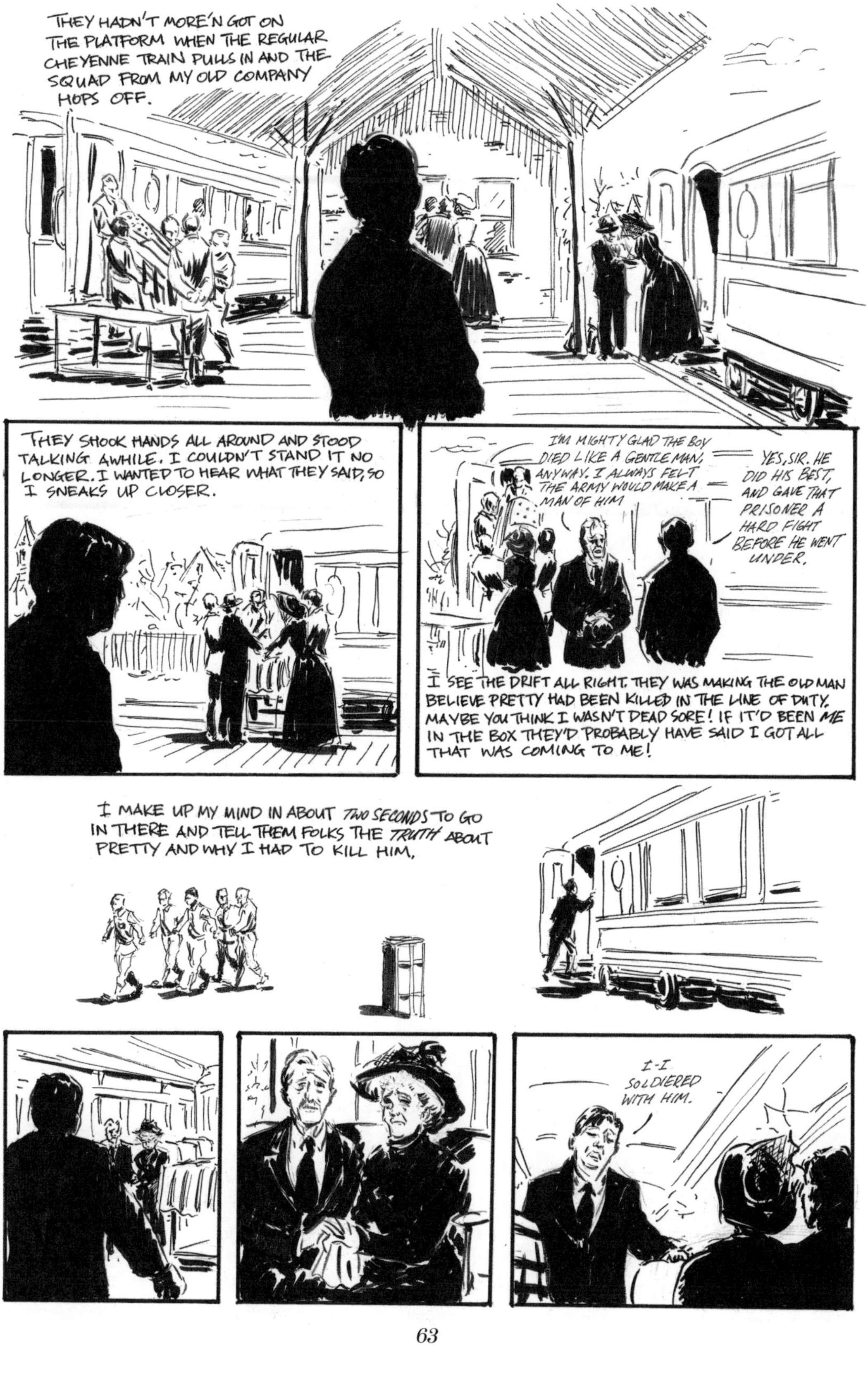
THEY HADN'T MORE'N GOT ON THE PLATFORM WHEN THE REGULAR CHEYENNE TRAIN PULLS IN AND THE SQUAD FROM MY OLD COMPANY HOPS OFF.
THEY SHOOK HANDS ALL AROUND AND STOOD TALKING AWHILE. I COULDN'T STAND IT NO LONGER. I WANTED TO HEAR WHAT THEY SAID, SO I SNEAKS UP CLOSER.
I'M MIGHTY GLAD THE BOY DIED LIKE A GENTLEMAN, ANYWAY. I ALWAYS FELT THE ARMY WOULD MAKE A MAN OF HIM
YES, SIR. HE DID HIS BEST, AND GAVE THAT PRISONER A HARD FIGHT BEFORE HE WENT UNDER.
I SEE THE DRIFT ALL RIGHT. THEY WAS MAKING THE OLD MAN BELIEVE PRETTY HAD BEEN KILLED IN THE LINE OF DUTY. MAYBE YOU THINK I WASN'T DEAD SORE! IF IT'D BEEN ME IN THE BOX THEY'D PROBABLY HAVE SAID I GOT ALL THAT WAS COMING TO ME!
I MAKE UP MY MIND IN ABOUT TWO SECONDS TO GO IN THERE AND TELL THEM FOLKS THE TRUTH ABOUT PRETTY AND WHY I HAD TO KILL HIM.
I-I SOLDIERED WITH HIM.

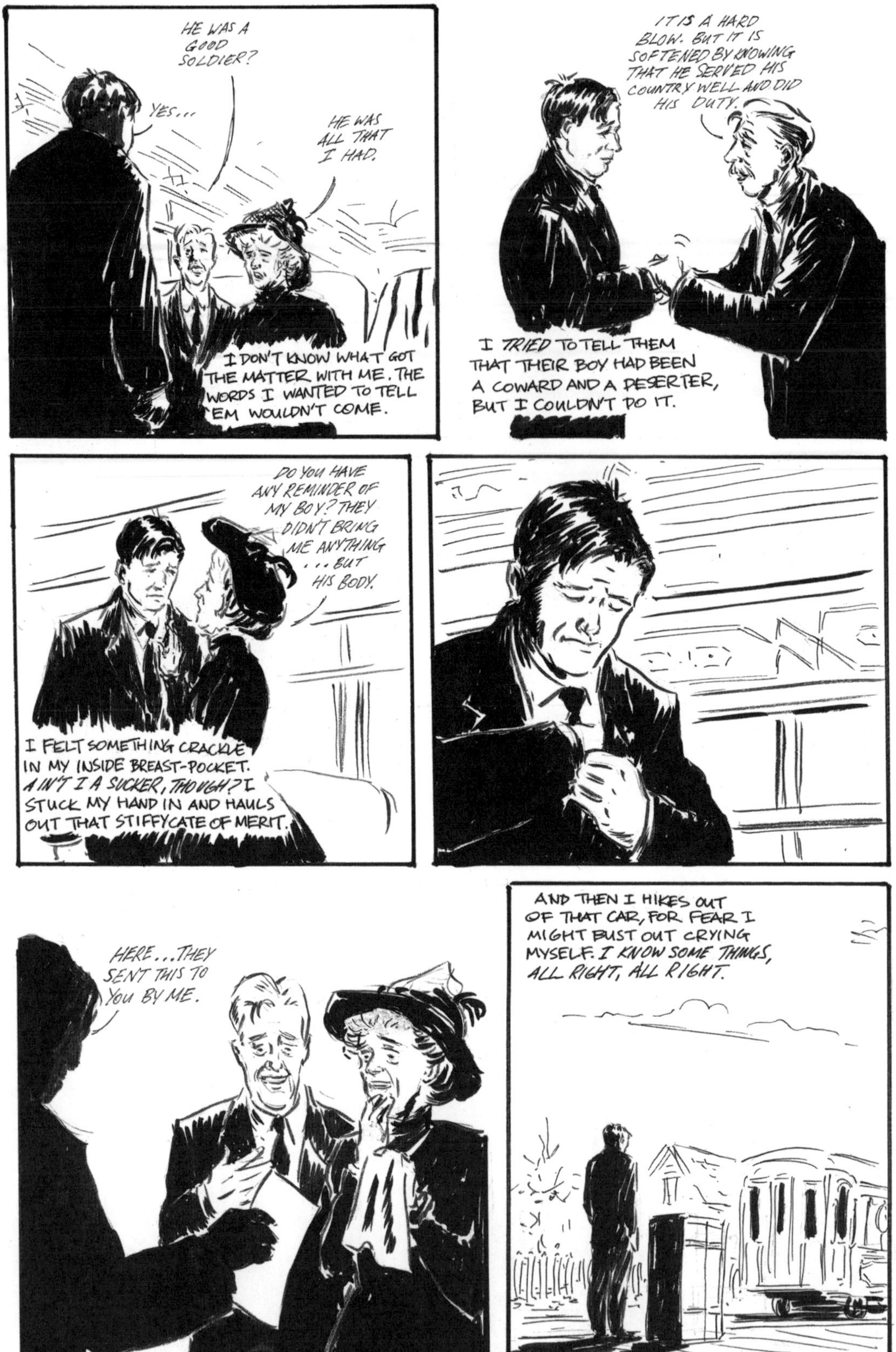
HE WAS A GOOD SOLDIER?
YES...
HE WAS ALL THAT I HAD.
I DON'T KNOW WHAT GOT THE MATTER WITH ME. THE WORDS I WANTED TO TELL 'EM WOULDN'T COME.
IT IS A HARD BLOW. BUT IT IS SOFTENED BY KNOWING THAT HE SERVED HIS COUNTRY WELL AND DID HIS DUTY.
I TRIED TO TELL THEM THAT THEIR BOY HAD BEEN A COWARD AND A DESERTER, BUT I COULDN'T DO IT.
DO YOU HAVE ANY REMINDER OF MY BOY? THEY DIDN'T BRING ME ANYTHING ... BUT HIS BODY.
I FELT SOMETHING CRACKLE IN MY INSIDE BREAST-POCKET. AIN'T I A SUCKER, THOUGH? I STUCK MY HAND IN AND HAULS OUT THAT STIFFYCATE OF MERIT.
HERE ... THEY SENT THIS TO YOU BY ME.
AND THEN I HIKES OUT OF THAT CAR, FOR FEAR I MIGHT BUST OUT CRYING MYSELF. I KNOW SOME THINGS, ALL RIGHT, ALL RIGHT.

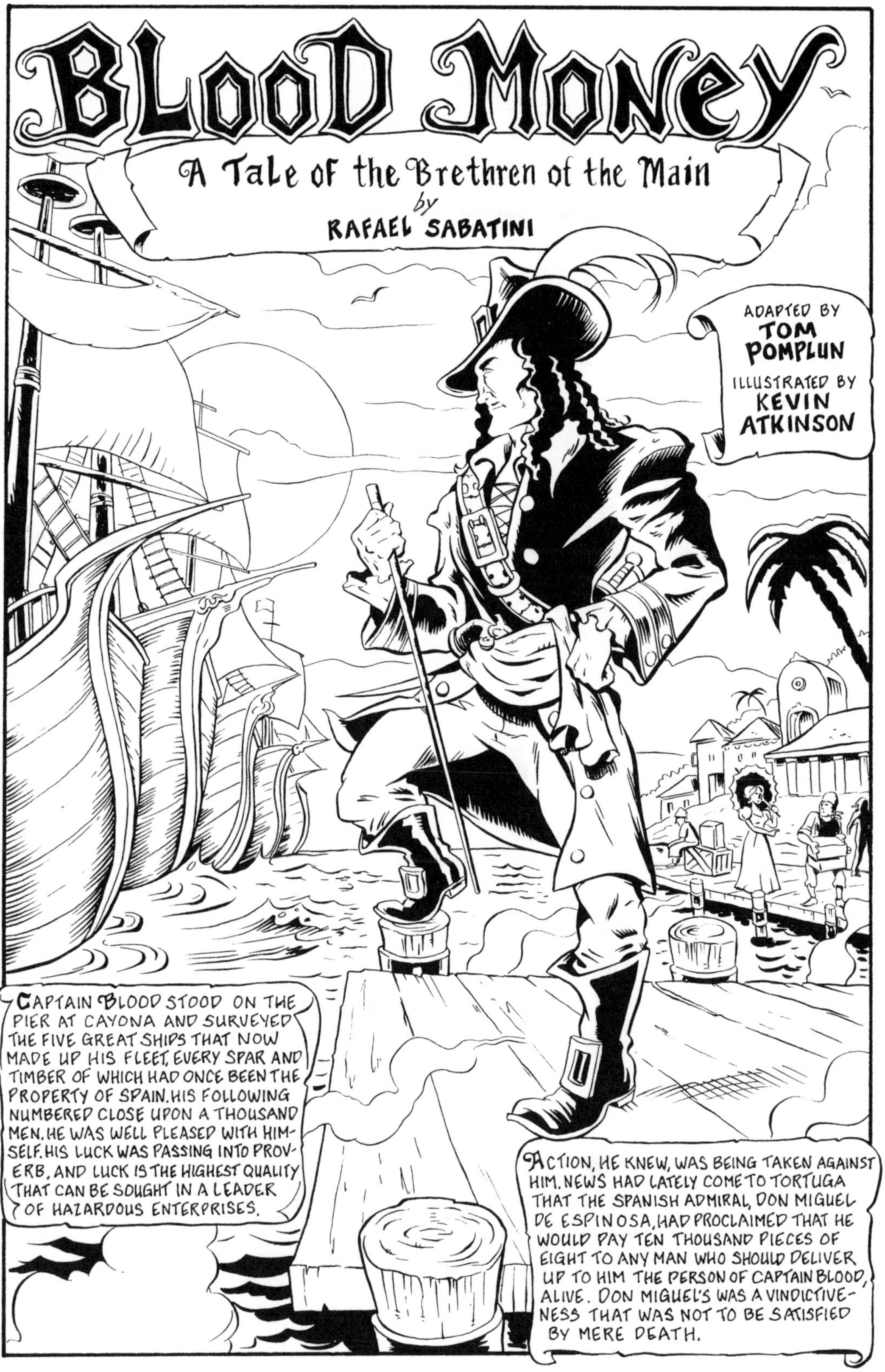
BLOOD MONEY
A Tale of the Brethren of the Main
by
RAFAEL SABATINI
ADAPTED BY
TOM POMPLUN
ILLUSTRATED BY
KEVIN ATKINSON
CAPTAIN BLOOD STOOD ON THE PIER AT CAYONA AND SURVEYED THE FIVE GREAT SHIPS THAT NOW MADE UP HIS FLEET, EVERY SPAR AND TIMBER OF WHICH HAD ONCE BEEN THE PROPERTY OF SPAIN. HIS FOLLOWING NUMBERED CLOSE UPON A THOUSAND MEN. HE WAS WELL PLEASED WITH HIMSELF. HIS LUCK WAS PASSING INTO PROVERB, AND LUCK IS THE HIGHEST QUALITY THAT CAN BE SOUGHT IN A LEADER OF HAZARDOUS ENTERPRISES.
ACTION, HE KNEW, WAS BEING TAKEN AGAINST HIM. NEWS HAD LATELY COME TO TORTUGA THAT THE SPANISH ADMIRAL, DON MIGUEL DE ESPINOSA, HAD PROCLAIMED THAT HE WOULD PAY TEN THOUSAND PIECES OF EIGHT TO ANY MAN WHO SHOULD DELIVER UP TO HIM THE PERSON OF CAPTAIN BLOOD, ALIVE. DON MIGUEL'S WAS A VINDICTIVENESS THAT WAS NOT TO BE SATISFIED BY MERE DEATH.

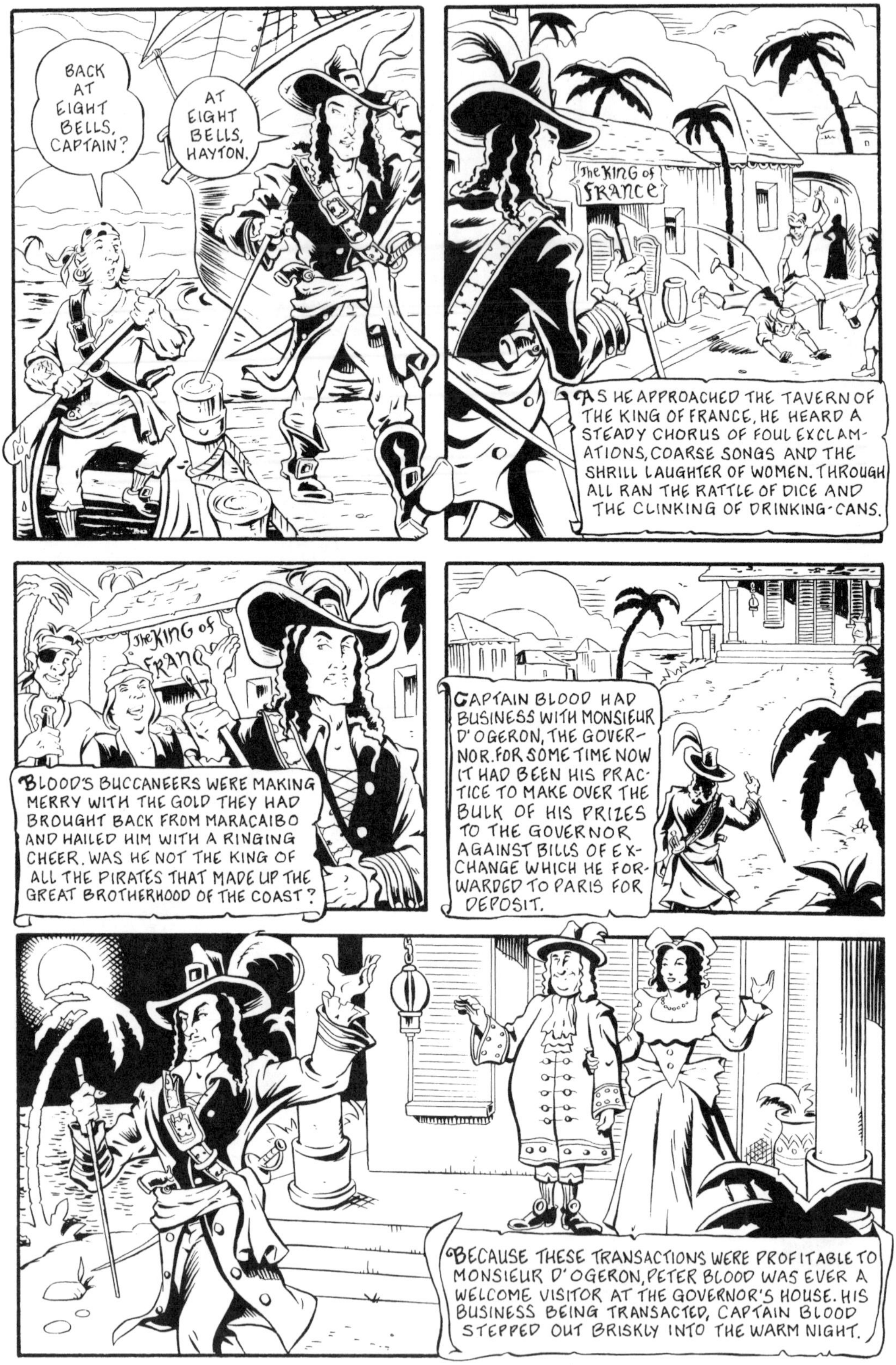
BACK AT EIGHT BELLS, CAPTAIN?
AT EIGHT BELLS, HAYTON.
The KING of FRANCE
AS HE APPROACHED THE TAVERN OF THE KING OF FRANCE, HE HEARD A STEADY CHORUS OF FOUL EXCLAMATIONS, COARSE SONGS AND THE SHRILL LAUGHTER OF WOMEN. THROUGH ALL RAN THE RATTLE OF DICE AND THE CLINKING OF DRINKING-CANS.
BLOOD'S BUCCANEERS WERE MAKING MERRY WITH THE GOLD THEY HAD BROUGHT BACK FROM MARACAIBO AND HAILED HIM WITH A RINGING CHEER. WAS HE NOT THE KING OF ALL THE PIRATES THAT MADE UP THE GREAT BROTHERHOOD OF THE COAST?
CAPTAIN BLOOD HAD BUSINESS WITH MONSIEUR D'OGERON, THE GOVERNOR. FOR SOME TIME NOW IT HAD BEEN HIS PRACTICE TO MAKE OVER THE BULK OF HIS PRIZES TO THE GOVERNOR AGAINST BILLS OF EXCHANGE WHICH HE FORWARDED TO PARIS FOR DEPOSIT.
BECAUSE THESE TRANSACTIONS WERE PROFITABLE TO MONSIEUR D'OGERON, PETER BLOOD WAS EVER A WELCOME VISITOR AT THE GOVERNOR'S HOUSE. HIS BUSINESS BEING TRANSACTED, CAPTAIN BLOOD STEPPED OUT BRISKLY INTO THE WARM NIGHT.

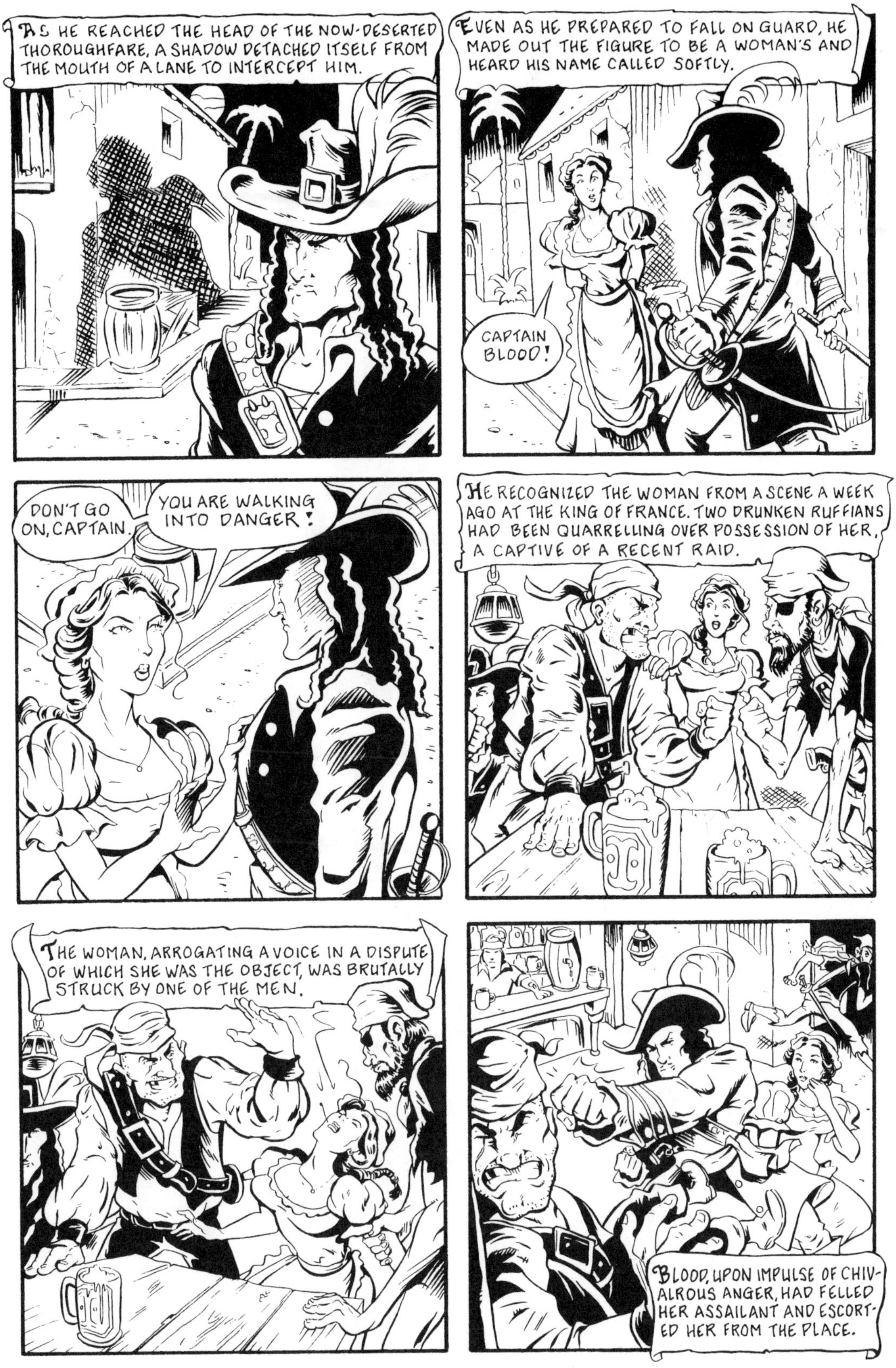
AS HE REACHED THE HEAD OF THE NOW-DESERTED THOROUGHFARE, A SHADOW DETACHED ITSELF FROM THE MOUTH OF A LANE TO INTERCEPT HIM.
EVEN AS HE PREPARED TO FALL ON GUARD, HE MADE OUT THE FIGURE TO BE A WOMAN'S AND HEARD HIS NAME CALLED SOFTLY.
CAPTAIN BLOOD!
DON'T GO ON, CAPTAIN.
YOU ARE WALKING INTO DANGER!
HE RECOGNIZED THE WOMAN FROM A SCENE A WEEK AGO AT THE KING OF FRANCE. TWO DRUNKEN RUFFIANS HAD BEEN QUARRELLING OVER POSSESSION OF HER, A CAPTIVE OF A RECENT RAID.
THE WOMAN, ARROGATING A VOICE IN A DISPUTE OF WHICH SHE WAS THE OBJECT, WAS BRUTALLY STRUCK BY ONE OF THE MEN.
BLOOD, UPON IMPULSE OF CHIVALROUS ANGER, HAD FELLED HER ASSAILANT AND ESCORTED HER FROM THE PLACE.

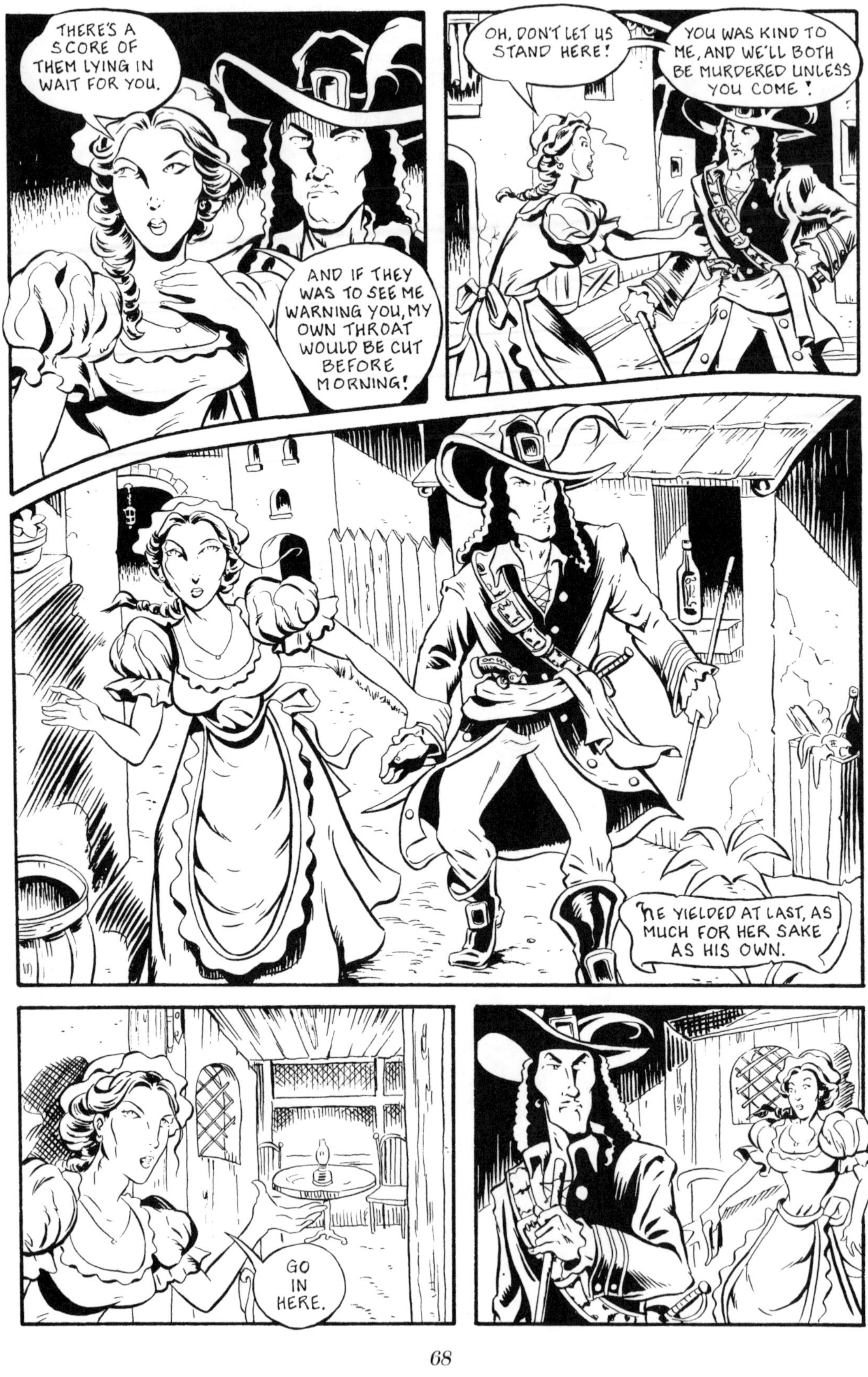
THERE'S A SCORE OF THEM LYING IN WAIT FOR YOU.
AND IF THEY WAS TO SEE ME WARNING YOU, MY OWN THROAT WOULD BE CUT BEFORE MORNING!
OH, DON'T LET US STAND HERE!
YOU WAS KIND TO ME, AND WE'LL BOTH BE MURDERED UNLESS YOU COME!
HE YIELDED AT LAST, AS MUCH FOR HER SAKE AS HIS OWN.
GO IN HERE.

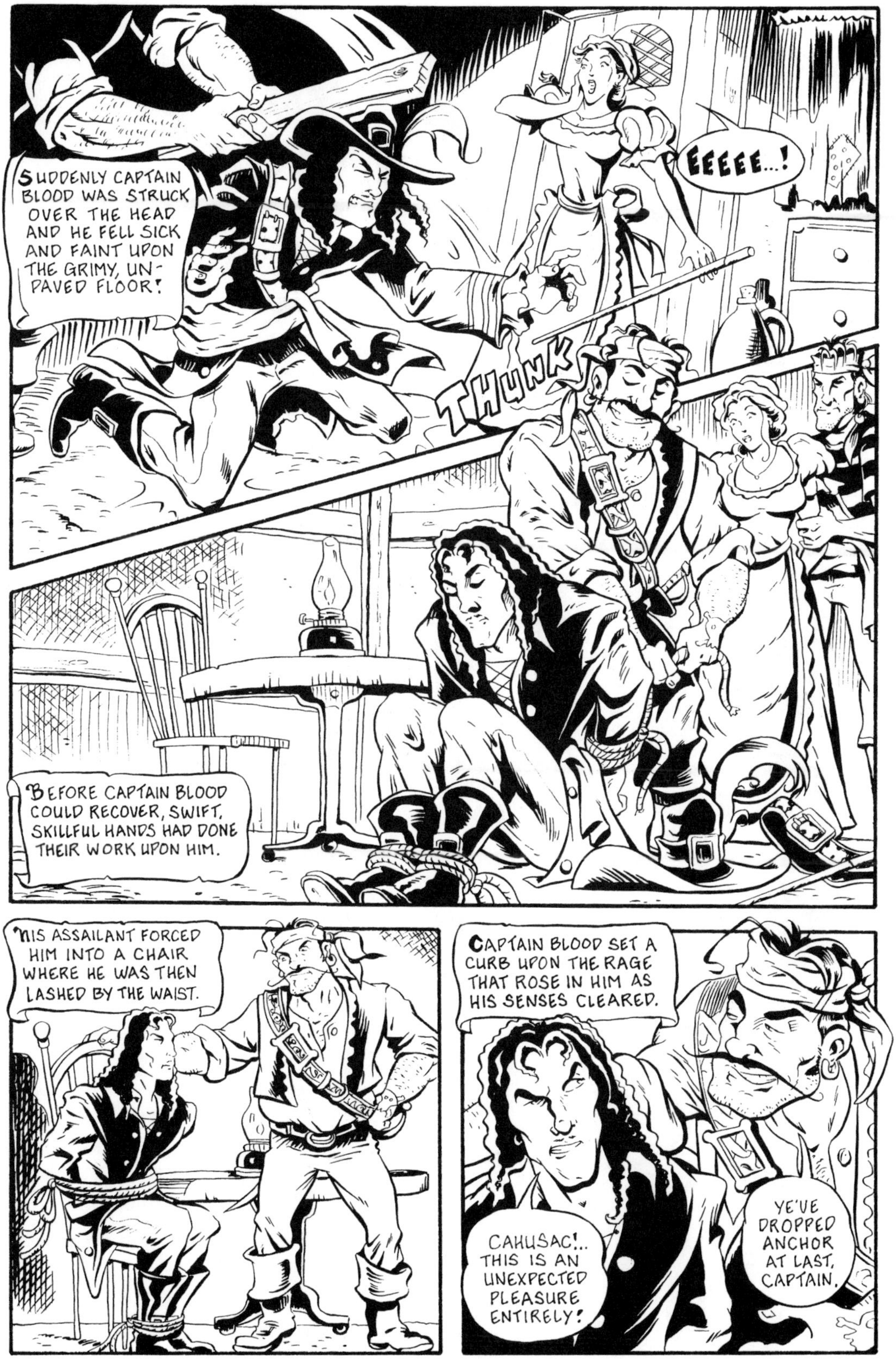
SUDDENLY CAPTAIN BLOOD WAS STRUCK OVER THE HEAD AND HE FELL SICK AND FAINT UPON THE GRIMY, UN-PAVED FLOOR!
EEEEE...!
THUNK
BEFORE CAPTAIN BLOOD COULD RECOVER, SWIFT, SKILLFUL HANDS HAD DONE THEIR WORK UPON HIM.
HIS ASSAILANT FORCED HIM INTO A CHAIR WHERE HE WAS THEN LASHED BY THE WAIST.
CAPTAIN BLOOD SET A CURB UPON THE RAGE THAT ROSE IN HIM AS HIS SENSES CLEARED.
CAHUSAC!.. THIS IS AN UNEXPECTED PLEASURE ENTIRELY!
YE'VE DROPPED ANCHOR AT LAST, CAPTAIN.

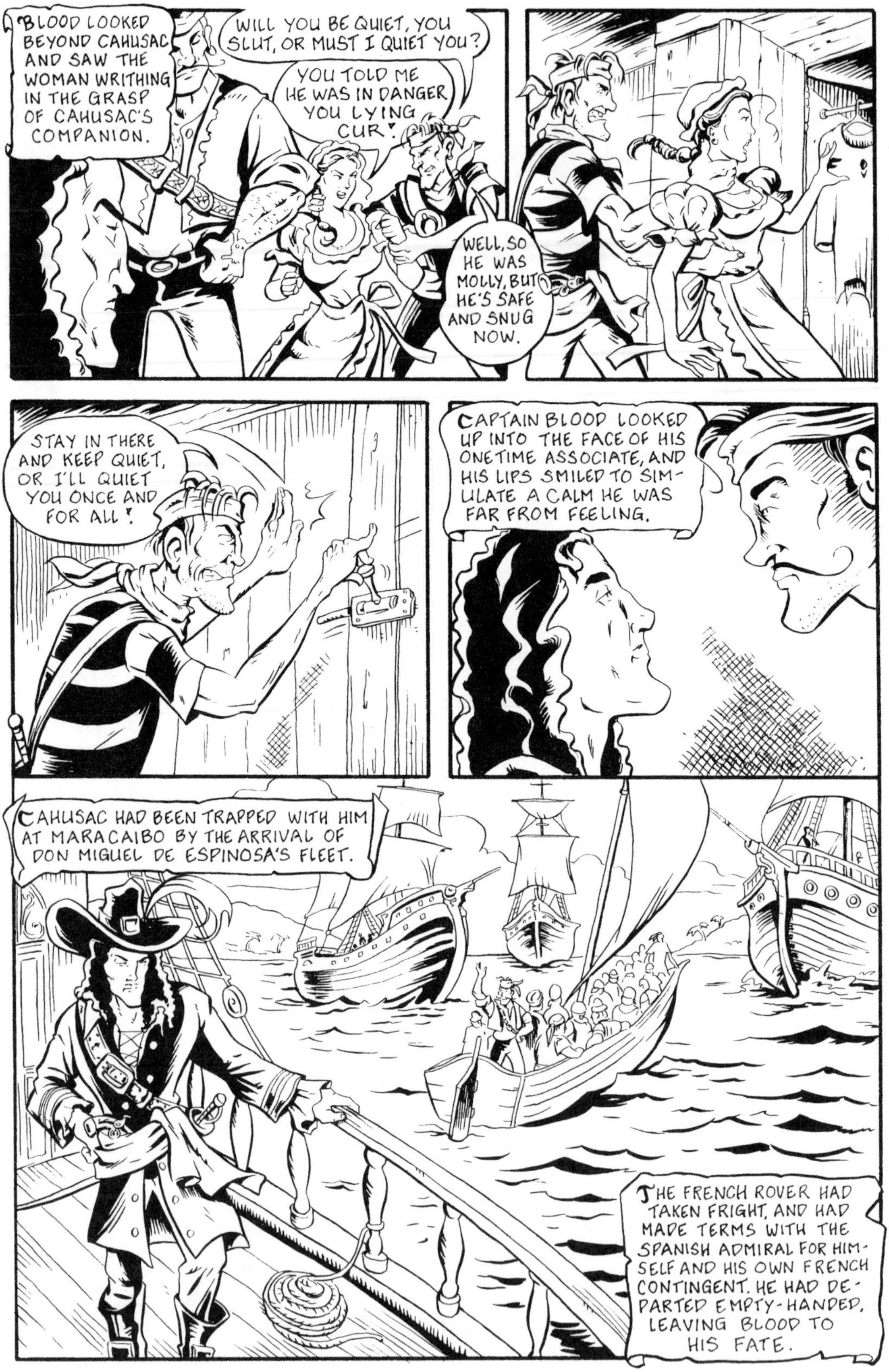
BLOOD LOOKED BEYOND CAHUSAC AND SAW THE WOMAN WRITHING IN THE GRASP OF CAHUSAC'S COMPANION.
WILL YOU BE QUIET, YOU SLUT, OR MUST I QUIET YOU?
YOU TOLD ME HE WAS IN DANGER YOU LYING CUR!
WELL, SO HE WAS MOLLY, BUT HE'S SAFE AND SNUG NOW.
STAY IN THERE AND KEEP QUIET, OR I'LL QUIET YOU ONCE AND FOR ALL!
CAPTAIN BLOOD LOOKED UP INTO THE FACE OF HIS ONETIME ASSOCIATE, AND HIS LIPS SMILED TO SIMULATE A CALM HE WAS FAR FROM FEELING.
CAHUSAC HAD BEEN TRAPPED WITH HIM AT MARACAIBO BY THE ARRIVAL OF DON MIGUEL DE ESPINOSA'S FLEET.
THE FRENCH ROVER HAD TAKEN FRIGHT, AND HAD MADE TERMS WITH THE SPANISH ADMIRAL FOR HIMSELF AND HIS OWN FRENCH CONTINGENT. HE HAD DEPARTED EMPTY-HANDED, LEAVING BLOOD TO HIS FATE.

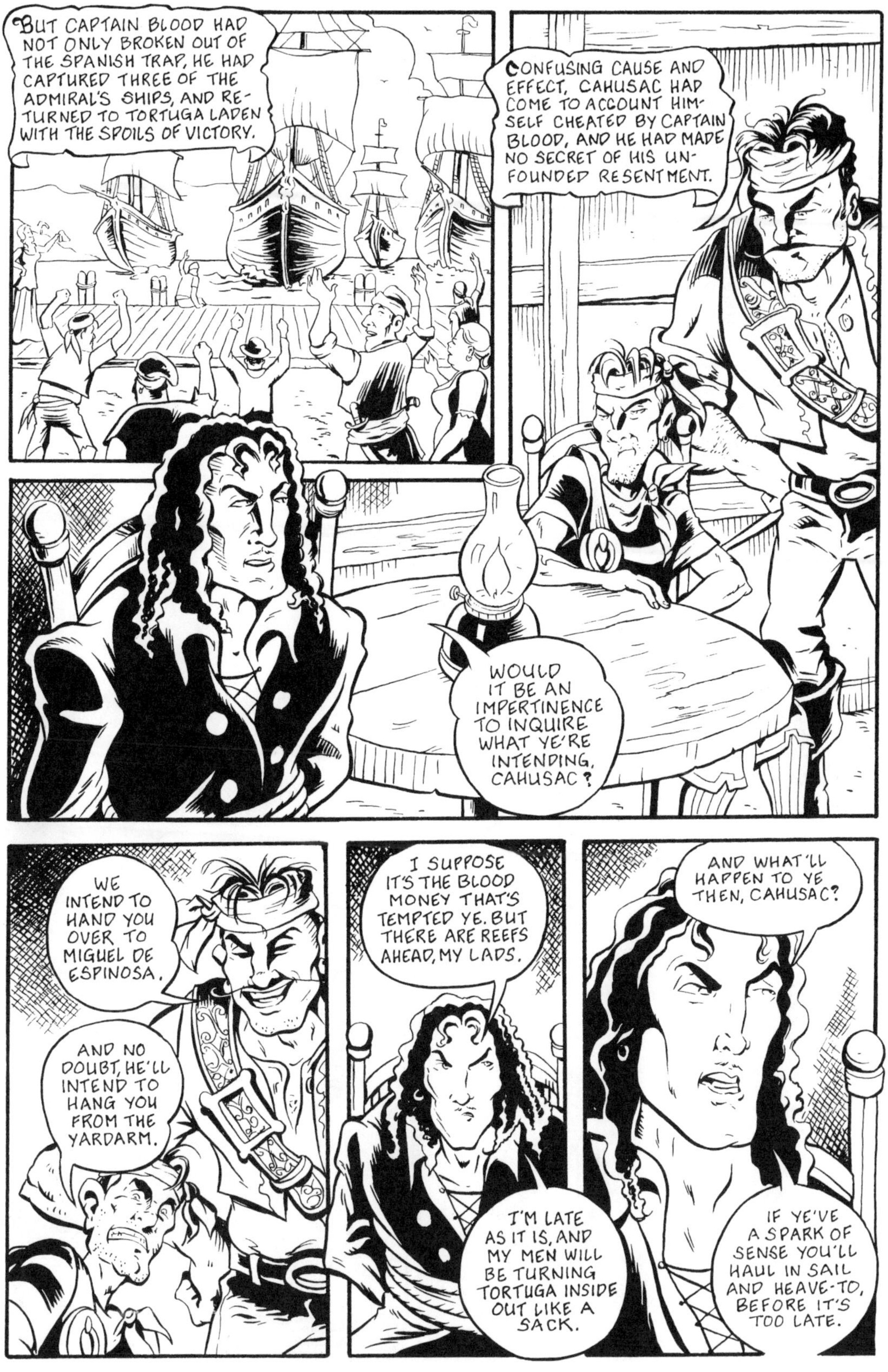
BUT CAPTAIN BLOOD HAD NOT ONLY BROKEN OUT OF THE SPANISH TRAP, HE HAD CAPTURED THREE OF THE ADMIRAL'S SHIPS, AND RETURNED TO TORTUGA LADEN WITH THE SPOILS OF VICTORY.
CONFUSING CAUSE AND EFFECT, CAHUSAC HAD COME TO ACCOUNT HIMSELF CHEATED BY CAPTAIN BLOOD, AND HE HAD MADE NO SECRET OF HIS UNFOUNDED RESENTMENT.
WOULD IT BE AN IMPERTINENCE TO INQUIRE WHAT YE'RE INTENDING, CAHUSAC?
WE INTEND TO HAND YOU OVER TO MIGUEL DE ESPINOSA.
AND NO DOUBT, HE'LL INTEND TO HANG YOU FROM THE YARDARM.
I SUPPOSE IT'S THE BLOOD MONEY THAT'S TEMPTED YE. BUT THERE ARE REEFS AHEAD, MY LADS.
I'M LATE AS IT IS, AND MY MEN WILL BE TURNING TORTUGA INSIDE OUT LIKE A SACK.
AND WHAT'LL HAPPEN TO YE THEN, CAHUSAC?
IF YE'VE A SPARK OF SENSE YOU'LL HAUL IN SAIL AND HEAVE-TO, BEFORE IT'S TOO LATE.

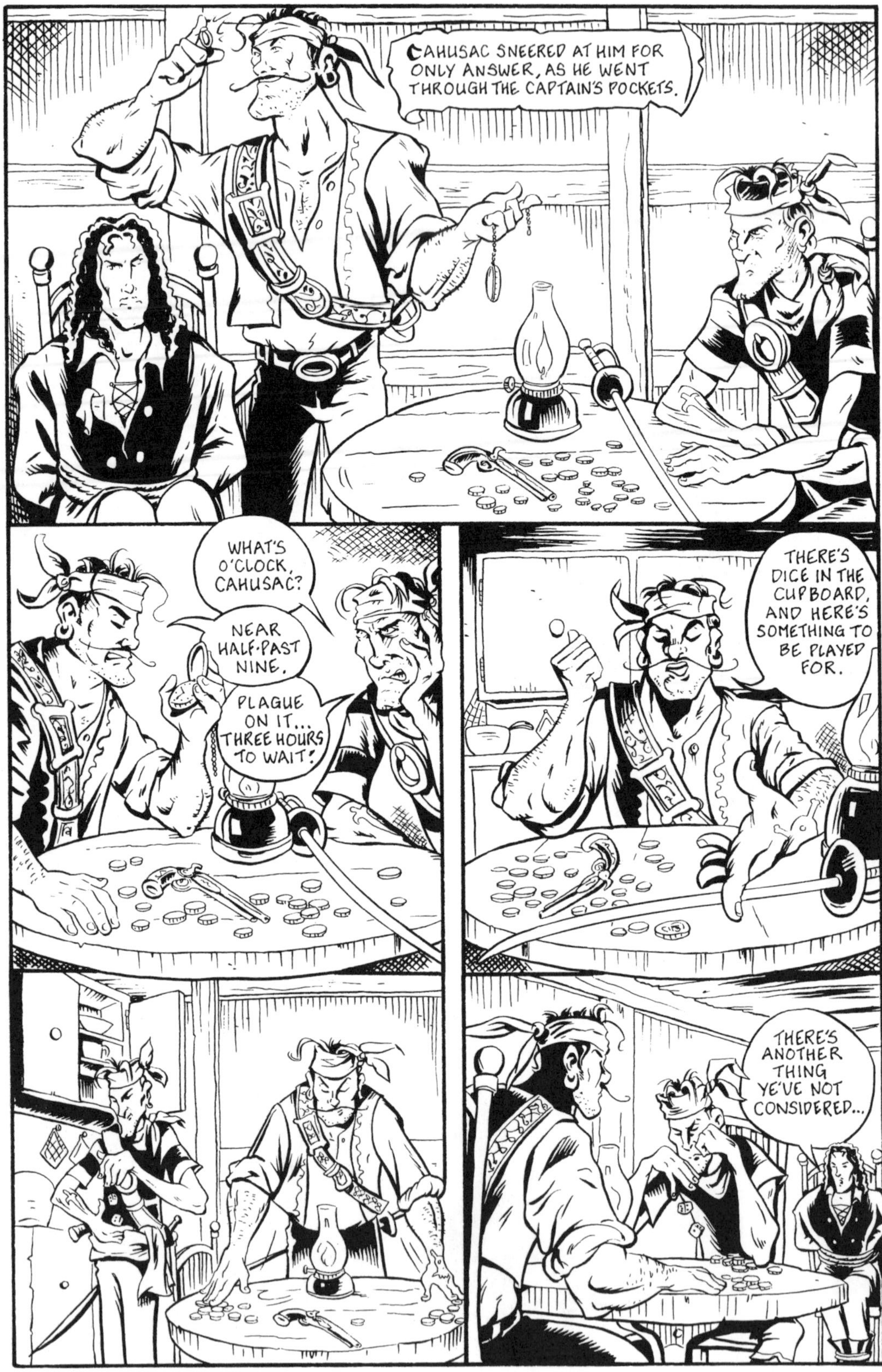
CAHUSAC SNEERED AT HIM FOR ONLY ANSWER, AS HE WENT THROUGH THE CAPTAIN'S POCKETS.
WHAT'S O'CLOCK, CAHUSAC?
NEAR HALF-PAST NINE.
PLAGUE ON IT... THREE HOURS TO WAIT!
THERE'S DICE IN THE CUPBOARD, AND HERE'S SOMETHING TO BE PLAYED FOR.
THERE'S ANOTHER THING YE'VE NOT CONSIDERED...

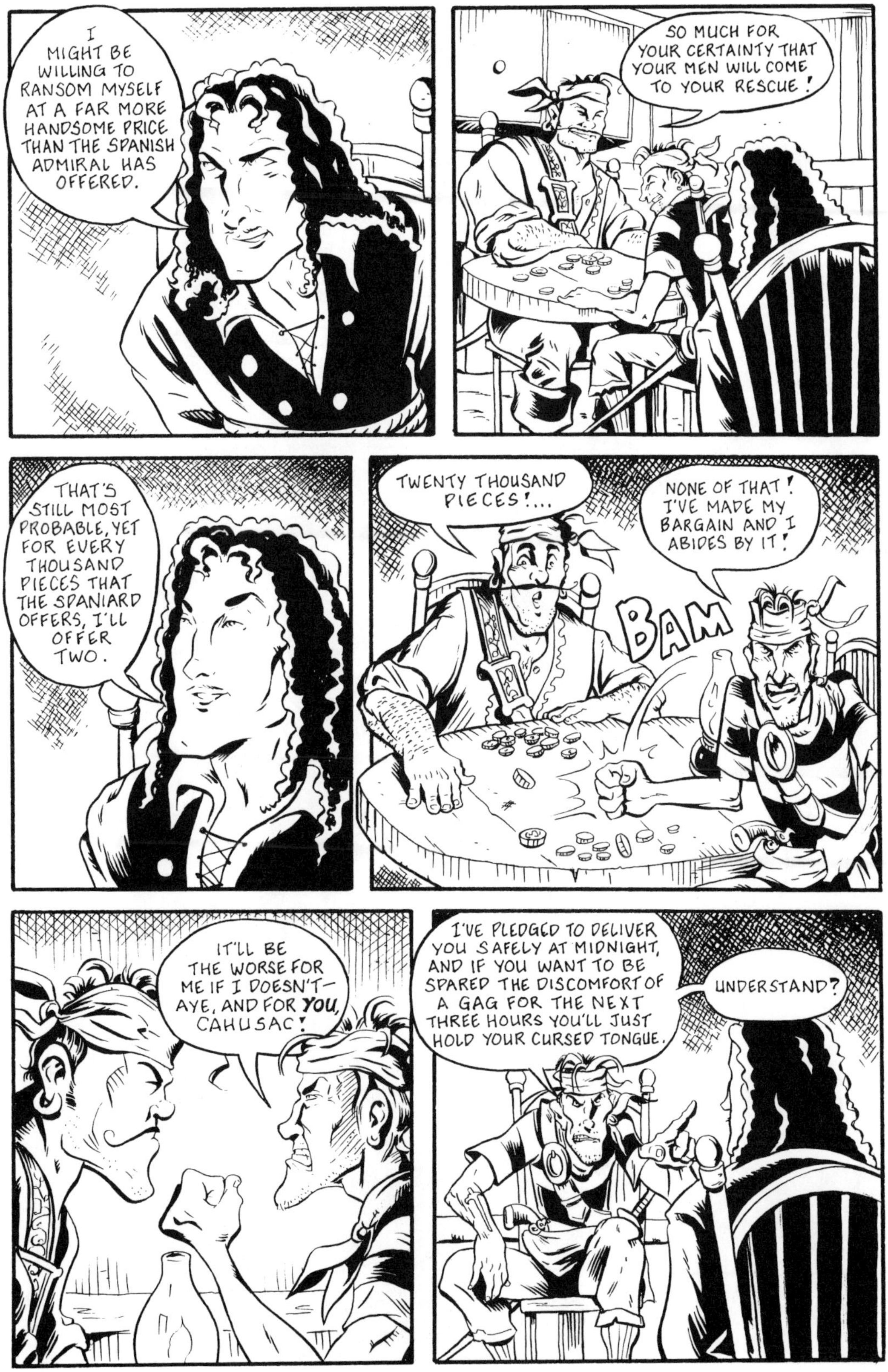
I MIGHT BE WILLING TO RANSOM MYSELF AT A FAR MORE HANDSOME PRICE THAN THE SPANISH ADMIRAL HAS OFFERED.
SO MUCH FOR YOUR CERTAINTY THAT YOUR MEN WILL COME TO YOUR RESCUE!
THAT'S STILL MOST PROBABLE, YET FOR EVERY THOUSAND PIECES THAT THE SPANIARD OFFERS, I'LL OFFER TWO.
TWENTY THOUSAND PIECES!...
NONE OF THAT! I'VE MADE MY BARGAIN AND I ABIDES BY IT!
BAM
IT'LL BE THE WORSE FOR ME IF I DOESN'T- AYE, AND FOR YOU, CAHUSAC!
I'VE PLEDGED TO DELIVER YOU SAFELY AT MIDNIGHT, AND IF YOU WANT TO BE SPARED THE DISCOMFORT OF A GAG FOR THE NEXT THREE HOURS YOU'LL JUST HOLD YOUR CURSED TONGUE.
UNDERSTAND?

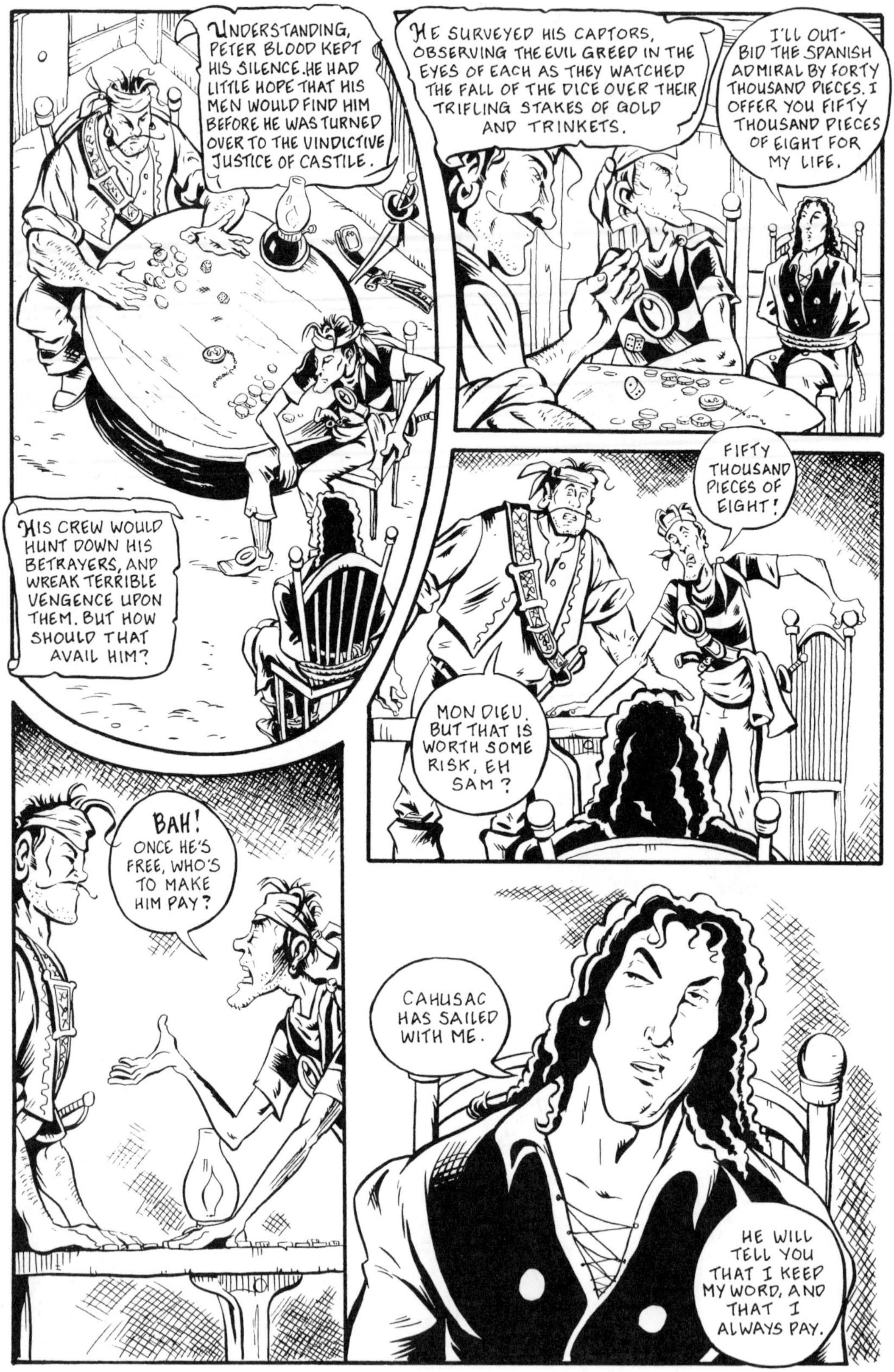
UNDERSTANDING, PETER BLOOD KEPT HIS SILENCE. HE HAD LITTLE HOPE THAT HIS MEN WOULD FIND HIM BEFORE HE WAS TURNED OVER TO THE VINDICTIVE JUSTICE OF CASTILE.
HIS CREW WOULD HUNT DOWN HIS BETRAYERS, AND WREAK TERRIBLE VENGENCE UPON THEM. BUT HOW SHOULD THAT AVAIL HIM?
HE SURVEYED HIS CAPTORS, OBSERVING THE EVIL GREED IN THE EYES OF EACH AS THEY WATCHED THE FALL OF THE DICE OVER THEIR TRIFLING STAKES OF GOLD AND TRINKETS.
I'LL OUT-BID THE SPANISH ADMIRAL BY FORTY THOUSAND PIECES. I OFFER YOU FIFTY THOUSAND PIECES OF EIGHT FOR MY LIFE.
FIFTY THOUSAND PIECES OF EIGHT!
MON DIEU. BUT THAT IS WORTH SOME RISK, EH SAM?
BAH! ONCE HE'S FREE, WHO'S TO MAKE HIM PAY?
CAHUSAC HAS SAILED WITH ME.
HE WILL TELL YOU THAT I KEEP MY WORD, AND THAT I ALWAYS PAY.

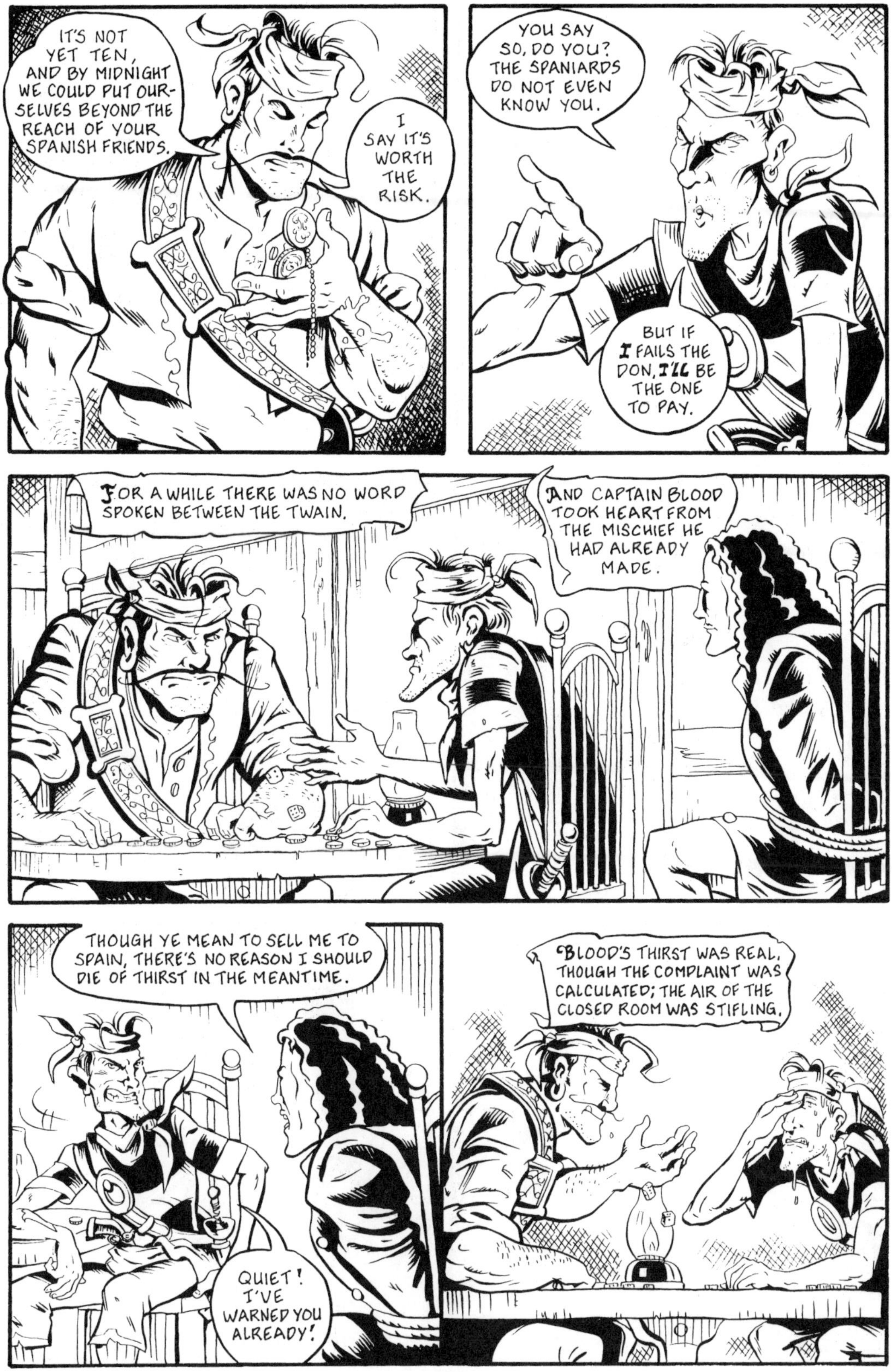
IT'S NOT YET TEN, AND BY MIDNIGHT WE COULD PUT OURSELVES BEYOND THE REACH OF YOUR SPANISH FRIENDS.
I SAY IT'S WORTH THE RISK.
YOU SAY SO, DO YOU? THE SPANIARDS DO NOT EVEN KNOW YOU.
BUT IF I FAILS THE DON, I'LL BE THE ONE TO PAY.
FOR A WHILE THERE WAS NO WORD SPOKEN BETWEEN THE TWAIN.
AND CAPTAIN BLOOD TOOK HEART FROM THE MISCHIEF HE HAD ALREADY MADE.
THOUGH YE MEAN TO SELL ME TO SPAIN, THERE'S NO REASON I SHOULD DIE OF THIRST IN THE MEANTIME.
QUIET! I'VE WARNED YOU ALREADY!
BLOOD'S THIRST WAS REAL, THOUGH THE COMPLAINT WAS CALCULATED; THE AIR OF THE CLOSED ROOM WAS STIFLING.

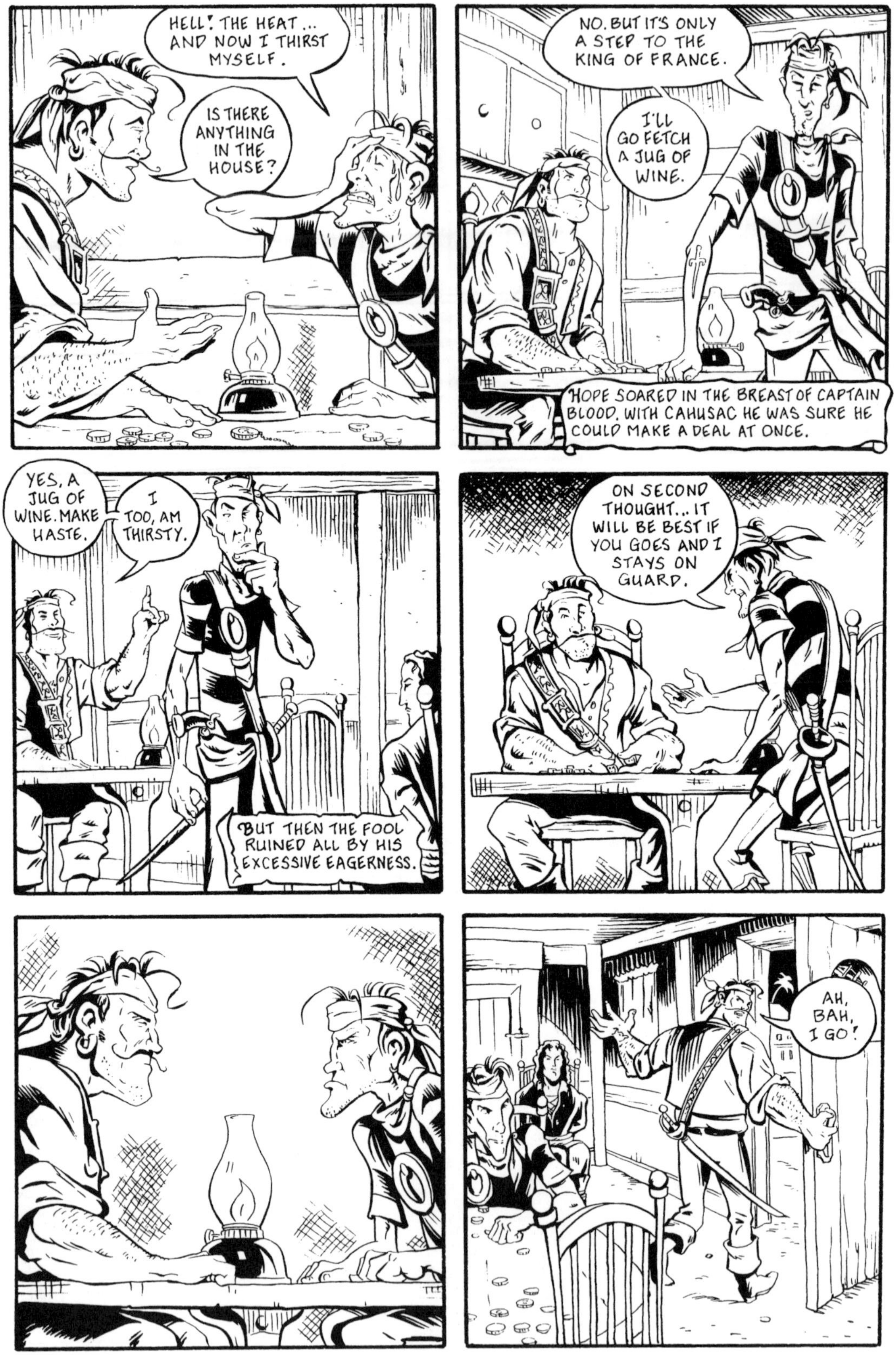
HELL! THE HEAT... AND NOW I THIRST MYSELF.
IS THERE ANYTHING IN THE HOUSE?
NO. BUT IT'S ONLY A STEP TO THE KING OF FRANCE.
I'LL GO FETCH A JUG OF WINE.
HOPE SOARED IN THE BREAST OF CAPTAIN BLOOD. WITH CAHUSAC HE WAS SURE HE COULD MAKE A DEAL AT ONCE.
YES, A JUG OF WINE. MAKE HASTE.
I TOO, AM THIRSTY.
BUT THEN THE FOOL RUINED ALL BY HIS EXCESSIVE EAGERNESS.
ON SECOND THOUGHT... IT WILL BE BEST IF YOU GOES AND I STAYS ON GUARD.
AH, BAH, I GO!

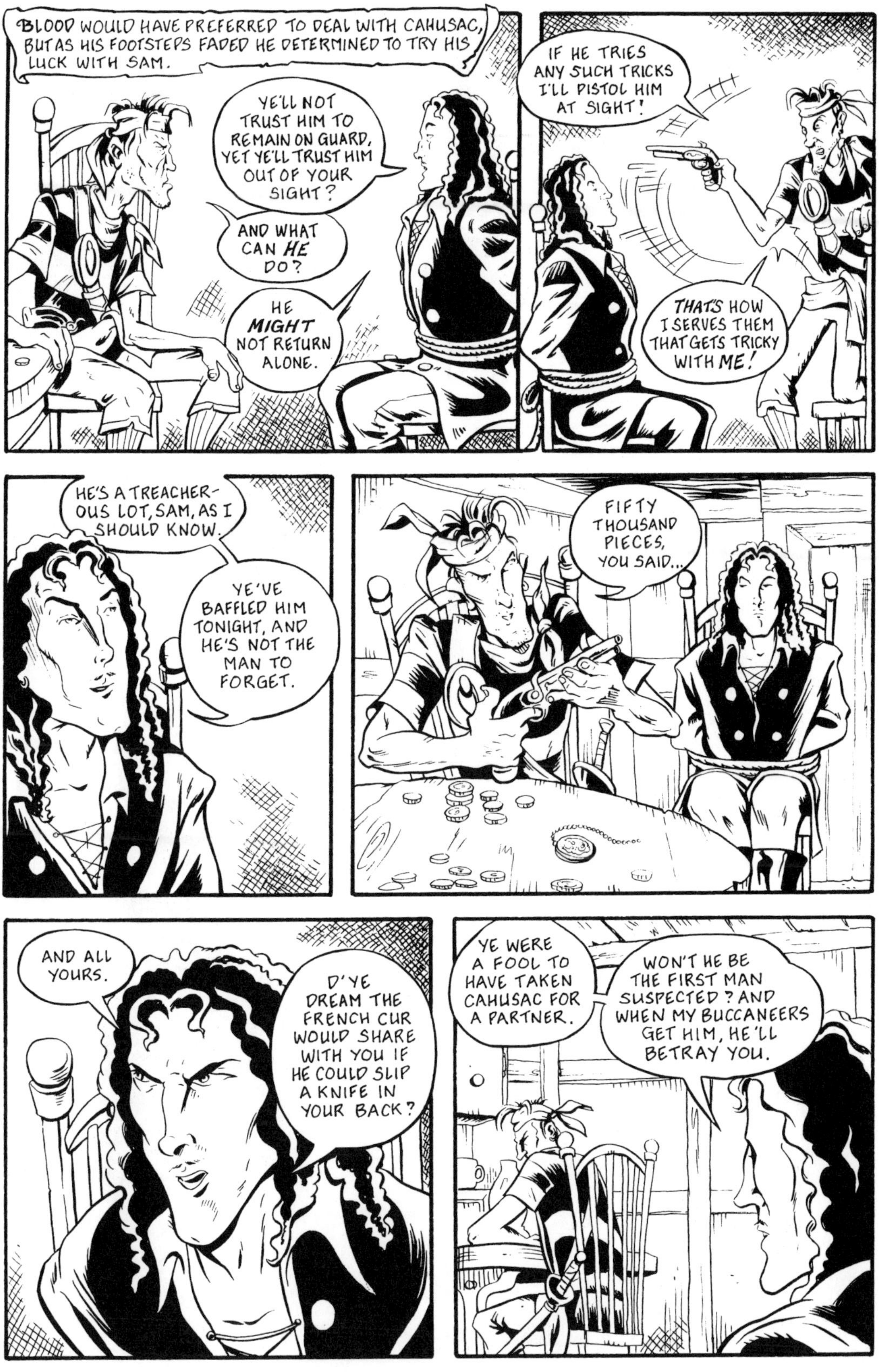
BLOOD WOULD HAVE PREFERRED TO DEAL WITH CAHUSAC, BUT AS HIS FOOTSTEPS FADED HE DETERMINED TO TRY HIS LUCK WITH SAM.
YE'LL NOT TRUST HIM TO REMAIN ON GUARD, YET YE'LL TRUST HIM OUT OF YOUR SIGHT?
AND WHAT CAN *HE* DO?
HE ***MIGHT*** NOT RETURN ALONE.
IF HE TRIES ANY SUCH TRICKS I'LL PISTOL HIM AT SIGHT!
THAT'S HOW I SERVES THEM THAT GETS TRICKY WITH *ME*!
HE'S A TREACHER-OUS LOT, SAM, AS I SHOULD KNOW.
YE'VE BAFFLED HIM TONIGHT, AND HE'S NOT THE MAN TO FORGET.
FIFTY THOUSAND PIECES, YOU SAID...
AND ALL YOURS.
D'YE DREAM THE FRENCH CUR WOULD SHARE WITH YOU IF HE COULD SLIP A KNIFE IN YOUR BACK?
YE WERE A FOOL TO HAVE TAKEN CAHUSAC FOR A PARTNER.
WON'T HE BE THE FIRST MAN SUSPECTED? AND WHEN MY BUCCANEERS GET HIM, HE'LL BETRAY YOU.

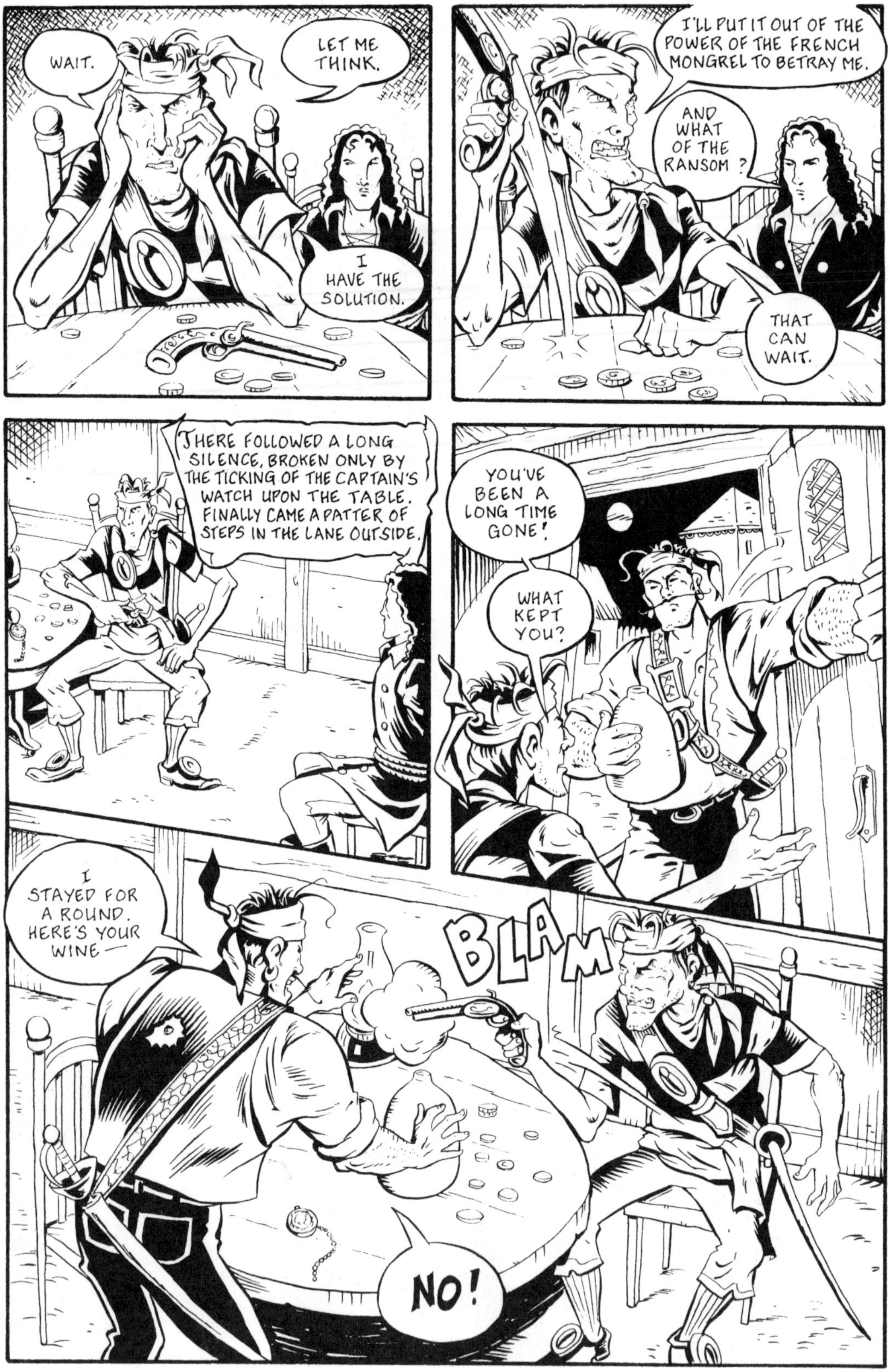
WAIT.
LET ME THINK.
I HAVE THE SOLUTION.
I'LL PUT IT OUT OF THE POWER OF THE FRENCH MONGREL TO BETRAY ME.
AND WHAT OF THE RANSOM ?
THAT CAN WAIT.
THERE FOLLOWED A LONG SILENCE, BROKEN ONLY BY THE TICKING OF THE CAPTAIN'S WATCH UPON THE TABLE. FINALLY CAME A PATTER OF STEPS IN THE LANE OUTSIDE.
YOU'VE BEEN A LONG TIME GONE!
WHAT KEPT YOU?
I STAYED FOR A ROUND. HERE'S YOUR WINE—
BLAM
NO!

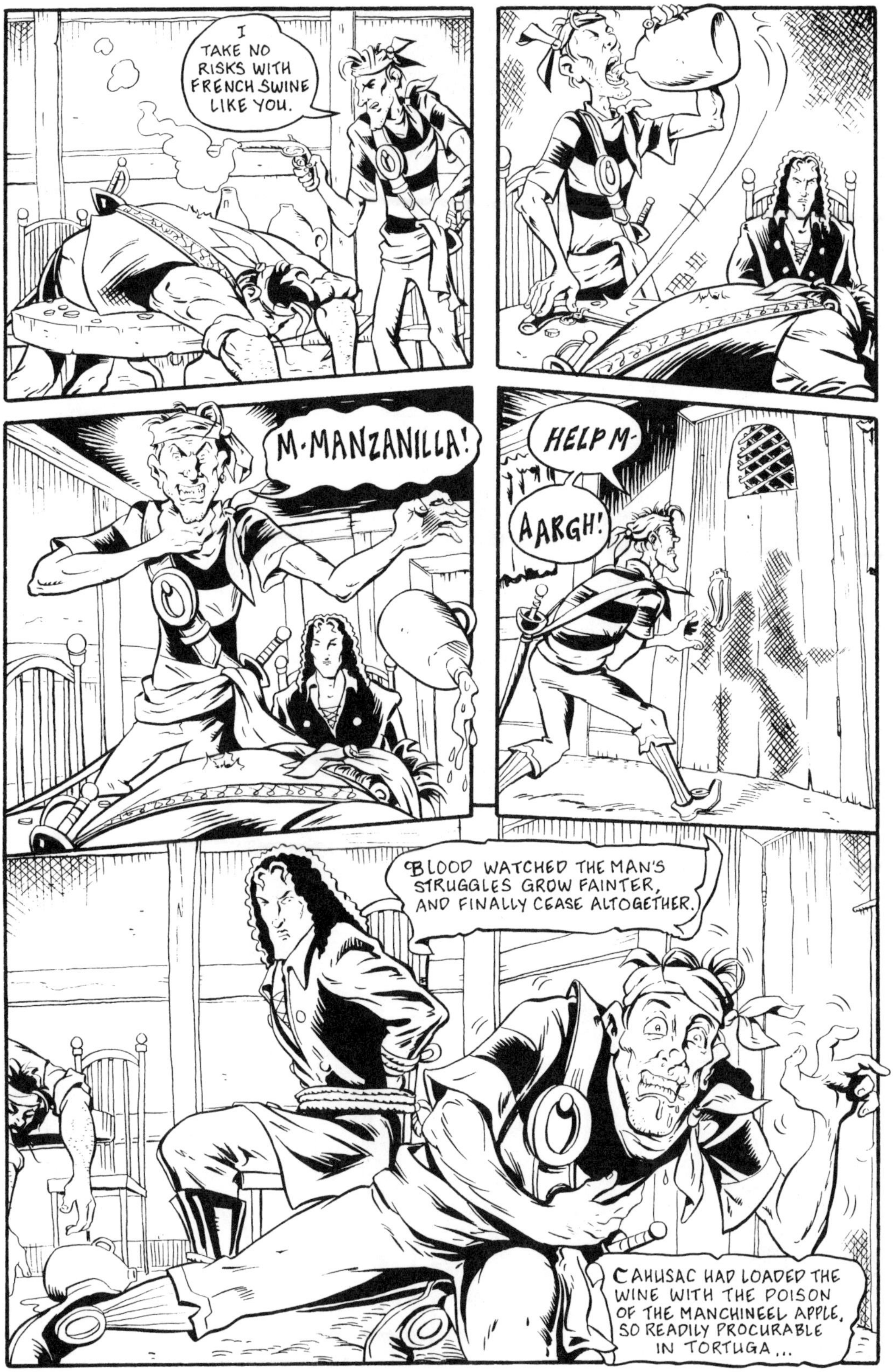
I TAKE NO RISKS WITH FRENCH SWINE LIKE YOU.
M-MANZANILLA!
HELP M-
AARGH!
BLOOD WATCHED THE MAN'S STRUGGLES GROW FAINTER, AND FINALLY CEASE ALTOGETHER.
CAHUSAC HAD LOADED THE WINE WITH THE POISON OF THE MANCHINEEL APPLE, SO READILY PROCURABLE IN TORTUGA...

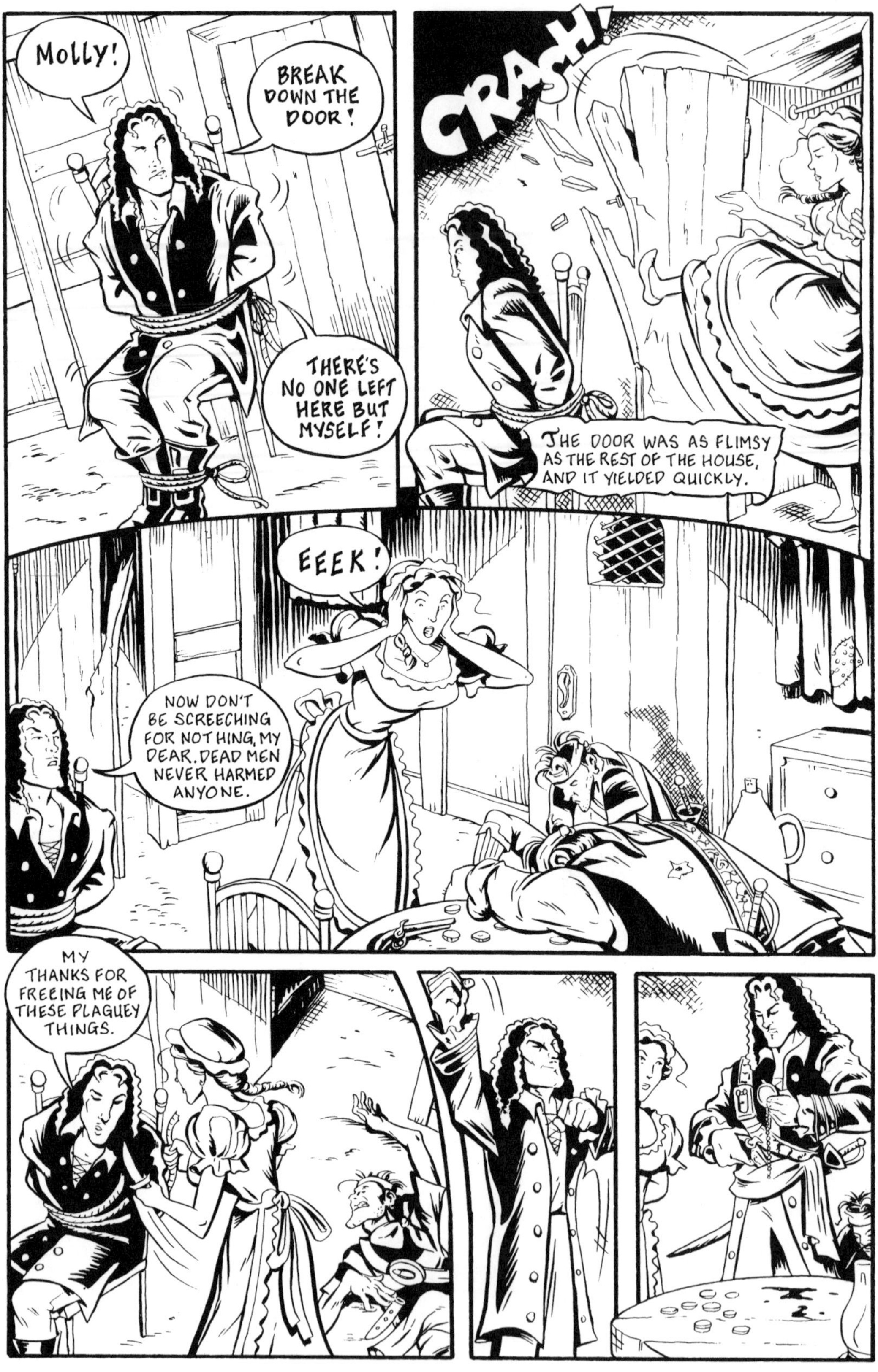
Molly!
BREAK DOWN THE DOOR!
THERE'S NO ONE LEFT HERE BUT MYSELF!
CRASH!
THE DOOR WAS AS FLIMSY AS THE REST OF THE HOUSE, AND IT YIELDED QUICKLY.
EEEK!
NOW DON'T BE SCREECHING FOR NOTHING, MY DEAR. DEAD MEN NEVER HARMED ANYONE.
MY THANKS FOR FREEING ME OF THESE PLAGUEY THINGS.

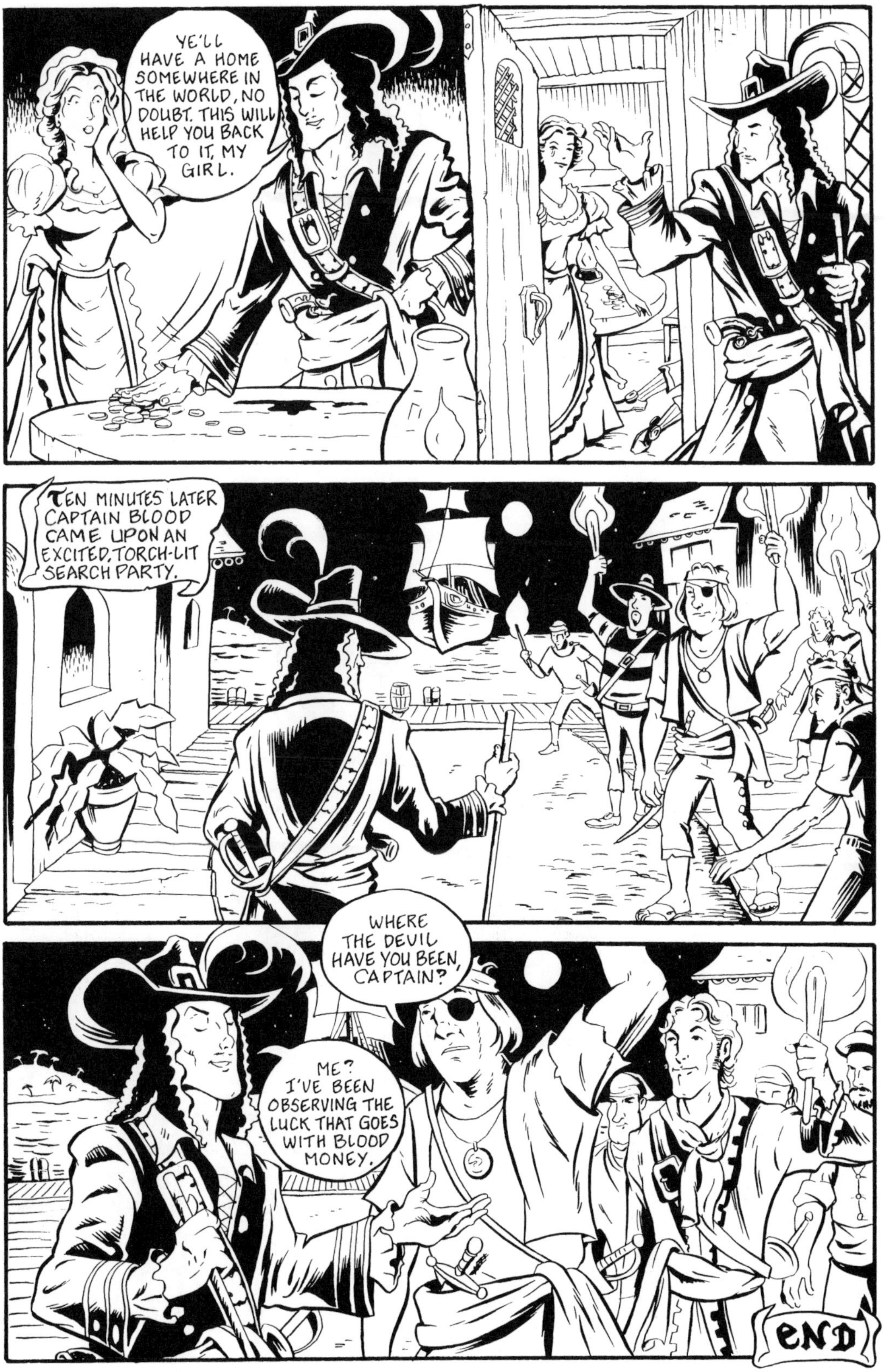
YE'LL HAVE A HOME SOMEWHERE IN THE WORLD, NO DOUBT. THIS WILL HELP YOU BACK TO IT, MY GIRL.
TEN MINUTES LATER CAPTAIN BLOOD CAME UPON AN EXCITED, TORCH-LIT SEARCH PARTY.
WHERE THE DEVIL HAVE YOU BEEN, CAPTAIN?
ME? I'VE BEEN OBSERVING THE LUCK THAT GOES WITH BLOOD MONEY.
END

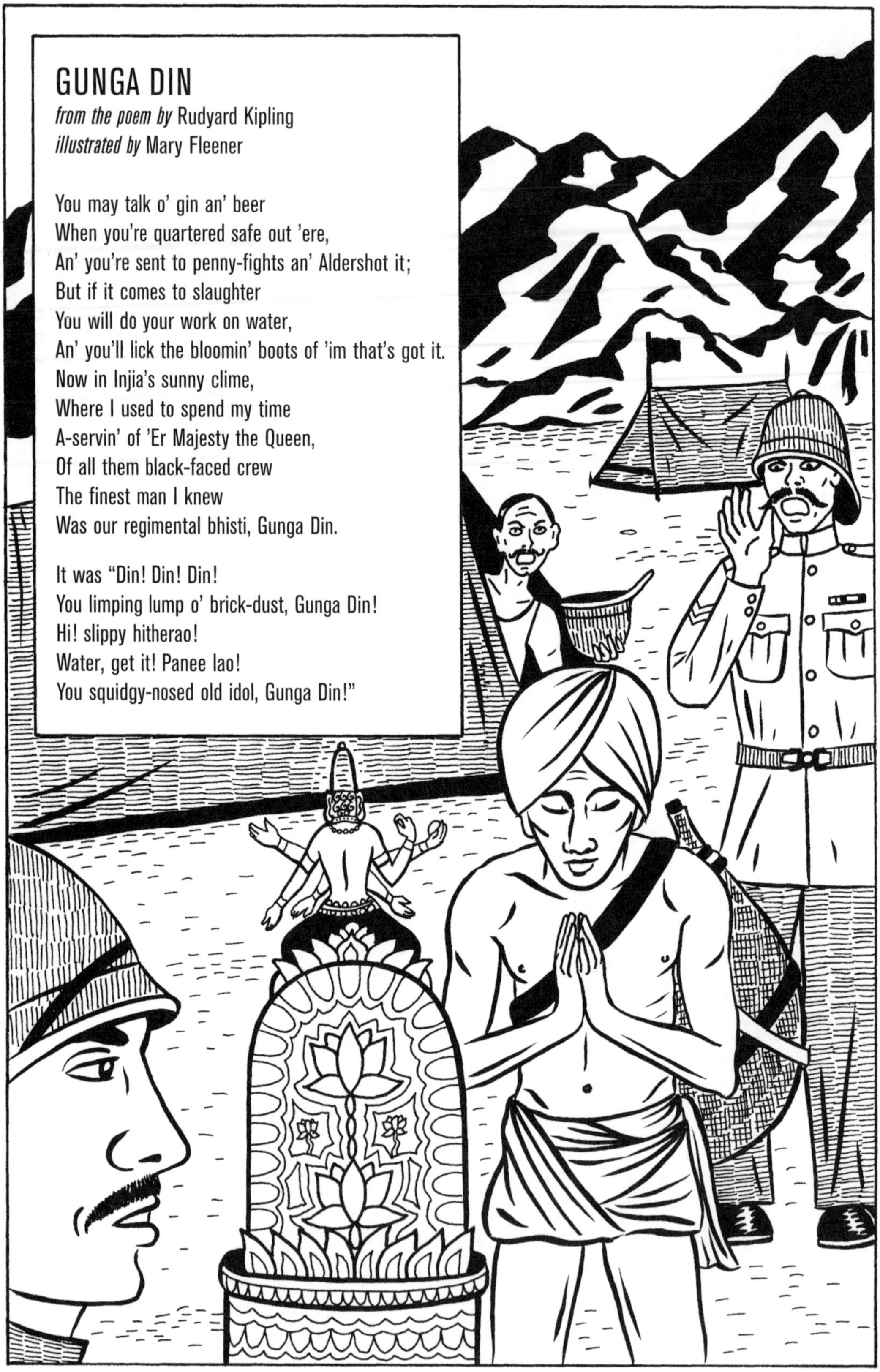
GUNGA DIN
from the poem by Rudyard Kipling
illustrated by Mary Fleener

You may talk o' gin an' beer
When you're quartered safe out 'ere,
An' you're sent to penny-fights an' Aldershot it;
But if it comes to slaughter
You will do your work on water,
An' you'll lick the bloomin' boots of 'im that's got it.
Now in Injia's sunny clime,
Where I used to spend my time
A-servin' of 'Er Majesty the Queen,
Of all them black-faced crew
The finest man I knew
Was our regimental bhisti, Gunga Din.

It was "Din! Din! Din!
You limping lump o' brick-dust, Gunga Din!
Hi! slippy hitherao!
Water, get it! Panee lao!
You squidgy-nosed old idol, Gunga Din!"

The uniform 'e wore
Was nothin' much before,
An' rather less than 'arf o' that be'ind,
For a twisty piece o' rag
An' a goatskin water-bag
Was all the field-equipment 'e could find.
When the sweatin' troop-train lay
In a sidin' through the day,
Where the 'eat would make your bloomin' eyebrows crawl,
We shouted "Harry By!"
Till our throats were bricky-dry,
Then we wopped 'im 'cause 'e couldn't serve us all.

It was "Din! Din! Din!
You 'eathen, where the mischief 'ave you been?
You put some juldee in it,
Or I'll marrow you this minute,
If you don't fill up my helmet, Gunga Din!"

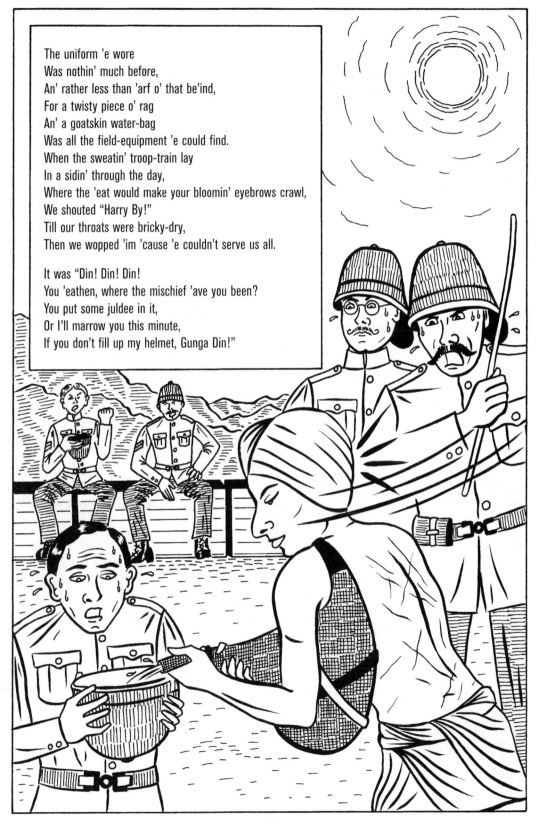

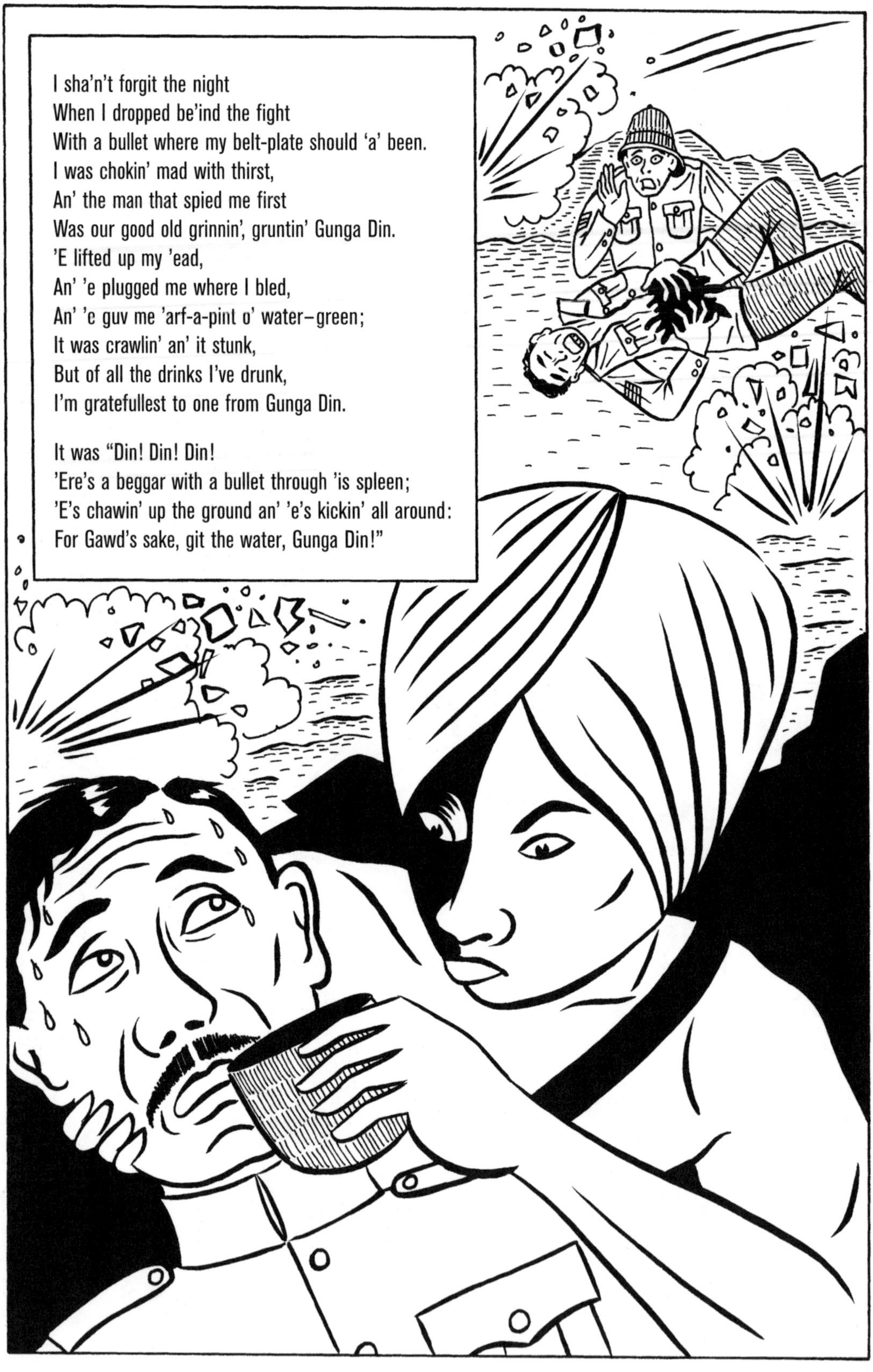
I sha'n't forgit the night
When I dropped be'ind the fight
With a bullet where my belt-plate should 'a' been.
I was chokin' mad with thirst,
An' the man that spied me first
Was our good old grinnin', gruntin' Gunga Din.
'E lifted up my 'ead,
An' 'e plugged me where I bled,
An' 'e guv me 'arf-a-pint o' water–green;
It was crawlin' an' it stunk,
But of all the drinks I've drunk,
I'm gratefullest to one from Gunga Din.
It was "Din! Din! Din!
'Ere's a beggar with a bullet through 'is spleen;
'E's chawin' up the ground an' 'e's kickin' all around:
For Gawd's sake, git the water, Gunga Din!"

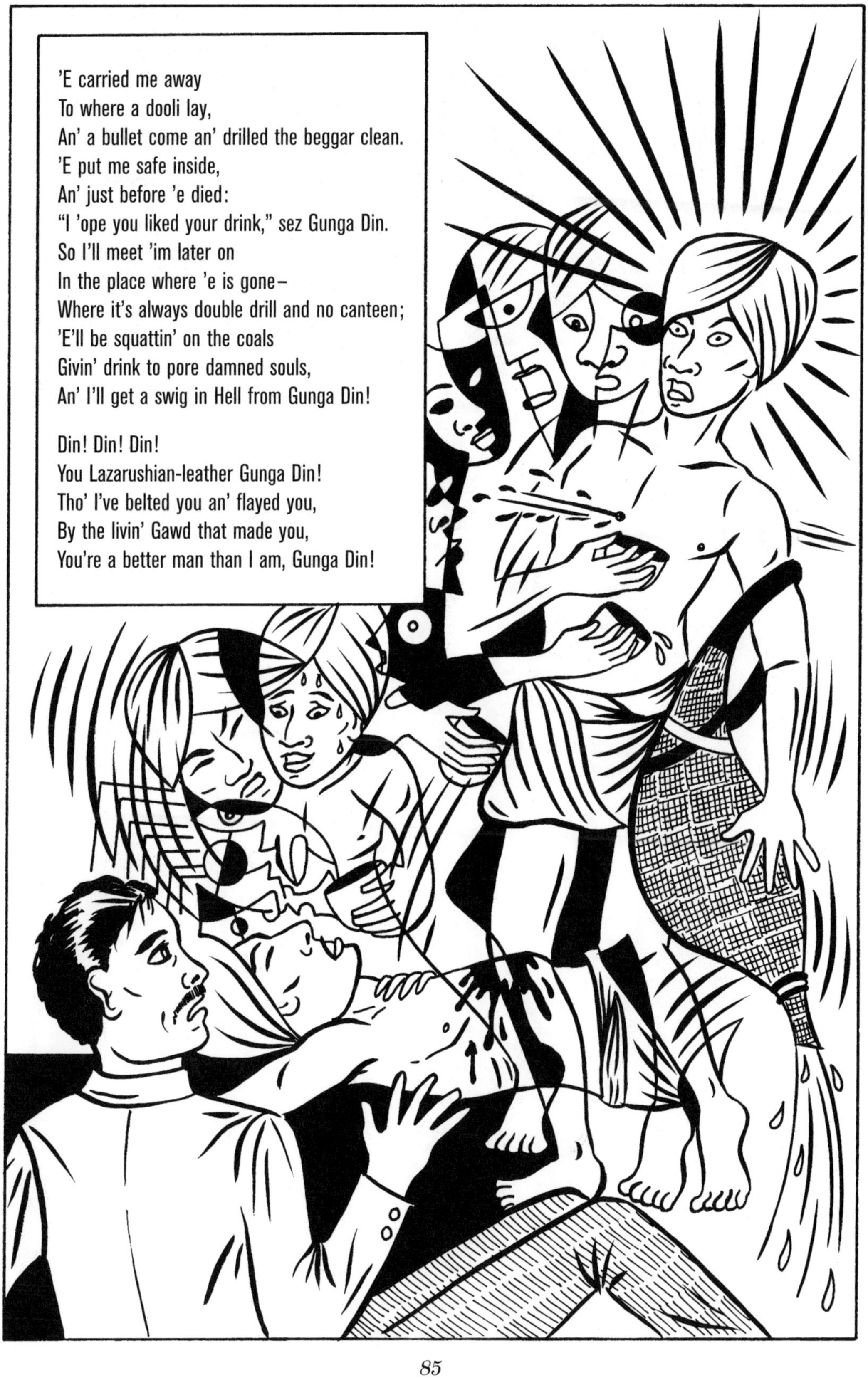
'E carried me away
To where a dooli lay,
An' a bullet come an' drilled the beggar clean.
'E put me safe inside,
An' just before 'e died:
"I 'ope you liked your drink," sez Gunga Din.
So I'll meet 'im later on
In the place where 'e is gone–
Where it's always double drill and no canteen;
'E'll be squattin' on the coals
Givin' drink to pore damned souls,
An' I'll get a swig in Hell from Gunga Din!
Din! Din! Din!
You Lazarushian-leather Gunga Din!
Tho' I've belted you an' flayed you,
By the livin' Gawd that made you,
You're a better man than I am, Gunga Din!

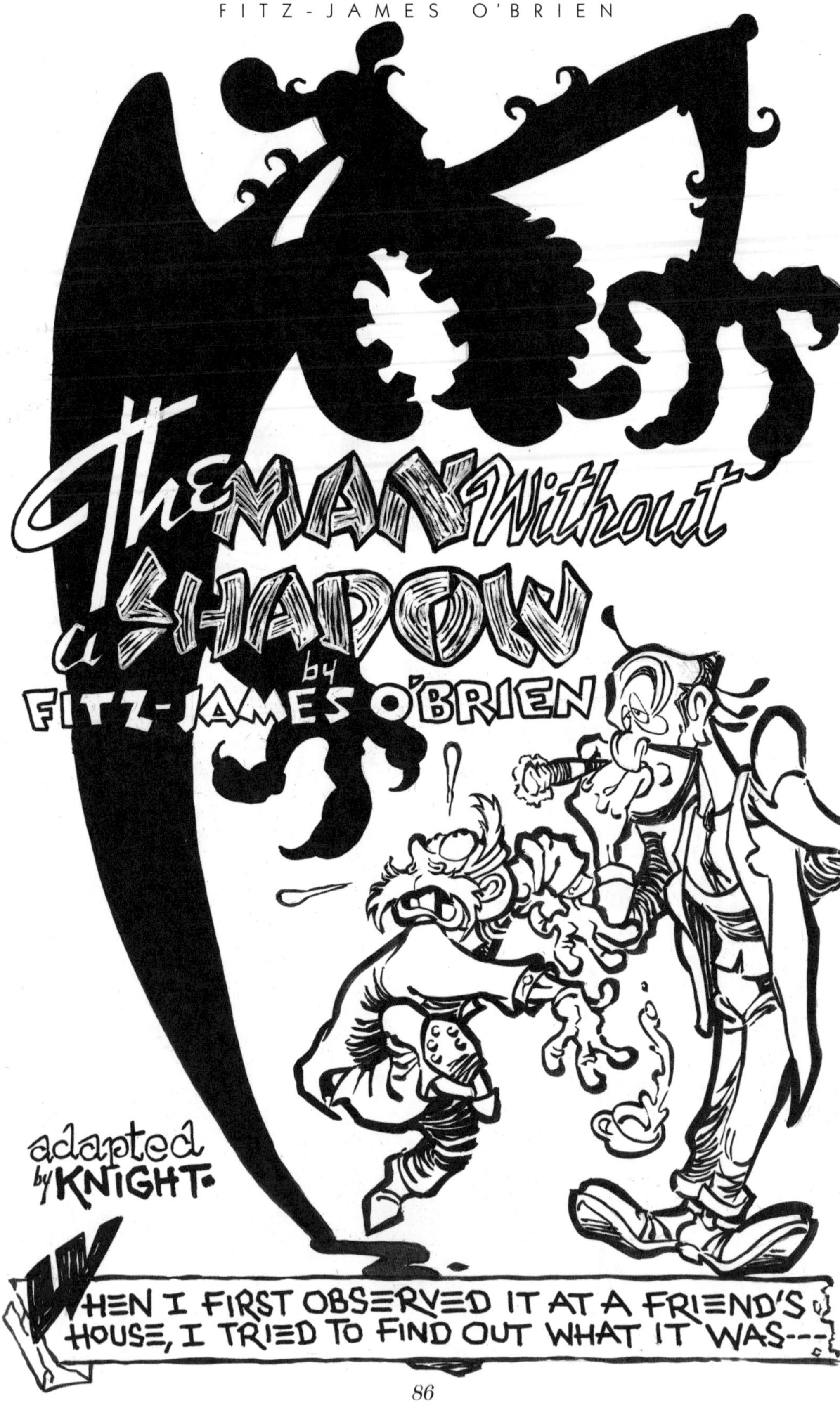
The MAN Without a SHADOW
by
FITZ-JAMES O'BRIEN
adapted by KNIGHT
WHEN I FIRST OBSERVED IT AT A FRIEND'S HOUSE, I TRIED TO FIND OUT WHAT IT WAS---

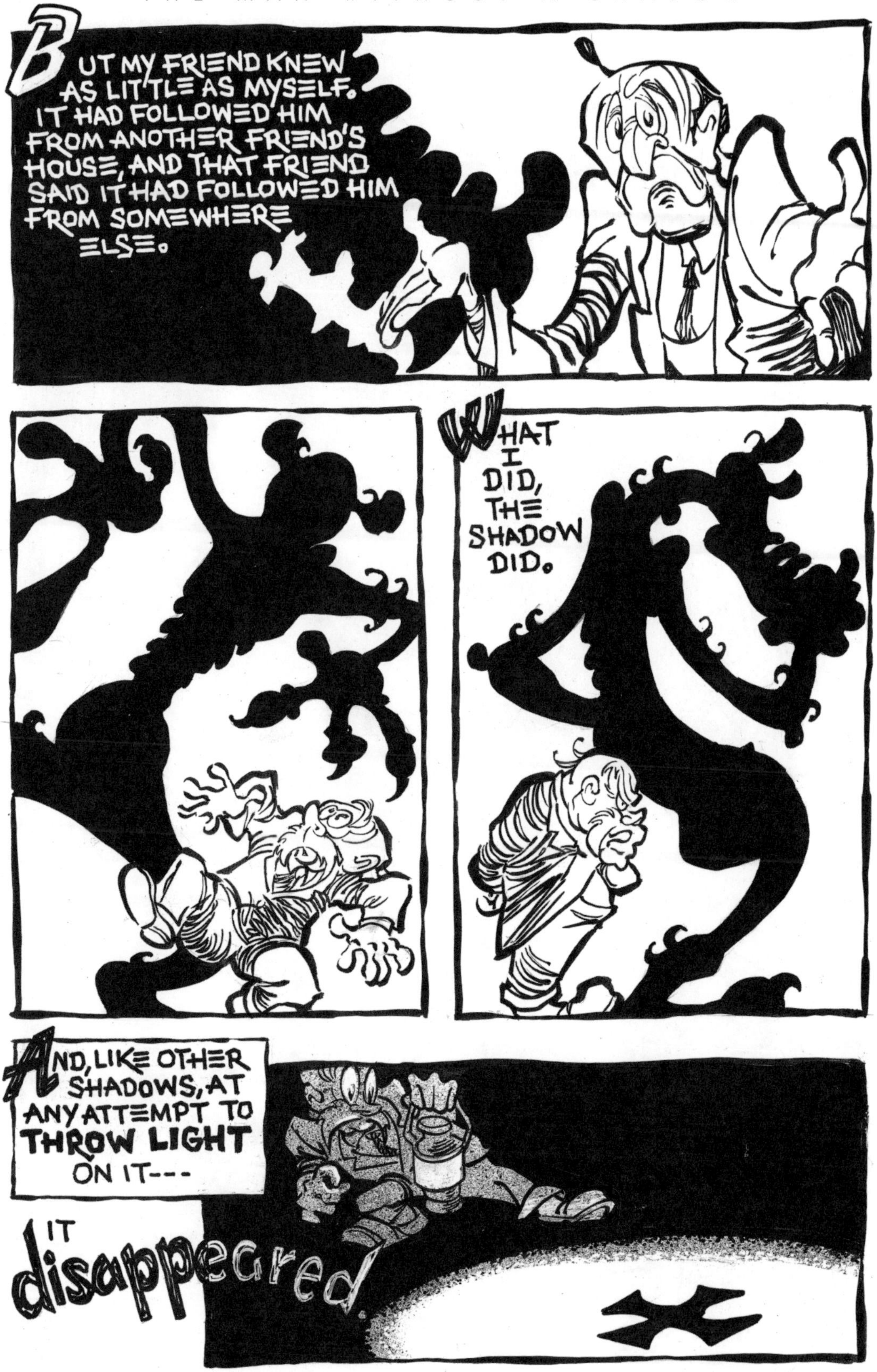
BUT MY FRIEND KNEW AS LITTLE AS MYSELF. IT HAD FOLLOWED HIM FROM ANOTHER FRIEND'S HOUSE, AND THAT FRIEND SAID IT HAD FOLLOWED HIM FROM SOMEWHERE ELSE.
WHAT I DID, THE SHADOW DID.
AND, LIKE OTHER SHADOWS, AT ANY ATTEMPT TO THROW LIGHT ON IT---
IT disappeared.

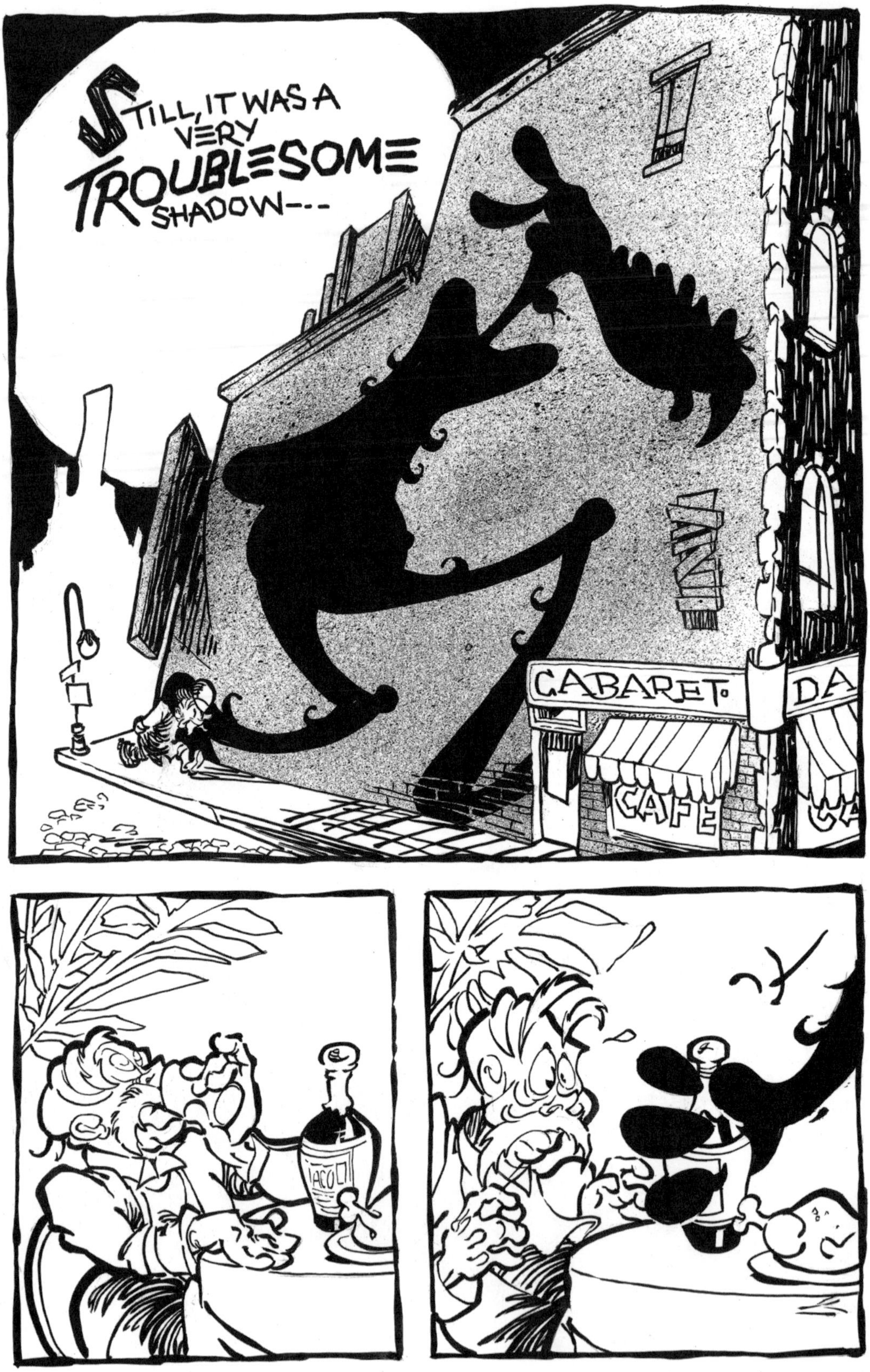
STILL, IT WAS A VERY TROUBLESOME SHADOW---
CABARET
DA
CAFE

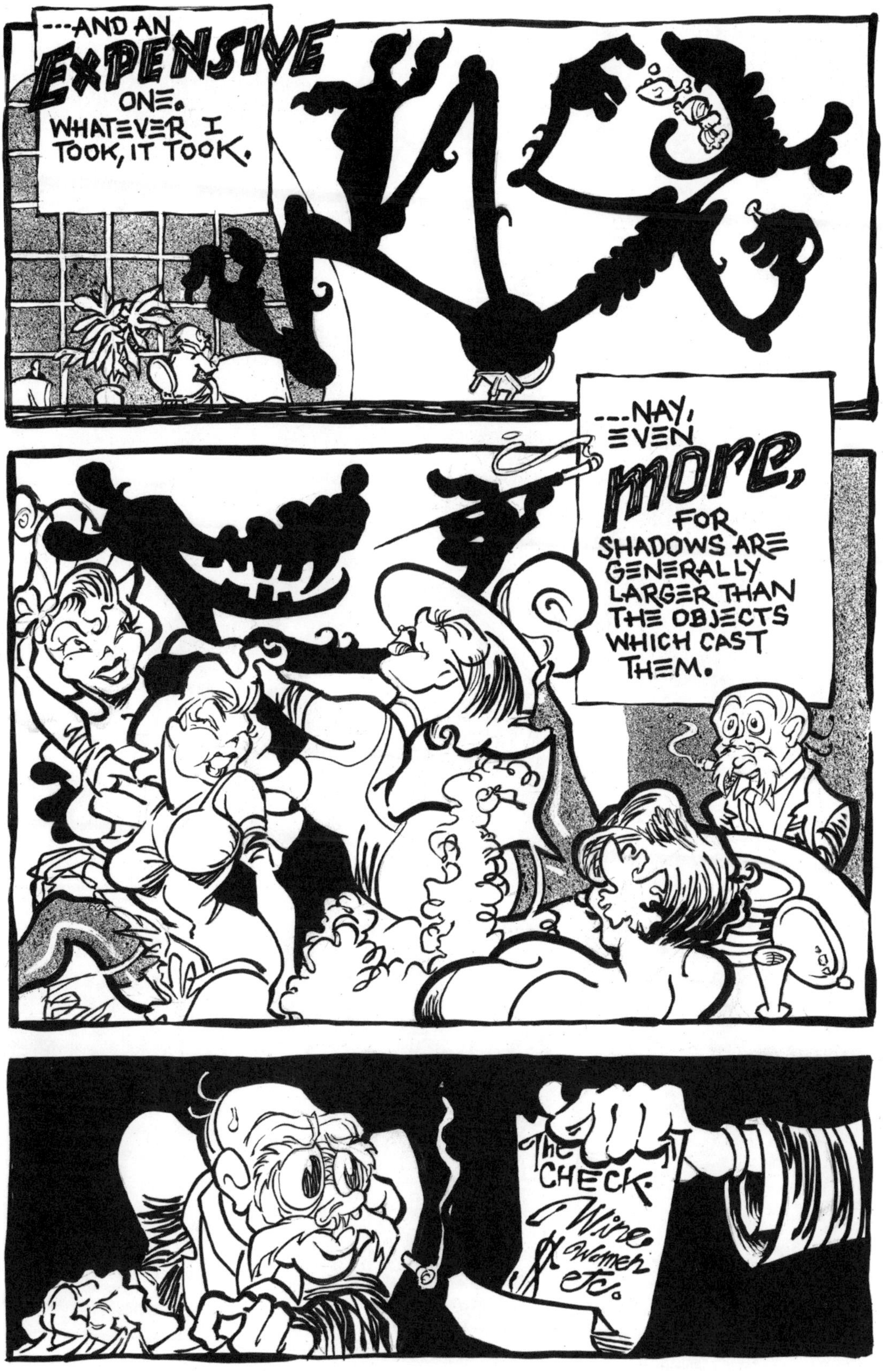
---AND AN EXPENSIVE ONE. WHATEVER I TOOK, IT TOOK.
---NAY, EVEN more, FOR SHADOWS ARE GENERALLY LARGER THAN THE OBJECTS WHICH CAST THEM.
The CHECK. Wine Women etc.

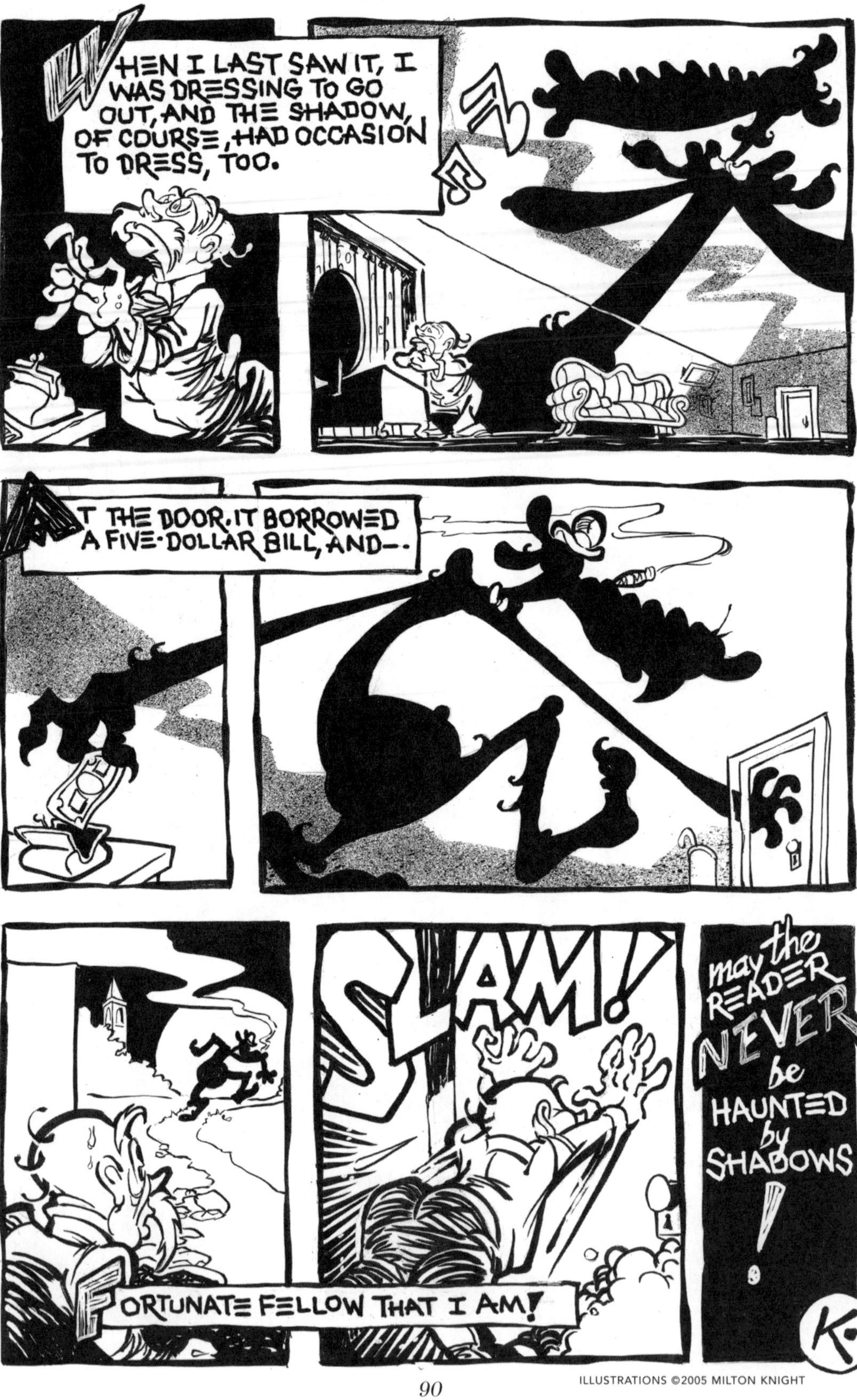
WHEN I LAST SAW IT, I WAS DRESSING TO GO OUT, AND THE SHADOW, OF COURSE, HAD OCCASION TO DRESS, TOO.
AT THE DOOR, IT BORROWED A FIVE-DOLLAR BILL, AND—.
SLAM!
FORTUNATE FELLOW THAT I AM!
may the READER NEVER be HAUNTED by SHADOWS!
K.

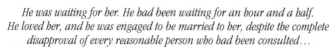

He was waiting for her. He had been waiting for an hour and a half.
He loved her, and he was engaged to be married to her, despite the complete
disapproval of every reasonable person who had been consulted…

The Mystery of the Semi-Detached

story by **Edith Nesbit** ~ *adapted by* **Antonella Caputo** ~ *illustrated by* **Mark A. Nelson**

EVENING, CONSTABLE!

EVENIN', SIR! CHILLY NIGHT, ISN'T IT?

And this half-clandestine meeting was tonight to take place because a certain rich uncle was visiting her house, and her mother was not the one to acknowledge to a moneyed uncle a match so deeply ineligible as hers with him.

His path led him by her house — desirable, commodious, semi-detached — she might, even now, be coming out. But she was not. There was no sign of movement about the house.

Then he noticed that the front door was opened. There was something about all this that did not please him.

91

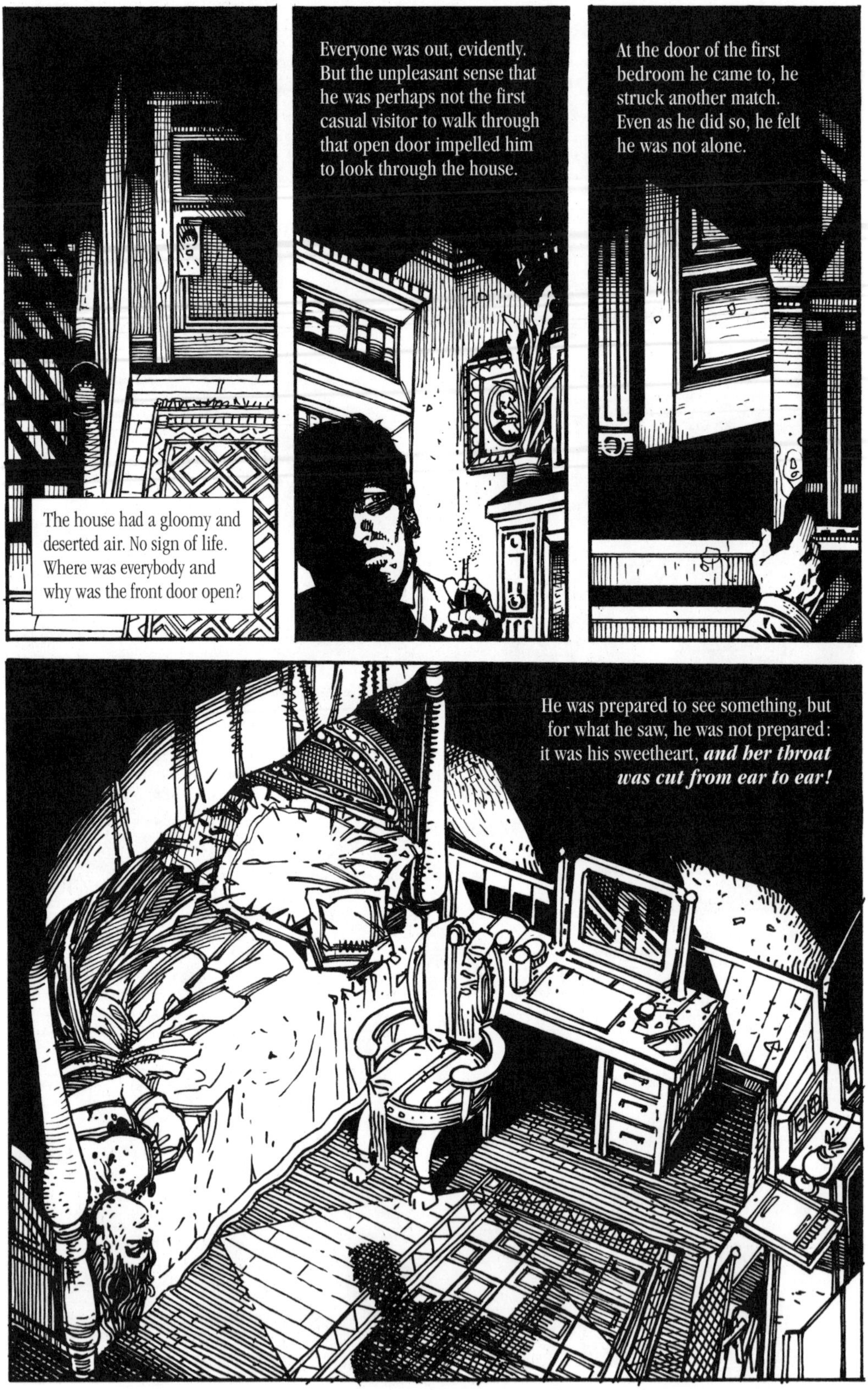
The house had a gloomy and deserted air. No sign of life. Where was everybody and why was the front door open?
Everyone was out, evidently. But the unpleasant sense that he was perhaps not the first casual visitor to walk through that open door impelled him to look through the house.
At the door of the first bedroom he came to, he struck another match. Even as he did so, he felt he was not alone.
He was prepared to see something, but for what he saw, he was not prepared: it was his sweetheart, ***and her throat was cut from ear to ear!***

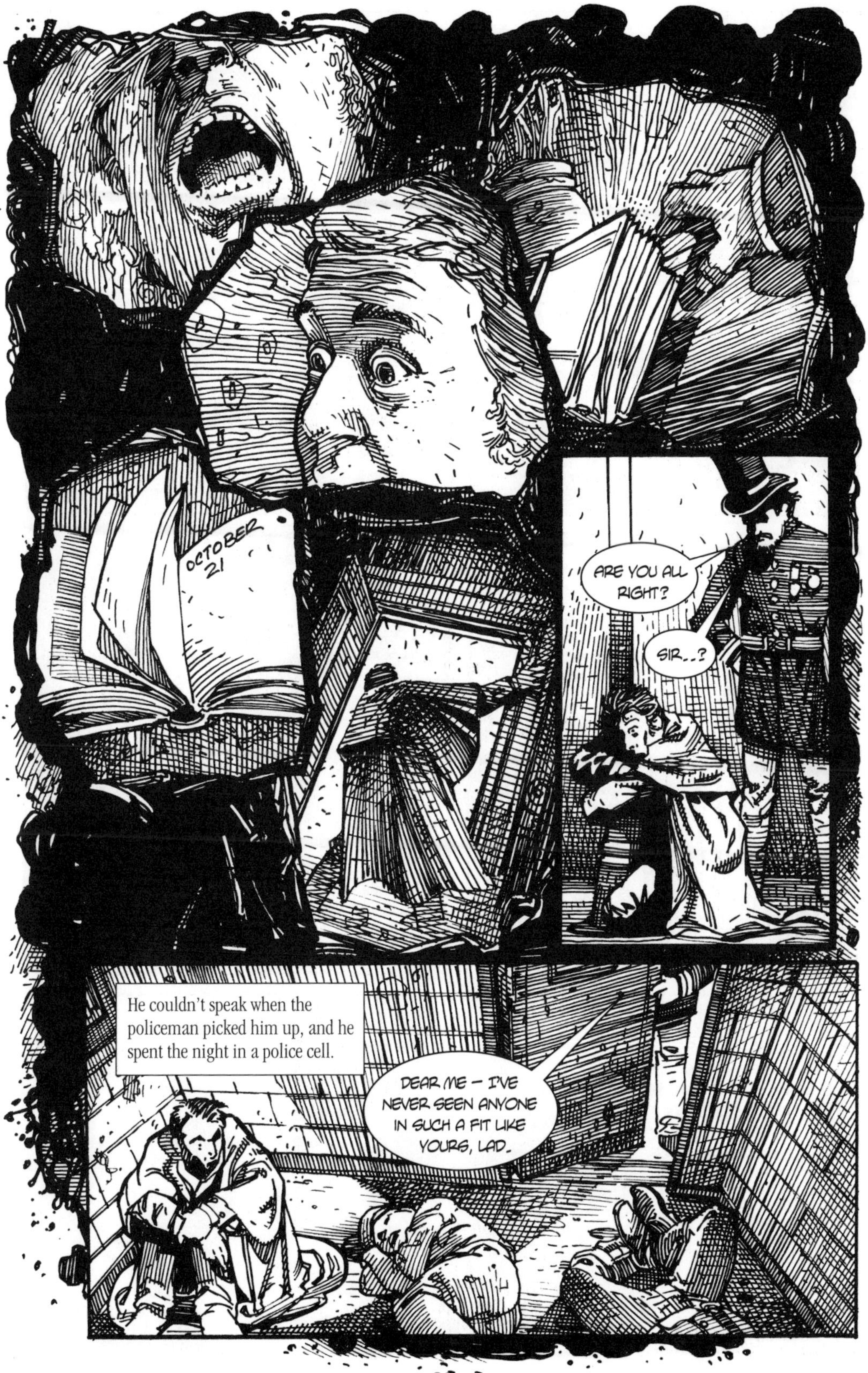
OCTOBER 21
ARE YOU ALL RIGHT?
SIR..?
He couldn't speak when the policeman picked him up, and he spent the night in a police cell.
DEAR ME — I'VE NEVER SEEN ANYONE IN SUCH A FIT LIKE YOURS, LAD.

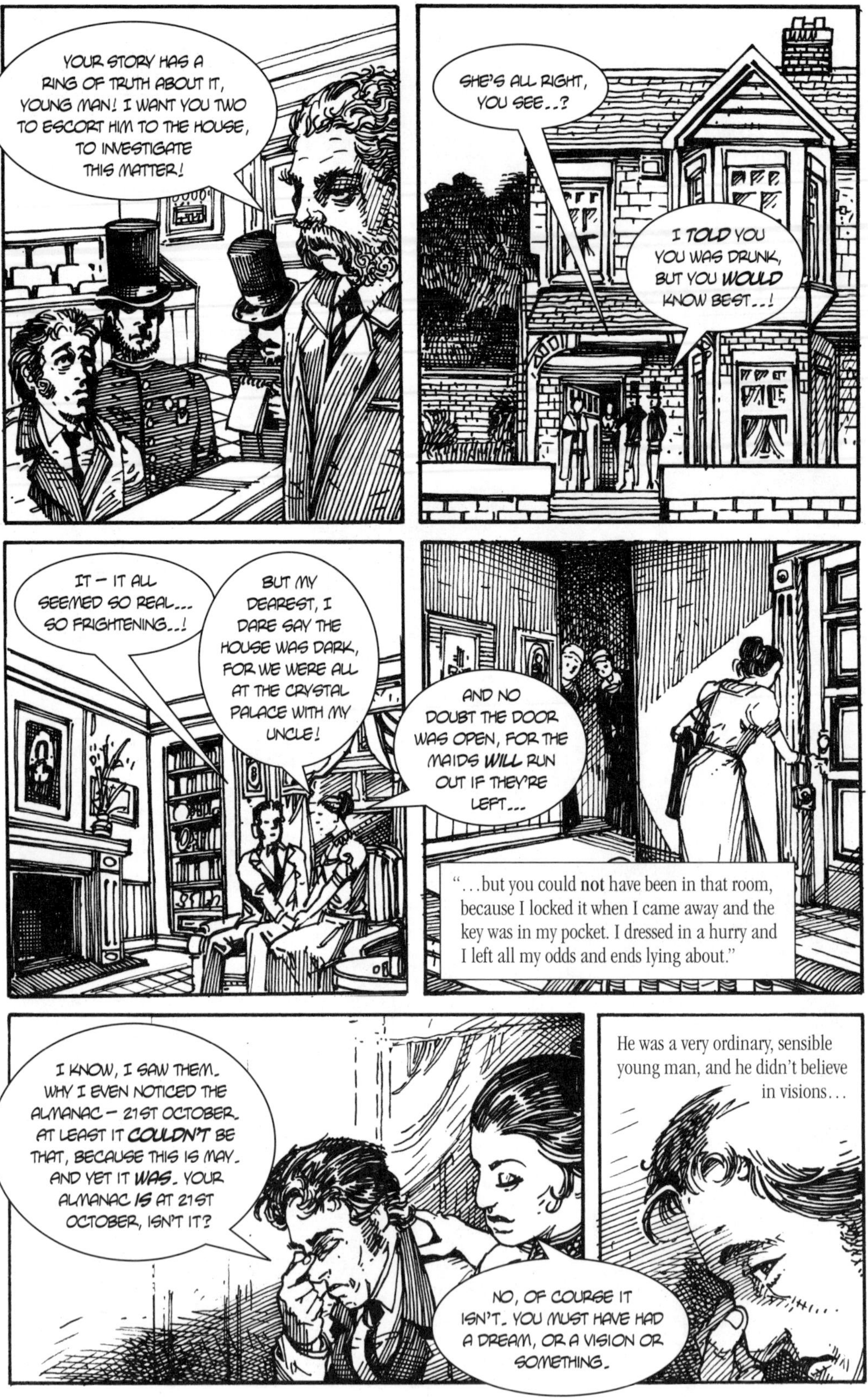
YOUR STORY HAS A RING OF TRUTH ABOUT IT, YOUNG MAN! I WANT YOU TWO TO ESCORT HIM TO THE HOUSE, TO INVESTIGATE THIS MATTER!
SHE'S ALL RIGHT, YOU SEE..?
I TOLD YOU YOU WAS DRUNK, BUT YOU WOULD KNOW BEST..!
IT – IT ALL SEEMED SO REAL... SO FRIGHTENING..!
BUT MY DEAREST, I DARE SAY THE HOUSE WAS DARK, FOR WE WERE ALL AT THE CRYSTAL PALACE WITH MY UNCLE!
AND NO DOUBT THE DOOR WAS OPEN, FOR THE MAIDS WILL RUN OUT IF THEY'RE LEFT...
"...but you could not have been in that room, because I locked it when I came away and the key was in my pocket. I dressed in a hurry and I left all my odds and ends lying about."
I KNOW, I SAW THEM. WHY I EVEN NOTICED THE ALMANAC – 21ST OCTOBER. AT LEAST IT COULDN'T BE THAT, BECAUSE THIS IS MAY. AND YET IT WAS. YOUR ALMANAC IS AT 21ST OCTOBER, ISN'T IT?
NO, OF COURSE IT ISN'T. YOU MUST HAVE HAD A DREAM, OR A VISION OR SOMETHING.
He was a very ordinary, sensible young man, and he didn't believe in visions...

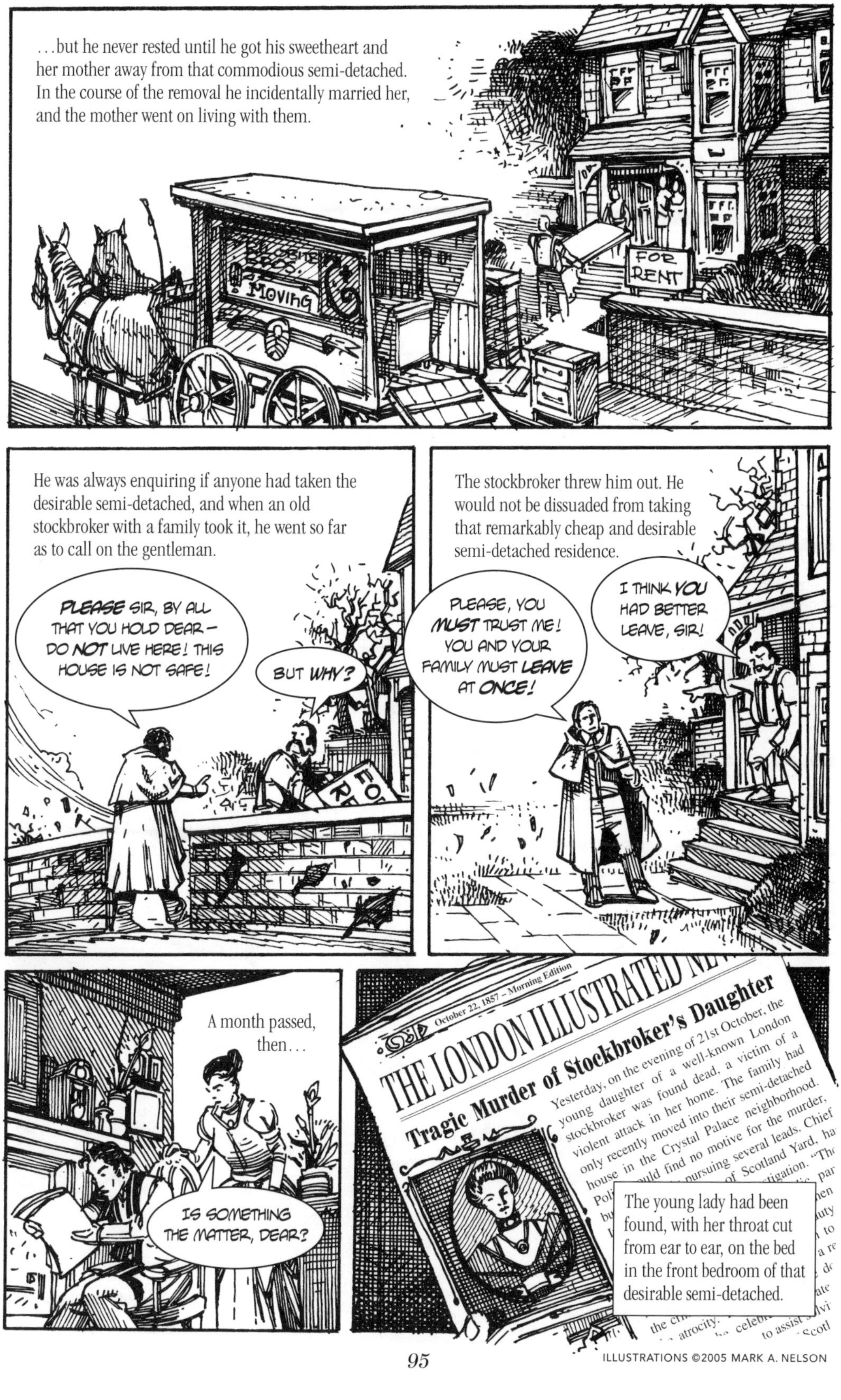
...but he never rested until he got his sweetheart and her mother away from that commodious semi-detached. In the course of the removal he incidentally married her, and the mother went on living with them.
MOVING
FOR RENT
He was always enquiring if anyone had taken the desirable semi-detached, and when an old stockbroker with a family took it, he went so far as to call on the gentleman.
PLEASE SIR, BY ALL THAT YOU HOLD DEAR—DO NOT LIVE HERE! THIS HOUSE IS NOT SAFE!
BUT WHY?
The stockbroker threw him out. He would not be dissuaded from taking that remarkably cheap and desirable semi-detached residence.
PLEASE, YOU MUST TRUST ME! YOU AND YOUR FAMILY MUST LEAVE AT ONCE!
I THINK YOU HAD BETTER LEAVE, SIR!
A month passed, then...
IS SOMETHING THE MATTER, DEAR?
October 22, 1857 – Morning Edition
THE LONDON ILLUSTRATED NE
Tragic Murder of Stockbroker's Daughter
Yesterday, on the evening of 21st October, the young daughter of a well-known London stockbroker was found dead, a victim of a violent attack in her home. The family had only recently moved into their semi-detached house in the Crystal Palace neighborhood.
The young lady had been found, with her throat cut from ear to ear, on the bed in the front bedroom of that desirable semi-detached.

John Branton wanted to become an author. In college, he had applied himself faithfully to the study of English and the classics, and in the four years since his graduation he had ably demonstrated the fact that a man may not ***himself*** create, merely because he appreciates the creations of others. Branton was long on technique, but short on ability to touch the heart. He had studied ***books*** to the exclusion of ***humanity*** – and it is ***humanity*** that successful authors write about.

He was holding down a humble clerkship that served to keep him in food and clothing. Regularly his compositions were returned to him by magazine editors who appreciated his command of English, but who knew that their readers never would get beyond the first paragraph.

The Stolen Story

by ***Johnston McCulley***

adapted by ***Tom Pomplun****, illustrated by* ***Chris Pelletiere***

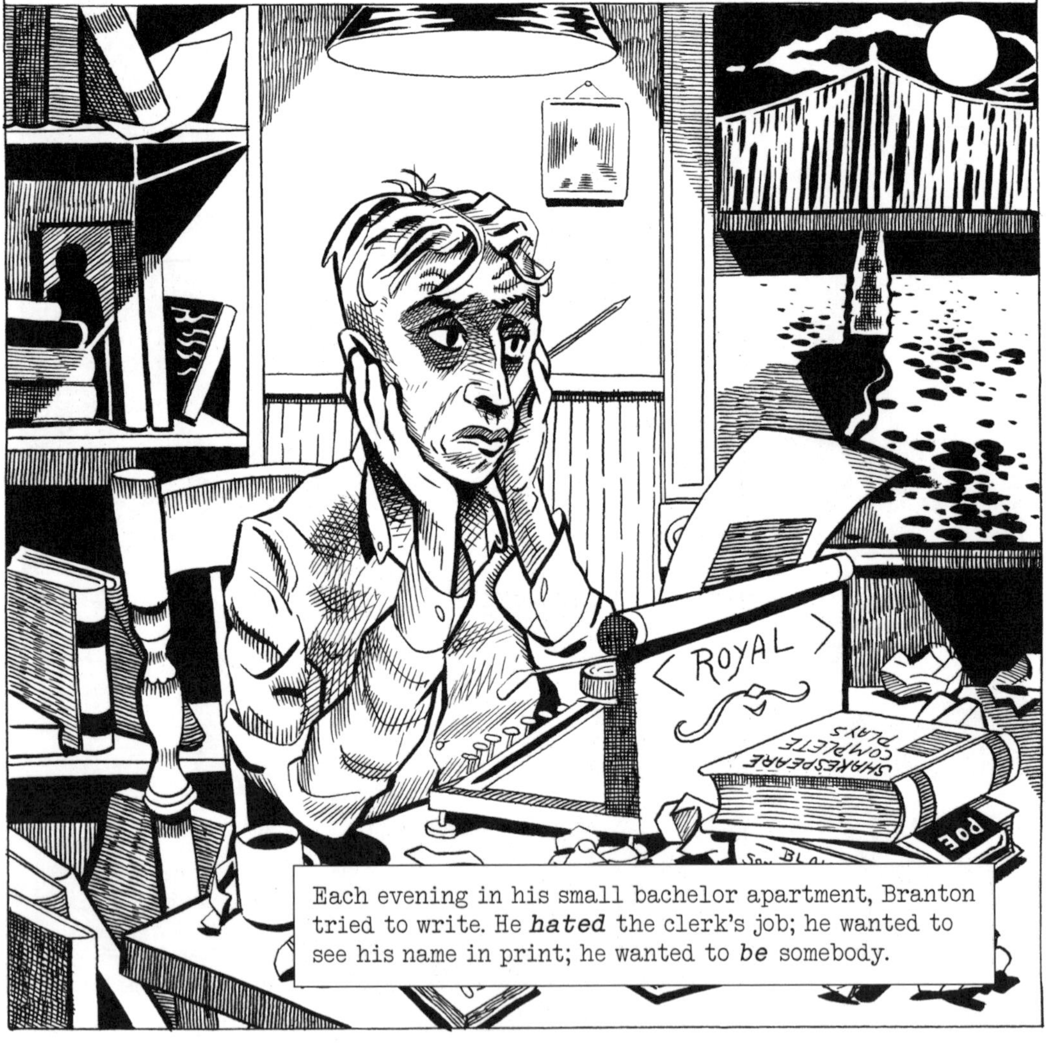
ROYAL
SHAKESPEARE COMPLETE PLAYS
POE
Each evening in his small bachelor apartment, Branton tried to write. He *hated* the clerk's job; he wanted to see his name in print; he wanted to *be* somebody.

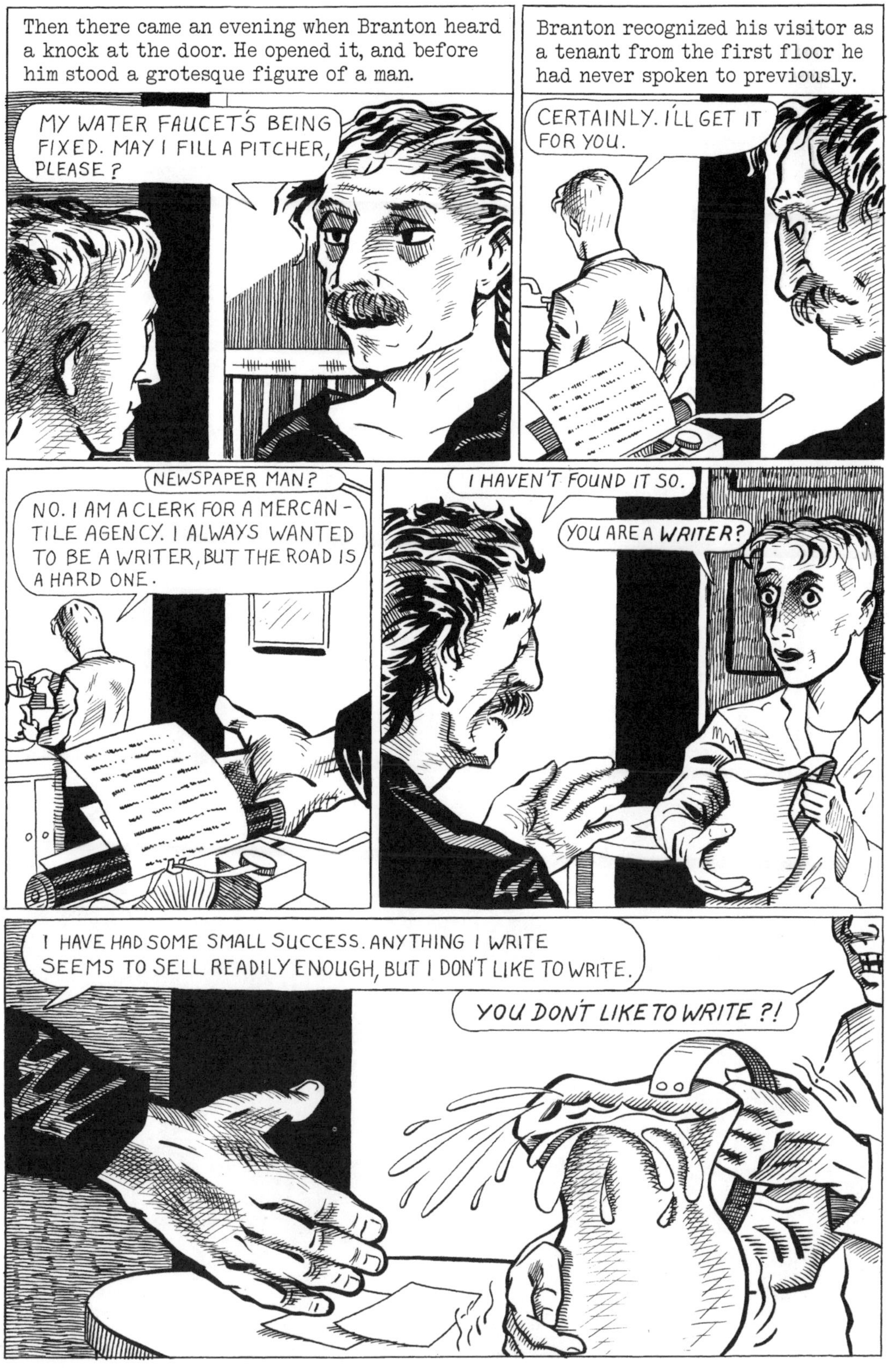
Then there came an evening when Branton heard a knock at the door. He opened it, and before him stood a grotesque figure of a man.
MY WATER FAUCET'S BEING FIXED. MAY I FILL A PITCHER, PLEASE?
Branton recognized his visitor as a tenant from the first floor he had never spoken to previously.
CERTAINLY. I'LL GET IT FOR YOU.
NEWSPAPER MAN?
NO. I AM A CLERK FOR A MERCANTILE AGENCY. I ALWAYS WANTED TO BE A WRITER, BUT THE ROAD IS A HARD ONE.
I HAVEN'T FOUND IT SO.
YOU ARE A WRITER?
I HAVE HAD SOME SMALL SUCCESS. ANYTHING I WRITE SEEMS TO SELL READILY ENOUGH, BUT I DON'T LIKE TO WRITE.
YOU DON'T LIKE TO WRITE?!

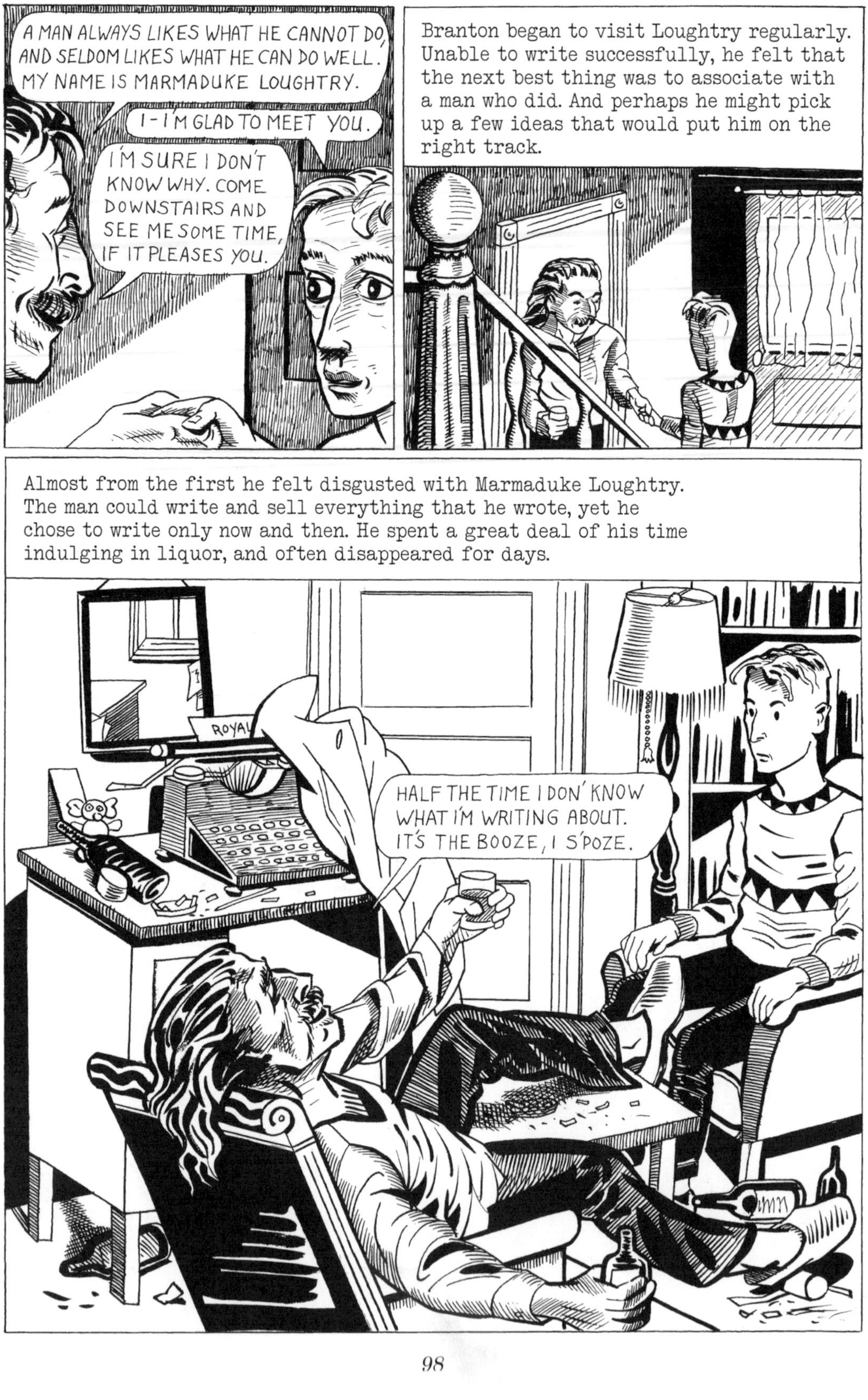
A MAN ALWAYS LIKES WHAT HE CANNOT DO, AND SELDOM LIKES WHAT HE CAN DO WELL. MY NAME IS MARMADUKE LOUGHTRY.
I-I'M GLAD TO MEET YOU.
I'M SURE I DON'T KNOW WHY. COME DOWNSTAIRS AND SEE ME SOME TIME, IF IT PLEASES YOU.
Branton began to visit Loughtry regularly. Unable to write successfully, he felt that the next best thing was to associate with a man who did. And perhaps he might pick up a few ideas that would put him on the right track.
Almost from the first he felt disgusted with Marmaduke Loughtry. The man could write and sell everything that he wrote, yet he chose to write only now and then. He spent a great deal of his time indulging in liquor, and often disappeared for days.
ROYAL
HALF THE TIME I DON' KNOW WHAT I'M WRITING ABOUT. IT'S THE BOOZE, I S'POZE.

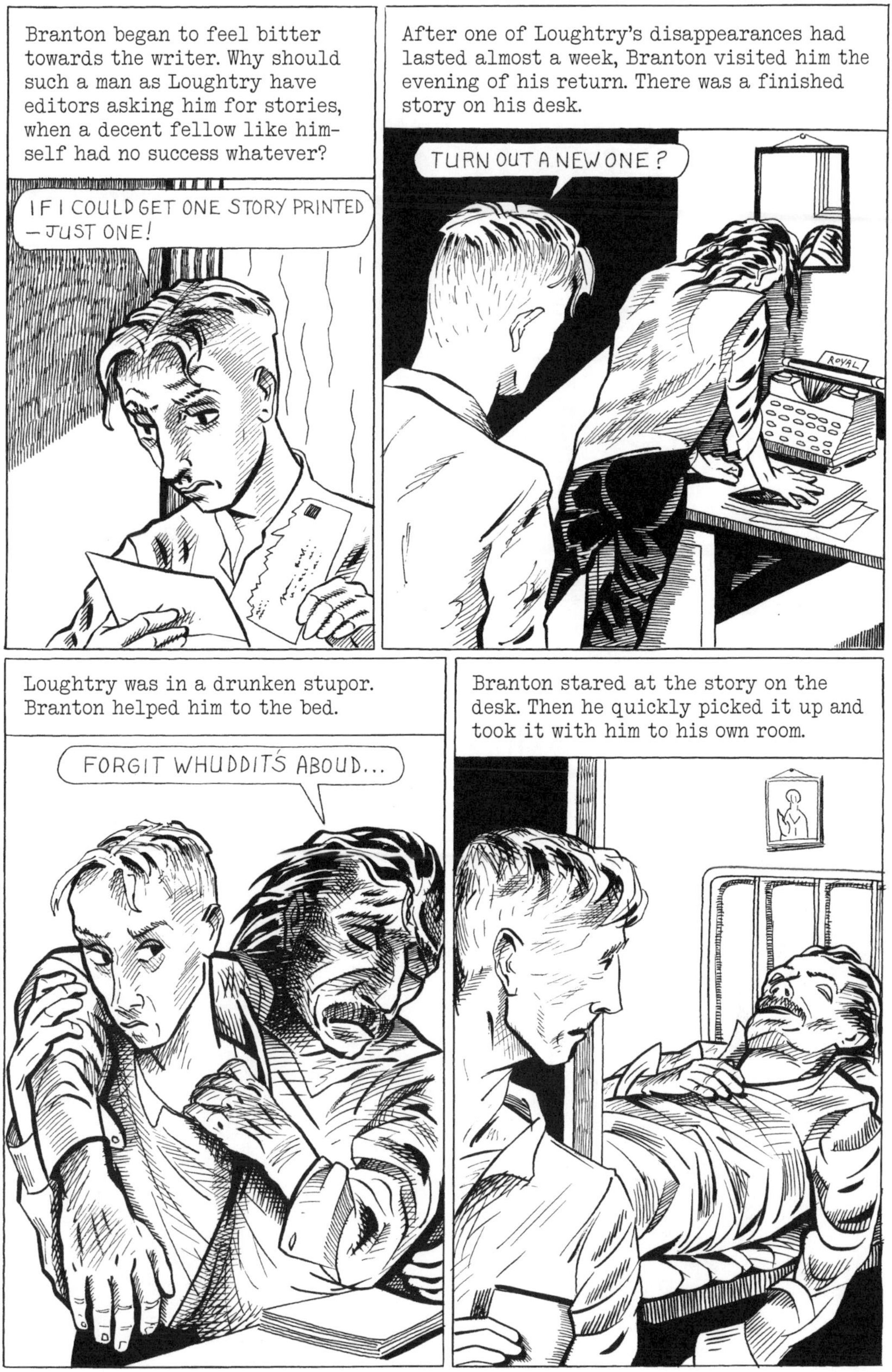
Branton began to feel bitter towards the writer. Why should such a man as Loughtry have editors asking him for stories, when a decent fellow like himself had no success whatever?
IF I COULD GET ONE STORY PRINTED —JUST ONE!
After one of Loughtry's disappearances had lasted almost a week, Branton visited him the evening of his return. There was a finished story on his desk.
TURN OUT A NEW ONE?
ROYAL
Loughtry was in a drunken stupor. Branton helped him to the bed.
FORGIT WHUDDIT'S ABOUD...
Branton stared at the story on the desk. Then he quickly picked it up and took it with him to his own room.

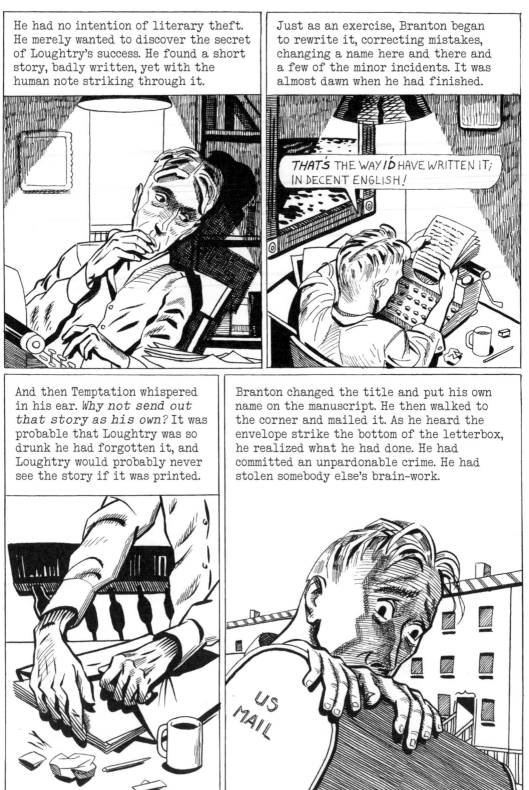

He had no intention of literary theft. He merely wanted to discover the secret of Loughtry's success. He found a short story, badly written, yet with the human note striking through it.

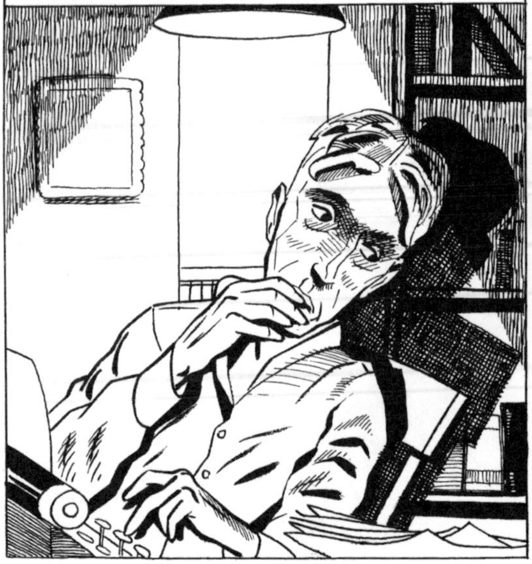

Just as an exercise, Branton began to rewrite it, correcting mistakes, changing a name here and there and a few of the minor incidents. It was almost dawn when he had finished.

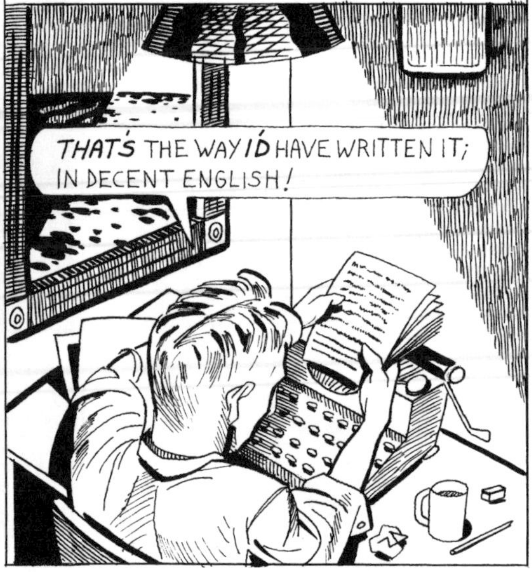
THAT'S THE WAY I'D HAVE WRITTEN IT; IN DECENT ENGLISH!

And then Temptation whispered in his ear. *Why not send out that story as his own?* It was probable that Loughtry was so drunk he had forgotten it, and Loughtry would probably never see the story if it was printed.

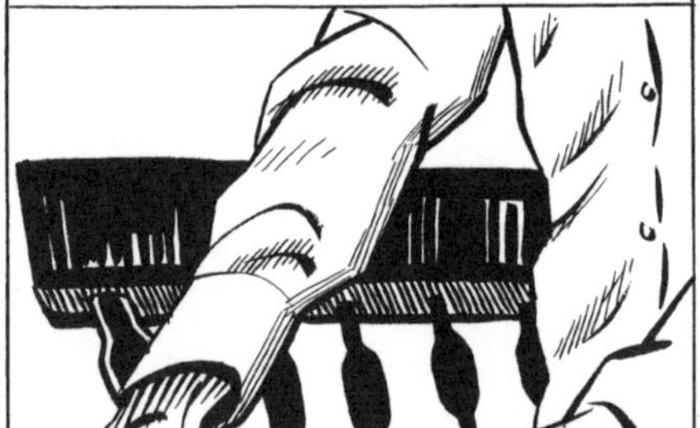

Branton changed the title and put his own name on the manuscript. He then walked to the corner and mailed it. As he heard the envelope strike the bottom of the letterbox, he realized what he had done. He had committed an unpardonable crime. He had stolen somebody else's brain-work.

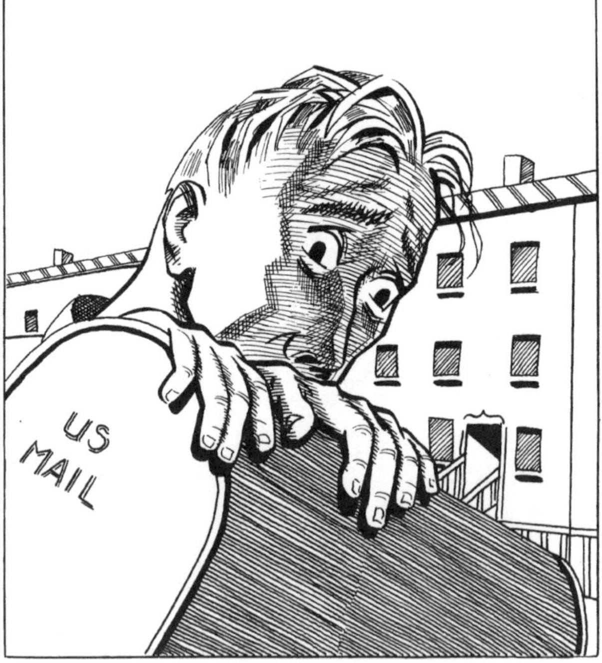
US MAIL

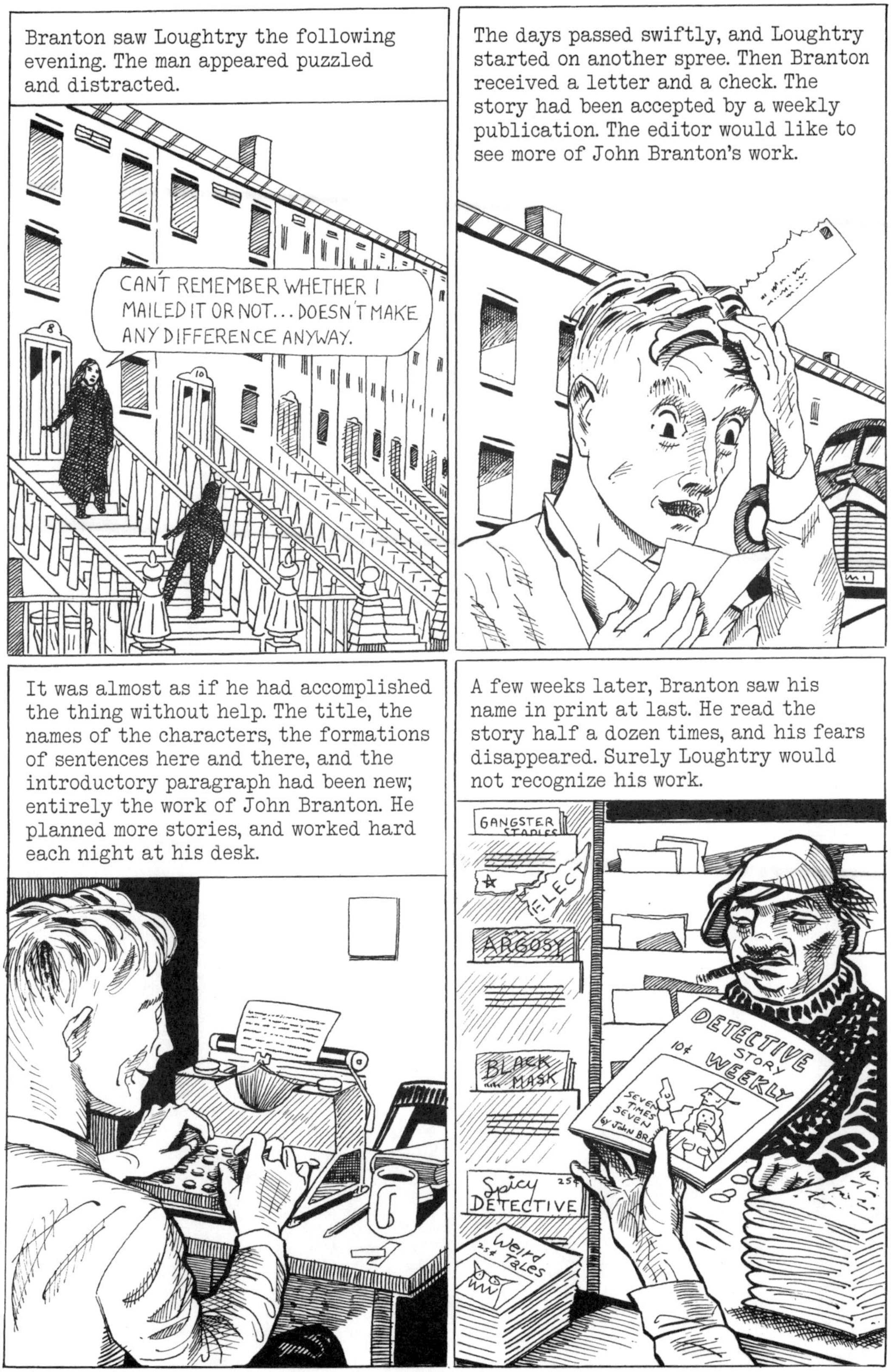
Branton saw Loughtry the following evening. The man appeared puzzled and distracted.
CAN'T REMEMBER WHETHER I MAILED IT OR NOT... DOESN'T MAKE ANY DIFFERENCE ANYWAY.
The days passed swiftly, and Loughtry started on another spree. Then Branton received a letter and a check. The story had been accepted by a weekly publication. The editor would like to see more of John Branton's work.
It was almost as if he had accomplished the thing without help. The title, the names of the characters, the formations of sentences here and there, and the introductory paragraph had been new; entirely the work of John Branton. He planned more stories, and worked hard each night at his desk.
A few weeks later, Branton saw his name in print at last. He read the story half a dozen times, and his fears disappeared. Surely Loughtry would not recognize his work.
GANGSTER
ARGOSY
BLACK MASK
DETECTIVE STORY WEEKLY
10¢
SEVEN TIMES SEVEN
Spicy DETECTIVE
25¢
Weird Tales
25¢

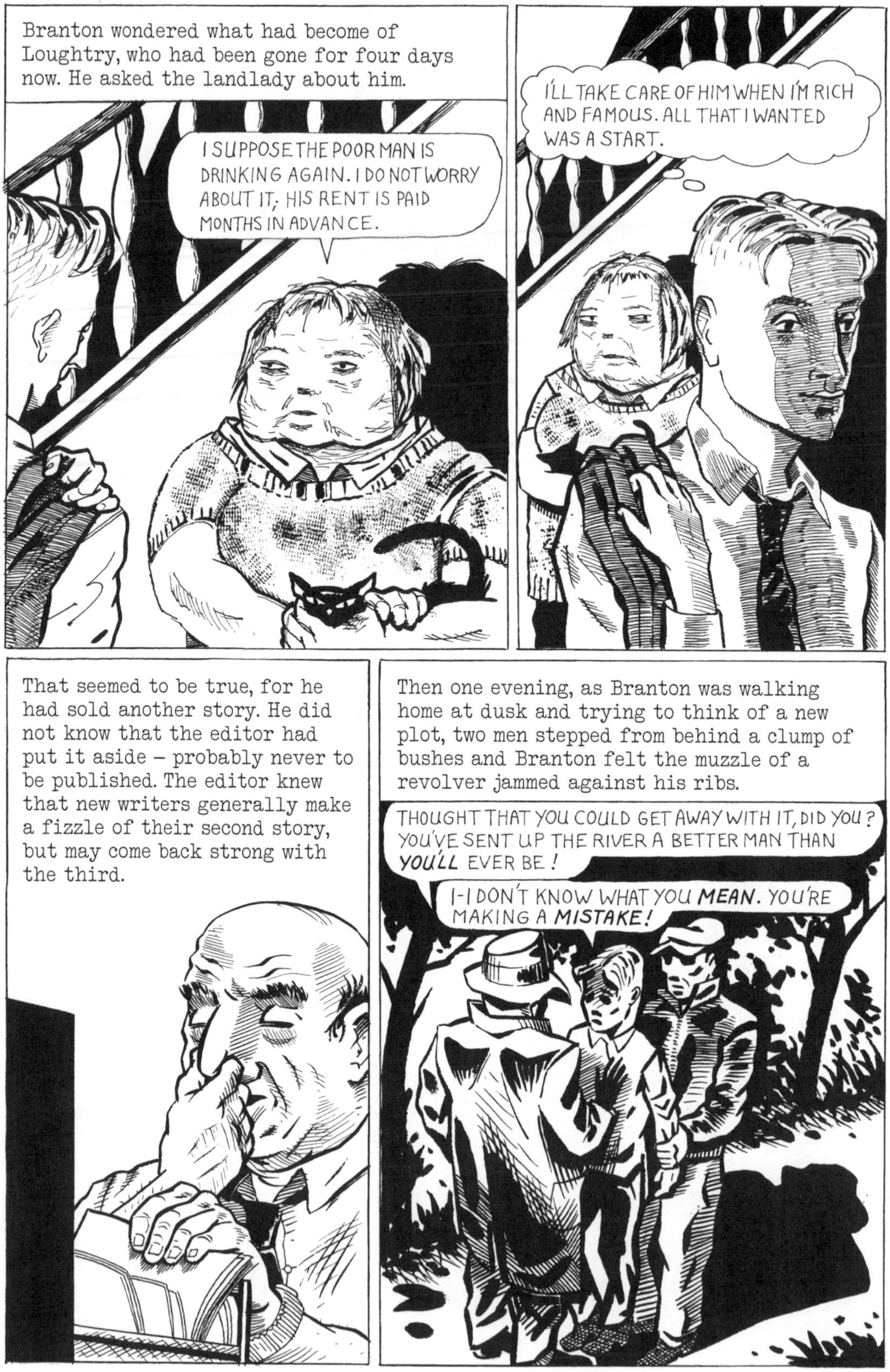
Branton wondered what had become of Loughtry, who had been gone for four days now. He asked the landlady about him.
I SUPPOSE THE POOR MAN IS DRINKING AGAIN. I DO NOT WORRY ABOUT IT; HIS RENT IS PAID MONTHS IN ADVANCE.
I'LL TAKE CARE OF HIM WHEN I'M RICH AND FAMOUS. ALL THAT I WANTED WAS A START.
That seemed to be true, for he had sold another story. He did not know that the editor had put it aside – probably never to be published. The editor knew that new writers generally make a fizzle of their second story, but may come back strong with the third.
Then one evening, as Branton was walking home at dusk and trying to think of a new plot, two men stepped from behind a clump of bushes and Branton felt the muzzle of a revolver jammed against his ribs.
THOUGHT THAT YOU COULD GET AWAY WITH IT, DID YOU? YOU'VE SENT UP THE RIVER A BETTER MAN THAN YOU'LL EVER BE!
I-I DON'T KNOW WHAT YOU MEAN. YOU'RE MAKING A MISTAKE!

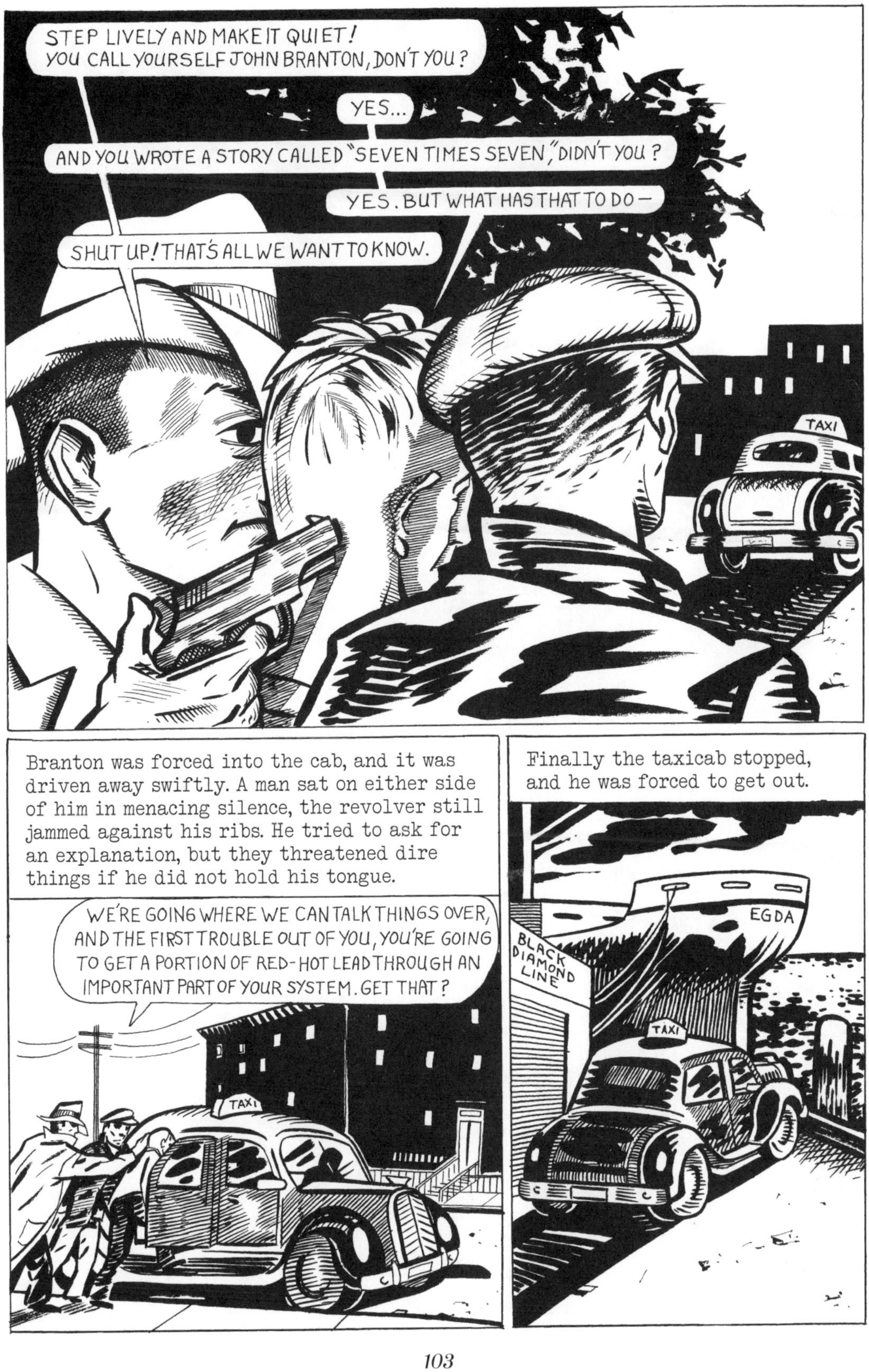
STEP LIVELY AND MAKE IT QUIET! YOU CALL YOURSELF JOHN BRANTON, DON'T YOU?
YES...
AND YOU WROTE A STORY CALLED "SEVEN TIMES SEVEN," DIDN'T YOU?
YES. BUT WHAT HAS THAT TO DO—
SHUT UP! THAT'S ALL WE WANT TO KNOW.
TAXI
Branton was forced into the cab, and it was driven away swiftly. A man sat on either side of him in menacing silence, the revolver still jammed against his ribs. He tried to ask for an explanation, but they threatened dire things if he did not hold his tongue.
WE'RE GOING WHERE WE CAN TALK THINGS OVER, AND THE FIRST TROUBLE OUT OF YOU, YOU'RE GOING TO GET A PORTION OF RED-HOT LEAD THROUGH AN IMPORTANT PART OF YOUR SYSTEM. GET THAT?
TAXI
Finally the taxicab stopped, and he was forced to get out.
EGDA
BLACK DIAMOND LINE
TAXI

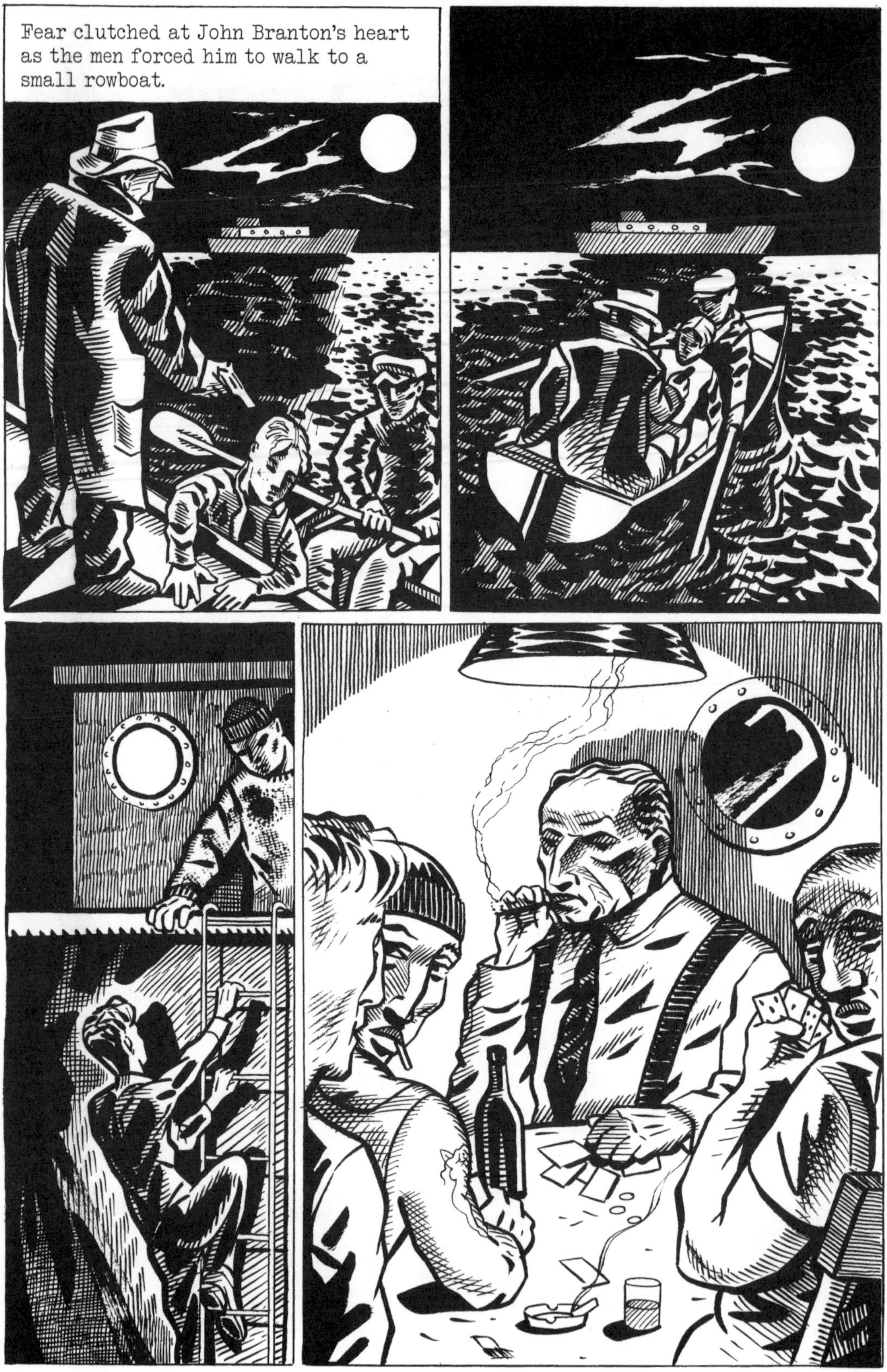
Fear clutched at John Branton's heart as the men forced him to walk to a small rowboat.

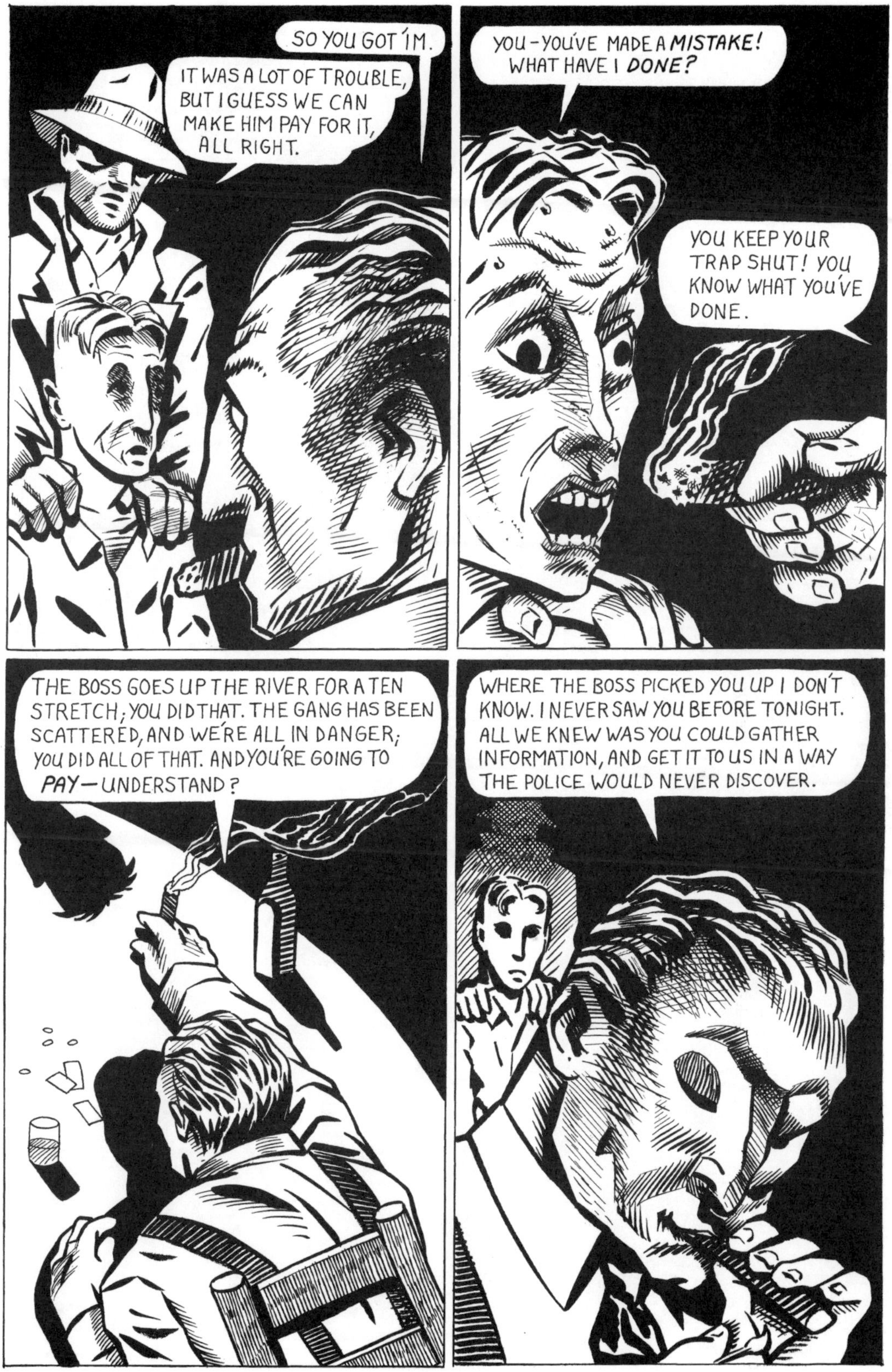
SO YOU GOT 'IM.
IT WAS A LOT OF TROUBLE, BUT I GUESS WE CAN MAKE HIM PAY FOR IT, ALL RIGHT.
YOU-YOU'VE MADE A MISTAKE! WHAT HAVE I DONE?
YOU KEEP YOUR TRAP SHUT! YOU KNOW WHAT YOU'VE DONE.
THE BOSS GOES UP THE RIVER FOR A TEN STRETCH; YOU DID THAT. THE GANG HAS BEEN SCATTERED, AND WE'RE ALL IN DANGER; YOU DID ALL OF THAT. AND YOU'RE GOING TO PAY—UNDERSTAND?
WHERE THE BOSS PICKED YOU UP I DON'T KNOW. I NEVER SAW YOU BEFORE TONIGHT. ALL WE KNEW WAS YOU COULD GATHER INFORMATION, AND GET IT TO US IN A WAY THE POLICE WOULD NEVER DISCOVER.

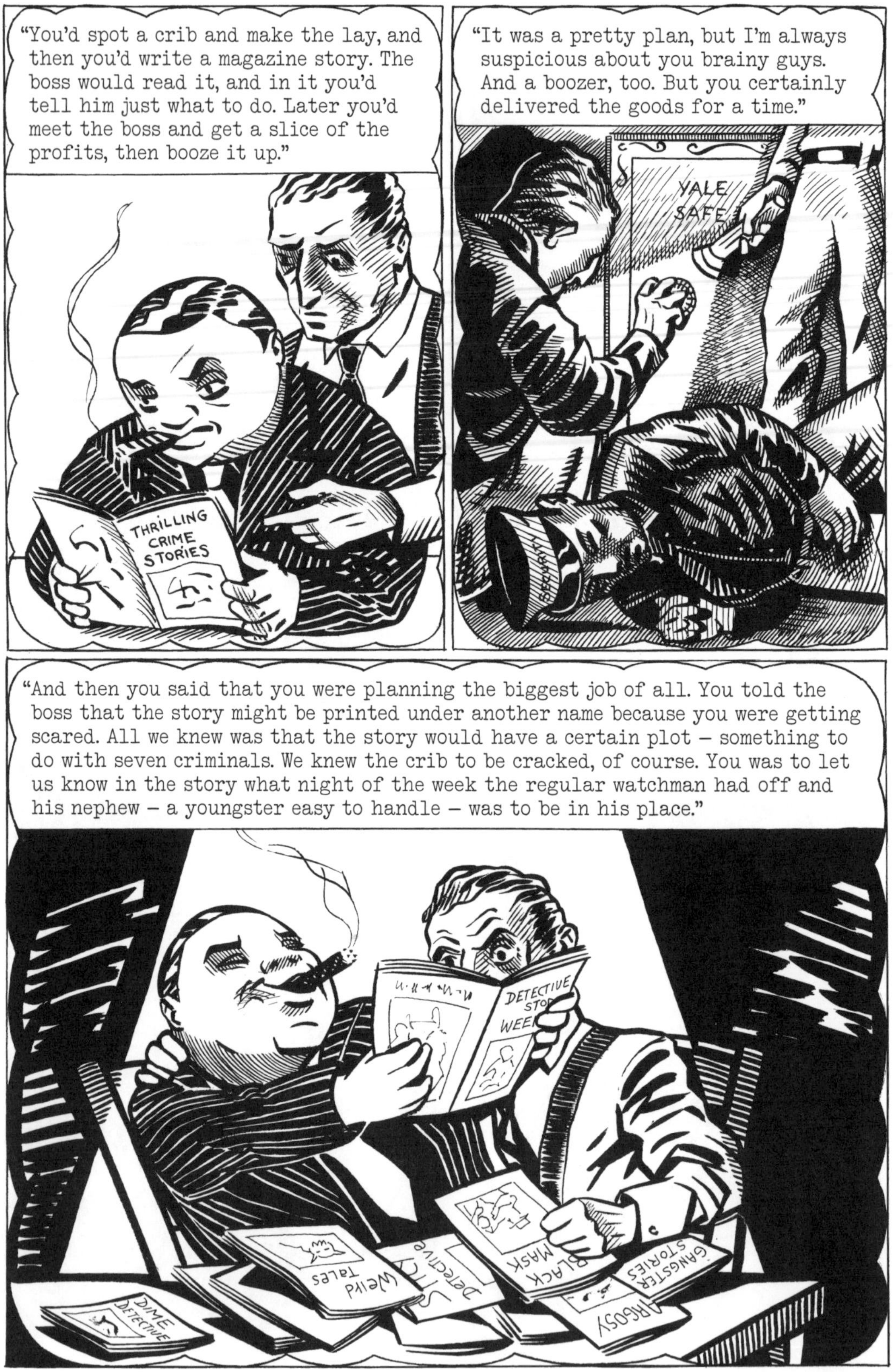
"You'd spot a crib and make the lay, and then you'd write a magazine story. The boss would read it, and in it you'd tell him just what to do. Later you'd meet the boss and get a slice of the profits, then booze it up."
THRILLING CRIME STORIES
"It was a pretty plan, but I'm always suspicious about you brainy guys. And a boozer, too. But you certainly delivered the goods for a time."
YALE SAFE
SECURITY
"And then you said that you were planning the biggest job of all. You told the boss that the story might be printed under another name because you were getting scared. All we knew was that the story would have a certain plot – something to do with seven criminals. We knew the crib to be cracked, of course. You was to let us know in the story what night of the week the regular watchman had off and his nephew – a youngster easy to handle – was to be in his place."
DETECTIVE
Weird Tales
Detective
BLACK MASK
GANGSTER STORIES
ARGOSY
DIME DETECTIVE

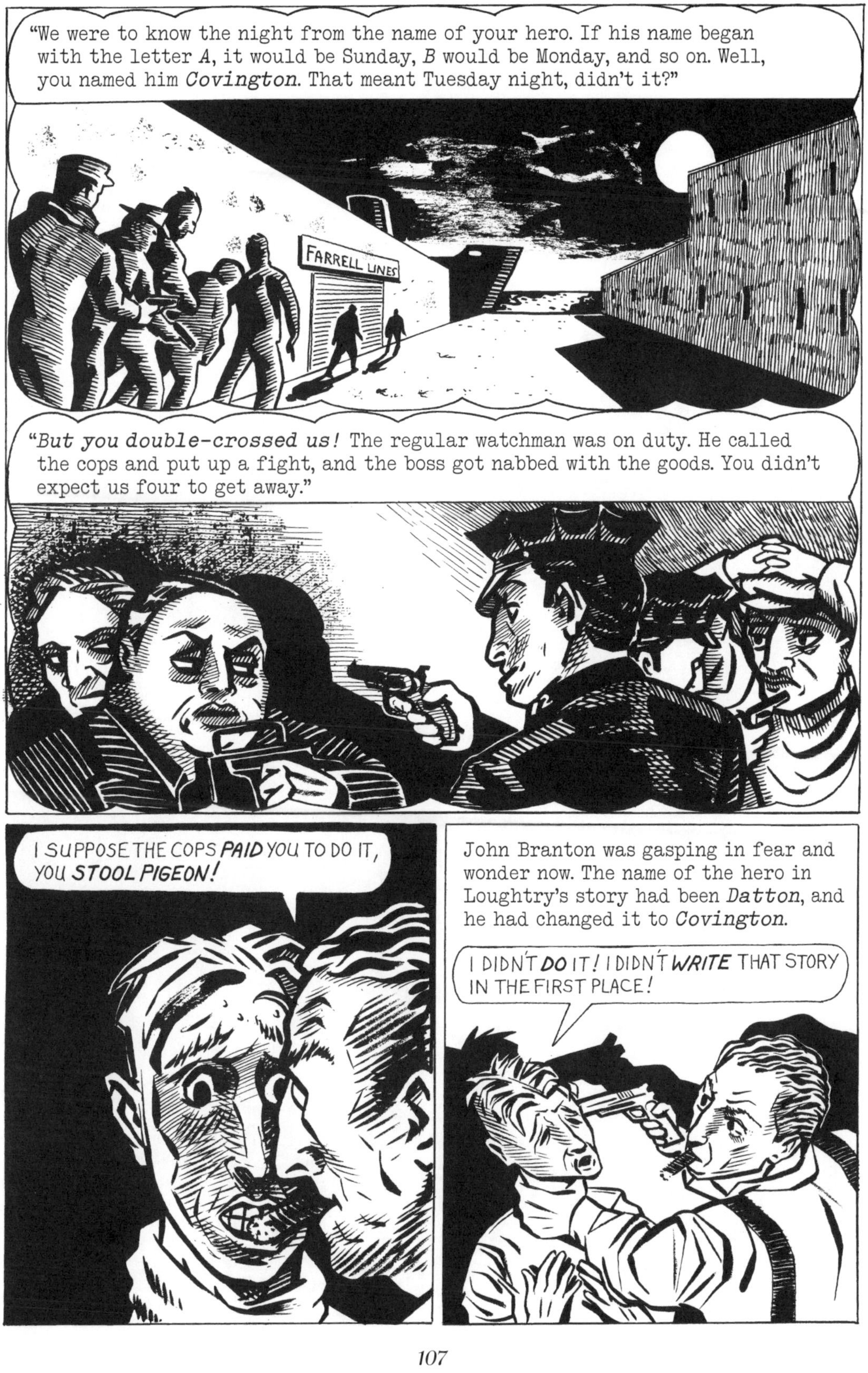
"We were to know the night from the name of your hero. If his name began with the letter A, it would be Sunday, B would be Monday, and so on. Well, you named him Covington. That meant Tuesday night, didn't it?"
FARRELL LINES
"But you double-crossed us! The regular watchman was on duty. He called the cops and put up a fight, and the boss got nabbed with the goods. You didn't expect us four to get away."
I SUPPOSE THE COPS PAID YOU TO DO IT, YOU STOOL PIGEON!
John Branton was gasping in fear and wonder now. The name of the hero in Loughtry's story had been Datton, and he had changed it to Covington.
I DIDN'T DO IT! I DIDN'T WRITE THAT STORY IN THE FIRST PLACE!

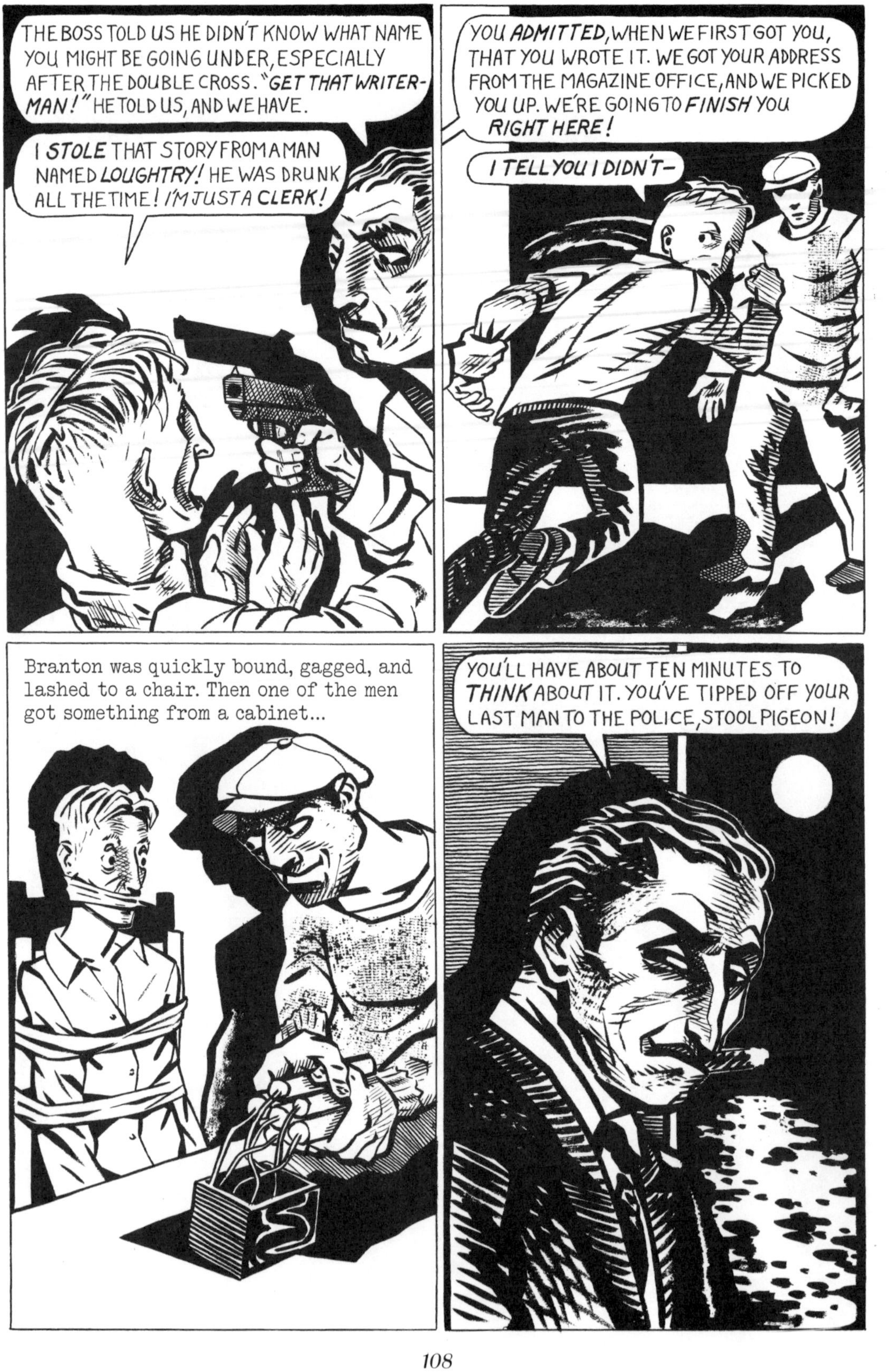
THE BOSS TOLD US HE DIDN'T KNOW WHAT NAME YOU MIGHT BE GOING UNDER, ESPECIALLY AFTER THE DOUBLE CROSS. "GET THAT WRITER-MAN!" HE TOLD US, AND WE HAVE.
I STOLE THAT STORY FROM A MAN NAMED LOUGHTRY! HE WAS DRUNK ALL THE TIME! I'M JUST A CLERK!
YOU ADMITTED, WHEN WE FIRST GOT YOU, THAT YOU WROTE IT. WE GOT YOUR ADDRESS FROM THE MAGAZINE OFFICE, AND WE PICKED YOU UP. WE'RE GOING TO FINISH YOU RIGHT HERE!
I TELL YOU I DIDN'T–
Branton was quickly bound, gagged, and lashed to a chair. Then one of the men got something from a cabinet...
YOU'LL HAVE ABOUT TEN MINUTES TO THINK ABOUT IT. YOU'VE TIPPED OFF YOUR LAST MAN TO THE POLICE, STOOL PIGEON!

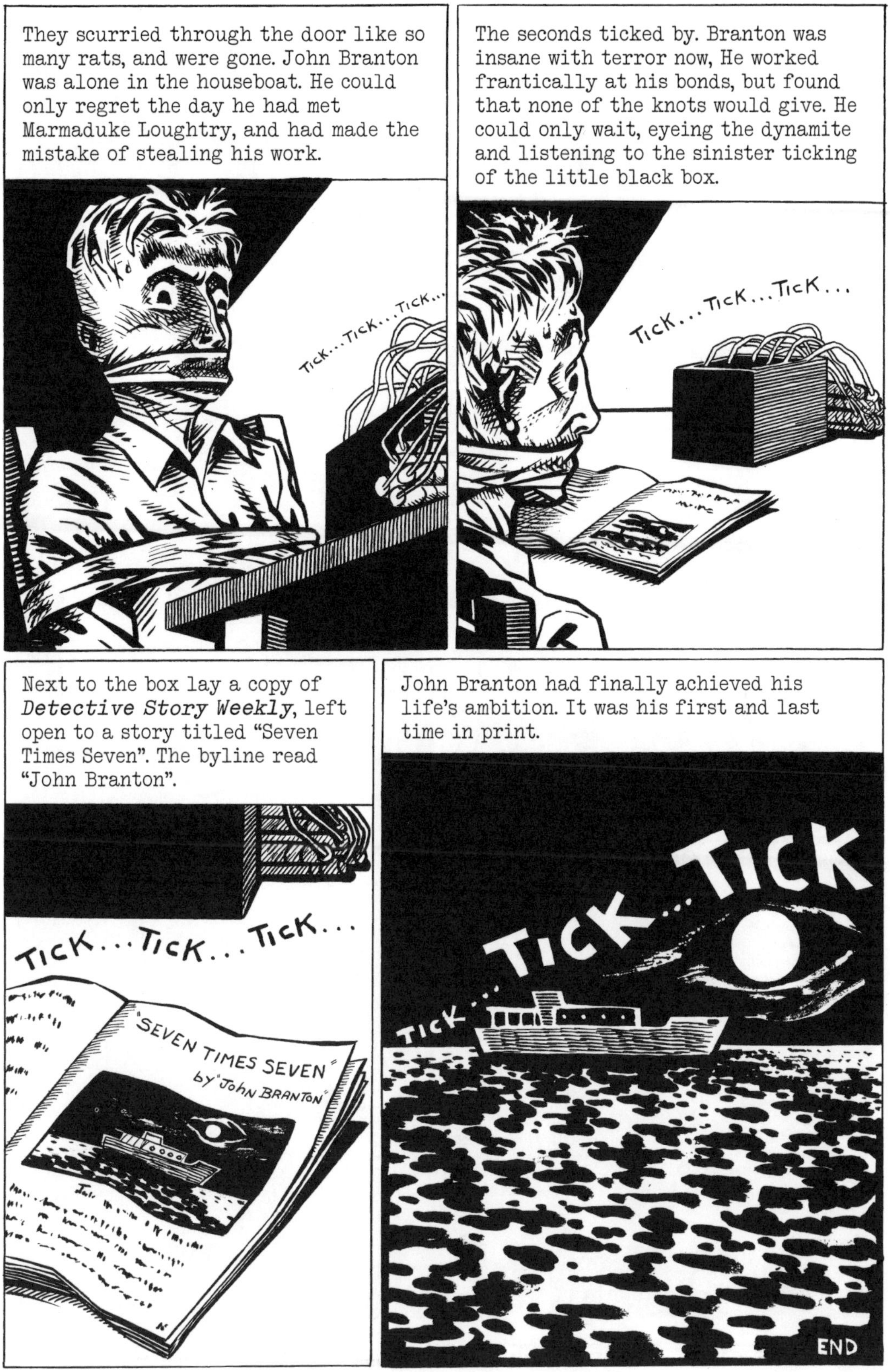
They scurried through the door like so many rats, and were gone. John Branton was alone in the houseboat. He could only regret the day he had met Marmaduke Loughtry, and had made the mistake of stealing his work.
TICK... TICK... TICK...
The seconds ticked by. Branton was insane with terror now, He worked frantically at his bonds, but found that none of the knots would give. He could only wait, eyeing the dynamite and listening to the sinister ticking of the little black box.
TICK... TICK... TICK...
Next to the box lay a copy of *Detective Story Weekly*, left open to a story titled "Seven Times Seven". The byline read "John Branton".
TICK... TICK... TICK...
"SEVEN TIMES SEVEN"
by "JOHN BRANTON"
John Branton had finally achieved his life's ambition. It was his first and last time in print.
TICK... TICK... TICK
END

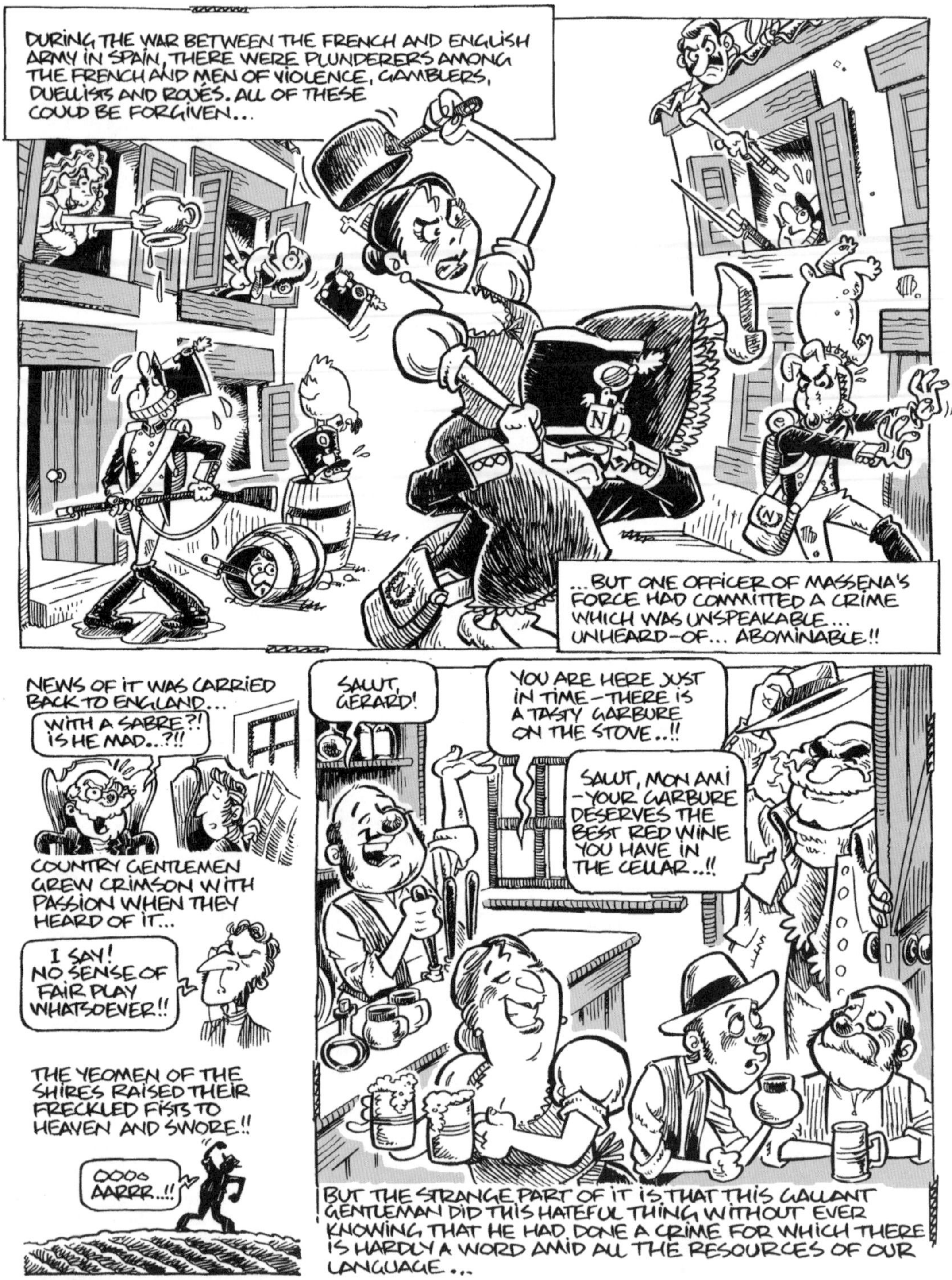
DURING THE WAR BETWEEN THE FRENCH AND ENGLISH ARMY IN SPAIN, THERE WERE PLUNDERERS AMONG THE FRENCH AND MEN OF VIOLENCE, GAMBLERS, DUELLISTS AND ROUÉS. ALL OF THESE COULD BE FORGIVEN...
...BUT ONE OFFICER OF MASSENA'S FORCE HAD COMMITTED A CRIME WHICH WAS UNSPEAKABLE... UNHEARD-OF... ABOMINABLE!!
NEWS OF IT WAS CARRIED BACK TO ENGLAND...
WITH A SABRE?! IS HE MAD..?!!
COUNTRY GENTLEMEN GREW CRIMSON WITH PASSION WHEN THEY HEARD OF IT...
I SAY! NO SENSE OF FAIR PLAY WHATSOEVER!!
THE YEOMEN OF THE SHIRES RAISED THEIR FRECKLED FISTS TO HEAVEN AND SWORE!!
OOOO AARRR..!!
SALUT, GERARD!
YOU ARE HERE JUST IN TIME—THERE IS A TASTY GARBURE ON THE STOVE..!!
SALUT, MON AMI —YOUR GARBURE DESERVES THE BEST RED WINE YOU HAVE IN THE CELLAR..!!
BUT THE STRANGE PART OF IT IS THAT THIS GALLANT GENTLEMAN DID THIS HATEFUL THING WITHOUT EVER KNOWING THAT HE HAD DONE A CRIME FOR WHICH THERE IS HARDLY A WORD AMID ALL THE RESOURCES OF OUR LANGUAGE...

The Crime of the Brigadier

BY **ARTHUR CONAN DOYLE**. SCRIPT BY **ANTONELLA CAPUTO**. ART BY **NICK MILLER**.

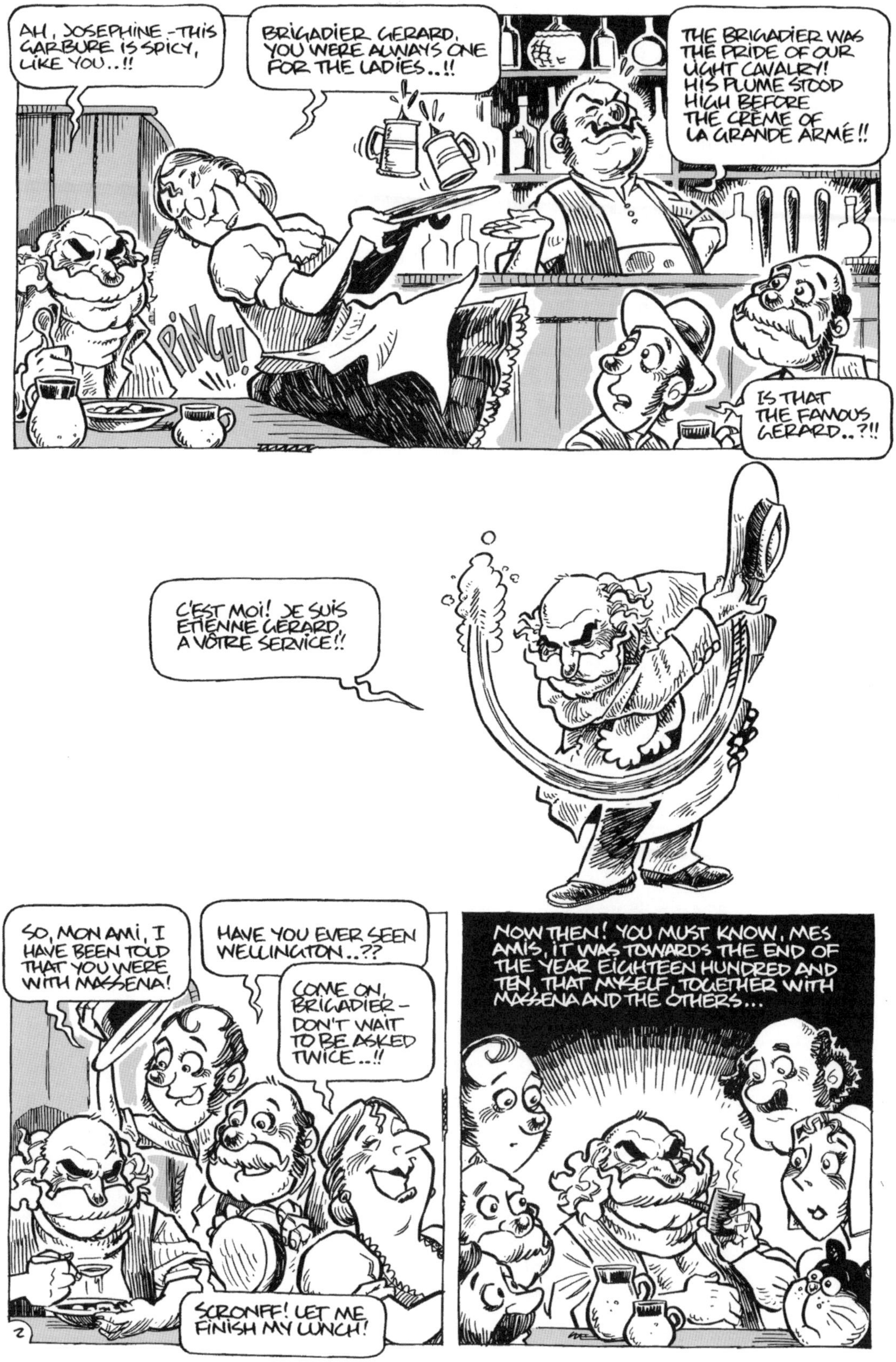
AH, JOSEPHINE - THIS GARBURE IS SPICY, LIKE YOU..!!
BRIGADIER GERARD, YOU WERE ALWAYS ONE FOR THE LADIES..!!
THE BRIGADIER WAS THE PRIDE OF OUR LIGHT CAVALRY! HIS PLUME STOOD HIGH BEFORE THE CRÈME OF LA GRANDE ARMÉ!!
PINCH!
IS THAT THE FAMOUS GERARD..?!!
C'EST MOI! JE SUIS ETIENNE GERARD, A VÔTRE SERVICE!!
SO, MON AMI, I HAVE BEEN TOLD THAT YOU WERE WITH MASSENA!
HAVE YOU EVER SEEN WELLINGTON..??
COME ON, BRIGADIER - DON'T WAIT TO BE ASKED TWICE..!!
SCRONFF! LET ME FINISH MY LUNCH!
NOW THEN! YOU MUST KNOW, MES AMIS, IT WAS TOWARDS THE END OF THE YEAR EIGHTEEN HUNDRED AND TEN, THAT MYSELF, TOGETHER WITH MASSENA AND THE OTHERS...

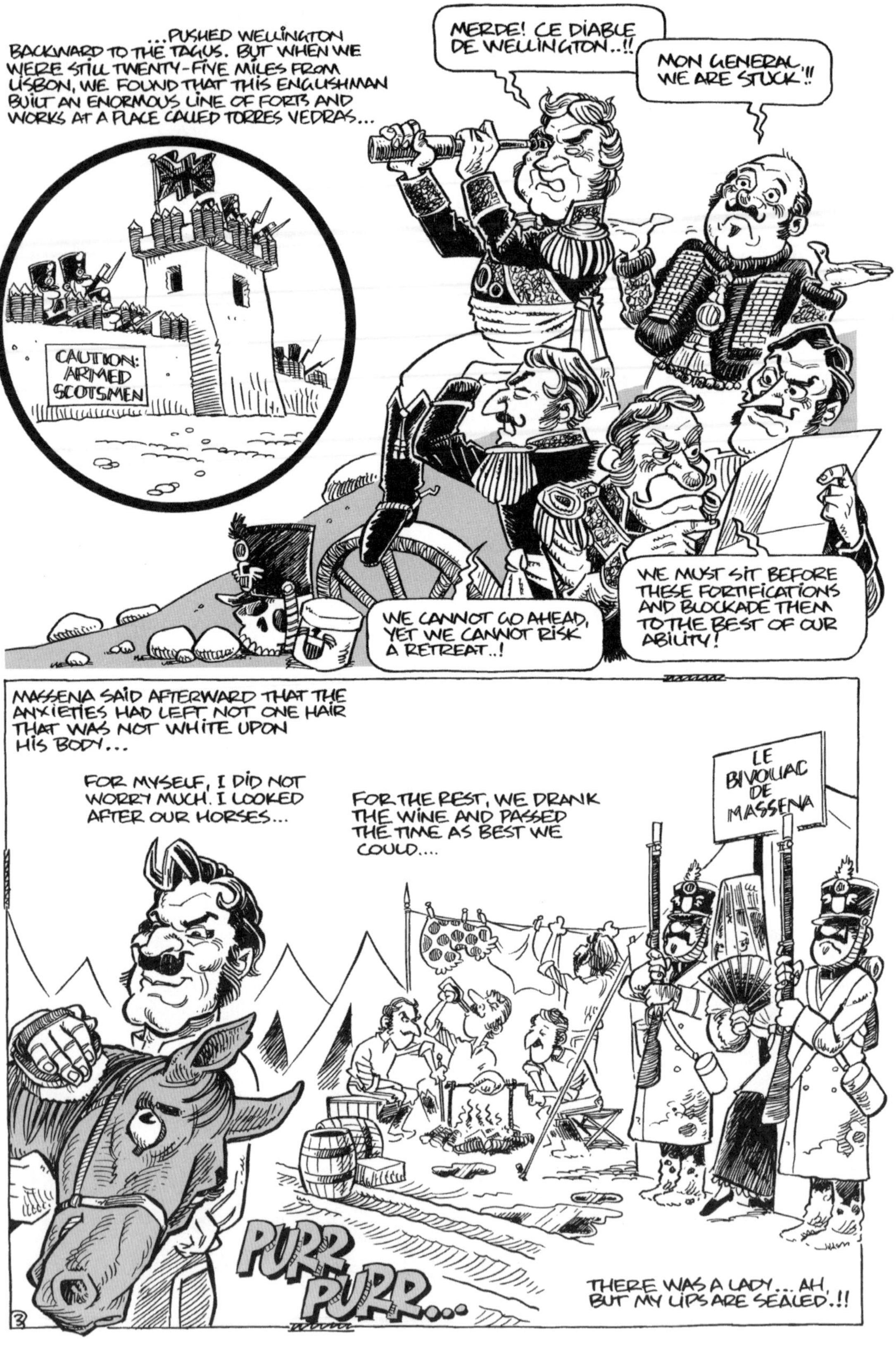
...PUSHED WELLINGTON BACKWARD TO THE TAGUS. BUT WHEN WE WERE STILL TWENTY-FIVE MILES FROM LISBON, WE FOUND THAT THIS ENGLISHMAN BUILT AN ENORMOUS LINE OF FORTS AND WORKS AT A PLACE CALLED TORRES VEDRAS...
MERDE! CE DIABLE DE WELLINGTON..!!
MON GENERAL, WE ARE STUCK!!
CAUTION: ARMED SCOTSMEN
WE CANNOT GO AHEAD, YET WE CANNOT RISK A RETREAT..!
WE MUST SIT BEFORE THESE FORTIFICATIONS AND BLOCKADE THEM TO THE BEST OF OUR ABILITY!
MASSENA SAID AFTERWARD THAT THE ANXIETIES HAD LEFT NOT ONE HAIR THAT WAS NOT WHITE UPON HIS BODY...
FOR MYSELF, I DID NOT WORRY MUCH. I LOOKED AFTER OUR HORSES...
FOR THE REST, WE DRANK THE WINE AND PASSED THE TIME AS BEST WE COULD....
LE BIVOUAC DE MASSENA
PURR PURR...
THERE WAS A LADY... AH, BUT MY LIPS ARE SEALED!!

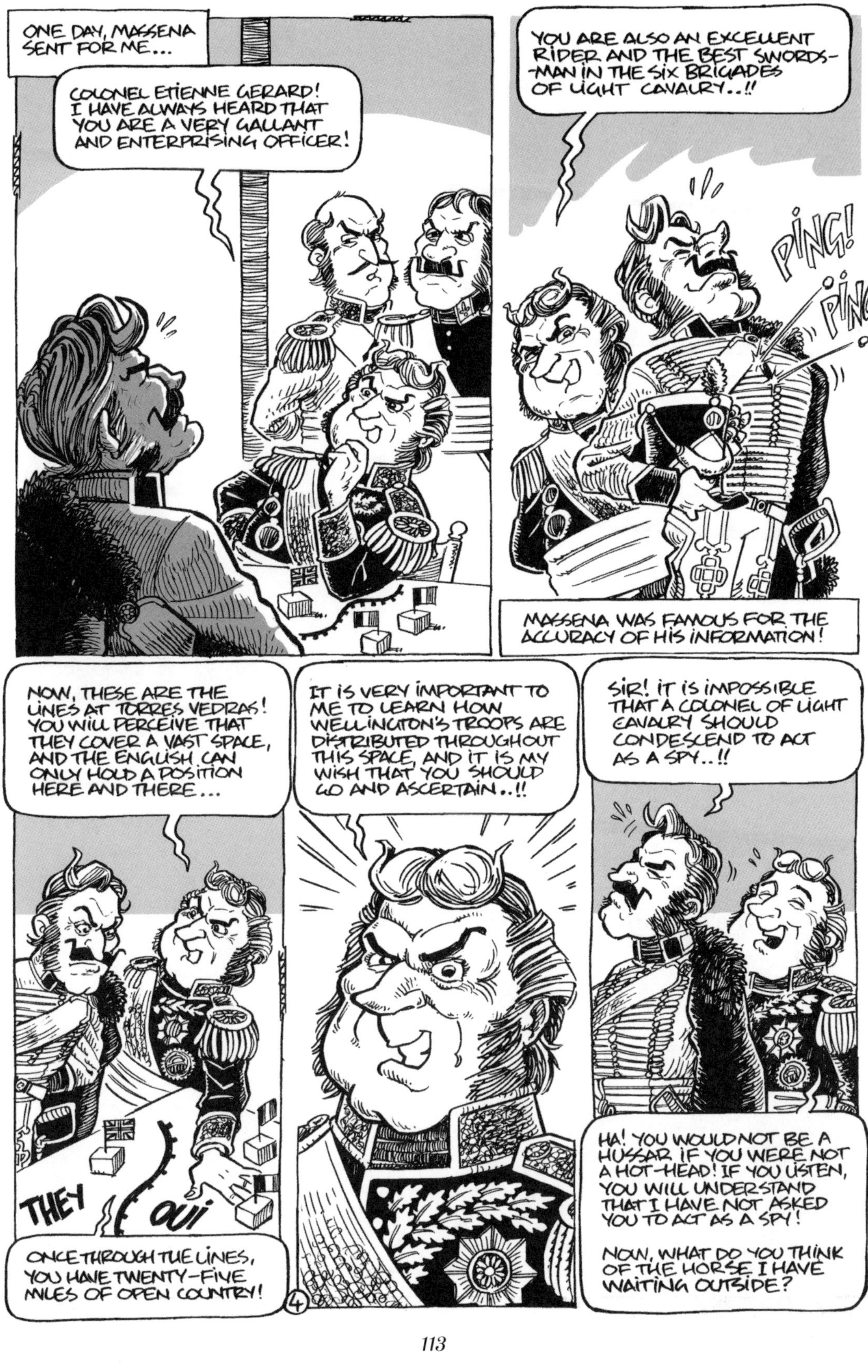

ONE DAY, MASSENA SENT FOR ME...
COLONEL ETIENNE GERARD! I HAVE ALWAYS HEARD THAT YOU ARE A VERY GALLANT AND ENTERPRISING OFFICER!
YOU ARE ALSO AN EXCELLENT RIDER AND THE BEST SWORDS--MAN IN THE SIX BRIGADES OF LIGHT CAVALRY..!!
PING!
PING!
MASSENA WAS FAMOUS FOR THE ACCURACY OF HIS INFORMATION!
NOW, THESE ARE THE LINES AT TORRES VEDRAS! YOU WILL PERCEIVE THAT THEY COVER A VAST SPACE, AND THE ENGLISH CAN ONLY HOLD A POSITION HERE AND THERE...
THEY
OUI
ONCE THROUGH THE LINES, YOU HAVE TWENTY-FIVE MILES OF OPEN COUNTRY!
IT IS VERY IMPORTANT TO ME TO LEARN HOW WELLINGTON'S TROOPS ARE DISTRIBUTED THROUGHOUT THIS SPACE, AND IT IS MY WISH THAT YOU SHOULD GO AND ASCERTAIN..!!
SIR! IT IS IMPOSSIBLE THAT A COLONEL OF LIGHT CAVALRY SHOULD CONDESCEND TO ACT AS A SPY..!!
HA! YOU WOULD NOT BE A HUSSAR IF YOU WERE NOT A HOT-HEAD! IF YOU LISTEN, YOU WILL UNDERSTAND THAT I HAVE NOT ASKED YOU TO ACT AS A SPY!
NOW, WHAT DO YOU THINK OF THE HORSE I HAVE WAITING OUTSIDE?

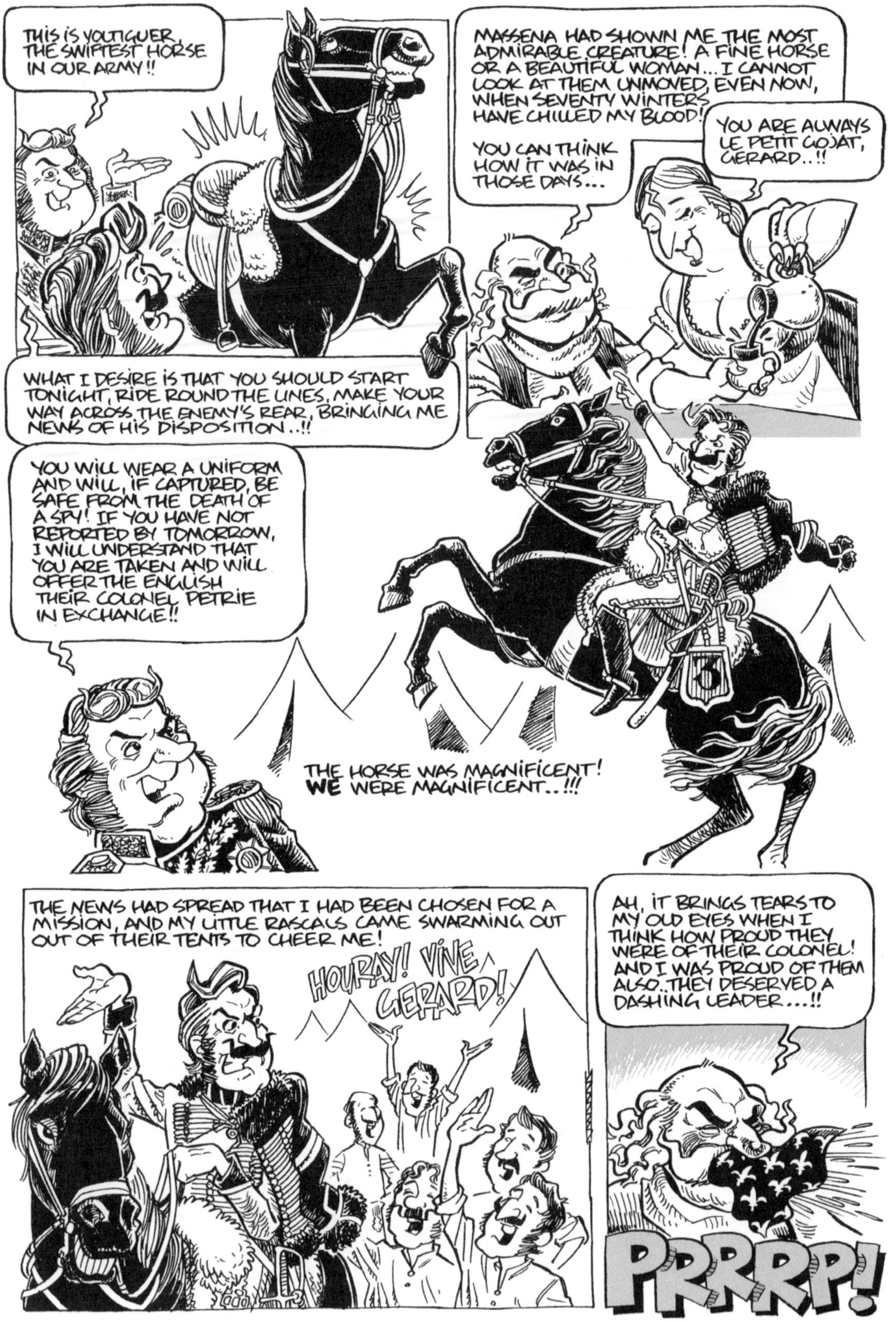
THIS IS VOLTIGUER, THE SWIFTEST HORSE IN OUR ARMY!!
MASSENA HAD SHOWN ME THE MOST ADMIRABLE CREATURE! A FINE HORSE OR A BEAUTIFUL WOMAN... I CANNOT LOOK AT THEM UNMOVED, EVEN NOW, WHEN SEVENTY WINTERS HAVE CHILLED MY BLOOD!
YOU CAN THINK HOW IT WAS IN THOSE DAYS...
YOU ARE ALWAYS LE PETIT GOJAT, GERARD..!!
WHAT I DESIRE IS THAT YOU SHOULD START TONIGHT, RIDE ROUND THE LINES, MAKE YOUR WAY ACROSS THE ENEMY'S REAR, BRINGING ME NEWS OF HIS DISPOSITION..!!
YOU WILL WEAR A UNIFORM AND WILL, IF CAPTURED, BE SAFE FROM THE DEATH OF A SPY! IF YOU HAVE NOT REPORTED BY TOMORROW, I WILL UNDERSTAND THAT YOU ARE TAKEN AND WILL OFFER THE ENGLISH THEIR COLONEL PETRIE IN EXCHANGE!!
THE HORSE WAS MAGNIFICENT! WE WERE MAGNIFICENT..!!!
THE NEWS HAD SPREAD THAT I HAD BEEN CHOSEN FOR A MISSION, AND MY LITTLE RASCALS CAME SWARMING OUT OUT OF THEIR TENTS TO CHEER ME!
HOURAY! VIVE GERARD!
AH, IT BRINGS TEARS TO MY OLD EYES WHEN I THINK HOW PROUD THEY WERE OF THEIR COLONEL! AND I WAS PROUD OF THEM ALSO..THEY DESERVED A DASHING LEADER...!!
PRRRP!

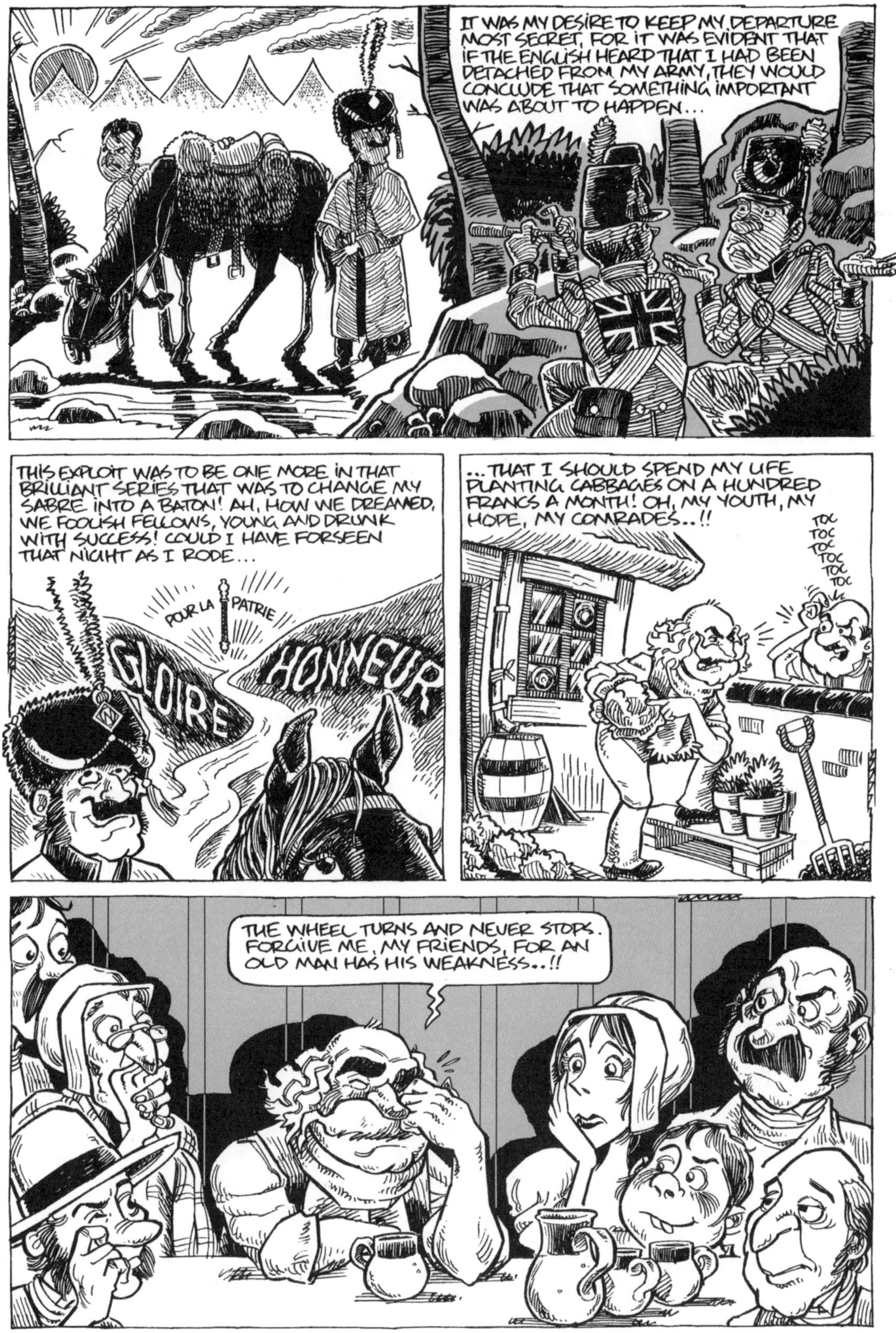
IT WAS MY DESIRE TO KEEP MY DEPARTURE MOST SECRET, FOR IT WAS EVIDENT THAT IF THE ENGLISH HEARD THAT I HAD BEEN DETACHED FROM MY ARMY, THEY WOULD CONCLUDE THAT SOMETHING IMPORTANT WAS ABOUT TO HAPPEN...
THIS EXPLOIT WAS TO BE ONE MORE IN THAT BRILLIANT SERIES THAT WAS TO CHANGE MY SABRE INTO A BATON! AH, HOW WE DREAMED, WE FOOLISH FELLOWS, YOUNG AND DRUNK WITH SUCCESS! COULD I HAVE FORSEEN THAT NIGHT AS I RODE...
POUR LA PATRIE
GLOIRE
HONNEUR
...THAT I SHOULD SPEND MY LIFE PLANTING CABBAGES ON A HUNDRED FRANCS A MONTH! OH, MY YOUTH, MY HOPE, MY COMRADES..!!
TOC TOC TOC TOC TOC TOC
THE WHEEL TURNS AND NEVER STOPS. FORGIVE ME, MY FRIENDS, FOR AN OLD MAN HAS HIS WEAKNESS..!!

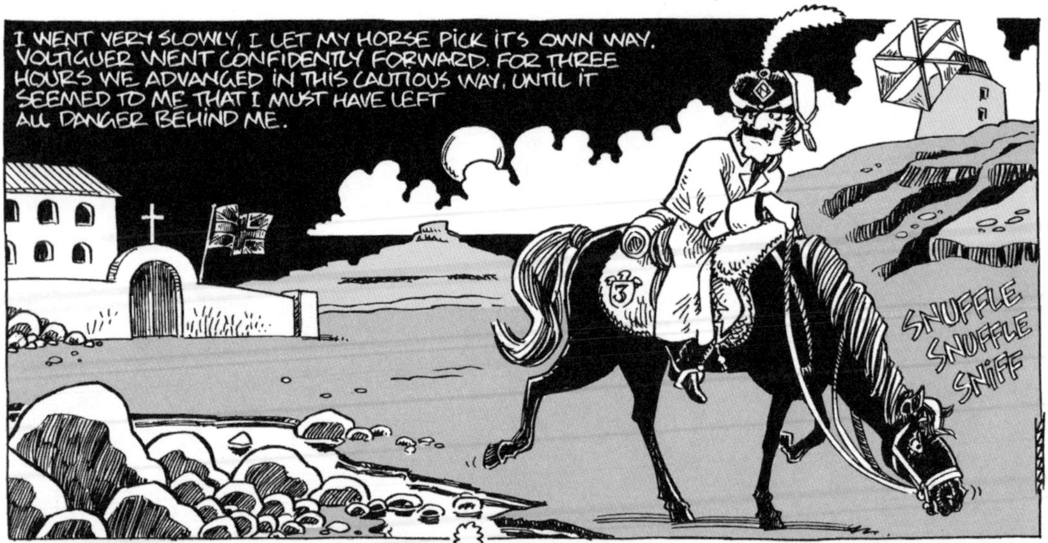
I WENT VERY SLOWLY, I LET MY HORSE PICK ITS OWN WAY. VOLTIGUER WENT CONFIDENTLY FORWARD. FOR THREE HOURS WE ADVANCED IN THIS CAUTIOUS WAY, UNTIL IT SEEMED TO ME THAT I MUST HAVE LEFT ALL DANGER BEHIND ME.
SNUFFLE
SNUFFLE
SNIFF

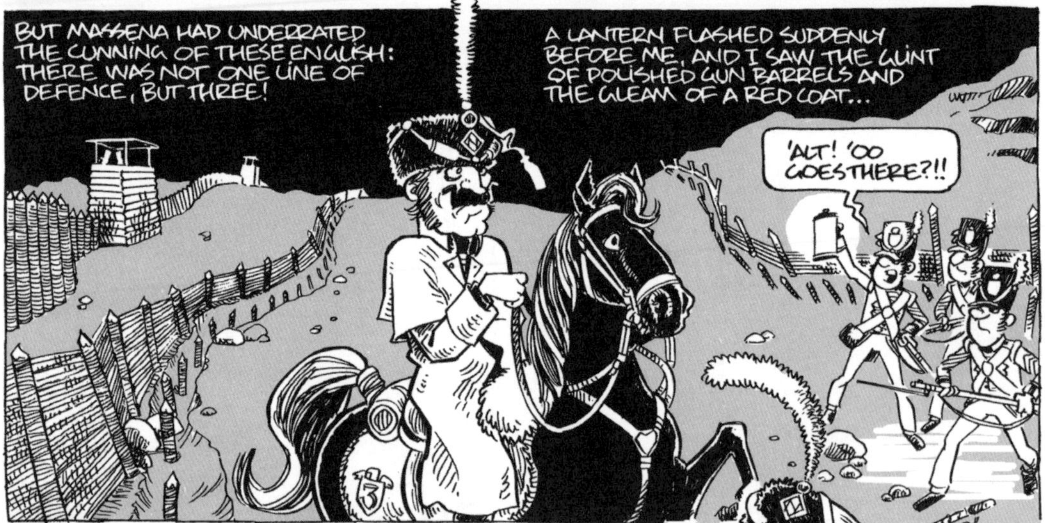
BUT MASSENA HAD UNDERRATED THE CUNNING OF THESE ENGLISH: THERE WAS NOT ONE LINE OF DEFENCE, BUT THREE!
A LANTERN FLASHED SUDDENLY BEFORE ME, AND I SAW THE GLINT OF POLISHED GUN BARRELS AND THE GLEAM OF A RED COAT...
'ALT! 'OO GOESTHERE?!!

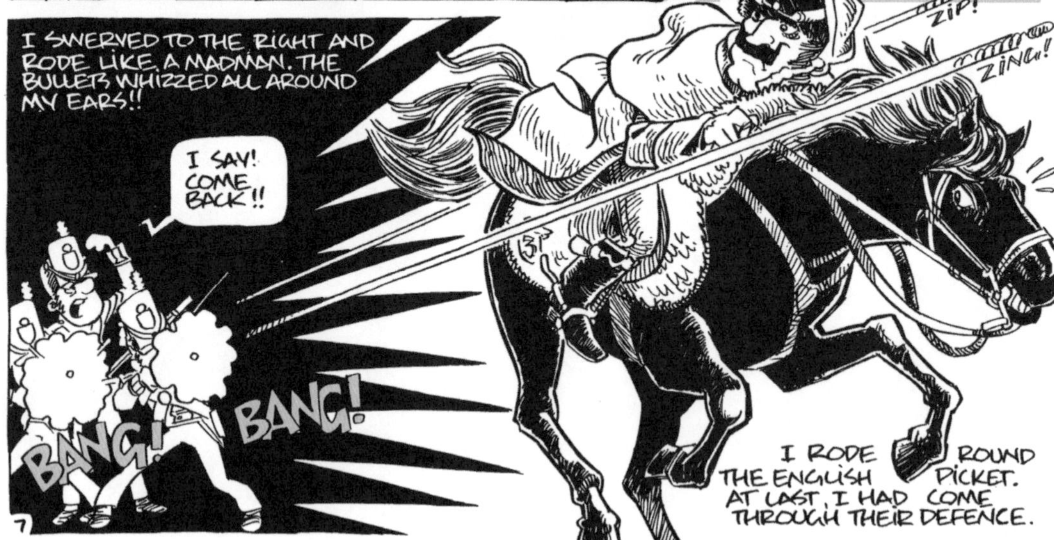
I SWERVED TO THE RIGHT AND RODE LIKE A MADMAN. THE BULLETS WHIZZED ALL AROUND MY EARS!!
ZIP!
ZING!
I SAY! COME BACK!!
BANG!
BANG!
I RODE ROUND THE ENGLISH PICKET. AT LAST, I HAD COME THROUGH THEIR DEFENCE.
7

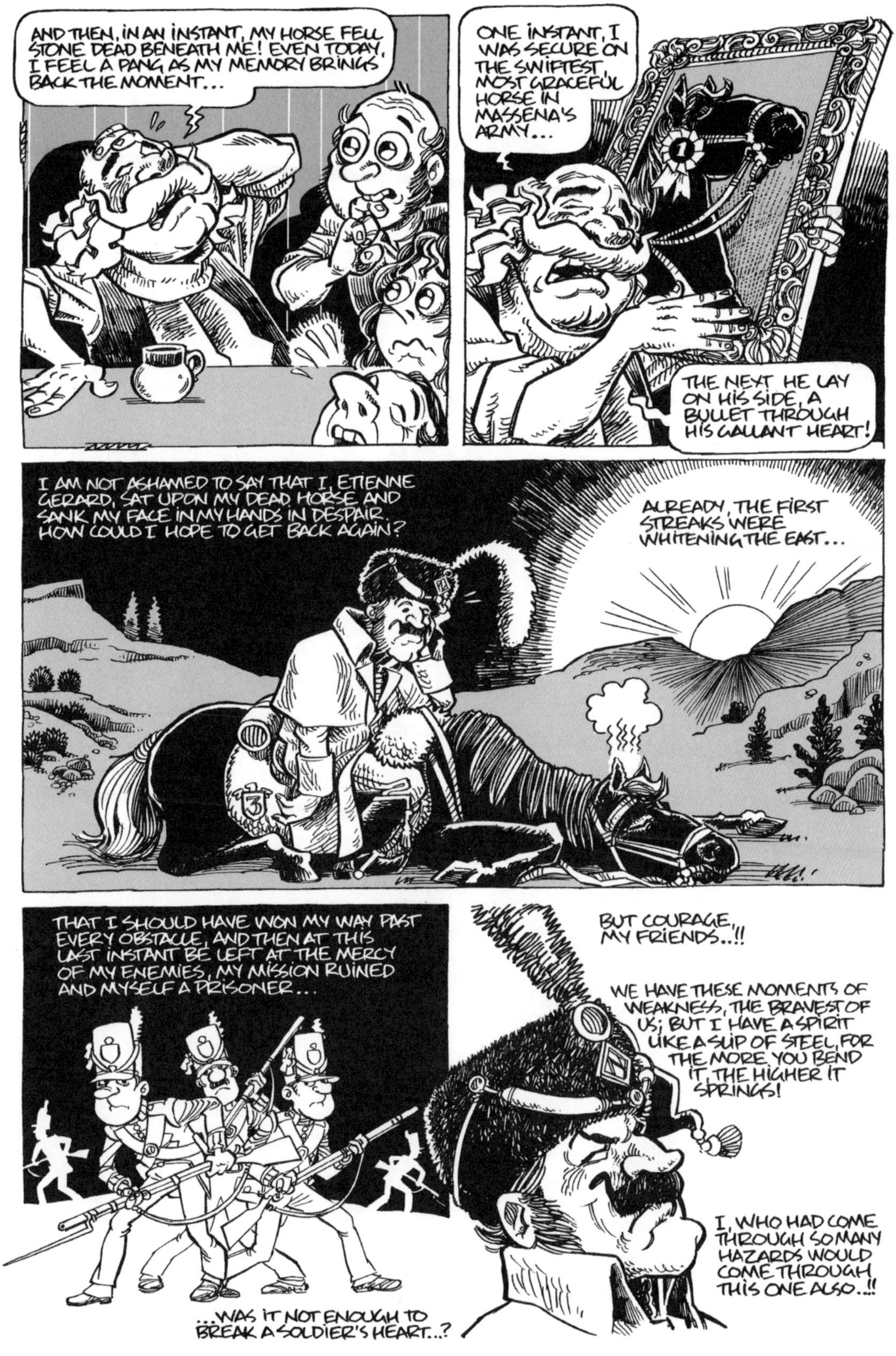
AND THEN, IN AN INSTANT, MY HORSE FELL STONE DEAD BENEATH ME! EVEN TODAY, I FEEL A PANG AS MY MEMORY BRINGS BACK THE MOMENT...
ONE INSTANT, I WAS SECURE ON THE SWIFTEST, MOST GRACEFUL HORSE IN MASSENA'S ARMY...
THE NEXT HE LAY ON HIS SIDE, A BULLET THROUGH HIS GALLANT HEART!
I AM NOT ASHAMED TO SAY THAT I, ETIENNE GERARD, SAT UPON MY DEAD HORSE AND SANK MY FACE IN MY HANDS IN DESPAIR. HOW COULD I HOPE TO GET BACK AGAIN?
ALREADY, THE FIRST STREAKS WERE WHITENING THE EAST...
THAT I SHOULD HAVE WON MY WAY PAST EVERY OBSTACLE, AND THEN AT THIS LAST INSTANT BE LEFT AT THE MERCY OF MY ENEMIES, MY MISSION RUINED AND MYSELF A PRISONER...
...WAS IT NOT ENOUGH TO BREAK A SOLDIER'S HEART...?
BUT COURAGE, MY FRIENDS..!!
WE HAVE THESE MOMENTS OF WEAKNESS, THE BRAVEST OF US; BUT I HAVE A SPIRIT LIKE A SLIP OF STEEL, FOR THE MORE YOU BEND IT, THE HIGHER IT SPRINGS!
I, WHO HAD COME THROUGH SO MANY HAZARDS WOULD COME THROUGH THIS ONE ALSO..!!

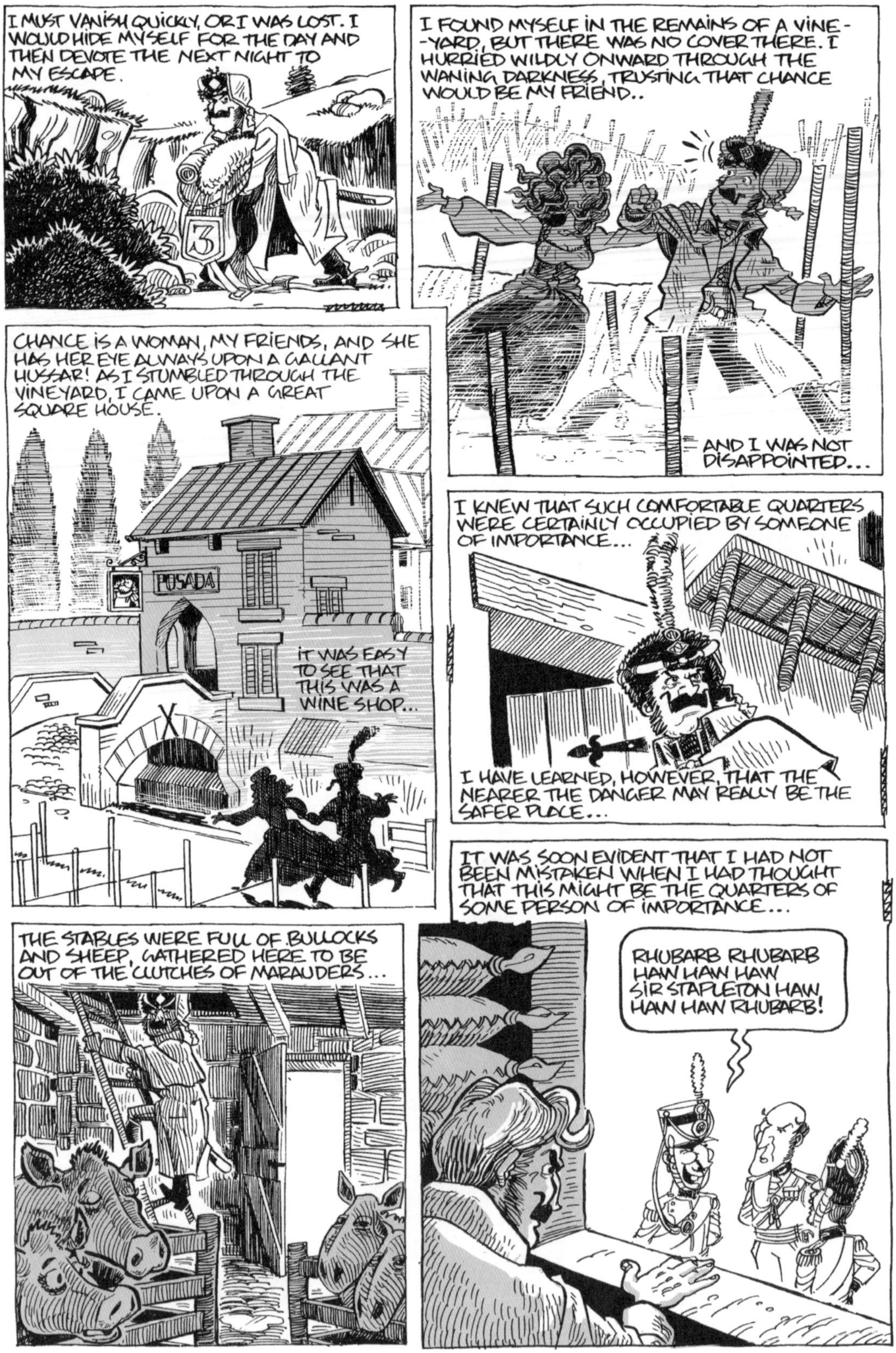
I MUST VANISH QUICKLY, OR I WAS LOST. I WOULD HIDE MYSELF FOR THE DAY AND THEN DEVOTE THE NEXT NIGHT TO MY ESCAPE.
3
I FOUND MYSELF IN THE REMAINS OF A VINE--YARD, BUT THERE WAS NO COVER THERE. I HURRIED WILDLY ONWARD THROUGH THE WANING DARKNESS, TRUSTING THAT CHANCE WOULD BE MY FRIEND..
AND I WAS NOT DISAPPOINTED...
CHANCE IS A WOMAN, MY FRIENDS, AND SHE HAS HER EYE ALWAYS UPON A GALLANT HUSSAR! AS I STUMBLED THROUGH THE VINEYARD, I CAME UPON A GREAT SQUARE HOUSE.
POSADA
IT WAS EASY TO SEE THAT THIS WAS A WINE SHOP...
I KNEW THAT SUCH COMFORTABLE QUARTERS WERE CERTAINLY OCCUPIED BY SOMEONE OF IMPORTANCE...
I HAVE LEARNED, HOWEVER, THAT THE NEARER THE DANGER MAY REALLY BE THE SAFER PLACE...
THE STABLES WERE FULL OF BULLOCKS AND SHEEP, GATHERED HERE TO BE OUT OF THE CLUTCHES OF MARAUDERS...
IT WAS SOON EVIDENT THAT I HAD NOT BEEN MISTAKEN WHEN I HAD THOUGHT THAT THIS MIGHT BE THE QUARTERS OF SOME PERSON OF IMPORTANCE...
RHUBARB RHUBARB HAW HAW HAW SIR STAPLETON HAW, HAW HAW RHUBARB!

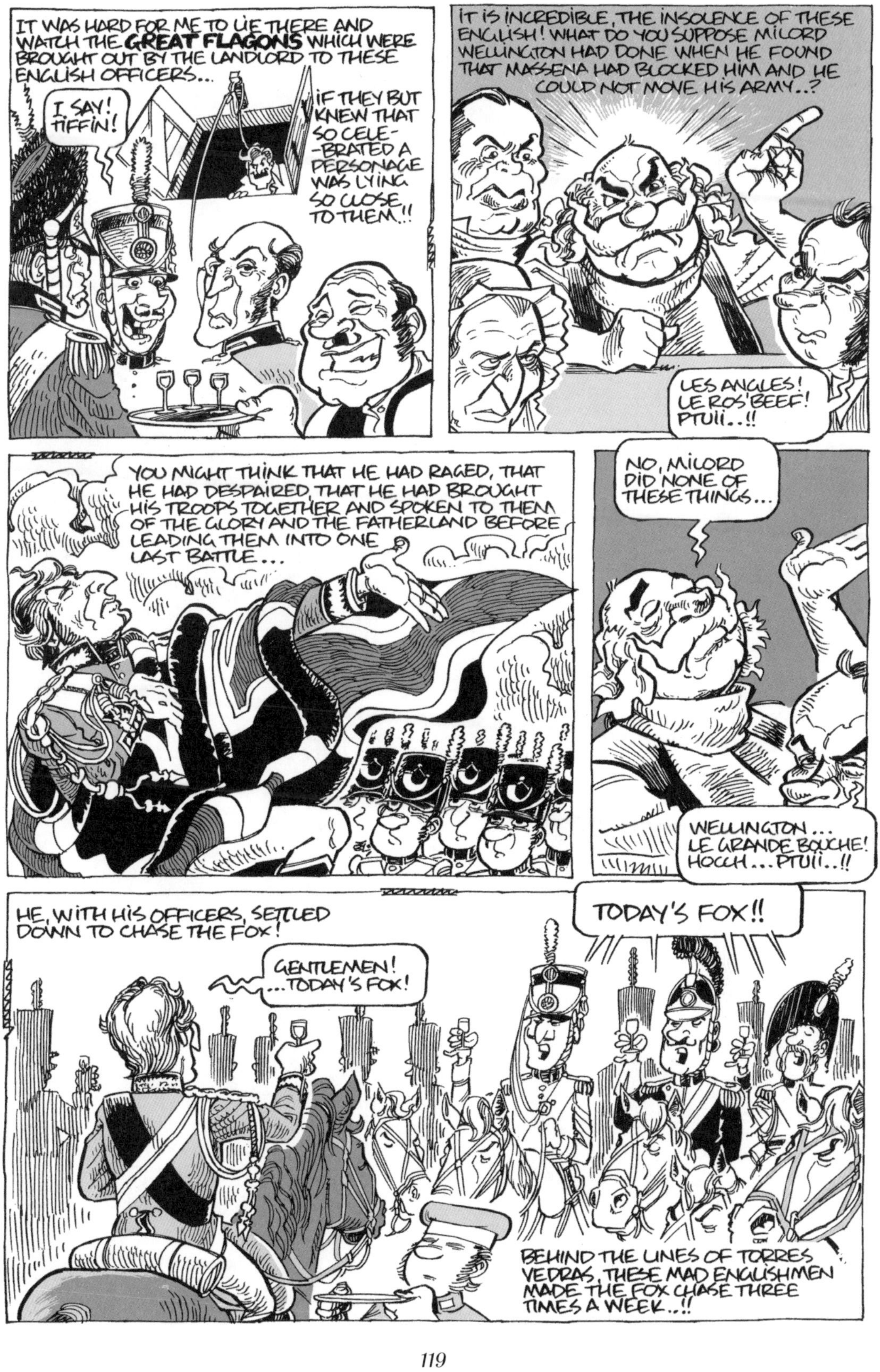
IT WAS HARD FOR ME TO LIE THERE AND WATCH THE **GREAT FLAGONS** WHICH WERE BROUGHT OUT BY THE LANDLORD TO THESE ENGLISH OFFICERS...
I SAY! TIFFIN!
IF THEY BUT KNEW THAT SO CELE- -BRATED A PERSONAGE WAS LYING SO CLOSE TO THEM!!
IT IS INCREDIBLE, THE INSOLENCE OF THESE ENGLISH! WHAT DO YOU SUPPOSE MILORD WELLINGTON HAD DONE WHEN HE FOUND THAT MASSENA HAD BLOCKED HIM AND HE COULD NOT MOVE HIS ARMY..?
LES ANGLES! LE ROS'BEEF! PTUII..!!
YOU MIGHT THINK THAT HE HAD RAGED, THAT HE HAD DESPAIRED, THAT HE HAD BROUGHT HIS TROOPS TOGETHER AND SPOKEN TO THEM OF THE GLORY AND THE FATHERLAND BEFORE LEADING THEM INTO ONE LAST BATTLE...
NO, MILORD DID NONE OF THESE THINGS...
WELLINGTON... LE GRANDE BOUCHE! HOCCH... PTUII..!!
HE, WITH HIS OFFICERS, SETTLED DOWN TO CHASE THE FOX!
GENTLEMEN! ...TODAY'S FOX!
TODAY'S FOX!!
BEHIND THE LINES OF TORRES VEDRAS, THESE MAD ENGLISHMEN MADE THE FOX CHASE THREE TIMES A WEEK..!!

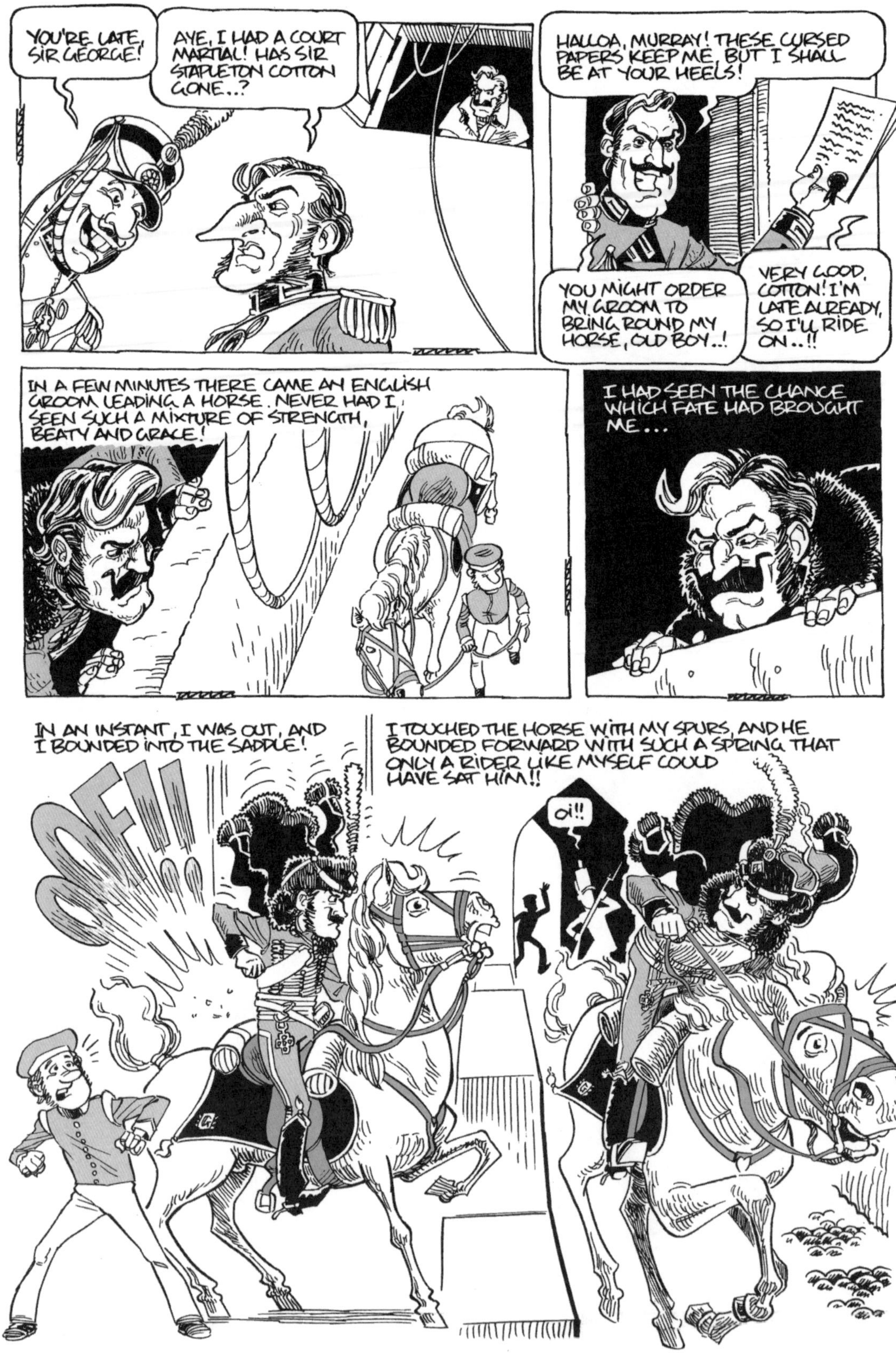
YOU'RE LATE, SIR GEORGE!
AYE, I HAD A COURT MARTIAL! HAS SIR STAPLETON COTTON GONE..?
HALLOA, MURRAY! THESE CURSED PAPERS KEEP ME, BUT I SHALL BE AT YOUR HEELS!
YOU MIGHT ORDER MY GROOM TO BRING ROUND MY HORSE, OLD BOY..!
VERY GOOD, COTTON! I'M LATE ALREADY, SO I'LL RIDE ON..!!
IN A FEW MINUTES THERE CAME AN ENGLISH GROOM LEADING A HORSE. NEVER HAD I SEEN SUCH A MIXTURE OF STRENGTH, BEATY AND GRACE!
I HAD SEEN THE CHANCE WHICH FATE HAD BROUGHT ME...
IN AN INSTANT, I WAS OUT, AND I BOUNDED INTO THE SADDLE!
OOF!!
I TOUCHED THE HORSE WITH MY SPURS, AND HE BOUNDED FORWARD WITH SUCH A SPRING THAT ONLY A RIDER LIKE MYSELF COULD HAVE SAT HIM!!
OI!!

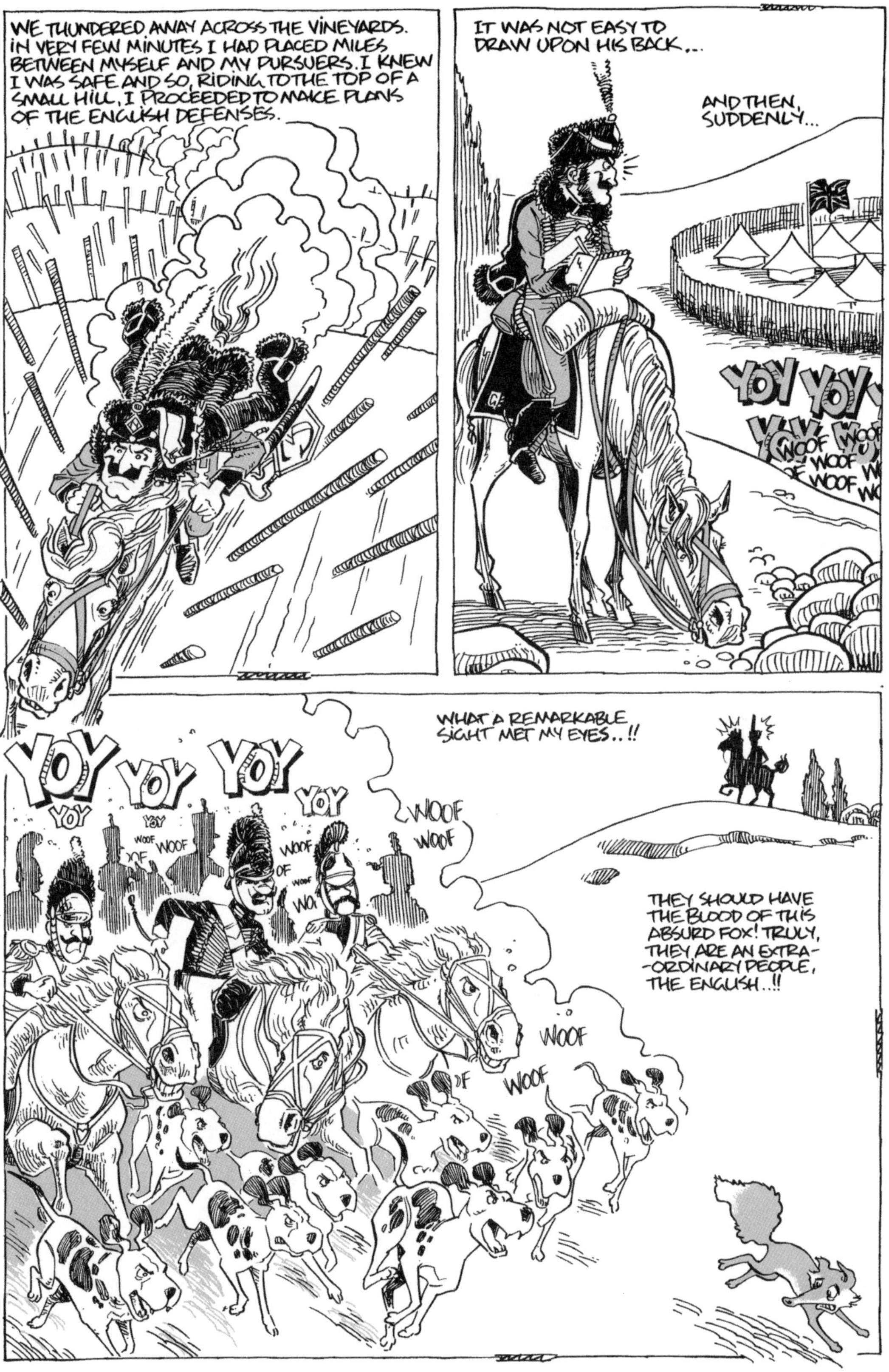
WE THUNDERED AWAY ACROSS THE VINEYARDS. IN VERY FEW MINUTES I HAD PLACED MILES BETWEEN MYSELF AND MY PURSUERS. I KNEW I WAS SAFE AND SO, RIDING TO THE TOP OF A SMALL HILL, I PROCEEDED TO MAKE PLANS OF THE ENGLISH DEFENSES.
IT WAS NOT EASY TO DRAW UPON HIS BACK...
AND THEN, SUDDENLY...
YOY YOY
WOOF WOOF WOOF
WHAT A REMARKABLE SIGHT MET MY EYES..!!
YOY YOY YOY
YOY YOY YOY
WOOF WOOF
WOOF WOOF
THEY SHOULD HAVE THE BLOOD OF THIS ABSURD FOX! TRULY, THEY ARE AN EXTRA-ORDINARY PEOPLE, THE ENGLISH..!!
WOOF
WOOF

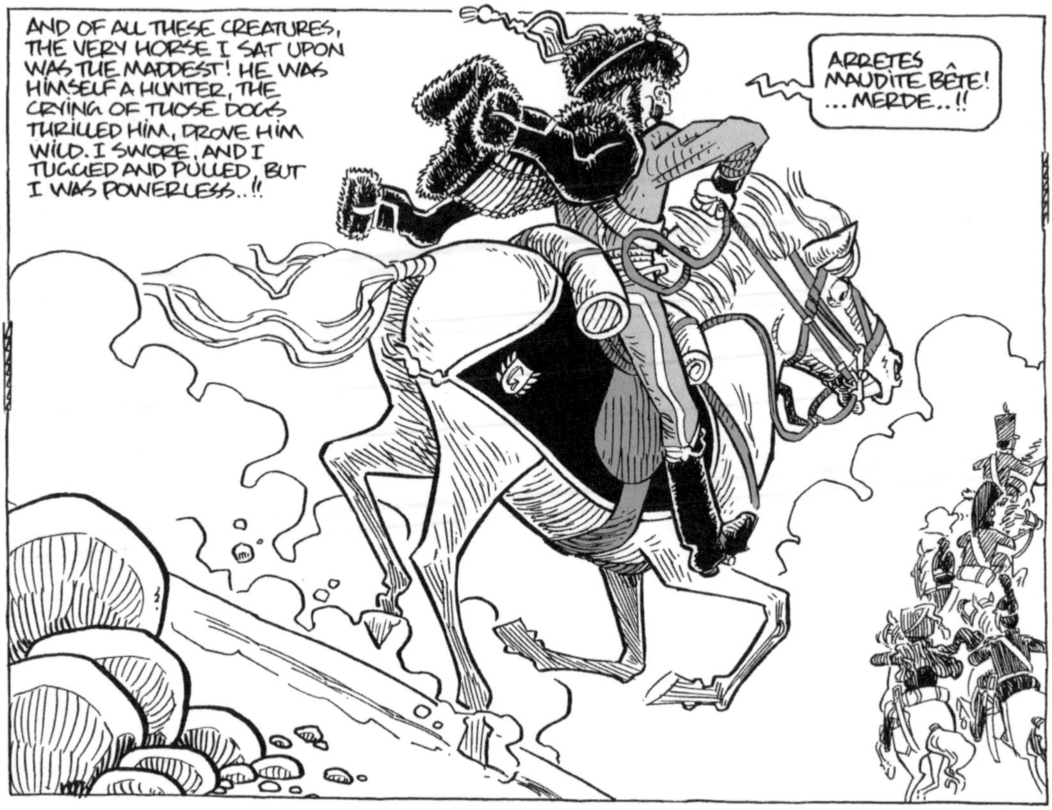
AND OF ALL THESE CREATURES, THE VERY HORSE I SAT UPON WAS THE MADDEST! HE WAS HIMSELF A HUNTER, THE CRYING OF THOSE DOGS THRILLED HIM, DROVE HIM WILD. I SWORE, AND I TUGGED AND PULLED, BUT I WAS POWERLESS..!!
ARRETES MAUDITE BÊTE! ...MERDE..!!

I WAS AS FINE A RIDER AS ANY, AND MY HORSE WAS THE BEST OF THEM ALL! IT WAS NOT LONG BEFORE HE HAD CARRIED ME TO THE FRONT...

I HAD TAKEN THE PRECAUTION OF REMOVING THE PLUME FROM MY HAT SO THAT I WOULD NOT BE RECOGNIZED.

THE IDEA THAT A FRENCH OFFICER MIGHT BE RIDING WITH THEM WAS TOO ABSURD TO ENTER THEIR MINDS!

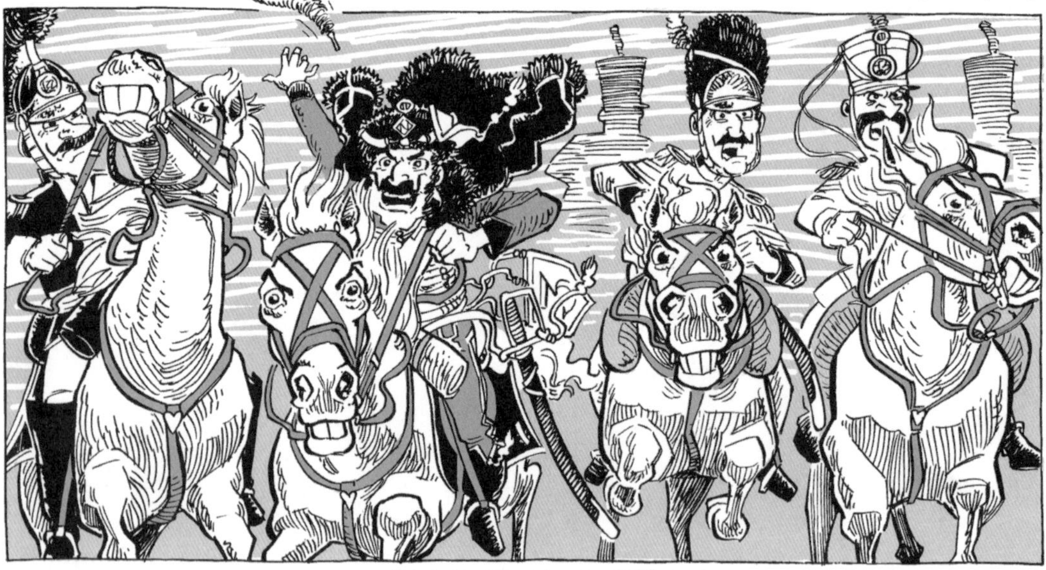

I LAUGHED AS I RODE! I, TOO, WENT MAD! I, ETIENNE GERARD..!!

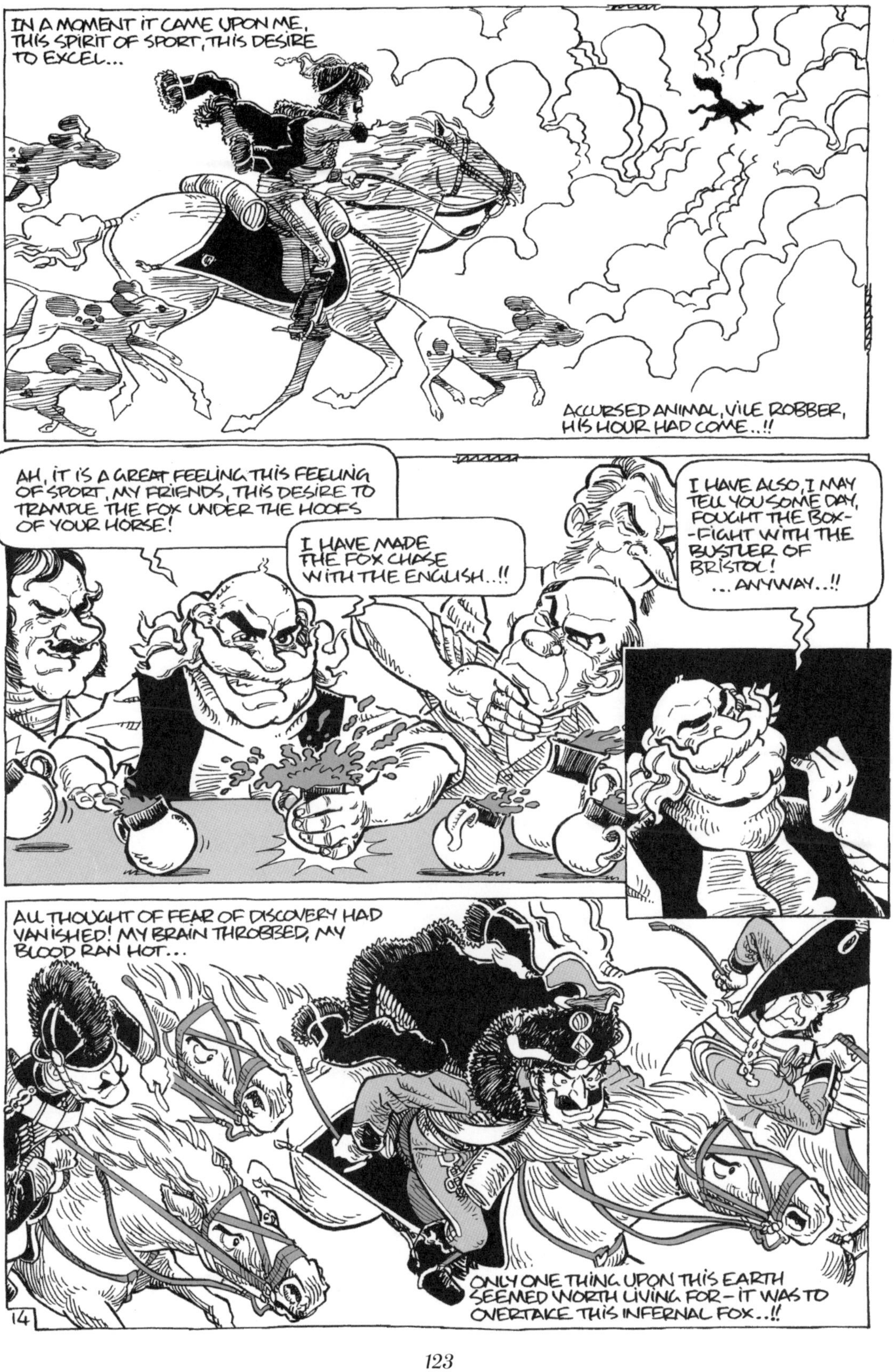
IN A MOMENT IT CAME UPON ME, THIS SPIRIT OF SPORT, THIS DESIRE TO EXCEL...
ACCURSED ANIMAL, VILE ROBBER, HIS HOUR HAD COME..!!
AH, IT IS A GREAT FEELING THIS FEELING OF SPORT, MY FRIENDS, THIS DESIRE TO TRAMPLE THE FOX UNDER THE HOOFS OF YOUR HORSE!
I HAVE MADE THE FOX CHASE WITH THE ENGLISH..!!
I HAVE ALSO, I MAY TELL YOU SOME DAY, FOUGHT THE BOX-FIGHT WITH THE BUSTLER OF BRISTOL! ...ANYWAY..!!
ALL THOUGHT OF FEAR OF DISCOVERY HAD VANISHED! MY BRAIN THROBBED, MY BLOOD RAN HOT...
ONLY ONE THING UPON THIS EARTH SEEMED WORTH LIVING FOR - IT WAS TO OVERTAKE THIS INFERNAL FOX..!!
14

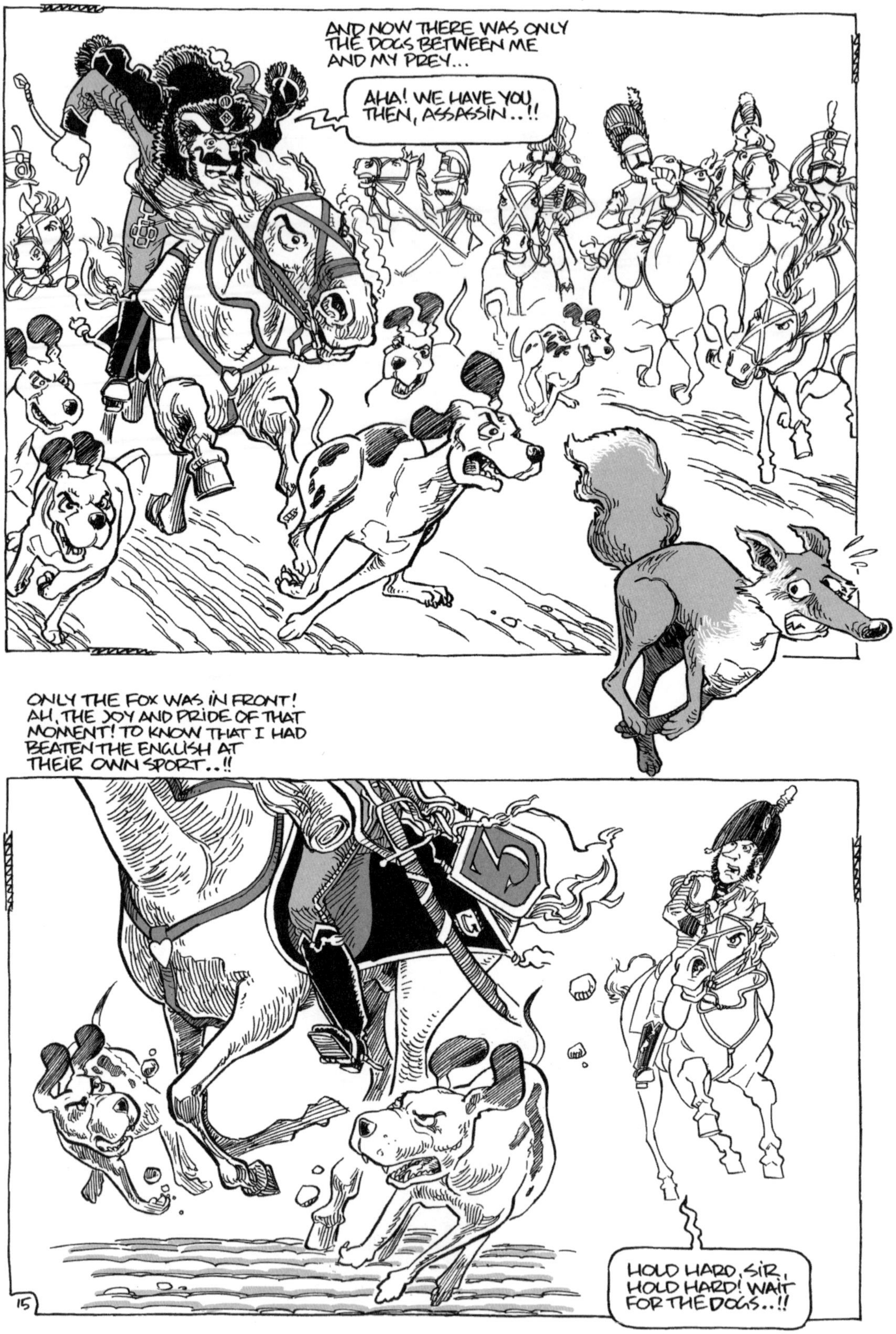
AND NOW THERE WAS ONLY THE DOGS BETWEEN ME AND MY PREY...
AHA! WE HAVE YOU, THEN, ASSASSIN..!!
ONLY THE FOX WAS IN FRONT! AH, THE JOY AND PRIDE OF THAT MOMENT! TO KNOW THAT I HAD BEATEN THE ENGLISH AT THEIR OWN SPORT..!!
15
HOLD HARD, SIR, HOLD HARD! WAIT FOR THE DOGS..!!

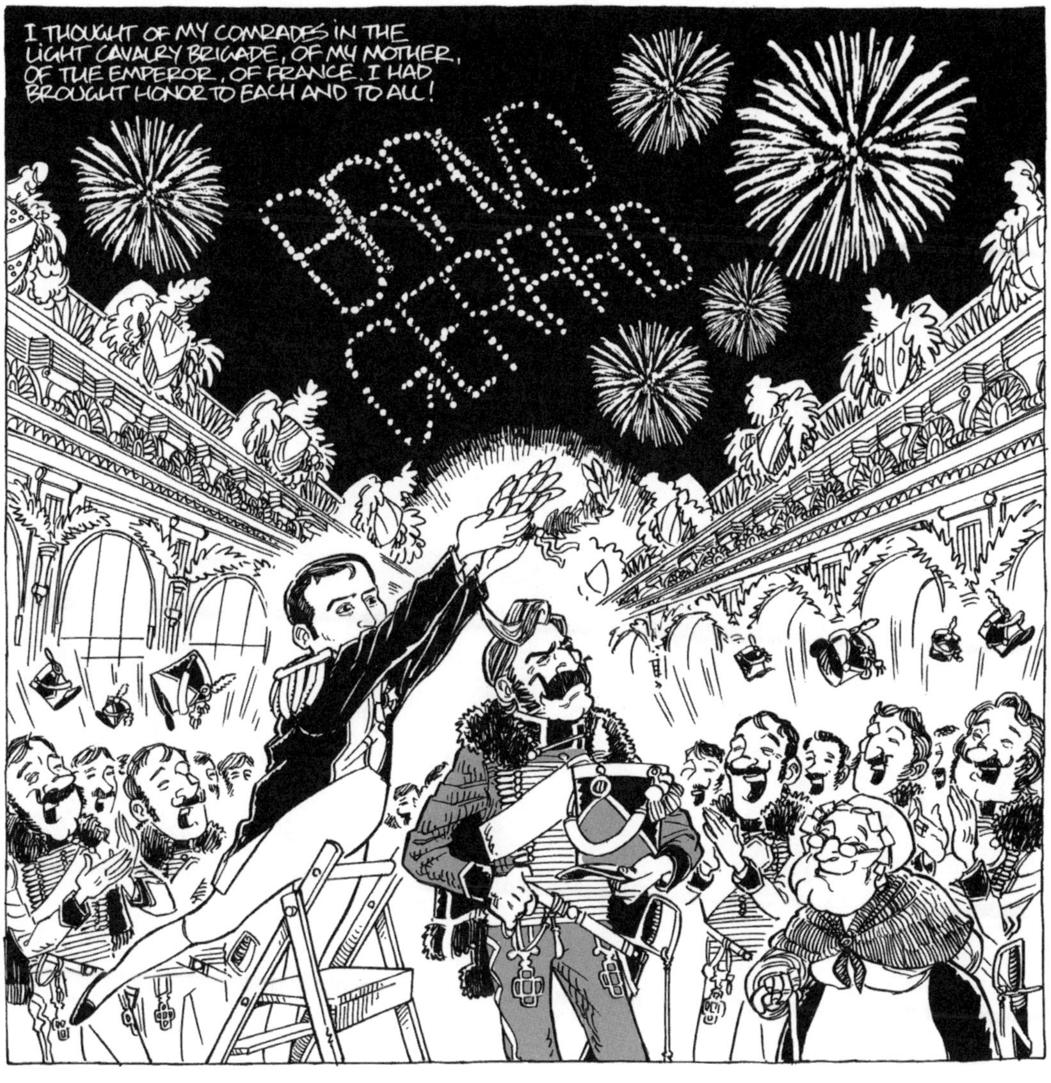
I THOUGHT OF MY COMRADES IN THE LIGHT CAVALRY BRIGADE, OF MY MOTHER, OF THE EMPEROR, OF FRANCE. I HAD BROUGHT HONOR TO EACH AND TO ALL!
BRAVO GERARD

AND THEN THE LAST SUPREME MOMENT OF TRIUMPH ARRIVED...

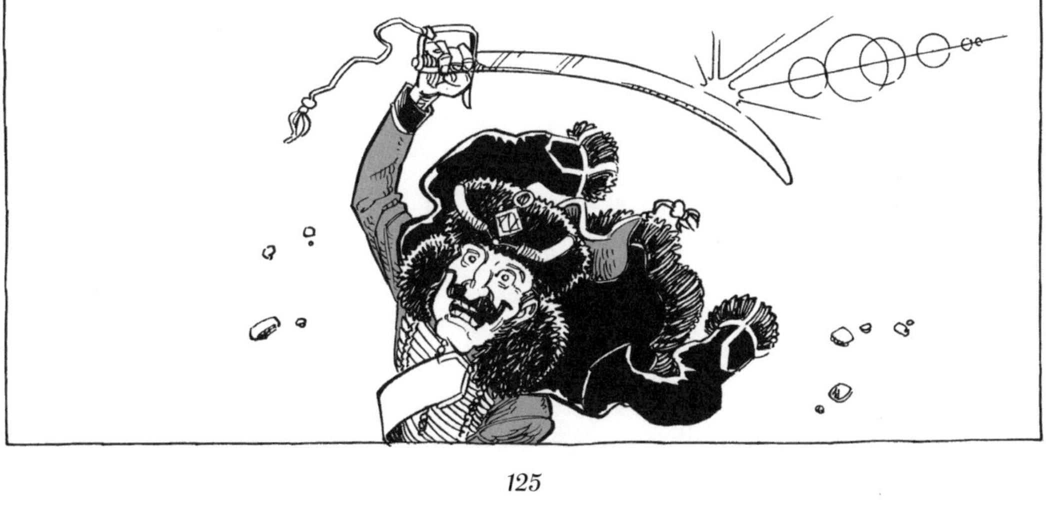

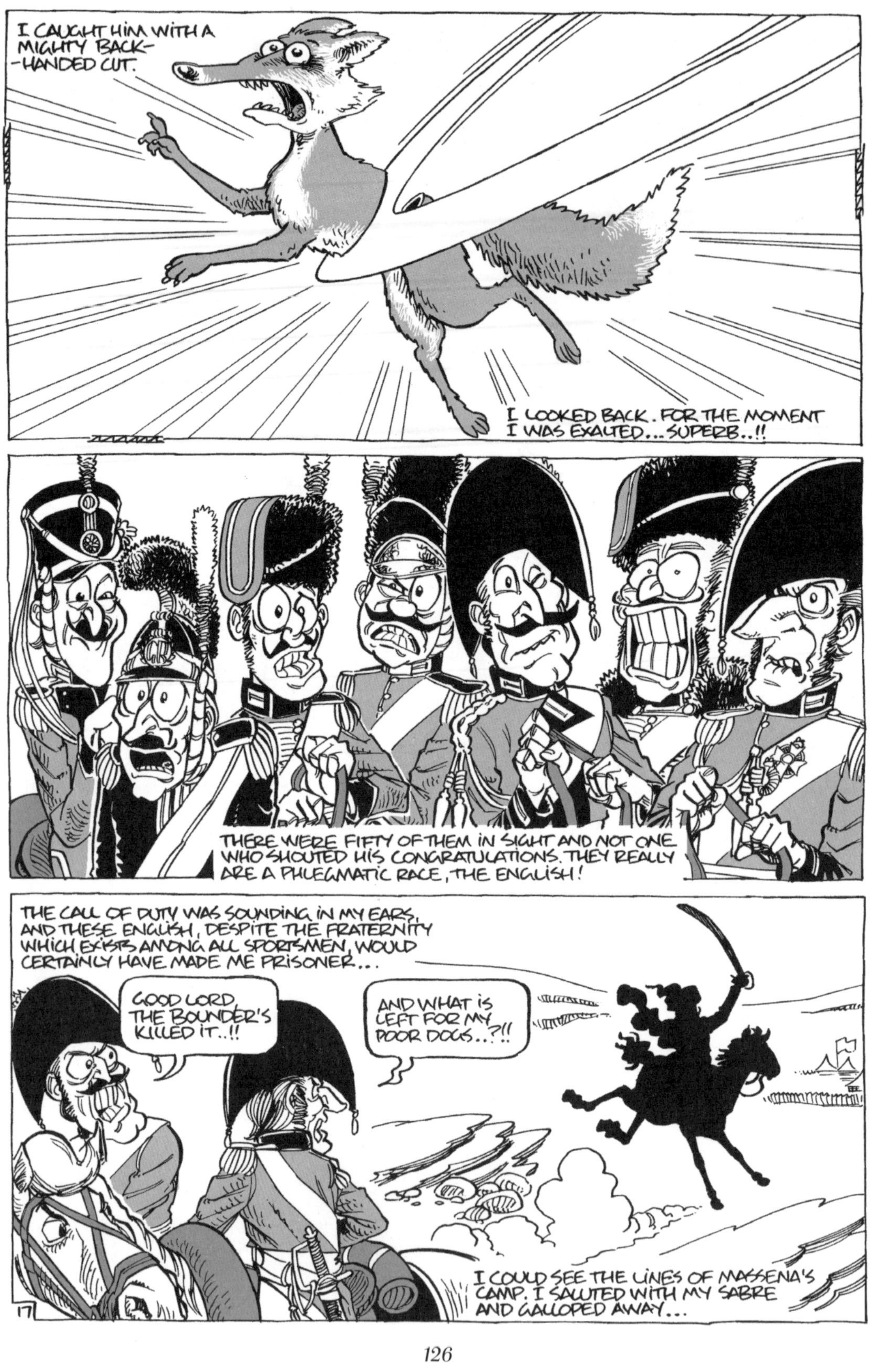
I CAUGHT HIM WITH A MIGHTY BACK-HANDED CUT.
I LOOKED BACK. FOR THE MOMENT I WAS EXALTED... SUPERB..!!
THERE WERE FIFTY OF THEM IN SIGHT AND NOT ONE WHO SHOUTED HIS CONGRATULATIONS. THEY REALLY ARE A PHLEGMATIC RACE, THE ENGLISH!
THE CALL OF DUTY WAS SOUNDING IN MY EARS, AND THESE ENGLISH, DESPITE THE FRATERNITY WHICH EXISTS AMONG ALL SPORTSMEN, WOULD CERTAINLY HAVE MADE ME PRISONER...
GOOD LORD, THE BOUNDER'S KILLED IT..!!
AND WHAT IS LEFT FOR MY POOR DOGS..?!!
I COULD SEE THE LINES OF MASSENA'S CAMP. I SALUTED WITH MY SABRE AND GALLOPED AWAY...
17

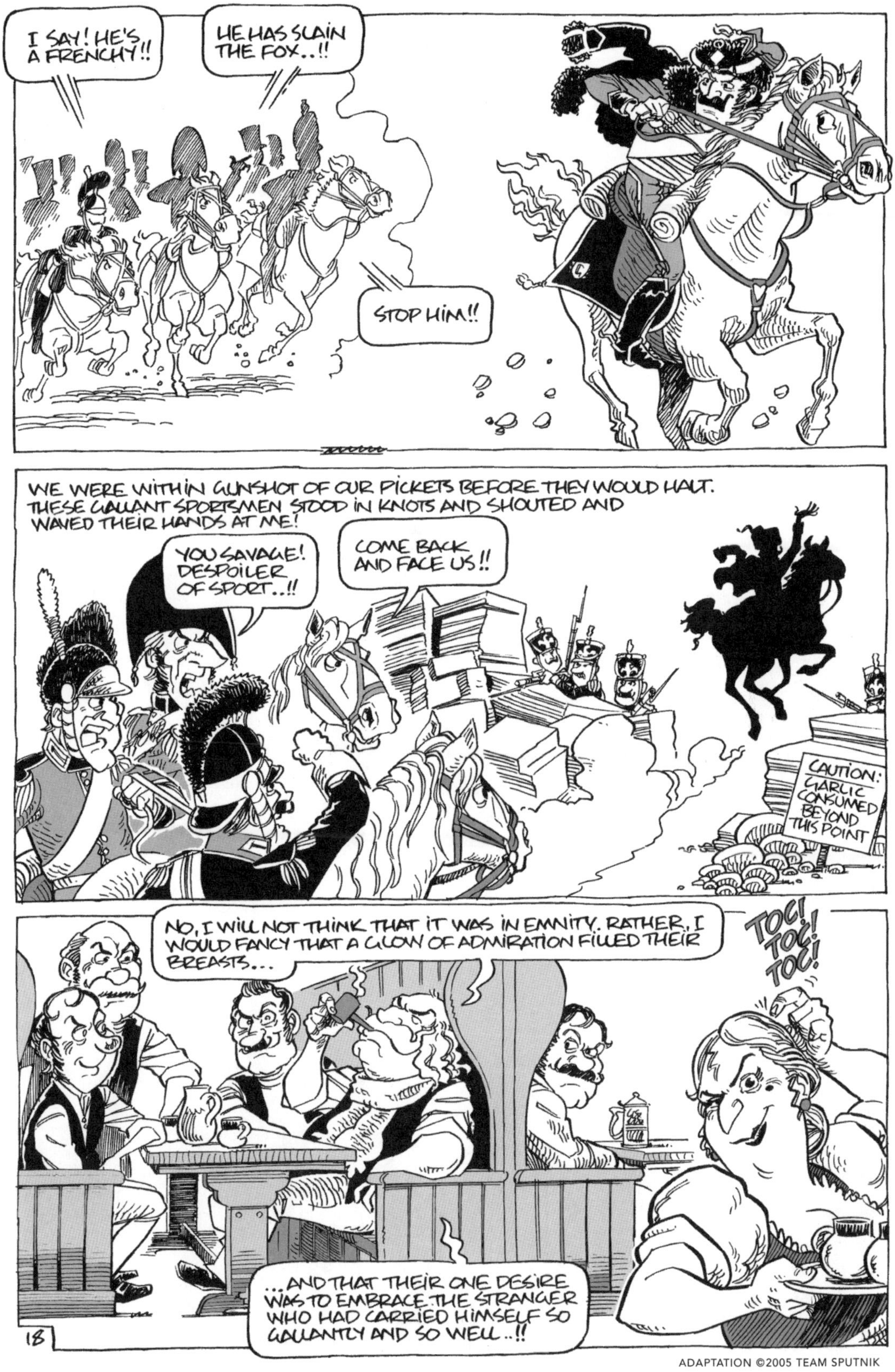
I SAY! HE'S A FRENCHY!!
HE HAS SLAIN THE FOX..!!
STOP HIM!!
WE WERE WITHIN GUNSHOT OF OUR PICKETS BEFORE THEY WOULD HALT. THESE GALLANT SPORTSMEN STOOD IN KNOTS AND SHOUTED AND WAVED THEIR HANDS AT ME!
YOU SAVAGE! DESPOILER OF SPORT..!!
COME BACK AND FACE US!!
CAUTION: GARLIC CONSUMED BEYOND THIS POINT
NO, I WILL NOT THINK THAT IT WAS IN ENMITY. RATHER, I WOULD FANCY THAT A GLOW OF ADMIRATION FILLED THEIR BREASTS...
TOC! TOC! TOC!
...AND THAT THEIR ONE DESIRE WAS TO EMBRACE THE STRANGER WHO HAD CARRIED HIMSELF SO GALLANTLY AND SO WELL..!!
18

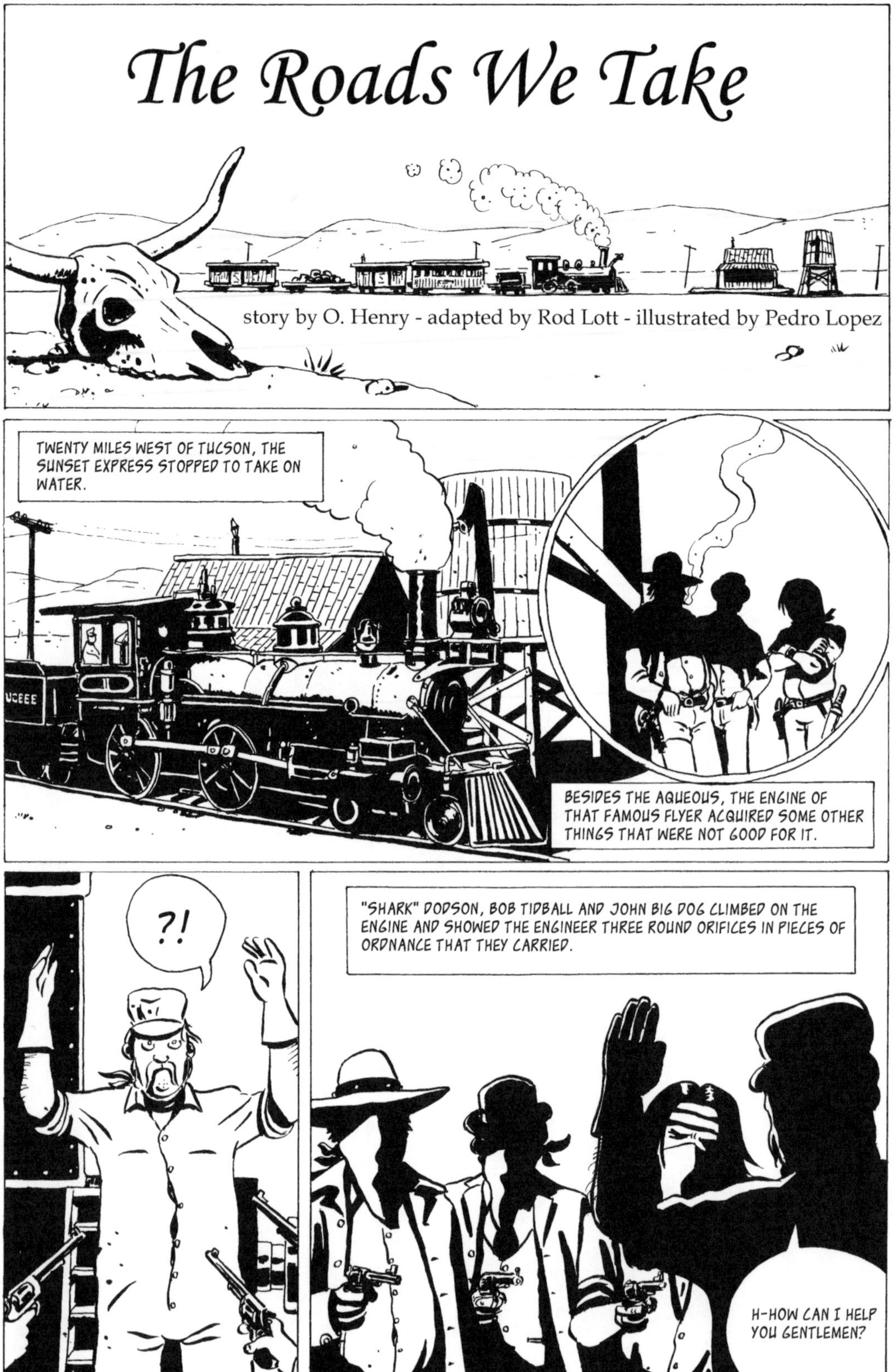
The Roads We Take
story by O. Henry - adapted by Rod Lott - illustrated by Pedro Lopez
TWENTY MILES WEST OF TUCSON, THE SUNSET EXPRESS STOPPED TO TAKE ON WATER.
BESIDES THE AQUEOUS, THE ENGINE OF THAT FAMOUS FLYER ACQUIRED SOME OTHER THINGS THAT WERE NOT GOOD FOR IT.
?!
"SHARK" DODSON, BOB TIDBALL AND JOHN BIG DOG CLIMBED ON THE ENGINE AND SHOWED THE ENGINEER THREE ROUND ORIFICES IN PIECES OF ORDNANCE THAT THEY CARRIED.
H-HOW CAN I HELP YOU GENTLEMEN?

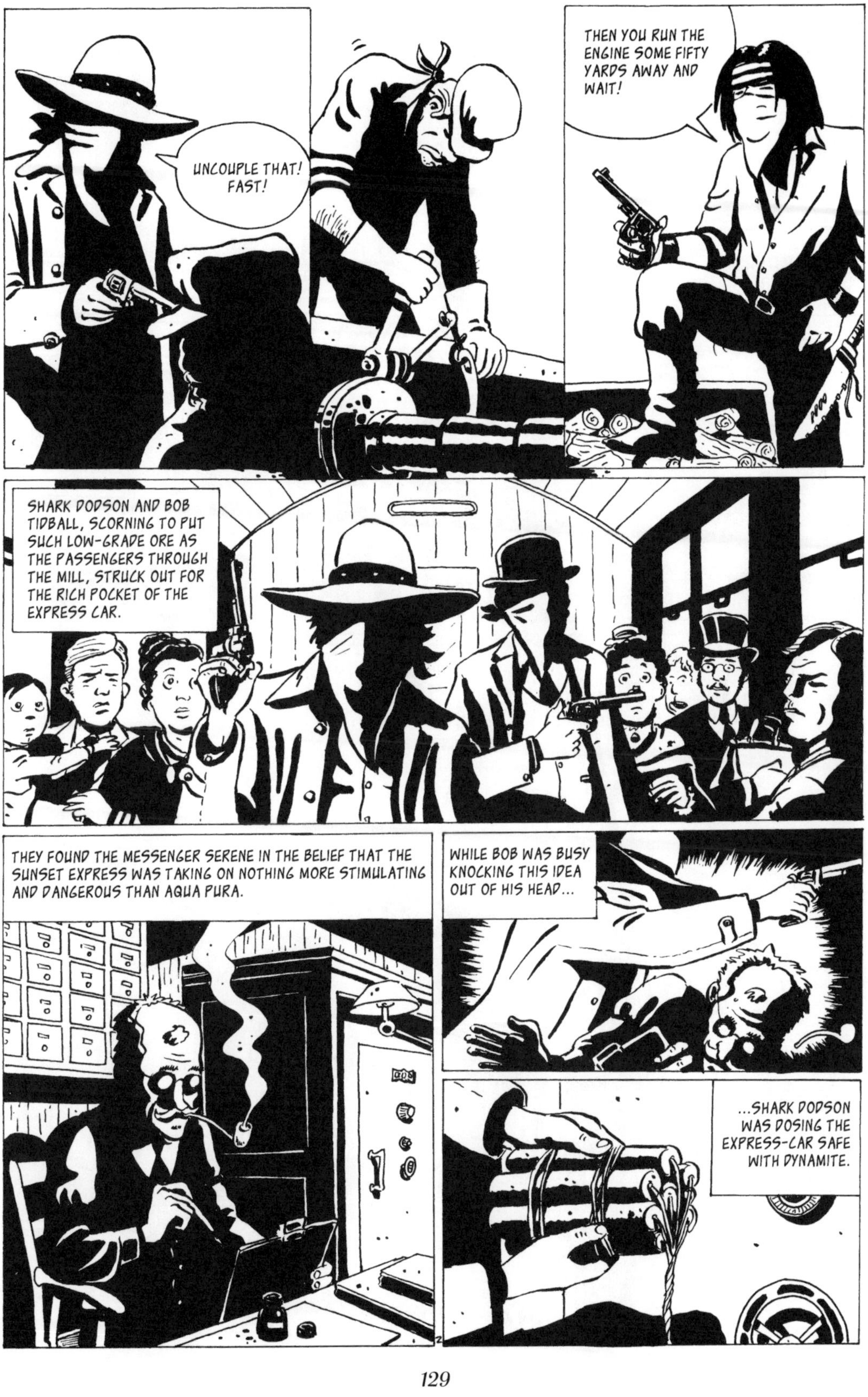
UNCOUPLE THAT! FAST!
THEN YOU RUN THE ENGINE SOME FIFTY YARDS AWAY AND WAIT!
SHARK DODSON AND BOB TIDBALL, SCORNING TO PUT SUCH LOW-GRADE ORE AS THE PASSENGERS THROUGH THE MILL, STRUCK OUT FOR THE RICH POCKET OF THE EXPRESS CAR.
THEY FOUND THE MESSENGER SERENE IN THE BELIEF THAT THE SUNSET EXPRESS WAS TAKING ON NOTHING MORE STIMULATING AND DANGEROUS THAN AQUA PURA.
WHILE BOB WAS BUSY KNOCKING THIS IDEA OUT OF HIS HEAD...
...SHARK DODSON WAS DOSING THE EXPRESS-CAR SAFE WITH DYNAMITE.

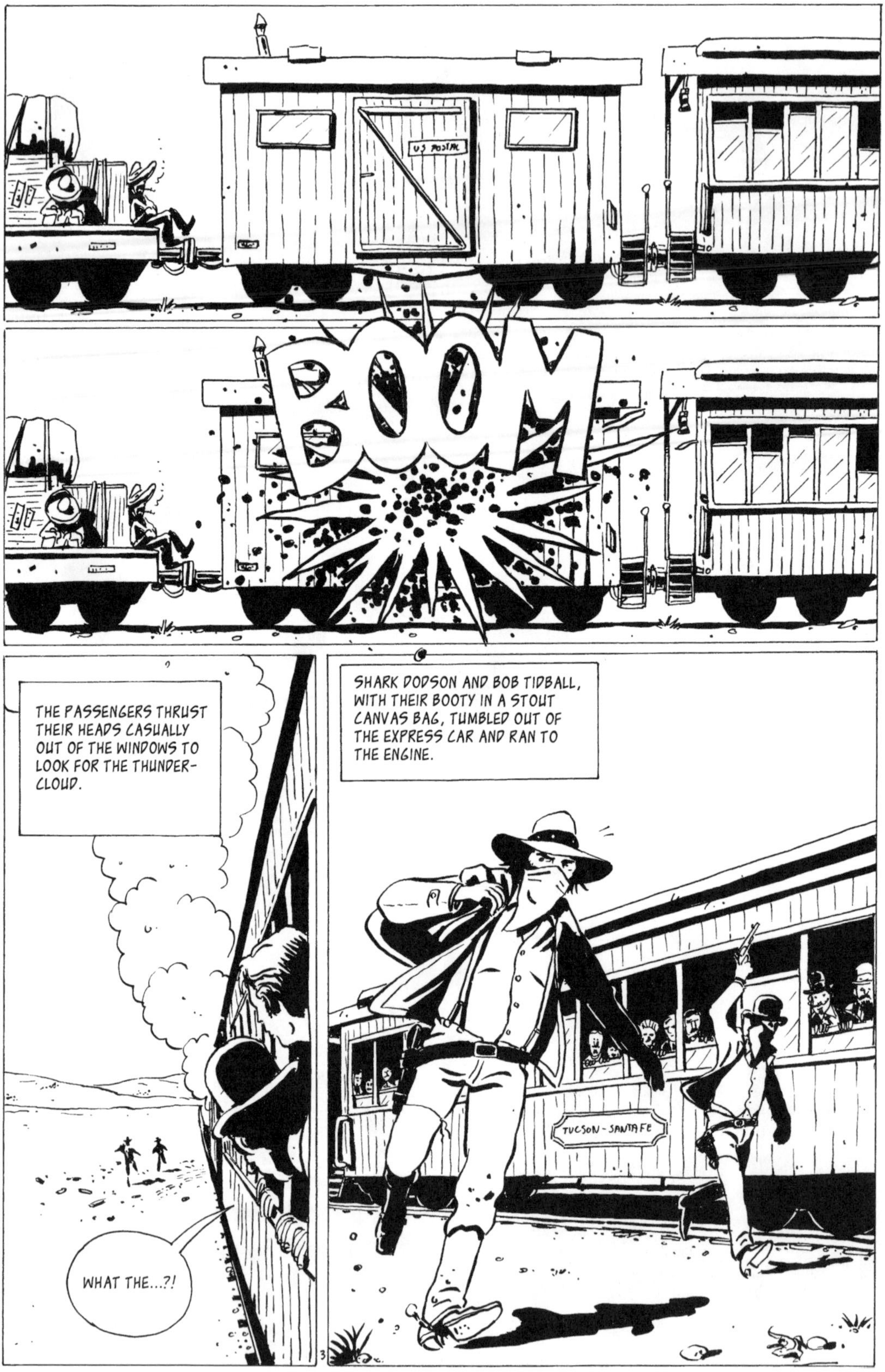
US POSTAL
BOOM
THE PASSENGERS THRUST THEIR HEADS CASUALLY OUT OF THE WINDOWS TO LOOK FOR THE THUNDER-CLOUD.
WHAT THE...?!
SHARK DODSON AND BOB TIDBALL, WITH THEIR BOOTY IN A STOUT CANVAS BAG, TUMBLED OUT OF THE EXPRESS CAR AND RAN TO THE ENGINE.
TUCSON-SANTAFE

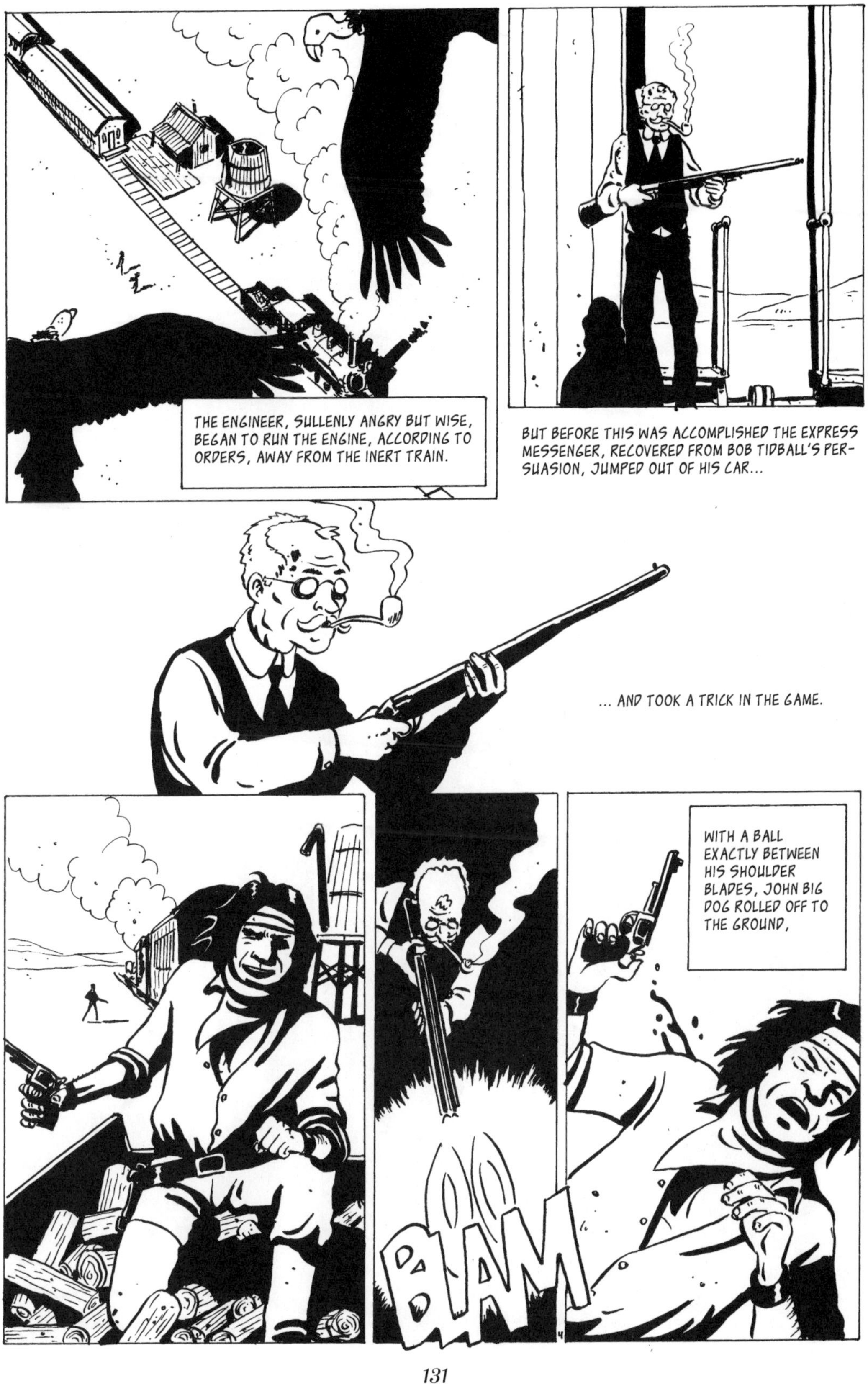
THE ENGINEER, SULLENLY ANGRY BUT WISE, BEGAN TO RUN THE ENGINE, ACCORDING TO ORDERS, AWAY FROM THE INERT TRAIN.
BUT BEFORE THIS WAS ACCOMPLISHED THE EXPRESS MESSENGER, RECOVERED FROM BOB TIDBALL'S PER-SUASION, JUMPED OUT OF HIS CAR...
... AND TOOK A TRICK IN THE GAME.
BLAM
WITH A BALL EXACTLY BETWEEN HIS SHOULDER BLADES, JOHN BIG DOG ROLLED OFF TO THE GROUND,

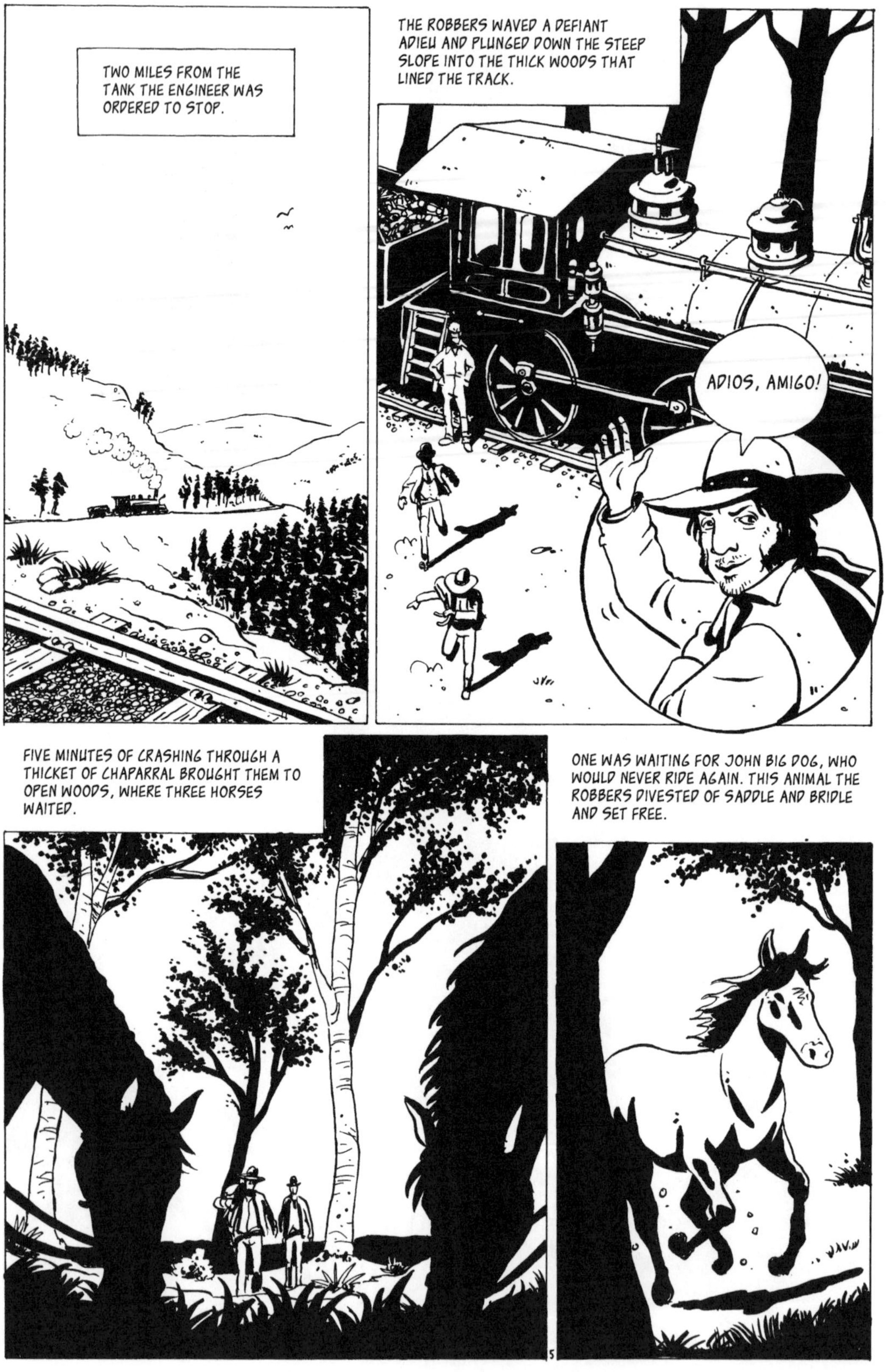
TWO MILES FROM THE TANK THE ENGINEER WAS ORDERED TO STOP.
THE ROBBERS WAVED A DEFIANT ADIEU AND PLUNGED DOWN THE STEEP SLOPE INTO THE THICK WOODS THAT LINED THE TRACK.
ADIOS, AMIGO!
FIVE MINUTES OF CRASHING THROUGH A THICKET OF CHAPARRAL BROUGHT THEM TO OPEN WOODS, WHERE THREE HORSES WAITED.
ONE WAS WAITING FOR JOHN BIG DOG, WHO WOULD NEVER RIDE AGAIN. THIS ANIMAL THE ROBBERS DIVESTED OF SADDLE AND BRIDLE AND SET FREE.

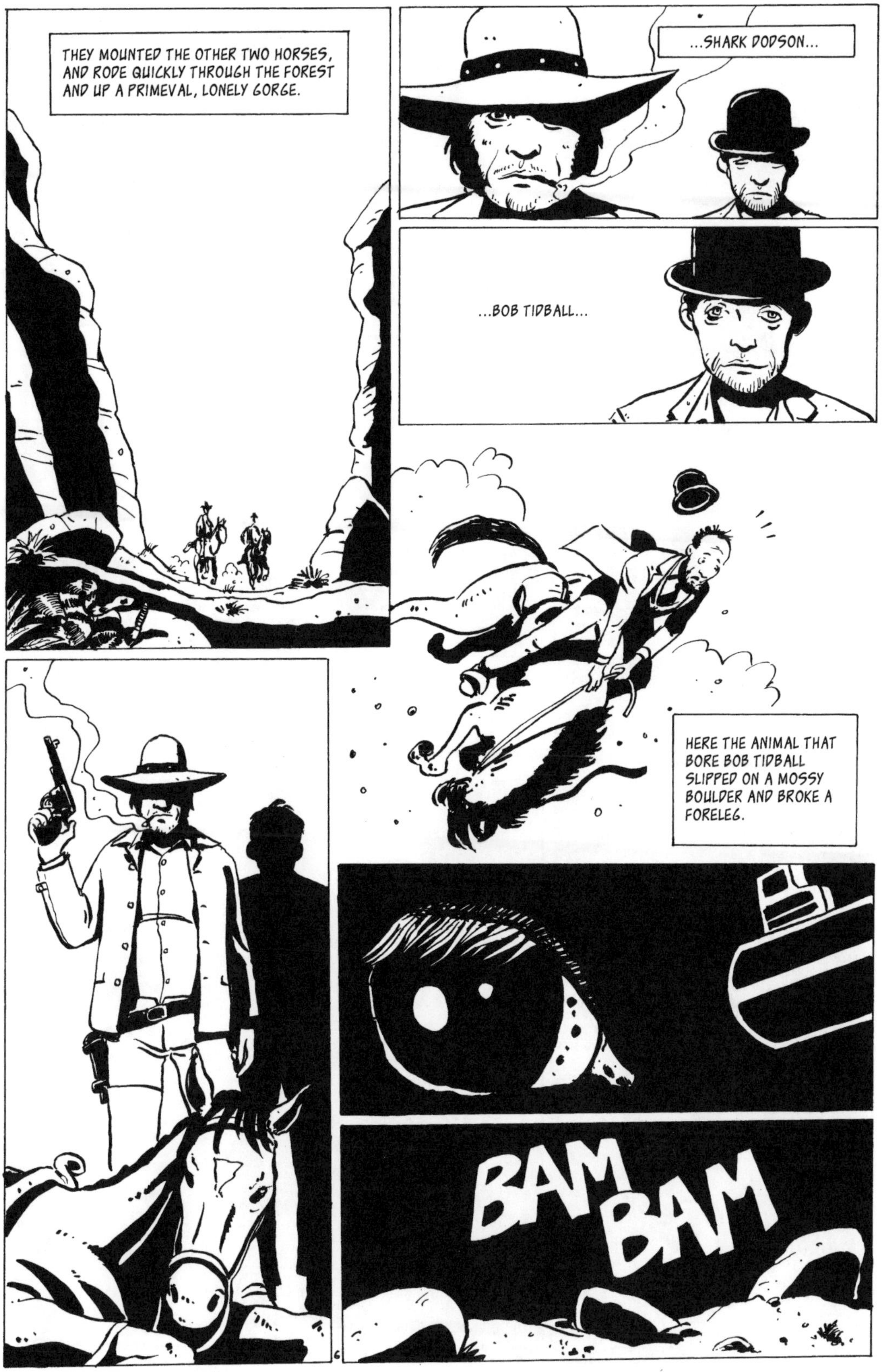
THEY MOUNTED THE OTHER TWO HORSES, AND RODE QUICKLY THROUGH THE FOREST AND UP A PRIMEVAL, LONELY GORGE.
...SHARK DODSON...
...BOB TIDBALL...
HERE THE ANIMAL THAT BORE BOB TIDBALL SLIPPED ON A MOSSY BOULDER AND BROKE A FORELEG.
BAM
BAM

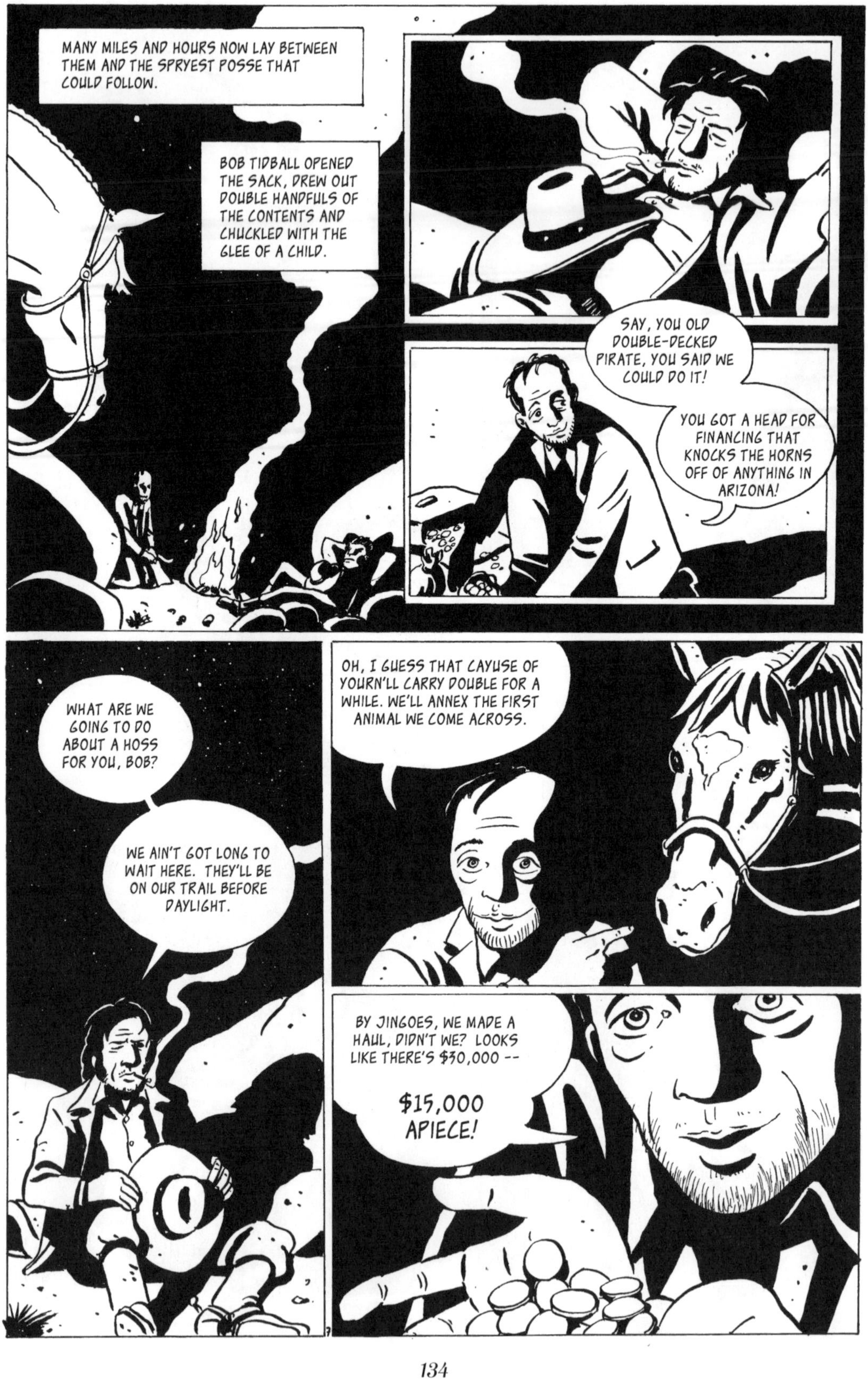
MANY MILES AND HOURS NOW LAY BETWEEN THEM AND THE SPRYEST POSSE THAT COULD FOLLOW.
BOB TIDBALL OPENED THE SACK, DREW OUT DOUBLE HANDFULS OF THE CONTENTS AND CHUCKLED WITH THE GLEE OF A CHILD.
SAY, YOU OLD DOUBLE-DECKED PIRATE, YOU SAID WE COULD DO IT!
YOU GOT A HEAD FOR FINANCING THAT KNOCKS THE HORNS OFF OF ANYTHING IN ARIZONA!
WHAT ARE WE GOING TO DO ABOUT A HOSS FOR YOU, BOB?
WE AIN'T GOT LONG TO WAIT HERE. THEY'LL BE ON OUR TRAIL BEFORE DAYLIGHT.
OH, I GUESS THAT CAYUSE OF YOURN'LL CARRY DOUBLE FOR A WHILE. WE'LL ANNEX THE FIRST ANIMAL WE COME ACROSS.
BY JINGOES, WE MADE A HAUL, DIDN'T WE? LOOKS LIKE THERE'S $30,000 --
$15,000 APIECE!

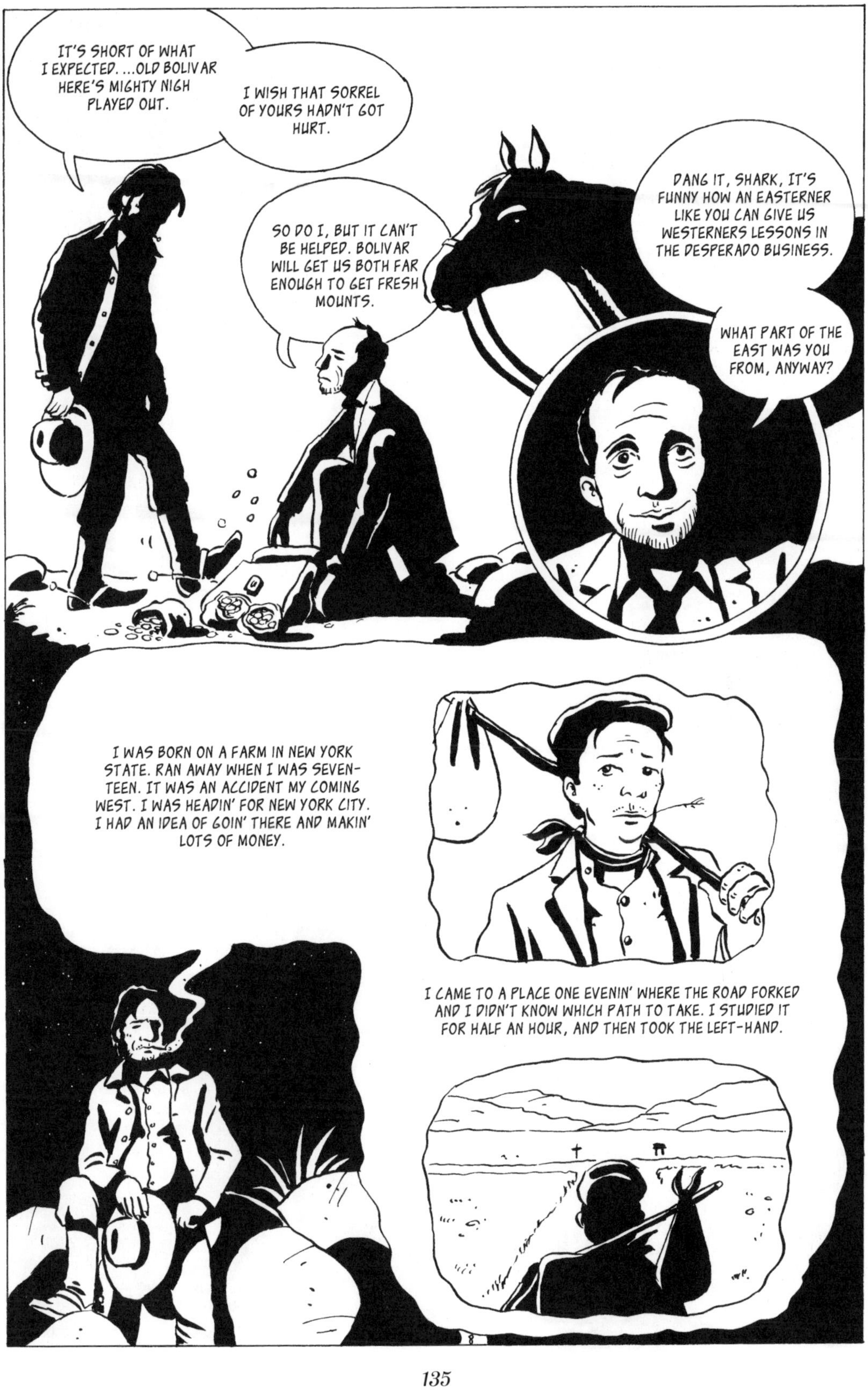
IT'S SHORT OF WHAT I EXPECTED. ...OLD BOLIVAR HERE'S MIGHTY NIGH PLAYED OUT.
I WISH THAT SORREL OF YOURS HADN'T GOT HURT.
SO DO I, BUT IT CAN'T BE HELPED. BOLIVAR WILL GET US BOTH FAR ENOUGH TO GET FRESH MOUNTS.
DANG IT, SHARK, IT'S FUNNY HOW AN EASTERNER LIKE YOU CAN GIVE US WESTERNERS LESSONS IN THE DESPERADO BUSINESS.
WHAT PART OF THE EAST WAS YOU FROM, ANYWAY?
I WAS BORN ON A FARM IN NEW YORK STATE. RAN AWAY WHEN I WAS SEVENTEEN. IT WAS AN ACCIDENT MY COMING WEST. I WAS HEADIN' FOR NEW YORK CITY. I HAD AN IDEA OF GOIN' THERE AND MAKIN' LOTS OF MONEY.
I CAME TO A PLACE ONE EVENIN' WHERE THE ROAD FORKED AND I DIDN'T KNOW WHICH PATH TO TAKE. I STUDIED IT FOR HALF AN HOUR, AND THEN TOOK THE LEFT-HAND.

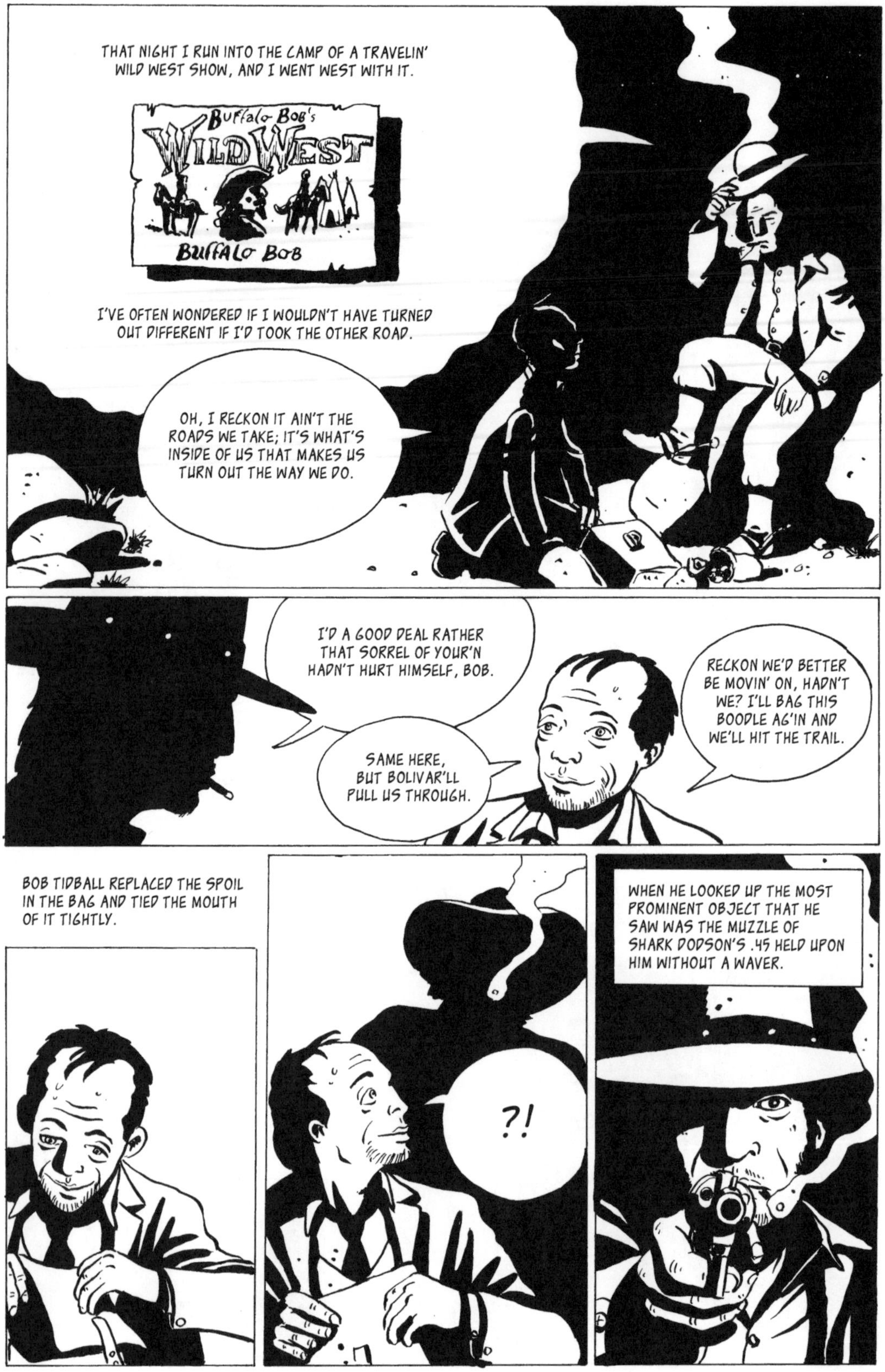
THAT NIGHT I RUN INTO THE CAMP OF A TRAVELIN' WILD WEST SHOW, AND I WENT WEST WITH IT.
Buffalo Bob's WILD WEST BUFFALO BOB
I'VE OFTEN WONDERED IF I WOULDN'T HAVE TURNED OUT DIFFERENT IF I'D TOOK THE OTHER ROAD.
OH, I RECKON IT AIN'T THE ROADS WE TAKE; IT'S WHAT'S INSIDE OF US THAT MAKES US TURN OUT THE WAY WE DO.
I'D A GOOD DEAL RATHER THAT SORREL OF YOUR'N HADN'T HURT HIMSELF, BOB.
SAME HERE, BUT BOLIVAR'LL PULL US THROUGH.
RECKON WE'D BETTER BE MOVIN' ON, HADN'T WE? I'LL BAG THIS BOODLE AG'IN AND WE'LL HIT THE TRAIL.
BOB TIDBALL REPLACED THE SPOIL IN THE BAG AND TIED THE MOUTH OF IT TIGHTLY.
?!
WHEN HE LOOKED UP THE MOST PROMINENT OBJECT THAT HE SAW WAS THE MUZZLE OF SHARK DODSON'S .45 HELD UPON HIM WITHOUT A WAVER.

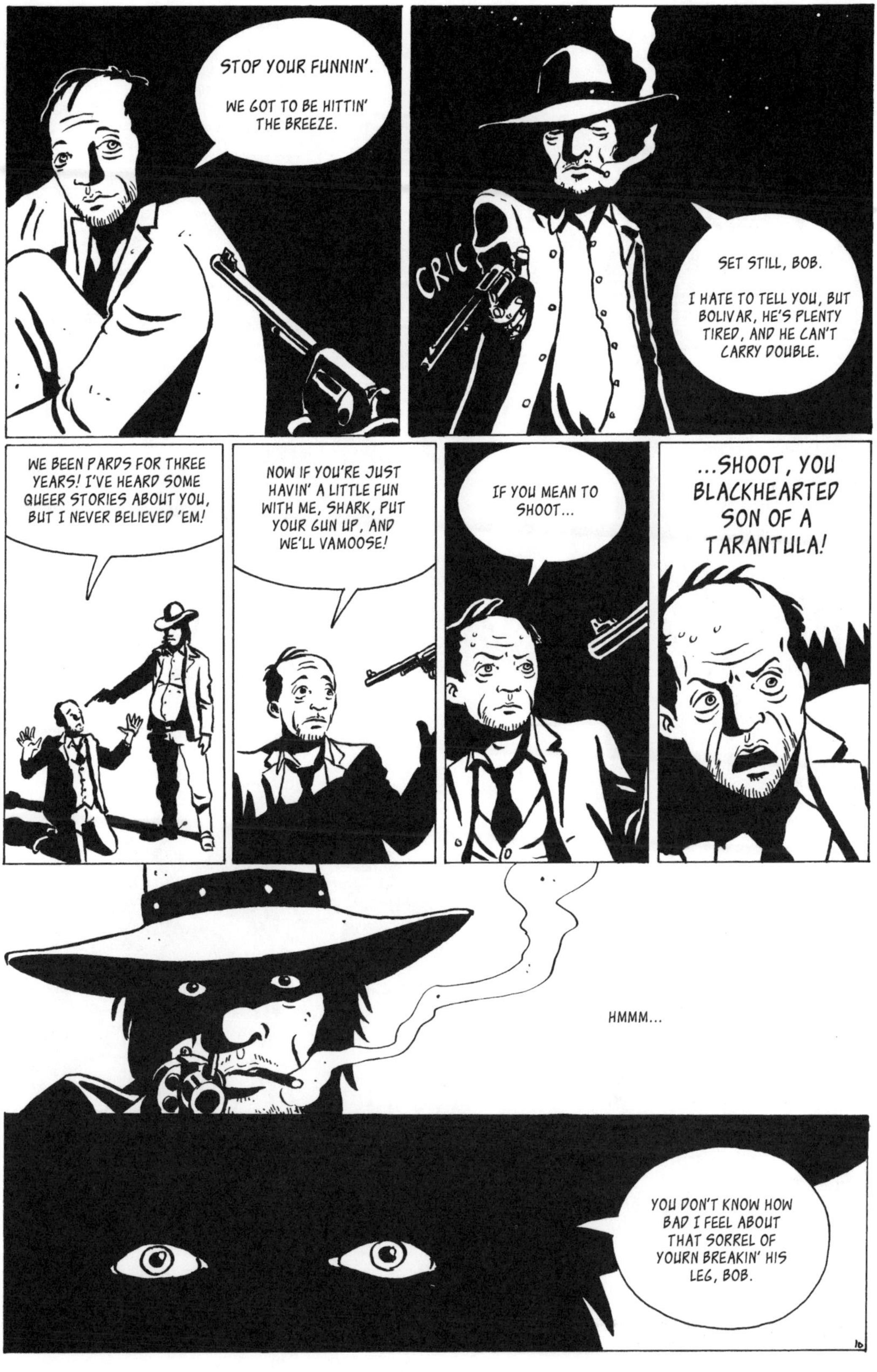
STOP YOUR FUNNIN'.
WE GOT TO BE HITTIN' THE BREEZE.
CRIC
SET STILL, BOB.
I HATE TO TELL YOU, BUT BOLIVAR, HE'S PLENTY TIRED, AND HE CAN'T CARRY DOUBLE.
WE BEEN PARDS FOR THREE YEARS! I'VE HEARD SOME QUEER STORIES ABOUT YOU, BUT I NEVER BELIEVED 'EM!
NOW IF YOU'RE JUST HAVIN' A LITTLE FUN WITH ME, SHARK, PUT YOUR GUN UP, AND WE'LL VAMOOSE!
IF YOU MEAN TO SHOOT...
...SHOOT, YOU BLACKHEARTED SON OF A TARANTULA!
HMMM...
YOU DON'T KNOW HOW BAD I FEEL ABOUT THAT SORREL OF YOURN BREAKIN' HIS LEG, BOB.
10

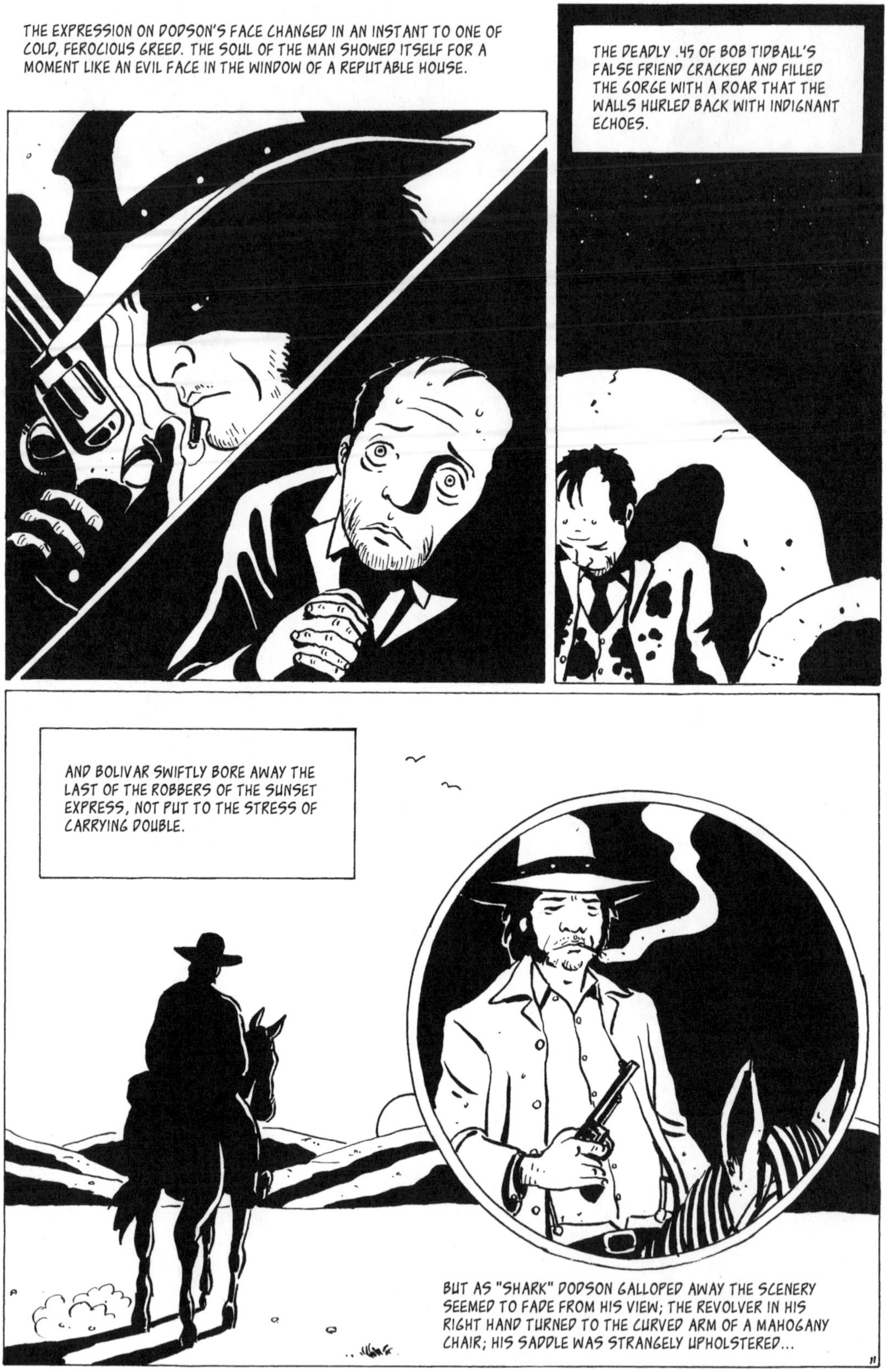
THE EXPRESSION ON DODSON'S FACE CHANGED IN AN INSTANT TO ONE OF COLD, FEROCIOUS GREED. THE SOUL OF THE MAN SHOWED ITSELF FOR A MOMENT LIKE AN EVIL FACE IN THE WINDOW OF A REPUTABLE HOUSE.
THE DEADLY .45 OF BOB TIDBALL'S FALSE FRIEND CRACKED AND FILLED THE GORGE WITH A ROAR THAT THE WALLS HURLED BACK WITH INDIGNANT ECHOES.
AND BOLIVAR SWIFTLY BORE AWAY THE LAST OF THE ROBBERS OF THE SUNSET EXPRESS, NOT PUT TO THE STRESS OF CARRYING DOUBLE.
BUT AS "SHARK" DODSON GALLOPED AWAY THE SCENERY SEEMED TO FADE FROM HIS VIEW; THE REVOLVER IN HIS RIGHT HAND TURNED TO THE CURVED ARM OF A MAHOGANY CHAIR; HIS SADDLE WAS STRANGELY UPHOLSTERED...

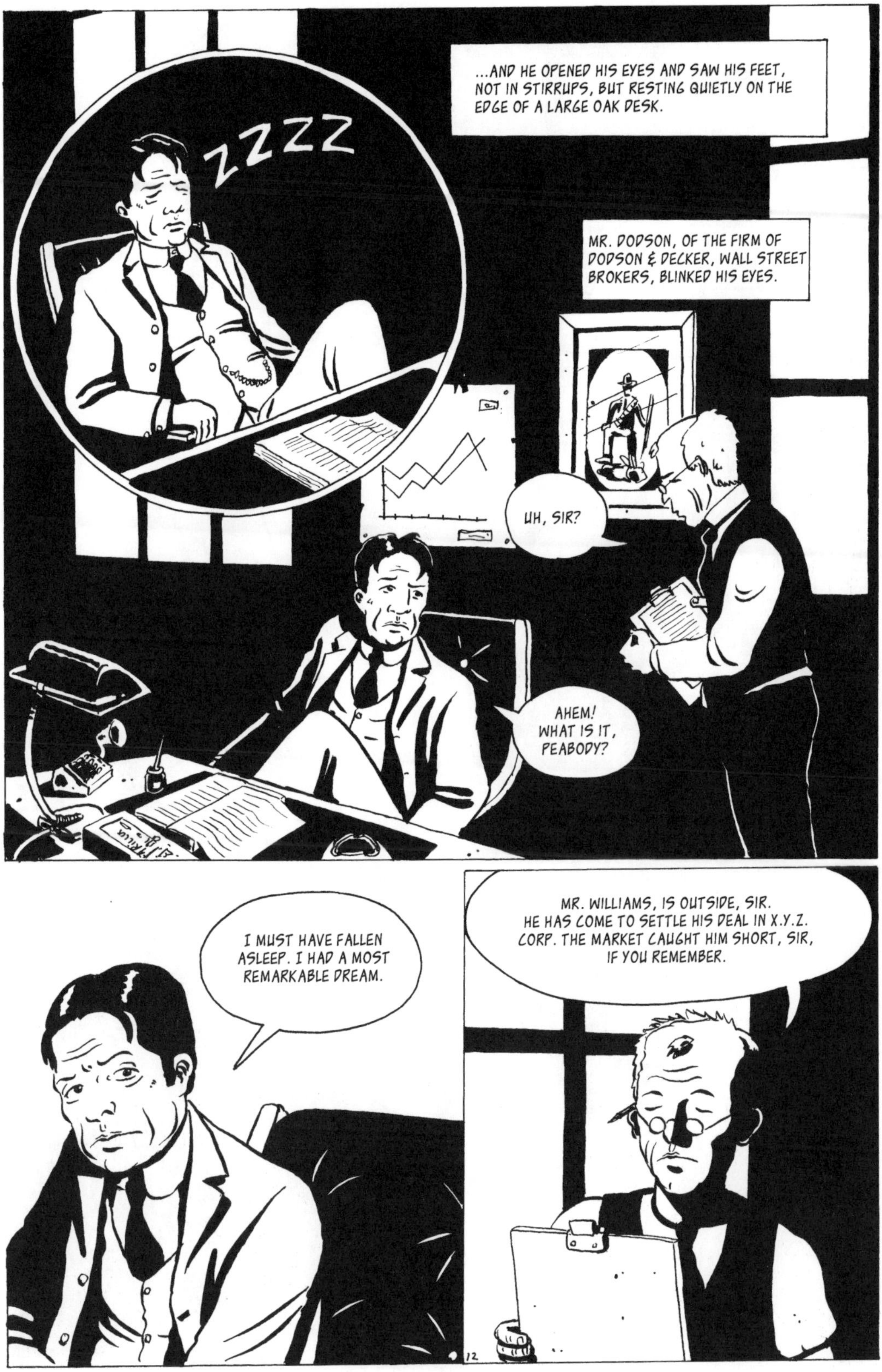
...AND HE OPENED HIS EYES AND SAW HIS FEET, NOT IN STIRRUPS, BUT RESTING QUIETLY ON THE EDGE OF A LARGE OAK DESK.
ZZZZ
MR. DODSON, OF THE FIRM OF DODSON & DECKER, WALL STREET BROKERS, BLINKED HIS EYES.
UH, SIR?
AHEM! WHAT IS IT, PEABODY?
I MUST HAVE FALLEN ASLEEP. I HAD A MOST REMARKABLE DREAM.
MR. WILLIAMS, IS OUTSIDE, SIR. HE HAS COME TO SETTLE HIS DEAL IN X.Y.Z. CORP. THE MARKET CAUGHT HIM SHORT, SIR, IF YOU REMEMBER.

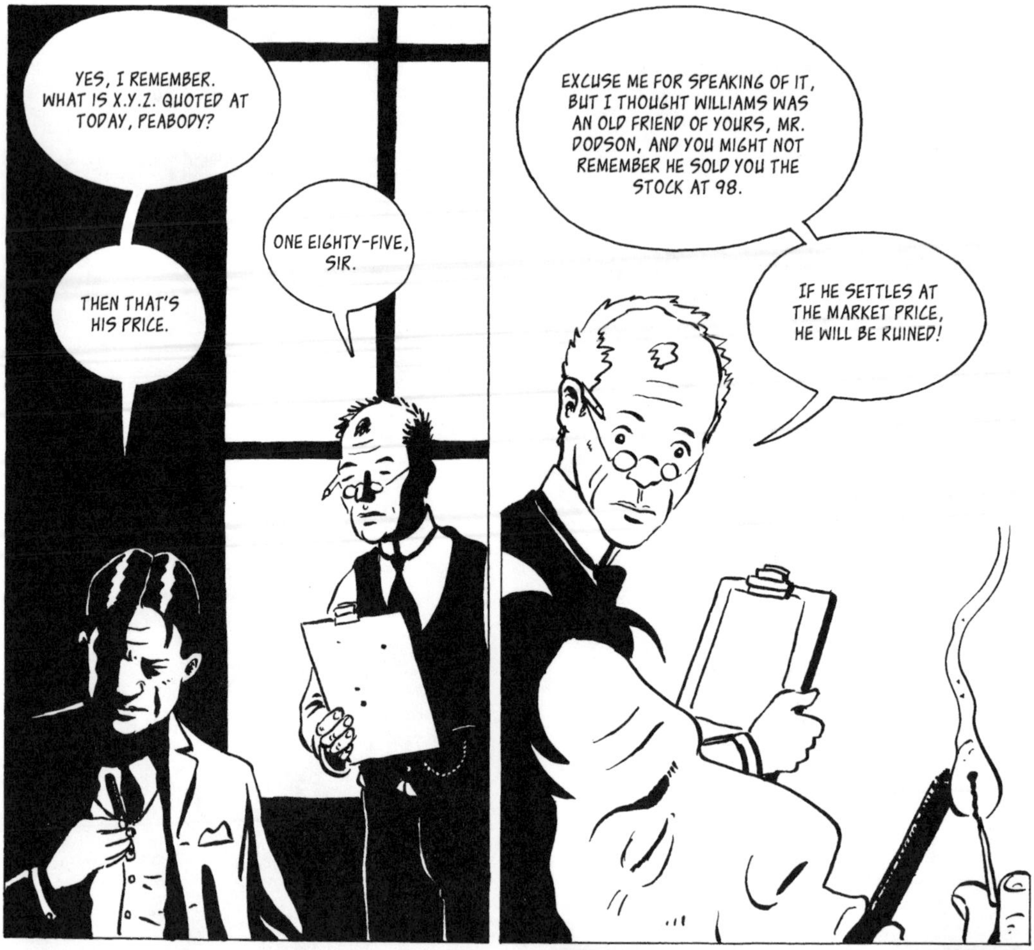
YES, I REMEMBER. WHAT IS X.Y.Z. QUOTED AT TODAY, PEABODY?
ONE EIGHTY-FIVE, SIR.
THEN THAT'S HIS PRICE.
EXCUSE ME FOR SPEAKING OF IT, BUT I THOUGHT WILLIAMS WAS AN OLD FRIEND OF YOURS, MR. DODSON, AND YOU MIGHT NOT REMEMBER HE SOLD YOU THE STOCK AT 98.
IF HE SETTLES AT THE MARKET PRICE, HE WILL BE RUINED!

THE EXPRESSION ON DODSON'S FACE CHANGED IN AN INSTANT TO ONE OF COLD, FEROCIOUS GREED. THE SOUL OF THE MAN SHOWED ITSELF FOR A MOMENT LIKE AN EVIL FACE IN THE WINDOW OF A REPUTABLE HOUSE.

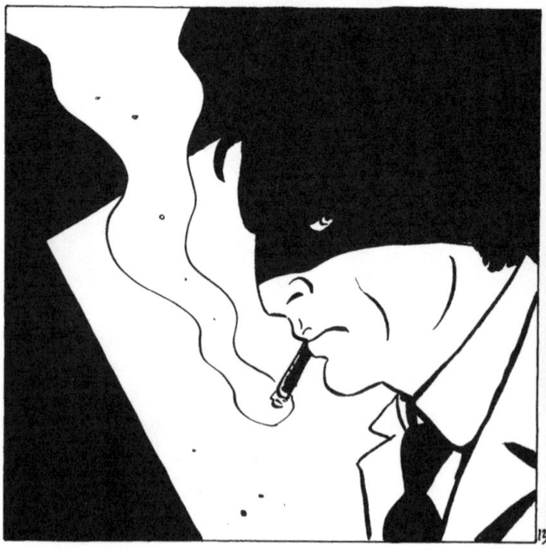

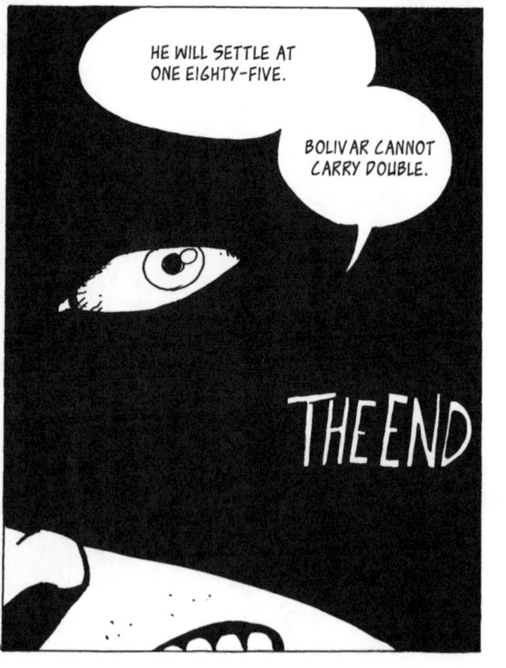
HE WILL SETTLE AT ONE EIGHTY-FIVE.
BOLIVAR CANNOT CARRY DOUBLE.
THE END

CHRIS MOORE (cover)

English artist Chris Moore is one of the premier illustrators of science fiction working today. In 1974 he did his first SF covers, for books by Alfred Bester and Philip K. Dick. He has specialized in the field ever since, and the roster of his covers reads like a Who's Who of the SF elite, including Isaac Asimov, Larry Niven, Frederick Pohl, Anne McCaffrey, Clifford D. Simak, Kurt Vonnegut, J.G. Ballard, Arthur C. Clarke and Samuel R. Delany. Chris Moore's art is featured in Graphic Classics: H.G. Wells, Rosebud 23, and in Fantasy Art Masters (1999, Watson-Guptill). Journeyman, a collection of his work, was published in 2000 by Paper Tiger. His website can be found at www.illust.demon.co.uk.

DON MARQUEZ (pages 1, 37, back cover)

Don, sometimes known as Donnie Jupiter, has been creating comics since 1985. In addition to The Lost World, which was reprinted in Graphic Classics: Arthur Conan Doyle, he adapted a second Professor Challenger adventure, The Poison Belt, in 1997. These books, plus Tiger Woman, The Nostradamus Chronicles, The Realm and The Land, are available from Caliber Press (www.calibercomics.com). Don is also a musician and painter. Selections from his Retro-Blast portfolio of space opera illustrations appeared in Rosebud 24. You can view the complete portfolio and other work by Don at www.cartuneland.com.

ROBERT LOUIS STEVENSON (page 2)

Novelist, essayist and poet, Robert Louis Stevenson is one of the world's most popular and beloved authors. Born in Edinburgh, Scotland in 1850, Stevenson was plagued with pulmonary trouble and ill health throughout his short life. He briefly studied engineering and law in college, but left school to travel and began his writing career with An Inland Voyage in 1879. His first major success was Treasure Island in 1881, followed quickly by A Child's Garden of Verses, Dr. Jekyll & Mr. Hyde, Kidnapped and more bestselling novels and collections. In 1880 he married Fanny Van de Grift Osbourne, and later collaborated on several books with his stepson, Lloyd Osbourne. The family moved to Samoa in 1888, seeking relief for Stevenson's health. His final novel, Weir of Hermiston, was still in progress when he died of a cerebral hemorrhage in 1894.

SKOT OLSEN (page 2)

While growing up in Connecticut, Skot and his parents spent their summers sailing up and down the coast of New England and all over the West Indies. It was on these long trips that he developed his love for the sea which forms the basis for much of his work. A 1991 graduate of the Joe Kubert School of Cartoon and Graphic Art, Skot now lives on the edge of the Florida Everglades, where he concentrates on paintings which have been featured in numerous publications and exhibited in galleries in Florida, New York and California. His illustrations are printed in Graphic Classics: H.P. Lovecraft, Graphic Classics: Bram Stoker, and on the cover of Graphic Classics: Edgar Allan Poe, and a large collection of his work is online at www.skotolsen.com.

SAX ROHMER (page 4)

Arthur Henry Sarsfield Ward was an English music hall sketch and song writer who took the pen name Sax Rohmer when he began to write thrillers for the British serial magazines. He wrote a number of stories with occult and Egyptian themes, including In the Valley of the Sorceress, which was collected in Tales of Secret Egypt in 1918. But Rohmer's greatest success was with his series of stories of Fu Manchu, the villainous oriental mastermind, which capitalized on the European "yellow peril" fears in the wake of the Chinese revolution in 1911. Rohmer's first Fu Manchu story was serialized in 1912, and the character was eventually featured in fifteen of Rohmer's books, and later in radio dramas, movies, television and comics. Sax Rohmer's work was never well-respected by literary critics, yet during the 1920s and '30s he was one of the most popular writers in the English language, and in 1955 sold the media rights to Fu Manchu for four million dollars.

ROD LOTT (pages 4, 128)

Based in Oklahoma City, Rod Lott is a freelance writer and graphic designer in the worlds of journalism, advertising and beyond. For the past ten years, he has served as editor and publisher of the more-or-less quarterly magazine Hitch: The Journal of Pop Culture Absurdity. Rod's humorous essays have been published in anthologies including More Mirth of a Nation, 101 Damnations and May Contain Nuts. He has adapted stories by Edgar Allan Poe, Clark Ashton Smith, O. Henry, Sax Rohmer and Arthur Conan Doyle for Graphic Classics, and is now working on a script for the upcoming Graphic Classics: Rafael Sabatini. You can learn more about Rod's work online at www.rodlott.com and www.hitchmagazine.com.

J. B. BONIVERT (page 4)

Jeffrey Bonivert is a Bay Area native who has contributed to independent comics as both artist and writer, in such books as The Funboys, Turtle Soup and Mister Monster. His unique adaptation of The Raven originally appeared in 1979 in Star*Reach, and was revised for Graphic Classics: Edgar Allan Poe. Jeff's art is also published in Graphic Classics: Arthur Conan Doyle, Graphic Classics: Jack London, Graphic Classics: Ambrose Bierce and Graphic Classics: Bram Stoker, and he was part of the unique four-artist team on Reanimator in Graphic Classics: H.P. Lovecraft. Jeff's biography of artist Murphy Anderson appears in Spark Generators, and Muscle and Faith, his Casey Jones / Teenage Mutant Ninja Turtles epic, can be seen online at www.flyingcolorscomics.com.

ALEXANDRE DUMAS (page 26)

The famed author of The Three Musketeers, The Count of Monte Cristo and The Man in the Iron Mask was the grandson of a French nobleman and a black Haitian slave, and the son of a general in Napoleon's army. When Alexandre was four years old, his father died, and thereafter the family lived in poverty. Dumas worked as a clerk and secretary before beginning his writing career as a successful playwright. But his greatest notoriety came with the historical novels which were originally serialized in French newspapers, making him a wealthy man. Unfortunately his large income was insufficient to support his lavish lifestyle, and he spent much of his life fleeing from creditors until his death in 1870. Dumas produced 250 books, with the aid of 73 assistants including his uncredited collaborator Auguste Maquet. A Masked Ball was originally published as Un Bal Masqué in 1835, and became the basis of a Giuseppe Verdi opera, *Un Ballo in Maschera*, in 1859.

MICHAEL MANNING *(page 26)*

Michael is the creator of the *Spider Garden* and *Tranceptor* erotic graphic novels series which are available from NBM/Amerotica. His latest release is *Inamorata*, a fine art collection published by Last Gasp. He studied at the School of the Museum of Fine Arts in Boston, and began publishing comics in 1987 while working as an animator and director of short films and music videos. A move to San Francisco's Mission District in 1991 coincided with Michael's decision to focus on erotic illustration and gallery shows full time. Michael's admiration for the Symbolist and Pre-Raphaelite movements as well as classical Japanese ukiyo-e and modern manga artists has contributed to the formulation of his distinct style. Michael's artwork can be seen online at www.thespidergarden.net and in the pages of *Graphic Classics: Robert Louis Stevenson*, *Graphic Classics: Bram Stoker* and *Horror Classics*.

ZANE GREY *(page 37)*

Zane Grey was born in 1872 in Zanesville, Ohio, named after the pioneering Zane family which founded the town. In his youth, Grey was a dentist and a semipro baseball player, and he later wrote stories about baseball, history and adventure, including *Tigre* (a.k.a. *Bernardos' Revenge*), originally published in 1912. He was also an avid angler, and wrote nine books concerning fishing. But his greatest fame was as the author of western novels including *Riders of the Purple Sage*. Zane Grey became the best-selling western author of all time, and during his lifetime more than 13 million copies of his nearly 90 books were sold. Dozens of his stories have been made into movies, from the 1920s to the present.

ROBERT W. SERVICE *(page 50)*

Robert William Service was born in England, raised in Scotland, and emigrated to Canada in 1894. There he worked a wide variety of jobs, from farm laborer to storekeeper. He was employed at a bank in Dawson City, in the Canadian Yukon, when he published his first book of poems, *Songs of a Sourdough*, in 1908. Service was a correspondent for the *Toronto Star* and an ambulance driver in France during World War I, and published *Rhymes of a Red Cross Man*, a series of poems relating the horrors of that war. He eventually published over 1,000 poems, two autobiographical works and six novels. Several novels were adapted to movies, as well as *The Shooting of Dan McGrew*, filmed in 1924. His 1958 obituary in the *Pittsburgh Sun-Telegraph* declared "He was a people's poet... they understood him, and knew that any verse carrying the by-line of Robert W. Service would be a lilting thing, clear, clean and power-packed, beating out a story with a dramatic intensity that made the nerves tingle."

HUNT EMERSON *(page 50)*

The dean of British comics artists, Hunt Emerson has drawn cartoons and comic strips since the early 1970s. His work appears in publications as diverse as *Fiesta*, *Fortean Times*, and *The Wall Street Journal Europe*, and he has also worked widely in advertising. Hunt has published over twenty comic books and albums, including *Lady Chatterley's Lover*, *The Rime of the Ancient Mariner*, and *Casanova's Last Stand*, and his

comics have been translated into ten languages. His hilarious adaptation of *Jan, the Unrepentant* appears in *Graphic Classics: Jack London*, he explains the nature of vampires in *Graphic Classics: Bram Stoker*, and he pictures the philosophical captain of a sinking ship in *Graphic Classics: Robert Louis Stevenson*. You can see lots of cartoons, comics, fun and laffs on Hunt's website at www.largecow.demon.co.uk.

DAMON RUNYON *(page 56)*

Born Alfred Damon Runyan in 1884, Runyon changed the spelling of his surname to match a typo in the *Pueblo Evening Press* where he worked at age 15, having been expelled from school in the sixth grade. In 1898 he lied about his age to enlist for the Spanish-American war and was sent to the Philippines, the background for *Two Men Named Collins*, published in 1907. He returned to Colorado and worked as a newspaper reporter in Denver until moving to New York in 1910, to become a sportswriter for the *New York American*. It is on Broadway where Runyon found the colorful characters who populated the tales of gambling and petty crime that made him most famous, including *The Idyll of Miss Sarah Brown*, which became the Broadway play *Guys and Dolls* in 1950, with a movie version in 1955. Runyon was the premier journalist of his time, and at the peak of his career his newspaper column had a daily readership of over ten million.

NOEL TUAZON *(page 56)*

Canadian artist Noel Tuazon has been working on and off within the comics industry since 1989, starting with Dave Sim's *Single Page* section of *Cerebus* reprints. This was followed by two issues of Rafael Nieves's *Arianne*, and the anthologies *Taboo Especial*, *Dennis Eichorn's Real Stuff*, *Reactor Girl*, *Frecklebean Stories*, *Fleshrot*, and *Drawing the Line*. His current project is the eight issue *Elk's Run* (written by Joshua Fialkov) from Hoarse and Buggy Productions. Noel says that although he still works in non-art related jobs to pay the bills, he's optimistic he'll someday be working full time just illustrating comics and children's books. Samples of his work can be viewed at: www.noeltuazon.creativesource.ca.

RAFAEL SABATINI *(page 65)*

Dubbed "the Prince of Storytellers," "the heir to Dumas" and "the Last of the Great Swashbucklers," Rafael Sabatini was, in the 1920s and '30s, one of the most popular authors in the world. Born in Italy in 1875, the son of professional opera singers, Sabatini attended schools in Portugal and Switzerland, and at the age of seventeen moved to England, the birthplace of his mother. His multilingual background landed him a job as translator for an import firm, but his real interest was in writing. Sabatini was fluent in Italian, French, German, Spanish and Portugese, but chose to write stories in English for the British magazines, as he believed "all the best stories are written in English." He wrote contemporary short stories, plays, and nonfiction histories, but his greatest success came with his historical adventures, including *Scaramouche*, *The Sea Hawk* and *Captain Blood*. *Blood Money* was published in *Adventure Magazine* in 1921 and collected in *Captain Blood Returns* in 1931. Captain Blood will again return in the pages of *Graphic Classics: Rafael Sabatini*, scheduled for January 2006.

KEVIN ATKINSON (page 65)

"I've lived in Texas my whole life with the exception of 1985–1988 when I went to New Jersey to study with [famed comics artist and teacher] Joe Kubert," says Kevin. Since then he has created short stories and full-length comics for various publishers. He wrote and drew two series, *Snarl* and *Planet 29*, and collaborated on another, *Rogue Satellite Comics*. Lately he's inked *The Tick* comics, and illustrated Drew Edward's *Halloween Man*, *The Celebrated Jumping Frog* for *Graphic Classics: Mark Twain* and *Some Words with a Mummy* for *Horror Classics*. More of Kevin's art can be seen at www.meobeco.com/pulptoons/index.htm.

RUDYARD KIPLING (page 82)

Rudyard Kipling was born in Bombay in 1865, but educated in England before returning to India from 1882 to 1889. Today he is celebrated as the author of *Captains Courageous* and *Kim*, and the children's classics *The Jungle Book* and *Just So Stories*. He is also reviled as an apologist for British colonialism, and the originator of the term "the white man's burden." He was a journalist and poet, but became chiefly known as a writer of short stories of adventure and military life. Kipling briefly lived in the United States, but soon moved back to England, where he came to be regarded as an unofficial poet laureate. He refused the official title, and many other honors, but accepted the Nobel Prize for Literature in 1907, and the Gold Medal of the Royal Society of Literature in 1926, ten years before his death.

MARY FLEENER (page 82)

Besides doing comics, like her biweekly strip *Mary-Land*, autobiographical collection *Life of the Party*, and Eros title *Nipplez 'n' Tum Tum*, Los Angeles native Mary has also produced illustrations for magazines and books such as *Guitar Player*, *Musician*, *Spin*, *Hustler*, *The Book of Changes*, *Guitar Cookbook*, and Poppy Z. Brite's *Plastic Jesus*. Her paintings have been shown at The American Visionary Art Museum, La Luz de Jesus Gallery, and the Laguna Beach Art Museum. She is currently painting on black velvet, and makes hand-thrown ceramics. Fleener also plays bass, and sings her own tunes in a band called The Wigbillies, with her husband. She loves to surf, and walks a lot. Her website is at www.maryfleener.com.

FITZ-JAMES O'BRIEN (page 86)

Born and educated in Ireland, O'Brien emigrated to the U.S. at age 24 in 1852. There he became a leader among the New York Bohemians as he began to publish fiction and poetry in various periodicals. He also wrote a number of plays which were very popular at the time, and was an accomplished short story writer who helped develop the American literary magazine, though today his work is little-known. O'Brien volunteered to fight with Union forces in the Civil War, and in 1862 he died of complications from a wound suffered in battle. *The Man Without a Shadow* is a companion piece to *A Day-Dream*, which appears in *Horror Classics*.

MILTON KNIGHT (page 86)

Milton Knight claims he started drawing, painting and creating his own attempts at comic books and animation at age two. "I've never formed a barrier between fine art and cartooning," says Milt. "Growing up, I treasured Chinese watercolors, Breughel, Charlie

Brown and Terrytoons equally." His work has appeared in magazines including *Heavy Metal*, *High Times*, *National Lampoon* and *Nickelodeon Magazine*, and he has illustrated record covers, posters, candy packaging and T-shirts, and occasionally exhibited his paintings. Labor on *Ninja Turtles* comics allowed him to get up a grubstake to move to the West Coast in 1991, where he became an animator and director on *Felix the Cat* cartoons. Milt's comics titles include *Midnite the Rebel Skunk*, *Slug and Ginger* and *Hugo*. He has contributed to the *Graphic Classics* volumes *Edgar Allan Poe*, *Jack London*, *Ambrose Bierce*, *Mark Twain*, *O. Henry* and *Horror Classics*, and is now working on an adaptation for the revised edition of *Graphic Classics: Arthur Conan Doyle*. Check the latest news at www.miltonknight.net.

EDITH NESBIT (page 91)

Known primarily as a prolific writer of stories for children, Edith Nesbit's novels included *The Story of the Treasure-Seekers*, *The Wouldbegoods*, and *The Railway Children*. She was also a poet, short story author and playwright, and, with her husband Hubert Bland, co-authored eight novels for adults. Bland and Nesbit were among the founders of the socialist Fabian Society, and practiced an open marriage. Their large family included Bland's mistress, her child, and other children fathered by Bland, as well as the three borne by Nesbit. Edith Nesbit herself mixed in bohemian circles and kept a circle of occasional lovers including author George Bernard Shaw. She was a lecturer on socialism in addition to her writing, and affected lavish dress and a long cigarette holder, from which she smoked incessantly. Nesbit died in 1924, of lung cancer, having published over forty books. The realism in her children's novels set her apart from the fantasies popular in her day, and her biographer Julia Briggs named her "the first modern writer for children."

ANTONELLA CAPUTO (pages 91, 110)

Antonella Caputo was born and educated in Rome, and is now living in England. She has been an architect, archaeologist, art restorer, photographer, calligrapher, interior designer, theater designer, actress and theater director. Antonella's first published work was *Casa Montesi*, a weekly comic strip that appeared in *Il Journalino*. She has since written comedies for children and scripts for comics in Europe and the U.S., before joining Nick Miller as a partner in Sputnik Studios. Antonella has collaborated with Nick, as well as with artists Francesca Ghermandi and Rick Geary in *Graphic Classics: Jack London*, *Graphic Classics: Ambrose Bierce*, *Graphic Classics: Mark Twain*, *Graphic Classics: O. Henry* and *Horror Classics*.

MARK A. NELSON (page 91)

Mark Nelson was a professor of art at Northern Illinois University for twenty years. From 1998 to 2004 he was a senior artist at Raven Software, doing conceptual work, painting digital skins and creating textures for computer games. Mark is now the lead instructor of the Animation Department of Madison Area Technical College in Madison, Wisconsin. His comics credits include *Blood and Shadows* for DC, *Aliens* for Dark Horse Comics, and *Feud* for Marvel. He has worked for numerous publishers, and his art is represented in *Spectrum #4, 5, 6, 8, 10* and *From Pencils to Inks: The Art of Mark A. Nelson* (2004 Baron Publishing). Mark's comics and illustrations have appeared in *Graphic Classics: Edgar Allan Poe, Graphic Classics: Arthur Conan Doyle, Graphic Classics: H. P. Lovecraft, Graphic Classics: Jack London, Graphic Classics: Ambrose Bierce, Graphic Classics: O. Henry, Horror Classics, Rosebud 18* and *The Best of Rosebud*, all from Eureka Productions.

JOHNSTON McCULLEY (page 96)

A former police reporter, Johnston McCulley became a prolific writer of westerns, adventure tales, and detective thrillers for the pulp magazines under his own name, as well as more than half-a-dozen pseudonyms. His stories were published from 1911 until his death in 1958, and featured numerous heroes including The Bat, Thubway Tham and The Black Star. But his greatest creation was Zorro, who debuted in *The Curse of Capistrano* in 1919 and continues as one of the most popular adventure heroes in history. McCulley went on to write sixty-four Zorro stories as well as another fifty novels featuring his other characters. *The Stolen Story* originally appeared in *Detective Story Magazine* in 1919.

CHRIS PELLETIERE (page 96)

Chris Pelletiere is a painter, illustrator, and cartoonist who cites his early influences as the pre-code crime and horror comics. His cartoons and illustrations have appeared in small horror and fantasy magazines from Fantico Press, and he was also a political cartoonist for *The Soho Weekly News*. His published work includes *The A to Z Encyclopedia of Serial Killers, Song* by Brigit Pegeen Kelly, *Art and the Law, Dagon* and *The Grabinski Reader* (vols. 4 & 5). His work is in many public and private collections including The Museum of Modern Art, The Metropolitan Museum, The Brooklyn Museum, The New York Public Library, Stephen King, Zak Norman, Robert Bloch, Roald Dahl, John Collier, Ramsey Campbell, and Albert Boime. His paintings can be seen online at www.newyorkartworld.com.

ARTHUR CONAN DOYLE (page 110)

Arthur Conan Doyle was born in 1859, studied in England and Germany and became a Doctor of Medicine at the University of Edinburgh. He built up a successful medical practice, but also wrote, and created his most famous character, Sherlock Holmes, in 1887. Following a less-successful practice as an oculist, Doyle concentrated on his writing career. He was proudest of his historical novels, such as *The White Company*, and in 1894 introduced his second popular character, Brigadier Gerard, and in 1912 a third, Professor Challenger. But Holmes continued to be his most famous creation. Doyle felt that Holmes was a distraction and kept him from writing the "better things" that would make him a "lasting name in English literature." He killed his detective in 1893 in *The Final Problem*, only to resurrect him in 1903 due to public demand. Doyle wrote an astonishing range of fiction including medical stories, sports stories, historical fiction, contemporary drama, and verse. He also wrote non-fiction, including the six-volume *The British Campaign in France and Flanders*. His defense of British colonialism in South Africa led to his being knighted in 1902. By 1916 Doyle's investigations into Spiritualism had convinced him that he should devote the rest of his life to the advancement of the belief. He wrote and lectured on the Spiritualist cause until his death in 1930.

NICK MILLER (page 110)

The son of two artists, Nick Miller learned to draw at an early age. After leaving college, he worked as a graphic designer before switching to cartooning full-time. Since then, his work has appeared in numerous adult and children's magazines as well as comics anthologies in Britain, Europe and the U.S. His weekly newspaper comics run in *The Planet on Sunday*. He shares his Lancaster, England house with two cats, a lodger and Antonella Caputo. His stories have appeared in *Graphic Classics: Jack London, Graphic Classics: Ambrose Bierce, Graphic Classics: Mark Twain* and *Horror Classics*. See more of Nick's work at www.cat-box.net/sputnik.

O. HENRY (page 128)

O. Henry is the pen name of William Sydney Porter. The master of the surprise ending was born in 1862 in Greensboro, North Carolina. Porter left school at age fifteen, worked a number of jobs, then moved to Texas in 1882 where he became a ranch hand, then a pharmacist, and a bookkeeper. He married in 1887, and briefly published a humorous weekly, *The Rolling Stone*. When that paper failed, he joined *The Houston Post* as a reporter and columnist. He also worked as, most unfortunately, a bank clerk. He was accused of embezzlement, and fled, first to New Orleans, and then to Honduras to escape trial. While in Honduras he received word that his wife was terminally ill. He returned to Austin, and shortly after her death in 1897 he was convicted and sentenced to five years in a federal penitentiary in Ohio. It was while in prison that he adopted the pen name O. Henry (taken from the name of one of his guards) and began to write fiction. He was released from prison after three years and moved to New York City, where he wrote for *The New York World* and other publications. O. Henry was a prolific and extremely popular writer, and before his death in 1910 published more than 600 short stories.

PEDRO LOPEZ (page 128)

Born in Denmark in 1974, Pedro is a comic artist inspired mostly by spaghetti westerns, Italian crime thrillers, and dark scifi movies. His passion for these movies is obvious when you read his comics. He is also inspired by French comic artists such as Tardi, Hermann, and Mézières. He has published comics in Denmark and adapted *The Cask of Amontillado* for *Graphic Classics: Edgar Allan Poe, The Suicide Club* for *Graphic Classics: Robert Louis Stevenson* and *Roads of Destiny* for *Graphic Classics: O. Henry*. He is now working on an online spaghetti western comic which you can see at www.pedrolopez.dk.

TOM POMPLUN

The designer, editor and publisher of the *Graphic Classics* series, Tom previously designed and produced *Rosebud*, a journal of poetry, fiction and illustration, from 1993 to 2003. He is now working on a revised edition of *Graphic Classics: Arthur Conan Doyle*, scheduled for October 2005, presenting over a hundred pages of new material including a new Sherlock Holmes adaptation by Simon Gane, Brigadier Gerard in *The Castle of Gloom*, and Doyle's fearsome pirate *Captain Sharkey*. Also in production is *Graphic Classics: Rafael Sabatini* for January 2006 with the origin of Captain Blood and six more tales of mystery, romance and adventure. You can see previews, sample art, and much more at www.graphicclassics.com.